Sex and Gender
in Medieval
and Renaissance Texts

SUNY Series in Medieval Studies
Paul E. Szarmach, Editor

Sex and Gender
in Medieval and Renaissance Texts

The Latin Tradition

EDITED BY

Barbara K. Gold,
Paul Allen Miller,
and
Charles Platter

State University of New York Press

Published by
State University of New York Press, Albany

© 1997 State University of New York

For information, address State University of New York
Press, State University Plaza, Albany, N.Y. 12246

Production by Diane Ganeles
Marketing by Nancy Farrell

Library of Congress Cataloging-in-Publication Data

Sex and gender in medieval and Renaissance texts : the Latin tradition
   /   edited by Barbara K. Gold, Paul Allen Miller, and Charles Platter.
        p.   cm. — (SUNY series in medieval studies)
      Includes bibliographical references and index.
      ISBN 0-7914-3245-9 (hc : alk. paper). — ISBN 0-7914-3246-7 (pbk.
   : alk. paper)
      1. Latin literature, Medieval and modern—History and criticism.
   2. Feminism and literature—Europe—History.   3. Women and
   literature—Europe—History.   4. Gender identity in literature.
   5. Sex role in literature.   6. Renaissance.   I. Gold, Barbara K.,
   1945– .   II. Miller, Paul Allen, 1959– .   III. Platter, Charles,
   1957– .   IV. Series.
PA8030.F45S48   1997
870.9'352042'0902—dc20   96-16249
                                                                   CIP

10   9   8   7   6   5   4   3   2   1

To Carl, Paul G., Alice, and Clara

Contents

Introduction

Barbara K. Gold, Paul Allen Miller, and Charles Platter

This collection has two goals: to reclaim some long-neglected Latin texts from the Middle Ages and the Renaissance and to examine the representations of the feminine and the female body in these texts. The volume asks what ideological values are explicitly encoded by the feminine in these texts; what other, less-articulated values the feminine implies; and what is the role of the Latin tradition in communicating those values. It is our expectation that this interrogation of the figure of the feminine—women both as subjects and as rhetorical constructions—will shed light on the wider dialogue about feminism that now pervades many disciplines, bringing a new historical perspective to current theoretical disputes and demonstrating the importance of the Medieval and Renaissance Latin traditions to later literature. Thus, texts that have long been the preserve of a relatively small group of specialists, who are concerned either with strictly philological issues or merely descriptive studies, will retake their rightful place in the mainstream of contemporary scholarly discourse on the humanities.[1]

The essays in this volume focus on works and authors from a long and important period of literature that has largely been excluded from both the college curriculum and modern debate. One result of this exclusion is that a vast amount of material on both women's history and the history of attitudes toward women has also been suppressed. The emphasis in this collection on the figure of the feminine will serve a twin function: it will provide a basis for discussion among scholars from various disciplines, and it will open up for Latin texts from the Middle Ages and Renaissance the kind of exciting dialogue that scholars of classical texts have already begun with critics of contemporary literature.[2]

There are complex historical reasons for the neglect of these Medieval and Renaissance texts. A full examination would require a volume of its own, but a general outline can be offered. The way that disciplinary boundaries have conventionally been drawn is partly responsible. Traditional studies of classical literature usually stop around the beginning of the fifth century c.e., although Latin continued to be the dominant literary and intellectual language of Europe until the latter half of the sixteenth century. Consequently, most classicists ignore over a thousand years of the Latin literary tradition. The reason for this is not hard to find. The classical era is traditionally thought to end with the fall of Rome in 476 c.e. Texts produced after that date customarily fall under the rubric of Medieval and Renaissance Studies, which are generally pursued within the framework of the various modern language departments and their corresponding national language sections.

But the notion of a national culture is anachronistic throughout most of this period. Indeed, how can we speak meaningfully of a French, Italian, or German culture in periods when the very idea of France, Germany, or Italy was either nonexistent or only in its formative stages? The concept of national literatures fails to account for the textual production of the premodern era.[3] The Middle Ages and Early Renaissance did not produce a set of ideal, homogeneous national cultures, but rather formed their cultural and ideological structures through an expansive and open-ended dialectical interchange. This interchange took place among various regional cultural centers and the larger international Latin culture whose primary, though not exclusive, mode of diffusion was the church.

Thus, although the Latin texts of the Medieval and Renaissance periods represent a huge, untapped scholarly reservoir, they tend to fall through the disciplinary cracks. On the one hand, they are postclassical and so outside the domain of classicists. On the other, the very international character of Medieval and Renaissance Latin culture defies classification according to the categories that were developed in the nineteenth century to chart the destinies of Europe's various national languages and literatures. As a result, these texts have been marginalized and seldom read. The progressive obscurity into which they have fallen has, in turn, provided modern scholars with a further *post facto* justification for their neglect.

This division of labor between Classical and Modern Language departments and their respective professional associations did, however, make some sense when it could be assumed that every educated person read Latin fluently. It was not at that time unreasonable to assume that scholars in French, Italian, English, and Spanish would read the Latin texts produced by those whom they claimed as their national authors. Today, however, we can no longer assume this level of linguistic competence. Few nonclassicists read Latin comfortably, and fewer still have a detailed understanding of the history of classical Latin literature, although a knowledge of this history was assumed by most Medieval and Neo-Latin writers, as well as by many of their contemporaries who wrote in the vernacular.[4] For writers of the Middle Ages and the Renaissance, the classical tradition was frequently both source and springboard for their creative work. Thus an understanding of the Latin texts of those periods themselves and their companion works in the vernacular often assumes a horizon of cultural and linguistic interpretation that no longer exists.

This is not to say that important work on women in Medieval and Renaissance literature has not been done. The past two decades have seen a large number of books devoted to women in Medieval and Renaissance vernacular literatures.[5] This work indicates a wide interest in the topic. Yet these studies largely ignore the influence of Latin culture. As a result, although they are valuable, they tend to be incomplete. Our volume will offer a partial corrective to this deficiency and suggest directions for further research.

More recently, classicists and neo-Latinists working on Medieval and Renaissance texts have begun to devote some attention to women writers and characters in literature and to feminist issues. For example, a volume from Routledge in 1993 on *Feminist Theory and the Classics* is the first explicitly theoretical work on the intersection of feminism and classical literature (both Greek and Latin).[6] Two anthologies and descriptive treatments of women writers in the Medieval period have also appeared,[7] and there are now several more specialized works (translations of works on women, articles on women and medicine in the Medieval period).[8] Nonetheless, little work exists on the figure of the feminine (both author and character) in the vast body of Medieval and Renaissance texts written in Latin and almost nothing of an interpretive or theoretical nature. The few interpretive works that are available cover only the Medieval period. Thus a growing body of work addresses gender issues in the Middle Ages and Renaissance in an increasingly theoretically sophisticated manner, yet too often it is innocent of Latin and the rich tradition that informs it, at the same time, the works currently produced on Medieval and Renaissance Latin texts remain largely untouched by both feminism and theory.

It is to this double lacuna that the present collection addresses itself. The essays deal with three interrelated topics in Medieval and Renaissance Latin literature: the status of women as writers, the status of women as rhetorical figures, and the status of women in society. The time period covered ranges from the fifth to the early seventeenth century C.E.; the papers proceed in chronological order. The aim of the volume is to make this vast body of literature better known to contemporary scholars and to demonstrate its relevance to current debates on feminism, the canon, and the nature and history of the western tradition. At the same time, the texts examined are interesting for their ability to problematize issues like originality and imitation that are now, since the publication of works like Gian Biaggio Conte's *The Rhetoric of Imitation*, in the forefront of the current critical reappraisal of Latin literature.[9] A more detailed knowledge of the heavily imitative texts of Renaissance and Medieval Latinity will deepen any Latinist's understanding of the intertextual relationships that produce literary imitation and of the interpretive problems that arise from it.

Finally, feminist theory often examines the terms of women's existence in a society dominated by men and male institutions. Several different approaches to this issue are possible: for example, an analysis of images of women created by men, whether in the texts of literature, philosophy, politics, art, or any other means of cultural production; and a focus on the voices of the women themselves. The latter introduces the difficulty of self-representation while using a language in which the domination of women has been encoded.

This volume addresses all these issues pragmatically, offering essays both about masculine representations of women and about women who speak in their own voices. It presents to feminist theorists a concrete body of work about women, available in most cases for the first time in English, which will contribute to the ongoing debate about the status of women in a male-dominated society. We hope that this volume will serve as a catalyst for Medieval and Renaissance Latin studies and will encourage more academicians to include Medieval and Renaissance women writers and works with a strong female presence in their classes and in their own work.

The first paper, "By Woman's Tears Redeemed: Female Lament in Saint Augustine's *Confessions* and the Correspondence of Abelard and Heloise" by Nancy A. Jones, starts by establishing in the works of Saint Augustine the centrality of the figure of the feminine in the iconography and symbolic economy of the Middle Ages at the very beginnings of the postclassical epoch. According to Jones, women's tears are a primary but deeply ambiguous form of power in late antique and Medieval literature. They signal women's roles as witnesses and intercessors in the scheme of salvation and thus identify women with a type of spiritual agency and authority. In this way, too, they figure in the climactic episodes of autobiographical conversion narratives. In her reading of two exemplary texts, Saint Augustine's *Confessions* and Peter Abelard's *Historia Calamitatum,* Jones shows that these narratives not only offer a framework for female authority within Medieval theology, but also continue a cultural discourse that seeks to contain the disturbing personal dimensions of lamentation and represents conversion as a fundamentally male experience. These are themes that will recur throughout the volume, with particular relevance to the character Augustinus in Petrarch's *Secretum* and the theology of the feminine as expounded by Cornelius Agrippa (see the essays by Paul Allen Miller and Diane S. Wood in this volume).

Through Nancy Jones' careful analysis, we discover how Augustine in his *Confessions* intertwines his mother's spiritual ordeal with his own. While Augustine praises his mother's "sacrificial tears" as a principal agent in his conversion, the rhetorical strategy of his text uses them to intensify the magnitude of the son's sins and, by extension, the importance of his conversion. In Abelard's *Historia Calamitatum* and the *Letters of Direction* addressed to Heloise and the nuns of the Paraclete, he imposes a Christological meaning on Heloise's expressions of grief and thereby perpetuates the hierarchical structure of their earlier relationship. He thus moves gradually from a stance of humility to one of authority, and he remains the subject of salvation within their common narrative. As is true of Monica and Augustine, so Heloise, despite having become Abelard's "sister" in their conversion, remains the instrument of his salvation. In both cases, the women's tears serve as a sign pointing the way towards salvation, but also function as vanishing mediators whose momentary presence is quickly reappropriated by the master narrative of masculine salvation.

In our second essay, "Hrotswitha Writes Herself: *Clamor Validus Gandeshemensis*" by Barbara K. Gold, we see that the figure of the feminine is central to men's writings but also occupies pride of place in the discourse of women themselves. Hrotswitha of Gandersheim, a tenth-century Saxon canoness, is the first known dramatist of Christianity and the first Medieval poet consciously to have attempted to remold the image of the literary depictions of women. Her six plays, in which her stated aim is to glorify the Christian church and to exalt the ideal of chastity, make extensive use of the Roman comic playwright, Terence. In this essay, Gold first discusses Hrotswitha's reputation as a female playwright and the misreading of her work as a result of various forms of bias in the scholarship. She then explores Hrotswitha's self-presentation in the prefaces to her plays and its echoes in her characters. Next Gold examines Hrotswitha's relationship to her male classical/pagan and hagiographic sources, as well as the role played by Hrotswitha's audience. Finally, she analyzes one of Hrotswitha's dramas, the *Passio Sanctarum Virginum Agapis Chioniae et Hirenae (Dulcitius)*. In her plays and prefaces, Hrotswitha vindicates her female protagonists, with whom she and her audience would presumably have identified, and establishes a space to define herself and the women's culture in which she lived. She thereby becomes a chronicler of women's tales and a creator of women's history, capable of shaping and influencing women's ways of knowing.

The understanding of the construction of a feminine voice begun in the investigation of Hrotswitha is continued in a more complex form in Phyllis Culham's "Gender and Negotiating Discourse: Mediated Autobiography and

Female Mystics of Medieval Italy." Culham discusses the vitae of Margherita of Cortona and Margherita of Faenza, as well as the Sermones of Umiltà of Faenza and the *Liber* of Angela of Foligno calling them "mediated autobiographies." In each case, the female "author" dictated her thoughts to a male who admits in the extant text to having edited what he was told by "removing excess words" or rearranging the text to improve the sense. The women associated with the texts deny all intentionality either as authors or as subjects of their own narratives; it was, they said, divine will that directed their thoughts and the making of the record. These women claim that their knowledge of divinity is direct and absolute but that their lengthy descriptions of the divine nature are deceptive. The male mediators claim no firsthand, mystical contact with the divine but still assert that the documents they generated are an absolutely authoritative source of knowledge.

In the past, various forms of historicist, phenomenological, and psychological criticism have been applied to these problematic texts with disappointing results. Phyllis Culham here presents a forceful case for the superior heuristic value of an archeological approach based on the works of Michel Foucault in examining these complex, many-layered documents. Culham suggests that, using a method derived from *Discipline and Punish*, *The Birth of the Clinic*, and volume one of the *History of Sexuality*, we can see how these mediated narratives participate in the negotiation of power and knowledge within their episteme. Foucault believed that the fourth Lateran Council in 1215 sparked a revolution in where and how people looked for the truth, and Culham argues that these texts continue that revolution. They seize the genre of the confession back from the confessor. They supply models for the assumption of religious authority by a prosperous urban elite, especially by wives and mothers who failed to conform to the earlier model of the saintly virgin. They move previously public shame and confession out of the squares of the communes into the vicarious experience of texts.

The final paper on the Medieval era is, "The Saint of the Womanly Body: Raimon de Cornet's Fourteenth Century Male Poetics" by St. John Flynn. Flynn's paper begins with the observation that the figure of the feminine is always open to a variety of appropriations. Indeed, from Eve to Pandora, to Dido, to the elegiac *domina* in the works of Propertius, Tibullus, and Ovid, and to the Blessed Virgin Mary, the icon of the feminine has been used to represent a variety of complex and often contradictory notions. The early fourteenth-century troubadour Raimon de Cornet was one of only two Medieval Provençal poets to write both vernacular and Latin lyrics. His two Latin pieces are testimonies to his Cistercian vocation: one a litany to the Virgin Mary, and the other a eulogy of the life of the great Cistercian founding father Bernard of Clairvaux. Using the theories of contemporary

French feminists such as Hélène Cixous and Luce Irigaray, Flynn seeks to show how both pieces are examples of male sexual poetics born of patriarchal sexual discourses. In each poem, Raimon seeks to establish a link between the figure of the Virgin and the Cistercian saint; in the litany Bernard provides a textual model for the Virgin, and in the eulogy the Virgin serves as a model for the life of Bernard. The figure of the Virgin is, therefore, a male poetic construct. She is not real in any subjective, autonomous sense but becomes a means of expressing Raimon's admiration for Bernard of Clairvaux. The male poet appropriates the female body of the Virgin such that she becomes what Cixous describes as "the uncanny stranger on display." As in secular poetry from the Medieval Provençal troubadours to the present, patriarchal strategies are used to present an idealized female who reflects the male. There is then a continuity between the practices of Augustine as outlined by Nancy Jones in the volume's opening essay, where his mother's tears are the sign of his own salvation (and hence a reflection of him rather than her), and those of Raimon, where the Virgin reflects the male Saint rather than vice versa.

The volume continues with two essays on Petrarch, the transitional figure from the Middle Ages to the Renaissance and, in many ways, the most widely read of the authors treated here. The first of the two papers is "Petrarch's Sophonisba: Seduction, Sacrifice, and Patriarchal Politics," by Donald Gilman. It argues that Petrarch's presentation of various female characters is particularly important to our understanding of the transition from the Middle Ages to the Renaissance. In most of the scholarship on Petrarch's *Africa* (1339–43), Petrarch is seen as reworking Livy's account of the Second Punic War, extolling the heroism and piety of Scipio Africanus while denouncing the subversion and snares of Sophonisba. Such a view is accurate but incomplete, and an analysis of Sophonisba within the contexts of patriarchal prerogatives elucidates the role of this problematic character in the *Africa* and so more fully defines Petrarch's thoughts on the place and function of women in early Renaissance society.

In the first section of the paper, "Neither Sinner nor Saint," Donald Gilman examines the portrayal of Sophonisba as a stereotypical seductress (e.g., Eve, Delilah) and a tragic victim (e.g., Phaedra, Dido). In the second segment, "From Marginalization to Legitimacy," Donald Gilman investigates Sophonisba's predicament in terms of patriarchal politics. Her allegiance to Carthage and her defiance of Roman rule compel her to shift from the domestic domain of women to a public arena reserved for men. Existentially, she assumes a legitimacy, but her suicide "neutralizes" and "naturalizes" her actions, consigning her to the eternal enclosures of Hades. In the third part, "Everywoman," Gilman compares her actions to those of Petrarch's representations of Medusa and Lucretia, who, through similar suffering, assure the restoration of temporal order. Finally, like Eve, who, according to patristic commentaries commits a *felix culpa*, Sophonisba reflects the condition of humankind that accounts for sin and sacrifice in the redemptive and recreative process of a divine design. Thus while her role is marginalized and problematized to a greater extent than what we have already seen in the cases of Monica's tears for Augustine or the figure of the Blessed Virgin Mary for Raimon de Cornet, the actions of Sophonisba, delineating both a character and a subject position, ultimately find their justification in their ability to insure male salvation (as in the case of Monica or Heloise; see Jones' paper in this volume). The real difference between the case of Sophonisba and that of her predecessors is that, in Sophonisba's case, the cost of male redemption is female damnation.

By the beginning of the Renaissance, then, woman's traditional position in the divine symbolic economy has begun to erode. Her relation to both male and female salvation has become much more problematic. It is this increased interrogation of the feminine that constitutes the focus of the second paper on Petrarch, "Laurel as the Sign of Sin: Laura's Textual Body in Petrarch's *Secretum*," by Paul Allen Miller. In this paper, Miller argues that the birth of humanism's commitment to rediscovering an authentic antiquity, stripped of the allegorical anachronisms of the Medieval world's reading of classical texts, is inseparable from the increasing problematization of the feminine's symbolic power in Petrarch's own textual economy. Miller argues that the *Secretum* is characterized by a fundamental ambivalence over the semiotic status of woman and that this ambivalence is a function of the poet's problematic historical position between the ideological and social worlds of the Middle Ages and Renaissance.

Paul Allen Miller begins by noting that Petrarch's simultaneous commitment to a world of piety and secular learning is particularly problematized in book three of the *Secretum*, where Augustine, in the character of Augustinus, tells the poet that he is bound by two chains that insure his damnation: love for Laura, and the pursuit of poetic glory. Miller maintains that the necessity of this collocation is inscribed in the epistemological, ideological, and sexual tensions that structure the *Secretum*. Laura, he argues, functions within Petrarch's work as a signifying body. Her physical beauty, Petrarch admits, is what makes possible her signifying function, but through that signifying function, Petrarch contends, he has been led from the love of Laura to the love of God. Augustinus replies that the poet has the order reversed: he should not love the creator because of the creature, but the creature because of the creator.

The debate between them centers around Laura's function as signifier both in Petrarch's life and his work. Does she make the ultimate transcendental signified, God's Logos, manifest to the senses, or does she deflect the poet's thoughts from the eternal to the merely temporal? In the light of such questions, the relationship between Petrarch's love of Laura and his pursuit of poetic glory comes into sharper focus. For poetry, like Laura, is a text that seduces by its beauty, while promising its lover the possibility of a transcendental signified in the form of a revelation of some fundamental truth or hidden meaning. If Petrarch is to give up one, he must also give up the other. The dialogue ends with his accepting the intellectual and theological force of Augustine's arguments but refusing to draw the necessary consequences from them. He will continue to write poetry and continue to love Laura, come what may.

Our next essay, "Woman, Space, and Renaissance Discourse" by Diana Robin, launches a discussion of Renaissance women's space as articulated by the discourse of women themselves. The essay begins with Foucault's intriguing suggestion that a whole history of spaces, that would at the same time be a history of powers, remains to be written. Robin notes that the humanism of Petrarch and those who followed in his wake was increasingly practiced by women, as well as men, although their work was not accorded the same prestige as that of their male counterparts. The same period also sees a growth in the production of "catalogues and encyclopedias of women's lives." These two phenomena, Robin argues, played key roles in what she labels "the literary production of women's space," a notion that she interprets in light of Kristeva's concept of the *chora*.

Diana Robin commences her investigation by noting that, at the beginning of the sixteenth century, the first printed encyclopedias of eminent women's lives began to appear in Italy. Like most learned source books in the Renaissance, they were in Latin. These biographical encyclopedias were, in turn, a logical consequence of the enormous interest in autobiography on the part of both readers and writers from the late fifteenth century onward. After Petrarch, it became almost de rigueur for writers to publish their familiar letters in Latin. These edited books of personal, Ciceronian letters (usually spanning several decades) offered an autobiographical portrait of their authors, among whose ranks were a few renowned women. Gender and the production of the figure of the feminine are focal concerns in both women's letter-books and encyclopedias of their lives. Both genres represent reactions, in one way or another, to the great European controversy of the period on the nature of woman, the *querelle des femmes*, and to Boccaccio's very influential *De Claris Mulieribus* (*Concerning Famous Women*). In this article, Robin argues that the Latin letter-books of two fifteenth-century Italian women in particular, Cassandra Fedele and Laura Cereta, represent alternately attempts within the format of the courtly

Quattrocento letter-book to respond to, or to accommodate and contest, certain older, Boccaccian traditions about gender difference and women's "nature." The result is the creation of a uniquely feminine literary space.

A male defense of women from the same period is the topic of Diane S. Wood's "In Praise of Woman's Superiority: Heinrich Cornelius Agrippa's *De nobilitate* (1529)." Here we see that the *querelle des femmes* continued to occupy a central position in Renaissance humanist debates. Wood focuses initially on the rhetorical techniques used by Agrippa in his *De nobilitate et praecellentia foemenei sexus* (1529) to undercut traditional and especially biblical injunctions that limited women's freedom and opportunities. Agrippa argues that the contemporary treatment of women is contrary to both divine and natural laws. According to him, laws, customs, and education all contribute to the suppression of women. Changing such human constructs is his implicit goal in writing the *De nobilitate*. Using both logic and hyperbole, his arguments subvert the rationale for the officially sanctioned gender oppression that had developed from the misogyny inherent in the writings of the early Church Fathers. Wood contends that an examination of his rhetoric illuminates his strategies and clarifies why his work is at the heart of the *querelle des femmes*. His arguments are used and reused throughout the sixteenth century, making an understanding of his approach vital to those interested in women's status during the period. Not content with proving that women are equal, Agrippa sets out to demonstrate their inherent superiority to men and thereby ensures through his rhetorical exuberance the great popularity of the *De nobilitate* among the partisans of women in the *querelle*. He reverses the conventional binary oppositions that are normally used to support the argument for male superiority in order to demonstrate the opposite view, and he thus reveals himself to be a kind of deconstructive feminist *avant la lettre*.

The next essay examines the intersection of classical imitation and sexual identity that was to remain problematic for humanists from the time of Petrarch to the end of the sixteenth century. Charles Platter's, "The Artificial Whore: George Buchanan's *Apologia pro lena*," focuses on the elegiac and erotic poetry of George Buchanan. This portion of Buchanan's oeuvre has received little critical attention compared to his political history and religious writing. Yet these poetic writings should be of considerable interests to all students of Renaissance literature, since they are among the clearest examples of Buchanan's intimate knowledge of and dialogue with the tradition of Latin poetry. One of the longest and most impressive examples of this erotic and elegiac strand in his poetry is his *Apologia pro lena*, an elegy written and circulated privately probably in the 1540s. The diction of this poem is so heavily laden with borrowings from Latin elegy that, at first glance, it might appear to be simply repetition rather than creative imitation. A closer reading, however, indicates that, although Buchanan appropriates all the machinery of elegy, he then transforms it to suit his rhetorical purposes.

The primary way in which this imitative strategy finds expression is through his construction of the *lena*. In Roman poetry, she is a sexually ambivalent figure, both a procuress and an obstacle who threatens the poet's exclusive possession of his *puella*. Buchanan attempts to reduce this power by depriving her of her ability to dispense sexual favors arbitrarily. He does so by first investing the *ars lenae* with the values and attributes of poets and poetry as described by Augustan elegy. At the same time, he downplays her status as a procuress in such a way that her "art" is, at times, indistinguishable from the connubial Venus she supposedly supplements. Charles Platter shows that, through these two strategies, Buchanan's poem attempts to reconstitute the Roman *lena* in such a way as to preserve her elegiac shape while simultaneously depriving her of sexual authority over poets. The poet thus achieves mastery over his medium, as defined by the humanist doctrine of classical imitation, without having to submit to the mastery of the *lena* or the elegiac *domina*, as was the case in Buchanan's Latin predecessors. As we saw in the works of Petrarch, sexual and literary agonistics are ultimately found to be one.

Our next essay " 'She Never Recovered her Senses': *Roxana* and Dramatic Representations of Women at Oxbridge in the Elizabethan Age" by Elizabeth M. Richmond-Garza, demonstrates how the figure of the feminine was bound up in concepts of national, as well as literary and historical, identity. Richmond-Garza begins by pointing out that, although many critics place the universities on the margins of Tudor England, Elizabeth I's own frequent and elaborate visits suggest that they occupied a central position in its intellectual and political construction. They produced a rich and ignored body of texts whose most outrageous examples are the plays presented by, and for, academic and aristocratic audiences. Often more incendiary than anything that could have been played on the London stage, these legitimate "exercises in rhetoric" were praised and funded by the authorities. Consistently politically irreverent and even subversive in their content, all the plays present challenges to modern critical expectations of what material was permitted a public hearing. In the contexts of the long period of female control represented by Elizabeth's reign and of the rapid international commercial expansion of the Elizabethan economy, one Cambridge play of 1592 stands out.

William Alabaster's *Roxana* assaults his audience not only with one of the bloodiest and most savage of revenge actions but also with a double problematic: its two antagonists are women, Atossa and Roxana, fighting over a single husband/lover, and their weapons are seduction, infanticide, and decapitation. The story takes place in Bactria, involving both a European orientalist representation of the Near East and its own internal xenophobic text: Roxana is from India. The play combines a consideration of the problems of the representation of women within the codes of marriage and alliance with an attempt to construct a new view of "the East" for an English audience. Richmond-Garza shows that this play, anticipating the comments of critics like Edward Saïd on the complicity of these two projects, challenges its voyeuristic male audience, who would have viewed the atrocities acted by and upon women necessarily within a perspective informed by the policies and self-construction of their own female monarch.

The volume concludes with a chapter by Holt Parker: "Latin and Greek Poetry by Five Renaissance Italian Women Humanists." This is a project in making visible. Even with the current revival of knowledge about the education of women, the existence of Latin and even Greek poetry from the hands of women remains largely unknown. They are absent from anthologies of Renaissance Latin poetry by reason of their sex and from anthologies of women's verse by reason of their language. They present a microcosmic view of the more general problems that this volume is meant to address. After a brief introduction outlining the place and importance of verse composition in humanist education and life, Parker provides short biographical sketches of five women educated in humanism: Angela Nogarola (fl. c. 1400), Isotta Nogarola (1418–66), Costanza Varano (1426–47), Alessandra Scala (1475–1506), and Fulvia Olympia Morata (1526–55). The sketches are followed by texts and translations of their surviving Latin and Greek poetry. In addition, he provides information for further research on the works of Luisa Sigea of Toledo (c. 1522–c. 1560), Elizabeth Jane Weston (1582–1612), and Elena Lucrezia Cornaro Piscopia, the first woman to win the Ph.D. (Parma, 1678).

Notes

1. See, for example, Jozef Ijsewijn's very useful *Companion to Neo-Latin Studies, Part 1: History and Diffusion of Neo-Latin Literature* (Atlanta, GA: Scholars Press, 1990). This is an immense work of true scholarly devotion, but its primary appeal is to fellow specialists.

2. See, for example, Helene Foley, ed., *Reflections of Women in Antiquity* (London and New York: Gordon and Breach, 1981); Averil Cameron and Amélie Kuhrt, eds., *Images of Women in Antiquity* (London: Croom Helm, 1983); John Peradotto and J. P. Sullivan, eds., *Women in the Ancient World: The Arethusa Papers* (Albany: State University of New York Press, 1984); Marilyn B. Skinner, ed., *Rescuing Creusa: New Methodological Approaches to Women in Antiquity, Helios*

13.2 (1986); three special issues of *Helios: Studies in Roman Women* parts. 1 and 2, 16.1 and 16.2 (Spring-Fall 1989) and *Helios* 17.2 (Autumn 1990); Nancy Sorkin Rabinowitz and Amy Richlin, eds., *Feminist Theory and the Classics* (London: Routledge,1993).

3. As the disciplines of comparative literature, semiotics, and postcolonial studies, as well as the current debates on the canon, show, it is not clear that the concept of national literatures is much more useful for modern texts.

4. Oswyn Murray, "The Idea of the Shepherd King from Cyrus to Charlemagne," *Latin Poetry and the Classical Tradition*, ed. Oswyn Murray and Peter Godman (Oxford: Oxford University Press, 1990), p. 2.

5. Joan M. Ferrante, *Woman as Image in Medieval Literature: From the Twelfth Century to Dante* (New York: Columbia University Press, 1975); Eileen Edna Power, *Medieval Women*, ed. M. M. Postan (Cambridge: Cambridge University Press, 1975); Susan Mosher Stuard, ed. *Women in Medieval Society* (Philadelphia: University of Pennsylvania Press, 1976); Pauline Stafford, *Queens, Concubines, and Dowagers: The King's Wife in the Early Middle Ages* (Athens: University of Georgia Press, 1983); Penny Schine Gold, *The Lady and the Virgin: Image, Attitude, and Experience in Twelfth-Century France* (Chicago: University of Chicago Press, 1985); Susan Mosher Stuard, ed. *Women in Medieval History and Historiography* (Philadelphia: University of Pennsylvania Press, 1987); Caroline Walker Bynum, *Holy Feast and Holy Fast: The Religious Significance of Food to Medieval Women* (Berkeley and Los Angeles: University of California Press, 1987); Mary Erler and Maryanne Kowaleski, eds. *Women and Power in the Middle Ages* (Athens: University of Georgia Press, 1988); Sheila Fisher and Janet E. Halley, eds. *Seeking the Woman in Late Medieval and Renaissance Writings: Essays in Feminist Contextual Criticism* (Knoxville: University of Tennessee Press, 1989); Kathryn Gravdal, *Ravishing Maidens: Writing Rape in Medieval French Literature and Law* (Philadelphia: University of Pennsylvania Press, 1991); R. Howard Bloch, *Medieval Misogyny and the Invention of Western Romantic Love* (Chicago: University of Chicago Press, 1991); E. Jane Burns, *Bodytalk: When Women Speak in Old French Literature* (Philadelphia: University of Pennsylvania Press, 1993); Roberta L. Krueger, *Women Readers and the Ideology of Gender in Old French Verse Romance* (Cambridge: Cambridge University Press, 1993). See also Nancy F. Partner, ed., *Studying Medieval Women: Sex, Gender, Feminism* (Cambridge, MA: The Medieval Academy of America, 1993), a collection that interrogates the role of sex, gender, and feminist thought in medieval studies today. There are also many journals that carry important reviews, updated bibliographies, and articles on women in Medieval and Renaissance vernacular literatures. See, for example, the list of journals and reviews in Partner, *Studying Medieval Women*, pp. 171–75.

6. See note 2.

7. Peter Dronke, *Women Writers of the Middle Ages: a Critical Study of Texts from Perpetua (d. 203) to Marguerite Porete (d. 1310)* (Cambridge: Cambridge

University Press, 1984), a presentation of selected Latin texts by women from the third to the thirteenth centuries and an appreciation of those texts; and Katharina M. Wilson, ed., *Medieval Women Writers* (Athens: University of Georgia Press, 1984), a collection of essays on women writers in the Medieval period (of whom only two write in Latin).

8. Helen Rodnite Lemay, *Women's Secrets: A Translation of Pseudo-Albertus Magnus's "De secretis mulierum" with Commentaries* (Albany: State University of New York Press, 1992); Monica Helen Green, "Women's Medical Practice and Health Care in Medieval Europe," *Signs* 14.2 (1989): pp. 434–73.

9. Gian Biaggio Conte, *The Rhetoric of Imitation: Genre and Poetic Memory in Virgil and Other Latin Poets*, ed. and trans. Charles Segal (Ithaca, NY: Cornell University Press, 1986).

By Woman's Tears Redeemed: Female Lament in St. Augustine's *Confessions* and the Correspondence of Abelard and Heloise

Nancy A. Jones

Ritual lamentation is a cross-cultural phenomenon studied by folklorists, anthropologists, and ethnomusicologists. It is characterized by a mixture of stylized weeping, singing, and ritual speech and gesture performed by women at death and wedding ceremonies in premodern societies. The ancient cultures of the West attributed a special power to the tears of female mourners and suppliants. In funerary ritual, as attested in cultures throughout the world, the weeping woman is a key actor. As anthropologist Maurice Bloch notes, "it falls to women to take on and take away the sorrow and pollution of death."[1] The woman lamenter's tears and utterances were believed to assure the safe passage of the dead kin member's soul to the afterlife and to channel the life force of the deceased back into the clan. In Homeric epic, the ritual mourning of women glorifies the fallen hero, as in the lament of the Muses over Achilles recounted in *Odyssey* 24.

Women's tears also commanded a certain sacral power within the traditional rite of supplication. Both biblical and classical narratives show how the tears of a suppliant mother or daughter could win mercy for a son, brother, or husband from a king or god. The figure of Thetis, whose tearful eyes move Zeus to grant special privileges for her son, Achilles, is the earliest classical example of the ability of the tearful female suppliant to win mercy for a son, brother, or husband from a king or god. The biblical figure who best incarnates the intercessional power of the female suppliant's tears is Rachel. Her combination of beauty and maternal solicitude gives her laments the power to soften God's anger against her sinful descendents, the tribe of Benjamin.

Appearing in Genesis as the beloved of Jacob, Rachel assumes a maternal guise in a prophetic passage from the book of Jeremiah. Here God hears Rachel weeping posthumously for her children, the people of Israel, as they are being led into the Babylonian exile. The passage became a favorite among Christian allegorists, for whom Rachel (and the mourning Virgin) was a figure for Christ's church.

> Haec dicit Dominus:
> Vox in excelso audita est lamentationis,
> luctus, et fletus Rachel plorantis filios suos,
> et nolentis consolari super eis,
> quia non sunt.
>
> Haec dicit Dominus:
> Quiescat vox tua a ploratu,
> et oculi tui a lacrymis,
> quia est merces operi tuo, ait Dominus,
> et revertentur de terra inimici . . .
> (31. 15–16)

[Thus says the Lord: "A voice is heard on high of lamentation, grieving, and weeping, of Rachel lamenting her children and refusing to be comforted for them because they are not."

Thus says the Lord: "Let your voice be quieted from its lamentation and your eyes from tears because your work has its reward," says the Lord; 'And they will return from the land of the enemy.]²

By the same token, Ovid, in the elegiac coloring that he gives to the tale of Andromeda and Perseus in *Metamorphoses* 4, depicts a woman's tears of distress as an attractive spectacle for men. Thus, in both classical texts and the Old Testament, tears flatter patriarchy's self-image: they make women's grief appear to serve the masculine cult of heroism rather than the women themselves, or else they make women appear both erotically receptive and dependent on male authority.

In Medieval literature, women's tears are one of the most ambiguous forms of female power. While the early Church fathers sought to suppress the lamentation rituals of women associated with pagan culture,³ the literary traditions of the Christian era perpetuated the cult of women's tears, celebrating above all maternal tears for a lost son, a theme that culminates in the figure of the Pietà.⁴ High in dignity, too, were the tears shed by wives and brides of fallen heroes. Dante's *Commedia* evokes the ancient belief in the power of women's tears in *Inferno* 2, relating how Virgil was sparked with zeal to rescue the despairing pilgrim, Dante, by the sight of Beatrice's tears of pity.⁵

Women's tears figure prominently in autobiographical conversion narratives. In such contexts, they signal a role for women in the scheme of salvation as witnesses and intercessors, for they implicitly identify women with a form of spiritual agency and authority. The figure of the lamenting woman in the letters of Abelard and Heloise may be understood in the context of the paradigmatic autobiographical conversion narrative of the Middle Ages, particularly Augustine's *Confessions*. Such a perspective illuminates the ways in which woman's tears of intercession were exploited by male autobiographers. Both the Abelard-Heloise correspondence and Augustine's *Confessions* identify a special role for women as tearful or prayerful witnesses and intercessors and, therefore, as agents of spiritual agency and authority. Yet, if these narratives offer a framework for female authority within Medieval theology, we must ask whether they do not help to perpetuate a cultural system that represents conversion as a primarily male experience and, while apparently glorifying women's spiritual experience, subordinates it to men's. Only in the correspondence of Abelard and Heloise do we find, in the voice of Heloise, a hint that a woman's lament may have other, non-male-centered, meanings.

The Son of Tears: Augustine's *Confessions*

In Augustine's account of his conversion, the tears and laments of a very human mother play a crucial role in the narrative. In this story, an errant son wins God's mercy through the agency of a mother's tearful prayer. Monica presents a particular variation of the *mater lacrimosa*. With its emphasis on the mother-son relationship and the role of affective relations in the divine order of things, Monica's story shares some important elements with this tradition. Nonetheless, Augustine's portrayal of his mother offers a particularly domestic and intimate portrait of the maternal intercessor. Monica, whom her son describes as "illa vidua casta, pia et sobria" [That chaste, god-fearing, and sober widow] (*Confessions*, book 3. xi.),[6] is a domestic Rachel whose tears over her wayward son's spiritual exile are exemplary but not allegorical in nature. In their personal, habitual quality, they signify Christianity's shift away from a concern with collective piety to a focus on individual salvation.

Throughout the *Confessions*, the narrative of Monica's spiritual ordeal intertwines with that of her son. Augustine depicts her struggle to see him converted to her faith as an unrelenting torrent of tears and prayers offered up to God. Once she becomes a widow and her son has reached adulthood, her devotional energies become focused almost exclusively on his salvation.

The magnitude of the son's sins can be measured by her daily flow of tears. Having caused her great suffering by his adherence to Manicheanism and by his worldly lifestyle, the young Augustine meets with a strong maternal reaction. He describes her demonstrations of grief as resembling ritual funerary behavior because she considers him spiritually dead: "cum pro me fleret ad te mea mater, fidelis tua, amplius quam flent matres corporea funera" [Because my mother, Your faithful one, wept to You for me more bitterly than mothers weep for the bodily deaths of their children].[7] Writing from the perspective of the converted, Augustine the narrator stresses the power of her tears and laments to find a sympathetic ear in God during the period when her son is in his deepest spiritual peril. Reflecting back upon these exhibitions of maternal grief, he finds in them an occasion for making a joyful prayer to God: "exaudisti eam nec despexisti lacrimas eius, cum profluentes rigarent terram sub oculis eius in omni loco orationis eius: exaudisti eam" (3. xi.) [You heard her and did not despise her tears when they flowed down and watered the earth against which she pressed her face whenever she prayed. You heard her].[8]

In the same chapter, he writes that she performs her ritual lament for him at each of her set prayers. Like the mothers of Greek tragedy, Monica weeps most profusely over her child's fate. Analyzing the passage cited above, Clarissa W. Atkinson notes that Monica's tears "resemble the water of baptism and the wine of the Eucharist." They are "sacramental fluids whose purposes are accomplished *ex opere operatio*" (in the performance of the rite).[9] In other words, the tears represent the pouring out of God's grace (as in the sacraments), rather than being the direct cause of Augustine's salvation. These maternal tears contrast implicitly with the tears of mourning that the young Augustine sheds over the death of his best friend from a fever. Without the love of God, such tears are characterized by the narrator as the "suavis fructus" of self-pity, not prayers for the resurrection of the beloved's body or soul.[10]

The narrator's prayer of thanksgiving precedes the first of two episodes in Book Three that stress the power of his mother's tears to make contact with the divine. In these episodes, Monica's weeping also becomes the occasion for prophecies of her son's salvation. Chapter 11 recounts Monica's dream in which an angelic young man appears to comfort her in her sorrow:

> vidit enim se stantem in quadam regula lignea et venientem ad se iuvenem splendidum hilarem atque arridentem sibi, cum illa esset maerens et maerore confecta.

> [She saw herself standing on a wooden rule and a youth all radiant coming to her cheerful and smiling upon her, whereas she was grieving and heavy with her grief.][11]

Like the risen Christ who greets the faithful Mary Magdalen at his tomb in the Gospel of Mark,[12] this smiling figure stills her laments by showing her that the son whose "perdition" [perditionem meam] she feared is in fact by her side "standing upon the same rule" [iuxta se in eadem stantem]. The wayward son's spiritual resurrection is thus prophesied.

In the following chapter, a certain tension emerges between the attitude of the protagonist and that of the narrator toward Monica's laments. Once again, Monica's tears over her wayward son receive official sanction, this time in the form of a bishop's blessing. Rendered distraught by her son's continued adherence to Manicheanism, she petitions a local bishop, asking that he argue with her stubborn son concerning the error of Manichean doctrine. When the bishop demurs, assuring her that he had himself outgrown a youthful infatuation with that heresy, she persists in her laments. Finally, unable to reason with her, he dismisses her with what the text suggests is a busy man's exasperation:

> ille iam substomachans: "vade," inquit. "a me; ita vivas, fieri non potest, ut filius istarum lacrimarum pereat." (3. xii)

> [He, losing patience, said: "Go your way; as sure as you live, it is impossible that the son of these tears should perish.]

Monica responds to his reply "ac si de caelo sonuisset" [as if an oracle had resounded from Heaven].[13]

Unlike the previous account of her dream with its heavenly consoler, the scene with the bishop allows a certain irony to creep in and undermine the exalted, oracular significance that Monica attaches to the bishop's words. From the latter's perspective, this is an overwrought mother whose tedious, hyperbolic laments can only be silenced by flattery. One wonders whether the narrator has fully mastered his own masculine desire to escape her outbursts. That the young Augustine was exasperated by her behavior is made clear in the later episode from book 5 when he embarks on his sea journey to Rome. Unable to silence her wails of opposition to his departure, Augustine resorts to deceit and steals aboard the ship one night after telling her that he meant only to bid farewell to a departing friend. Her complaints and lamentations upon discovering his ruse are here denied any intercessional powers by the narrator. Blending his hindsight with God's foresight, he notes that God's plan for his conversion necessitated that Monica's tearful petitions go unheard and that he make the voyage to Italy. Monica's intense and emotional devotion to her son's salvation does not endow her with a greater knowledge of God's plan for him; indeed, Augustine sees in this episode proof that her laments stem in part from a "carnal affection" [carnale desiderium] for him that "was justly punished by the scourge of sorrows" [iusto dolorum flagello vapularet]. In her ignorance of God's plan, Monica shows herself to be a mere daughter of Eve, condemned to seek with sorrow what she had brought forth in sorrow.[14] Monica's tears are thus as inescapable and inevitable as a mother's physical travails in childbirth, the "sorrow" originally imposed upon Eve as punishment for her sins. Her spiritual grief, though sincere and more vehement than her human concern for her son's physical welfare, cannot fully transcend the latter. She thus remains vulnerable to physical and moral collapse should her son die without being converted.

When Augustine suffers his spiritual crisis in Milan, having abandoned Manicheanism while yet lacking faith, Monica's rescue of her son is vividly told. As the latter "walked through dark and slippery places" and "had come into the depths of the sea" in his quest for God, a parallel scene is juxtaposed in the narrative: we are told how Monica, anxious to help her son, leaves Africa for Italy on a literal voyage over the perilous sea. Her son writes that, fortified by the courage of piety, she was undaunted by the dangers of the journey (6. i). Once in Milan, Monica does not confront Augustine directly but relies on her own tears and the eloquence of the great bishop Ambrose to do their work on her son's soul.

The line between maternal possessiveness and maternal piety blurs throughout the *Confessions*, but one thing remains clear: the emphasis on Monica's tears intensifies the magnitude of Augustine's sins and, by extension, the miraculous significance of his conversion. While celebrating these proofs of Monica's powerful faith, initially so superior to his own, Augustine frames his praise and awe of her tears with the superior knowledge of grace which he shares with his interlocutor, God.

Consolation or Lamentation? The *Historia calamitatum*

Augustine describes his spiritual peril and the role of a female intercessor as the means and sign of his salvation from the viewpoint of the converted narrator. A different perspective appears in Peter Abelard's *Historia calamitatum*, in which the protagonist writes from the position of one who is converted and who can console others, but who is as yet imperiled by Fortune.[15] There is little to indicate any direct influence of the *Confessions* on Abelard's text, although Abelard mentions Augustine three times. Of Abelard's narrative, Mary M. McLaughlin writes: "[t]here is in the *Story of Calamities* little of the reflectiveness, the profound spiritual and psychological insight, of the *Confessions*."[16] Yet the same critic goes on to assert that Abelard, like Augustine, succeeded "in imposing on the confusions of experience an order in which both the shape of a life and the paradoxes of a personality are clearly disclosed," noting that he endowed his life experience with a unity and coherence by depicting his career "through the lens of calamity."[17] If Abelard is less introspective on the subject of his troubles and errors than is Augustine, nonetheless he depicts himself, as we shall see, as the object of public pity and lamentation on the part of his supporters.

The theme of lament is closely connected to Abelard's penchant for self-dramatization in the *Historia calamitatum*. His innovative excursion into autobiography unites rhetorical self-fashioning with a theatrical view of life as a series of scenes played out before an audience. Through quotation and allusion, he assumes many different identities culled from literature and history: most are victims of Fortune. Abelard closes his "Letter of Consolation"[18] with an affirmation of personal fortitude—"Whatever befalls the righteous man it shall not sadden him" (Proverbs xii, 21)—but his narrative's highly rhetorical character hardly suits Abelard's putative homiletic concerns. By quoting the passage from Proverbs, he attempts to throw a cloak of pious resignation over what is largely the lament of an unredeemed Boethius. Abelard sees himself engaged in a lifelong epic struggle with infamous adversaries. His sufferings on behalf of intellectual rigor, professional integrity, and monastic reform and his downfall brought on by lust and pride are recounted in highly charged rhetoric. He is by turns a figurative soldier for Knowledge, a Jerome set upon by envious rivals, a Samson in bondage because of Woman, and, finally, a saintly, even Christlike martyr for Truth. Each of these rhetorical stances makes him into a potential figure for lament. Such is clearly Heloise's initial response to his account of his persecutions:

> Que cum siccis oculis neminem vel legere vel audire posse estimem, tanto dolores meos amplius renovarunt quanto diligentius singula expresserunt, et eo magis auxerunt quo in te adhuc pericula crescere retulisti; ut omnes pariter de vita tua desperare cogamur, et cotidie ultimos illos de nece tua rumores trepidantia nostra corda et palpantia pectora expectent. (112)

> [No one, I think, could read or hear it dry-eyed; my own sorrows are renewed by the detail in which you have told it, and redoubled because you say your perils are still increasing. All of us here are driven to despair of your life, and every day we await in fear and trembling the final word of your death.] (110)

Although Heloise's response has been seen as rhetorical exaggeration, it conforms to the tearful reactions of Abelard's supporters in his own narrative.[19] By their emotional impact upon the reader, the collective force of his calamities compromises, if not undercuts, the author's expressions of humble penitance. And finally, the Christian stoicism of the concluding consolatory lines must be weighed against the work's assertion of the exemplary, larger-than-life nature of its subject's suffering.

The ideological contradiction between consolation and lamentation is difficult to resolve in the *Historia calamitatum*. The contradiction is partly formal. While consolation is associated with the quasi-private epistolary form, Abelard's highly visible career as a goliardic philosopher caused his misfortunes to become public spectacle, and he evokes the spontaneous laments of his supporters as a way of impressing the reader with the magnitude of his travails. Both of his greatest calamities, his castration by Fulbert's henchmen and the burning of his book on the Trinity at the Council of Soissons, were public events causing Abelard an acute sense of shame. In both instances, he himself shed tears for his broken reputation. He describes the scene in the streets of Paris after his castration as a situation of public mourning:

> Mane autem facto, tota ad me civitas congregata, quanta stuperet ammiratione, quanta se affligeret lamentatione, quanto me clamore vexarent, quanto planctu perturbarent, difficile, immo impossibile est exprimi. Maxime vero clerici ac precipue scolares nostri intolerabilibus me lamentis et ejulatibus cruciabant, ut multo amplius ex eorum compassione quam ex vulneris lederer passione, et plus erubescentiam quam plagam sentirem. (80)

> [Next morning the whole city gathered before my house, and the scene of horror and amazement, mingled with lamentations, cries and groans which exasperated and distressed me, is difficult, no, impossible to describe. In particular, the clerks and, most of all, my pupils tormented me with their unbearable weeping and wailing until I suffered more from their sympathy than from the pain of my wound, and felt the misery of my mutilation less than my shame and humiliation.] (75)

The students' histrionic behavior over the lost manhood of their teacher conveys the idea of Abelard's personal charisma. It thus links his masculine sexuality and aggression to his reputation as an intellectual leader. In literary terms, however, the scene evokes the collective outpourings of grief over fallen warriors and heroes common to epic. Although Abelard distances himself from the students' lament, their wailing is a natural response to a central feature of his self-portrait.

Abelard's combativeness in intellectual debate in fact made him into a kind of warrior, as he asserts at the outset of the *Historia calamitatum*.

Having "withdrawn from the court of Mars in order to kneel at the feet of Minerva" (63) [Martis curie penitus abdicarem ut Minerve gremio educarer (58)], he transferred his combative energy and self-confidence into a new arena that called for other weapons. As he depicts it, his goliardic career paralleled that of the fictional knight errant on a quest for glorifying combats. For both knight and philosopher, the object was fame. When Abelard arrived at the height of his fame as a logician, he commanded an army of devoted students and clerks who exulted and gloried with him but who also identified with his defeats, as the passage cited above indicates.

From this perspective, his self-portrayal recalls that of the Roman general Pompey in Lucan's *De Bello Civili*, from which Abelard quotes both in the *Historia calamitatum* and in his second letter to Heloise. The structure and rhetoric of Lucan's narrative in books 8 and 9 of *De Bello Civili*, with its protracted laments, play an important role in shaping Abelard's autobiographical letter and, we shall see, Heloise's response to it. The parallel between Abelard and Lucan's tragic protagonist is less explicit than the one that he repeatedly draws between himself and Jerome but is nevertheless clear from several common motifs. Pompey enjoyed the intense devotion of his army in his doomed fight against Julius Caesar: like Abelard, he was initially Fortune's favorite; like Abelard, his lust for fame was enormous; and like Abelard, his body was mutilated when he was betrayed by the treachery of lesser men. His courage in enduring a gruesome death was a model of stoic heroism. More important, he appears as a husband, as well as a military hero, for his wife shows intense devotion to him in adversity. In its gruesomeness, Pompey's fate hangs over the *Historia calamitatum*.

This parallel with a protagonist from classical epic suggests that Abelard's motives as a philosopher are influenced by pagan, as well as strictly Christian, conceptions of fame. Rather than Augustine's notion of *fama* as a kind of moral and public reputation,[20] Abelard seeks fame as a form of immortality. This is hardly surprising on the part of an author steeped in Roman literature. But the importance of fame, or, more precisely, lost fame, to the writing of the *Historia calamitatum* has been underestimated. It is significant that Abelard wrote his autobiographical epistle at the nadir of his professional and personal fortunes, during his disastrous tenure as abbot of St. Gildas in Brittany.[21] McLaughlin argues convincingly that Abelard writes to console himself as well as others during this period of despair and that "the writing of his letter became the act of catharsis" enabling him to return to creative activity.[22] However, one can offer another interpretation of Abelard's decision to record his troubles in epistolary form.[23] If the earlier period of triumphant teaching and disputations represented the apex of his public career, the abbacy at St. Gildas represented the loss of all his former powers and status. Like Pompey, he made a disastrous choice of refuge in defeat. Above all, St. Gildas, with its isolated location and hostile inmates, threatened to bring a miserable, demeaning finale to a brilliant, if controversial, career. Writing the *Historia calamitatum* thus represents a bid to escape obscurity and reclaim his fame by composing a literary monument to himself in which he is portrayed as the fitting object of public lament. He therefore appropriates the framework of the consolatory epistle in order to cast a veil of resigned piety over a proud man's desire for public recognition.

Desire for immortality, befitting a hero in the classical sense, can also be seen as a motive in his founding of his oratory, the Paraclete. Erected by Abelard in Champagne, the Paraclete (meaning "God the Comforter") holds a special meaning within Abelard's autobiography. The Paraclete has been called the "citadel of his better self,"[24] but one can discern a less psychological meaning. Abelard, I suggest, also viewed the Paraclete as a kind of literary and quasi-sacred monument to his stature as a great man, fusing in the process Christian and classical meanings. Once Heloise and her nuns settle there, its symbolic and structural function becomes closely bound up with the figure of the female intercessor.

The Paraclete was initially a retreat in the wilderness for the intellectual renegade Abelard became at midlife. The episode in which he recounts its founding and early days conveys Abelard's conflicted nature as a man sincerely converted from worldly pursuits who nevertheless wants to leave his mark on that world. He writes how, upon being released from the abbey of St. Denis, he sought refuge in the wilds of Champagne as a sort of latter-day John the Baptist who shunned the Pharisees of his time. What begins as an attempt to console himself by turning to God for private comfort becomes a professional enterprise. Obliged to earn his living, Abelard begins to teach again, founding a rustic, antiestablishment school in opposition to those of his enemies in Paris. In his account, however, the lonely spot with its makeshift chapel is transformed into a bustling intellectual center when Abelard's reputation once again attracts large bands of students. When they flock down from Paris and other towns to receive his instruction, the students turn the site into a small city of tents and cabins and rebuild his oratory in wood and stone.[25] In recounting these events, Abelard stresses his own passivity and nonparticipation in the success of his school, in remarkable contrast to his earlier attitude. He is strangely absent, as if his reputation has, in fact, replaced him. The Paraclete is a place in which, Abelard writes, he can hide from his envious enemies, while remaining in the public consciousness.

> Hoc autem loco me corpore latitante, sed fama tunc maxime universum mundum perambulante et illius poetici figmenti quod

Equo dicitur instar penitus retinente, quod videlicet plurimum vocis habet sed nichil substantie . . . (97)

[Meanwhile, though my person lay hidden in this place, my fame travelled all over the world, resounding everywhere like that poetic creation Echo, so called because she has so large a voice but no substance.] (93)

Paradoxically, he is now more famous for being absent from Paris. The passage shifts the image of the Paraclete from that of lively open-air school to that of a figurative tomb enclosing Abelard's body. Unjustly punished and scorned like the mythical Echo, the garrulous debator and teacher retreats to the wilds and is ostensibly silenced. Yet by disappearing physically within his remote citadel, as the passage asserts, Abelard ensures the perpetuation of his fame as a philosopher, much as his epistle will spread his fame and function as a kind of disembodied voice. The comparison to Echo is a good example of Abelard's ability to wrest a victorious identity as martyr out of his victimization by casting himself as figuratively dead. Looking back, the episode as a whole suggests that the Paraclete has become a place of quasi-religious pilgrimage from which emanates the power of a martyr's relics. It is thus possible to view Abelard's edifice with its surrounding "city" as his initial attempt to create a shrine comparable to other monastic monuments of the period such as St. Denis and Fontevrault.[26] There is, however, a fundamental difference between fame (associated with pagan hero cults) and sanctity in the Christian sense. This flirtation with a pagan form of commemoration, as much as the oratory's unusual name, may have been what scandalized some of his contemporaries. The narrator's identification with such saintly exiles as Paul and Jerome further blurs the distinction between pagan fame and Christian sainthood.

In any case, the Paraclete did not long endure in this form. Abelard writes how he made the fateful decision to leave his oratory and accept the abbacy of St. Gildas out of a fear of persecution by hostile rivals who sought his condemnation as a heretic.[27] One may also conjecture that the contradiction between martyr and active teacher forced Abelard to resort to a different tactic to retrieve his reputation. Or, more importantly, one could infer that the aura of the place and his image could not be sustained by his male students. In the final section of this essay, I shall argue that the Paraclete's meaning as tomb and monument to his memory is fulfilled by the installation there of Heloise and her community of nuns. Only in a transferral of guardianship of the site to his spouse and figurative women kinfolk could Abelard ensure the lasting power of his fame. The gesture, as we shall see, requires a rhetorical appropriation of the Christian cult of women's tears and a reconquest of Heloise's defiant form of lament.

Cornelia or Mary Magdalen? The Correspondence of Heloise and Abelard

The lament of women over a man becomes a central theme in the correspondence of Abelard and Heloise. Here the two former lovers debate the proper response to their (mostly Abelard's) suffering through evocations of lament, tears, prayer, and tombside vigils. Their contrasting versions of female lament reveal directly opposed interpretations of their personal fates.

The *Historia calamitatum* tells how Abelard, tormented by his abandonment of his oratory, bestowed the establishment upon Heloise and her sister nuns who had been expelled from their convent at Argenteuil. The gift of the Paraclete to Heloise is a complex gesture. On the one hand, it is an act of generosity and solicitude toward the woman he had seduced, bullied, and forced into monastic life ten years earlier. On the other hand, by moving Heloise and her nuns to the Paraclete, Abelard was able to rescue his oratory from oblivion. Under Heloise's leadership, the Paraclete was saved from ruin and achieved great prosperity and fame.[28] Heloise became a widely revered figure, as Peter the Venerable's later panegyric of her attests.[29] Although Abelard felt obliged to defend his association with a women's convent at the end of the *Historia calamitatum*, the Paraclete's good fortune could only reflect favorably upon its founder, Abelard.[30]

As founder and spiritual director of the Paraclete, Abelard writes, he enjoyed there a "haven of peace and safety from the raging storms" (102) that eluded him in his previous roles as monk and abbot. Throughout the *Historia calamitatum*, Abelard speaks with premonitions of his death, much as Christ spoke to his apostles. His narrative ends with the bleak forecast of his doom at the hands of the evil monks at St. Gildas. This provokes the alarmed outburst from Heloise quoted earlier as she responds to the idea of his imminent peril. In its intensity, her fear for his bodily safety recalls Monica's fears for her son's soul. Unlike Monica, however, the cloistered nun's only means of reaching him is by letter. The strong emotions Heloise expresses in her first two letters to Abelard strengthen the association made between her and Lucan's Cornelia in the *Historia calamitatum*. There Abelard depicts her as quoting the grieving wife of Pompey at the moment when Heloise takes up the veil:

> O maxime conju[n]x!
> O thalamis indigne meis, hoc juris habebat
> In tantum fortuna capud? Cur impia nupsi,
> Si miserum factura fui? Nunc accipe penas.
> Sed quas sponte luam. . . . (81)

[O greatest husband! O unworthy of my marriage bed! Did Fortune have so much power over one so great? Why did I marry you, wrongfully, if I was to make you wretched? Now receive the punishment, but a punishment that I myself shall pay of my own accord.][31]

The similarities between Heloise and Lucan's character led one critic to call Heloise a "new Cornelia."[32] Heloise's voicing of Cornelia's lament reflects her identification with the Roman heroine: they both gave themselves in love before marriage, and they both blamed themselves for having doomed their beloved by marrying him. Heloise's outburst at the altar is usually taken as a kind of suicide speech, as she herself confirms when she writes later that she thus destroyed herself by his command.[33] Cornelia goes on to declare that she will sacrifice herself voluntarily to bring victory to her husband, implicitly contrasting herself with the unwilling victim Iphigenia.[34] Heloise may also wish to convey this kind of violent self-surrender. In taking a nun's vows, she was surrendering both her sexual and intellectual self out of obedience to Abelard. By quoting Cornelia, Heloise not only underscores their circumstantial similarities but also gives her own moment of crisis a sense of epic drama and pathos. In Lucan's text, Cornelia's speech provokes the tears of her husband and a sympathetic crowd, and such is no doubt the effect Heloise desires to make. There is evidence, moreover, that the lament from *De Bello Civili* was a performance piece during the twelfth century.[35] Like Cornelia, moreover, the vow she makes to pay the penalty (p[o]enas) is utterly futile. The histrionic quality of her speech, with its ultraliterary quality, also conveys the degree of her powerlessness to affect her husband's fortunes and her own.

In her letters, Heloise again adopts extravagantly emotional stances in response to Abelard's voiced premonitions of death. The formal devices and rhetorical strategies of her first two letters have been sensitively analyzed by Peter Dronke in terms of the Medieval epistolary and *planctus* traditions.[36] He convincingly shows how poetically accomplished and carefully structured her letters are. Heloise skillfully manipulates arguments and conventions drawn from the great Latin *auctores* Seneca, Lucan, Cicero, Ovid, and the Church Fathers. She may have modeled her second, more passionate letter on the Epistle of Briseis to Achilles in Ovid's *Heroides*.[37] More to our point, she evokes elements of the ritual lamentation in her passionate rhetoric. To be sure, her laments are highly stylized, as Dronke and others have made clear. These texts are not improvisational in nature. It is likely that what she knew of ritual lamentation was drawn from the literary tradition. Nevertheless, some of the elements in her letters, which appear to be pure hyperbole and rhetorical (or psychological) ploys, gain new meaning if they are recognized as conventions and themes associated with ritual lament.

First, the rhetorical situation of Heloise's letters resembles pagan funeral ritual. As we have seen, Abelard has presented himself in his autobiography as a repeatedly lamented victim. He concludes his narrative with overt premonitions of his death. Heloise's reponses to the situation that he presents, therefore, have the urgency and the emotional intensity of a lament for one who is dead or about to die. We imagine her figuratively standing before a dead man.

The parallels with funerary lament can be taken even further when we compare Heloise's rhetoric with conventional elements of ritual lamentation studied (in the Greek tradition) by Margaret Alexiou. Heloise alternatively writes in a collective voice on behalf of the nuns of the Paraclete and in her own personal voice. Interpreters have noted how these shifts between the first person singular and first person plural pronouns reveal the intensification of her private feelings about Abelard and their mutual past. At the same time, the collective "we" is probably a screen for her own intense involvement in Abelard's situation. This alternation between collective and individual voice becomes even more meaningful if it is seen in terms of ritual lament. Typically lament rituals feature a principal lamenter and a chorus. Ritual laments, as Alexiou observes of the Greek tradition, begin with an opening question or series of questions expressing the plight of the mourner.[38] This is exactly the form in which Heloise expresses her emotional involvement at the beginning of her second letter. She quotes the end of Abelard's letter to her: "but if the Lord should deliver me into the hands of my enemies so that they overcome and kill me. . . . ?" and then goes on: "My dearest, how could you think such a thought? How could you give voice to it?" Shortly after, she again quotes Abelard and asks: "But how could you suppose that our memory of you could ever fade? Besides, what time will there be then which will be fitting for prayer when extreme distress will allow us no peace . . . ?" (128).

Another frequent feature of ritual lament is the contrast between past and present in which "the mourner turned to reflect on what the dead was in his lifetime and what he has come to now. . . . "[39] This pattern, too, informs Heloise's letters: "What king or philosopher could match your fame? What district, town or village did not long to see you when you appeared in public? Who did not hurry to catch a glimpse of you or crane his neck or strain his eyes to follow your departure?" (115). Still another pattern of ritual lament applies to Heloise, namely the contrast between the dead, addressed in the second person, and the mourner who speaks of his or her condition in the first person. In these contrasts, the mourner calls upon the dead as more fortunate for having escaped the pain of continuing grief.[40] For Heloise, Abelard's castration makes him dead to her. As in the laments cited by Alexiou, she writes that God has given her a greater suffering than Abelard because "a single wound of the body" ends his torments whereas her sufferings continue unabated (133). Finally, the traditional lament often includes a wish that the survivor had died or else that death had come differently. Such statements often take the form of a "should have." So Heloise writes: "The proper course would be for you to perform our funeral rites, for you to commend our souls to God. . . . " (127). Or shortly afterwards, "I would not even have us live to see that day . . . God grant that we never live on to perform this duty . . . in this may we go before, not after you!" (128).

As I have already shown, Abelard, by drawing on the heroic models in classical literature, has portrayed himself as worthy of lament. He has also developed the pathos of his situation. In this way, he elicits these emotional responses from Heloise. How then does Abelard respond? In fact, he does direct Heloise and her nuns in a program of lament for him, and he writes prayers for them to recite on his behalf, while neutralizing their intensity.[41] He begins by acknowledging the special power of women's lament, especially the lament of wives. He cites the case of David and the wife of Nabal the Carmelite:

> Quod diligenter ipse Psalmista considerans, ad supplicationem uxoris Nabal Carmeli iuramentum quod ex iustitia fecerat, de viro eius scilicet et ipsius domo delenda per misericordiam cassavit. (74)
>
> [The Psalmist himself considered this carefully when at the entreaty of the wife of Nabal the Carmelite, as an act of mercy he broke the oath he had justly sworn concerning her husband and the destruction of his house.]

He instructs her and her nuns at length to imitate the Holy Women who followed Christ and came to mourn him at the tomb. Unlike the earlier Christian writers, Abelard finds the behavior of the Holy Women exemplary. Donald K. Frank's study of the correspondence between Abelard and Heloise points out the many passages in which Abelard expresses his desire for the prayers and the thoughts of the nuns of the Paraclete. Frank also notes how Abelard exaggerates the qualities of faithfulness and courage attributed to the Holy Women in the Scriptures: "He would perhaps have the biblical circumstance accord more readily with the type of vigil he wished Heloise and her nuns to have."[42] In the ritual laments examined above, the lamenter takes an active, confrontative role in addressing the mourned dead person and those viewed as responsible for the death. Abelard's instructions about the Holy Women, however, recast Heloise's lament into a much more passive mode. His mourners weep but do not speak directly in the text.

Throughout his two letters to Heloise, moreover, Abelard blurs the distinction between lament and prayer. In his initial reply to Heloise's voiced distress over his sufferings and continuing peril, he turns the nuns' expressions of anxiety into the ordered, more ceremonial idiom of liturgical chant, inserting a prayer of his own composition into a psalter that she had requested of him. Rather than acknowledge their laments, he puts prayers into their mouths. His second letter, written in response to her much more fully developed *planctus*, takes this strategy even further. In his final instructions to Heloise, he appends a prayer for mercy that she, in particular, is directed to recite:

> ne despicias ancillulae tuae preces, quas pro meis ipsis carique mei excessibus in conspectu maiestatis tuae supplex effundo. (93)

> [despise not the prayers of thy humble handmaid which I pour out as a suppliant in the presence of thy majesty for my own excesses and those of my beloved. . . .] (155)

Having completely taken over her voice, Abelard is able to fortify his prayer for himself and, in essence, to lament himself.

The example of the three Holy Women becomes the means through which Abelard beats down Heloise's emotional and sexual attachment to his body. In her second letter she confesses her inability to stop dwelling on their past lovemaking, even during the Mass.[43] Abelard, however, wishes to portray Heloise as a kind of Mary Magdalen, the courtesan-turned-hermit saint.[44] Faced with such impious resistance to his program of sublimation, however, Abelard resumes his sermon on the Holy Women and addresses a series of injunctions or devotional exercises to Heloise that are designed to turn her thoughts away from the corporeal images that haunt her. In a series of commands, he sets before her a substitute body on which to meditate; it is the broken body of Christ rather than his own:

> Hunc semper, soror, verum tuum et totius Ecclesiae sponsum prae oculis habe, mente gere. Intuere hunc exeuntem ad crucifigendum pro te et bajulantem sibi crucem. [. . .] Patienti sponte pro redemptione tua compatere et super crucifixo pro te compungere, Sepulcro eius mente semper assiste, et cum fidelibus feminis lamentare et luge. De quibus etiam ut iam supra memini scriptum est: Mulieres sedentes ad monumentum lamentabantur flentes

Dominum. [. . .] Plange tuum reparatorem, non corruptorem, redemptorem, non scortatorem, pro te mortuum Dominum, non viventem servum, immo nunc primum de morte vere liberatum. (91–92)

[Think of him always, sister, as your true spouse and the spouse of all the Church. Keep him in mind. Look at him going to be crucified for your sake, carrying his own cross. . . . Have compassion on him who suffered willingly for your redemption, and look with remorse on him who was crucified for you. In your mind be always present at his tomb, weep and wail with the faithful women, of whom it is written, as I said, 'The women sitting at the tomb wept and lamented for the Lord.' . . . Mourn for your Saviour and Redeemer, not for the seducer who defiled you, and for the Master who died for you, not for the servant who lives and, indeed for the first time, is truly freed from death.] (151–53)

Then, in a startling about-face, he turns from Scripture and liturgy back to Lucan and issues a final rebuke:

Cave, obsecro, ne quod dixit Pompeius maerenti Corneliae tibi improperetur turpissime:
  Vixit post proelia Magnus!
  Sed fortuna perit. Quod defles, illud amasti. (92)

[I beg you, beware lest Pompey's reproach to weeping Cornelia is applied to you, to your shame:
  The battle ended, Pompey the Great
  Lived, but his fortune died. It is this you now mourn
  And loved.] (153)[45]

Abelard has saved this rejection of Cornelia's laments for the conclusion of his sermon as if to deal Heloise a final blow by scorning her identification with the Roman heroine she had quoted so dramatically ten years earlier. This gesture rebukes the core of Heloise's identity: her longing for grandeur, her selfless love for Abelard, her passionate spirit, and her learning. The quotation also points to the paradox of Abelard's relation to the female lament. On the one hand, he dismisses Cornelia's (i.e., Heloise's) laments as belonging to the lower realm of the body and the emotions rather than the soul. Yet, on the other hand, he desires the commemoration that these laments offer. Thus the passage from Lucan evokes the self-effacing gesture of one who is not interested in being lamented. On the other hand, there is an implicit comparison to a heroic figure, Pompey the Great.

These contradictions play around the instructions he gives to Heloise and her nuns. The Paraclete, tended by Heloise's able leadership, was to be his final resting place, a monument to his memory not unlike the architectural shrines being erected by the French royalty during this period. In their correspondence, Heloise reveals how Abelard has remained a powerful though absent figure at the Paraclete and that the nuns' devotions center around him. By playing the role of the absent yet beloved spiritual director (mutilated and banished by envious men), Abelard presents himself as a Christlike figure, who is the redeemer of women. In exchange for his ministrations in life, he would be lamented by holy women under his former mistress and wife, Heloise.

Furthermore, Heloise's later request for hymns suggests that she, too, thought of her nuns as a medium for Abelard's creations rather than an audience. In a figurative sense, Abelard's gift of prayers, hymns, and sequences turns the women of the Paraclete into a choir of professional mourners who will sing his songs over him in an imaginative antiphonal song with the kinswoman-wife, Heloise. Behind Abelard's sermonizing on the Holy Women and, by extension, his dwelling on God's favoring of women's tears and supplications (ceremonialized into liturgical matter), one can see a strategy to deflect Heloise's own personal complaint into institutionalized passivity by imposing a Christological meaning on her experience. Abelard's schema, which becomes the frame for all future exchanges between them, serves as a compliment to Heloise's womanly and religious dignity as an abbess and is calculated to defuse her passion and anger. Yet it also perpetuates the hierarchical structure of their earlier relationship, for, despite Abelard's self-deprecating disclaimers and his confessions of his unworthiness of Heloise's love, he gradually moves away from his initial acknowledgment of dependence on her prayers and intercession to reassert his authority as male spiritual director who assigns her and her nuns a purely institutional intercessionary role. Furthermore, he remains the subject of salvation within their common narrative, whereas she, despite having become his "sister" in their conversion, remains its instrument. Her grief and anger over her own destiny are degendered and silenced by the combination of his personal authority over her and by her institutional obligation to pray for the souls of the dead. Heloise's tears, which initially fell for herself as well as for him, are reinterpreted and thereby denied their healing power, having lost all relation to her own suffering.

Conclusion

Both Augustine and Abelard relate narratives of conversion in which the powers of women's tears have the important role of supplication and intercession. This role operates in retrospect in Augustine as he recounts Monica's supplications, prayers, and laments for his spiritual salvation and in prospect for Abelard as he solicits the prayers of Heloise and her community and directs them to his own models. These laments enhance the importance of each writer's spiritual struggle and eventual conversion, but, at the same time, both authors separate themselves from the women's subjection to the total experience, both physical and emotional, of sorrow.

In these textual operations, both Augustine's and Abelard's male narrators draw upon a deeply rooted cultural opposition between female emotionality and male knowledge and control. In the narrative form of the *Confessions,* Monica's voice appears only in the third person as a component of the narrator's spiritual growth. Because the *Confessions* are written in the form of a prayer, her voice is absorbed into the implicit dialogue between Augustine and God. Both Augustine and Abelard are critical of the female laments even as they profit from them, and, in the process, they implicitly deny spiritual autonomy to the women. These texts represent conversion as a primarily, if not exclusively, male experience.

As we have seen, Augustine lightly ironizes Monica's laments, whereas Abelard casts the traditional motifs of funeral laments in Heloise's letters into the more passive form of the Holy Women's lamentation over Christ's body. Only Heloise's letters retain the emotive power of the traditional female lament, with its question-and-answer form, its intense personal quality, anger, and implied gestural expressiveness. In this context, it is moving to see Heloise accepting Abelard's criticism and authority but still insisting on a sorrow that can be repressed in writing but not in the speech of tongue and heart:

> Ne me forte in aliquo de inobedientia causari queas, verbis etiam immoderati doloris tuae frenum impositum est iussionis ut ab his mihi saltem in scribendo temperem a quibus in sermone non tam difficile quam impossibile est providere. Nihil enim minus in nostra est potestate quam animus, eique magis obedire cogimur quam imperare possimus. Unde et cum nos eius affectiones stimulant, nemo earum subitos impulsus ita repulerit ut non in effecta facile prorumpant, et se per verba facilius effluant quae promptiores animi passionum sunt notae, secundum quod scriptum est: "Ex abundantia enim cordis os loquitur." Revocabo itaque manum a scripto in quibus linguam a verbis temperare non valeo. Utinam sic animus dolentis parere promptus sit quemadmodum dextra scribentis.

> [I would not want to give you cause for finding me disobedient in anything, so I have set the bridle of your injunction on the words which issue from my unbounded grief; thus in writing at least I

may moderate what it is difficult or rather impossible to forestall
in speech. For nothing is less under our control than the heart—
having no power to command it we are forced to obey. And so
when its impulses move us, none of us can stop their sudden
promptings from easily breaking out, and even more easily overflowing into words which are the ever-ready indications of the
heart's emotions: as it is written, "A man's words are spoken from
the overflowing of the heart." I will therefore hold my hand from
writing words which I cannot restrain my tongue from speaking;
would that a grieving heart would be as ready to obey as a writer's
hand!] (159)[46]

Even after all of Abelard's rebuke and redirection, she does not entirely
surrender the emotions that here, as in so much of the tradition before her,
are expressed through the tears and laments of women.

Notes

1. "Death, Women, and Power" in *Death and the Regeneration of Life*,
ed. Maurice Bloch and Jonathan Parry (Cambridge: Cambridge University
Press, 1982), p. 226.
2. *Biblia sacra. Juxta Vulgatam Clementinam* (Madrid: Biblioteca de
Autores Cristianos, 1965).
3. Johannes Quasten, *Music and Worship in Pagan and Christian
Antiquity*, trans. Boniface Ramsey, O. P. (Washington, DC: NPM Studies in
Church Music and Liturgy, National Association of Pastoral Musicians, 1983),
p. 161. See also Frederick S. Paxton, *Christianizing Death: The Creation of
a Ritual Process in Early Medieval Europe* (Ithaca, NY: Cornell University
Press, 1991), p. 43.
4. Clarissa W. Atkinson, *The Oldest Vocation: Christian Motherhood in the Middle Ages* (Ithaca, NY: Cornell University Press, 1991), pp.
105–06.
5. In *Inferno* 2, Dante becomes paralyzed with doubt and fear at the
idea of journeying through the "alto passo" as a mere mortal. To encourage
him, Virgil reveals that it was Beatrice who had ordained their journey
during an extraordinary appearance to Virgil in Hell. Virgil then reports
Beatrice's narrative to him in the so-called "prologue in heaven" scene.
Listening to Virgil, Dante learns how "three blessed ladies in the court of
Heaven" took pity on him in his impediment, and how Virgil, finally, was
inspired to rescue Dante, by the sight of Beatrice's tears:

> Poscia che m'ebbe ragionato questo,
> li occhi lucenti lagrimando volse,
> per che mi fece del venir pu presto.
> (2. 115–17)

[When she had said this to me, she turned her eyes, which shone with tears, making me the more eager to come. . . .]

Text and translation from *The Divine Comedy*, trans. Charles S. Singleton (Princeton: Princeton University Press, 1970, repr. 1977), vol. 1, *Inferno*, pp. 20–21.

Clearly, for Virgil and his listener Dante, the tears heighten the suppliant's feminine vulnerability and virtue and spur Virgil with a greater urgency than mere respect would dictate. More than anything Beatrice actually says, the tears in her eyes persuade her male interlocutor to heed her wish.

6. I cite throughout the Latin text of Augustine's *Confessions* from the Loeb Classical Library edition (Cambridge: Harvard University Press, 1912; repr. 1977), which is based on P. Knöll's Teubner text (Leipzig, 1909). All subsequent quotations from the *Confessions* will be taken from this edition. The present citation is from vol. 1, p. 140.

7. Augustine, *Confessions*, vol. 1, Book 3, chap. xi, p. 136. English text from *The Confessions of St. Augustine*, trans. F. J. Sheed (New York: Sheed and Ward, 1942), p. 45. I cite Sheed's translation throughout. The page numbers of the translation will always be cited after those of the original.

8. *Confessions*, p. 136/pp. 45–46.

9. Clarissa W. Atkinson, " 'Your Servant, My Mother': The Figure of St. Monica in the Ideology of Christian Motherhood," in *Immaculate and Powerful: The Female in Sacred Image and Social Reality*, ed. Clarissa W. Atkinson, Constance H. Buchanan, and Margaret R. Miles (Boston: Beacon Press, 1985), pp. 142–43.

10. "Unde igitur suavis fructus de amaritudine vitae carpitur gemere et flere et suspirare et conqueri? an hoc ibi dulce est, quod speramus exaudire te? recte istud in precibus, quia desiderium perveniendi habent. num in dolore amissae rei et luctu, quo tunc operiebar?" (4. v) (*Confessions*, p. 162) [How does it come then that from the bitterness of life we can pluck fruit so sweet as is in mourning and weeping and sighing and the utterance of our woe? Are all these things such relief to our misery because of our hope that You hear them? Obviously this is so of our prayers, because they are uttered with the sole aim of reaching You. But is it so also of the sorrow and grief for a thing lost, in which I was then overwhelmed?] (p. 55). Meditating further on the bonds of human friendship that give rise to such

grief, Augustine notes that the man who loves his friend in God finds no sorrow in the friend's death, for there can be no loss if the human love is subsumed in a greater love of God (4. ix.).

11. *Confessions*, p. 138/p. 46.

12. Mark vv. 2–8. This scene is not mentioned in the Gospel of Matthew.

13. *Confessions*, p. 142/p. 47.

14. *Confessions* 5, viii; pp. 236–38.

15. By aligning Abelard's text with Augustine's *Confessions*, I am implicitly agreeing with those scholars who consider the manuscript attribution of the *Historia calamitatum* and the collection of letters to Abelard and Heloise to be largely authentic rather than a case of forgery. For the most vigorous defenses of the authenticity of the collection, and especially Heloise's letters, see Peter Dronke, *Abelard and Heloise in Medieval Testimonies*, W. P. Kerr Memorial Lecture, no. 26 (Glasgow: University of Glasgow Press, 1976) and ibid., "Excursus: Did Abelard Write Heloise's Third Letter?" in *Women Writers of the Middle Ages: A Critical Study of Texts from Perpetua (d. 203) to Marguerite Porete (d. 1310)* (Cambridge: Cambridge University Press, 1984), pp. 140–43. For an explicitly feminist refutation of the forgery theories as they concern Heloise's authorship, see Barbara Newman, "Authority, Authenticity, and the Repression of Heloise," *Journal of Medieval and Renaissance Studies* 22.2 (1992): pp. 121–57. Citations from the *Historia calamitatum* and Heloise's first two letters are taken from the edition of Jacques Monfrin, *Abélard. Historia calamitatum. texte critique* (Paris: Vrin, 1959). Heloise's first two letters appear in the appendix. The passage quoted above appears on p. 207. Translations are taken from Betty Radice, *The Letters of Abelard and Heloise* (Harmondsworth, England: Penguin, 1974). Page numbers for futher citations refer to this edition and translation which I quote with minor changes.

16. Mary H. McLaughlin, "Abelard as Autobiographer: The Motives and Meaning of his 'Story of Calamities,'" *Speculum* 42 (1967): p. 471.

17. McLaughlin, "Abelard," p. 472.

18. *Abaelardi ad Amicum suum consolatoria* is the title given to Abelard's text in the most authoritative manuscript, MS Troyes 802.

19. Peter Dronke, "Heloise," in *Women Writers of the Middle Ages* (Cambridge: Cambridge University Press, 1984), pp. 121–22. Dronke provides a fine poetic analysis of her lament as an example of the literary *planctus*. In addition to the laments of his students and those of Heloise, are the tears shed by the Geoffrey, the bishop of Chartres (Monfrin, *Abélard*, p. 87).

20. Such seems to be the meaning of *fama* when Abelard quotes Augustine: "Qui, fidens conscientie sue, negligit famam suam, crudelis est."

(102) [He who relies on his conscience to the neglect of his reputation is cruel. (99)]

21. Not only did Abelard fail to reform the wild and unruly Breton monks at St. Gildas, he incurred their animosity to the extent that he feared for his life. He recounts the various attempts against his life and the peril he felt himself to be in toward the end of his letter. Monfrin, *Abélard*, pp. 98–101.

22. McLaughlin, "Abelard," pp. 469, 473.

23. Scholars have debated the intended audience for Abelard's "Letter of Consolation to a Friend" and how it fell into the hands of Heloise. Some see the "Friend" as a fiction; others not. Whether or not his text was intended as an open letter, the consolatory epistle was from classical times on a literary form, and thus public in nature.

24. McLaughlin, "Abelard," p. 476.

25. "Cum autem oratorium nostrum modicam eorum portionem capere non posset, necessario ipsum dilataverunt, et de lapidibus et lignis construentes melioraverunt" (94). [As my oratory could not hold even a modest proportion of their numbers, they were obliged to enlarge it, and improved it by building in wood and stone (90)]. The students' building activities suggest a way of compensating for the physical mutilation of their teacher which they earlier had lamented.

26. The comparison to St. Denis is, of course, ironic, since Abelard had fled his persecutors in that abbey that he depicts as being highly corrupt. The similarity to Fontevrault will be enhanced when Abelard converts the Paraclete into a convent for Heloise and her nuns.

27. "Deus ipse mihi testis est, quotiens aliquem ecclesiasticarum personarum conventum adunari noveram, hoc in dampnationem meam agi credebam. Stupefactus ilico quasi supervenientis ictum fulguris, expectabam ut quasi hereticus aut prophanus in conciliis traherer aut sinagogis" (97). [God is my witness that I never heard that an assembly of ecclesiastics had met without thinking this was convened to condemn me. I waited like one in terror of being struck by lightening to be brought before a council or synod and charged with heresy or profanity . . . (93)]. His flight from possible condemnation and execution for heresy seems ironically unheroic.

28. In the *Historia calamitatum* Abelard attributes the success of the convent to women's natural ability to attract assistance and to Heloise's piety and wisdom. Monfrin, *Abélard*, pp. 100–01. For information about the various charters connected with the Paraclete under Heloise, see Mary Martin McLaughlin, "Peter Abelard and the Dignity of Women: Twelfth Century 'Feminism' in Theory and Practice," in *Pierre Abélard-Pierre le Vénérable: Les courants philosophiques, littéraires et artistiques en occident au milieu du XIIe siècle*, Colloques Internationaux du Centre National de la

Recherche Scientifique, no. 546 (Paris: Editions du Centre National de la Recherche Scientifique, 1975), p. 317, note 100. McLaughlin argues (p. 315) that one of the goals of the *Historia calamitatum* "appears to have been the defense of his role as founder and guide of the Paraclete."

29. Giles Constable, ed., *The Letters of Peter the Venerable* , 2 vols. (Cambridge, MA: Harvard University Press, 1967) 1. 115, pp. 303–08.

30. Monfrin, *Abélard*, pp. 101–05. See also the discussion of Abelard as monastic reformer in McLaughlin, "Abelard and the Dignity of Women," pp. 315–20.

31. My translation. Heloise is quoting *De Bello Civili* 8. 94–98.

32. Etienne Gilson, *Héloïse et Abélard* (Paris: J. Vrin, 1948). A study of the Heloise-Cornelia parallel in terms of the *consolatio* tradition can be found in Peter von Moos, "Cornelia und Heloise," *Latomus* 34 (1975): pp. 1024–59. Von Moos provides a bibliography of the discussions of the parallel on p. 1025.

33. Monfrin, *Abélard*, p. 114.

34. Her speech continues: "quo sit tibi mollius aequor, / Certa fides regum totusque paratior orbis, / Sparge mari comitem" (8. 98–100) [So that the waves may be gentler for you and the firm faith of kings and the whole world more ready for you, throw [me] your companion into the sea.].

35. Peter von Moos, "Cornelia und Heloise," *Latomus* 34 (1975): pp. 1029–30.

36. Dronke, *Women Writers*, pp. 112–26.

37. Dronke, *Women Writers*, p. 126.

38. Margaret Alexiou, *The Ritual Lament in Greek Tradition* (Cambridge: Cambridge University Press, 1974), pp. 161–65.

39. Alexiou, p. 165.

40. Alexiou, pp. 173–77.

41. Text from J. T. Muckle, ed. "The Personal Letters between Abelard and Heloise," *Mediaeval Studies* 15 (1953): p. 76. Further references to this edition appear parenthetically in the text. Translation from Radice.

42. Donald K. Frank, "Abelard as Imitator of Christ," *Viator* 1 (1970): p. 110.

43. Monfrin, *Abélard*, p. 122.

44. Abelard does not mention the Magdalen by name and simply refers to the three Holy Women who followed Christ and tended his tomb. However, the specific parallels between Heloise and Mary Magdalen (the latter was Christ's devoted companion and most demonstrative mourner) are worth noting. The Magdalen's cult was reaching its peak in twelfth-century France, and contemporary commentaries on the Gospel passages about her praise her loyalty and affective piety. See Victor Saxer, *Le culte de Marie Madeleine*

en occident, des origines à la fin du Moyen-Age, 2 vols. (Paris: Librairie philosophique, 1959).

45. Lucan, *The Civil War*, ed. and trans. J. D. Duff. Loeb Classical Library. Cambridge: Harvard University Press, 1962. 8. 84–85.

46. Text: J. T. Muckle, C. S. B., "The Letter of Heloise on Religious Life and Abelard's First Reply," *Mediaeval Studies* 17 (1955): p. 241. Translation from Radice, p. 159.

Hrotswitha Writes Herself: *Clamor Validus Gandeshemensis*

Barbara K. Gold

Background

In a 1907 book entitled *Plays of our Forefathers*, C. M. Gayley describes the plays of Hrotswitha of Gandersheim: "Terence, the dear delight of the mediaeval monastery, was in the tenth [century] pruned of his pagan charm and naughtiness, and planted out in six persimmon comedies by a Saxon nun of Gandersheim, Hrotsvitha—comedies of tedious saints and hircine sinners and a stuffy Latin style."[1] Since the rediscovery of Hrotswitha's works by the German humanist Conrad Celtis in 1494 after nearly 500 years of obscurity, Hrotswitha has suffered many harsh judgments and received a wide variety of notice, both critical and laudatory.[2] Debate has centered on particular areas of concern: Hrotswitha's relationship to Terence, the pagan, Roman dramatist to whom she declares a debt in the Prefaces to her plays[3]; Hrotswitha's unusual position as a religious woman writer of plays, epics, poetry, and history in tenth-century Saxony; her understanding of and concern with eroticism and passion in a religious milieu; her double-edged depiction of her female characters as weak yet heroic; and her originality, or her dependence on pagan writers and Church Fathers.

Hrotswitha seems, by all accounts, an anomaly. She lived in the tenth century in the Benedictine Abbey of Gandersheim in Saxony, founded in the mid-ninth century.[4] By the mid-tenth century, Saxony was ruled by the Ottos, who presided over and hoped to make Germany a world power. They welcomed scholars, founded and supported monastic and cathedral schools, and fostered an atmosphere of increasing cosmopolitanism and intellectualism. During this period, Gandersheim had become a wealthy imperial abbey and a center of intellectual activity. It was given much independence by Otto the Great and ruled by Gerberga II, his niece. Those who lived at Gandersheim were from aristocratic families, and it is thought that Hrotswitha must therefore have been of noble Saxon parentage. She came to Gandersheim after Gerberga II became abbess (in the 950s), and Gerberga became Hrotswitha's teacher, friend, and patron. Hrotswitha was a canoness at Gandersheim and thus had considerably more freedom, more interchange with outsiders, and more opportunity to express herself than the nuns did.[5] She benefitted from the teachers and libraries at Gandersheim (and possibly at the court of Otto) and was enmeshed in the religious life of the convent, but she also had the advantage of the intellectual, political, and social connections of Gandersheim with the Ottonian court and perhaps the ability to read and to speak on a wider range of literature and subjects than the nuns.

Hrotswitha was a woman of great learning and was acquainted with a wide variety of Roman authors, ancient commentaries, Christian writers, lives of saints and martyrs, and liturgical texts.[6] Her corpus contains an astounding variety of works: a life of the Virgin Mary, an account of Christ's ascension, and six saints' lives and legends (all in verse); six plays in rhymed prose; and an account of the *res gestae* of Otto I and a history of the monastery of Gandersheim down to 919 (both in hexameter verse). She can lay claim to many firsts: first poet of Saxony, first female German poet, first female German historian, first dramatist of Germany and of Christianity, and only female writer of extant Latin epic.

Hrotswitha was also the first medieval poet who made a conscious attempt to remold the image of women found in ancient literary depictions.[7] It has continued to amaze her critics and commentators that a woman of her background, education, and religious situation would have the ingenuity, creativity, and boldness to try to provide a human and humane characterization of women within a Christian theological context.[8] In her plays, she was able to mediate with marvelous facility among the generic and aesthetic demands of her dramas, the strictures of her religious life, and the historical reality of the legends upon which her plays are based and, at the same time, to use these plays as a vehicle for a redefinition of women's qualities, characters, and motivations.

It is Hrotswitha's redefinition of women that I will explore further in this paper. I will first discuss Hrotswitha's own reputation as a female playwright and the misreadings of Hrotswitha and her works as a result of sexist bias in the scholarship on her; then explore her professed feminine perspective and self-presentation in her works, her identity with her female characters, and her relationship to her male sources; next examine the role played by Hrotswitha's audience in the composition of her dramas and her female characters; and, finally, analyze one specific play, the *Passio Sanctarum Virginum Agapis Chioniae et Hirenae* (*Dulcitius*) as evidence of Hrotswitha's treatment of women in her works.[9]

The critical scholarship on Hrotswitha has replicated, in many respects, the difficulties she must have faced as a woman writing about women in her own cultural context. Almost no one has treated her kindly. She is generally seen as an anomaly, "an artist without precedent and without succession."[10] We should not, however, relegate her to "the literary periphery as a curious and unconnected phenomenon having neither roots nor influence,"[11] as we so often do to women of letters. She was an important part of the Carolingian and Ottonian cultural revival, and, as Peter Dronke shows in *Women Writers of the Middle Ages*, she belongs to a long tradition of women writers from Perpetua to Marguerite Porete and beyond. She is also an important part of the dramatic and hagiographical traditions.

Misreadings of Hrotswitha have appeared in conflicting guises. Some critics have simply found this writer an enigma, a *rara avis*[12]—a female religious figure who was educated and worldly enough to write plays in good Latin, who based her religious dramas on a pagan, Roman comic writer, and who wrote in a century that was long regarded as the nadir of cultural and intellectual production,[13] "a literary prodigy in the arid desert of 10th-century cultural stagnation."[14] So disturbing a figure was Hrotswitha to early critics of medieval women writers that a nineteenth-century Austrian historian, Joseph Aschbach, claimed that she was a historical impossibility.[15] He went so far as to suggest that Conrad Celtis, the fifteenth-century discoverer of Hrotswitha's works, and his friends had forged her writings, a fraud perpetrated to glorify German literature.

Although Aschbach's theory was almost immediately challenged, it took until the twentieth century to prove Hrotswitha's authenticity,[16] and lingering biases have remained in the scholarship on her.[17] To be able to take Hrotswitha's writings seriously, many critics have ignored the fact of her gender and any ramifications that it might have for her writings. They have, instead, regarded Hrotswitha as just another tenth-century monk whose "sex is assumed to have little or no significance" and whose "choice of women as the chief characters of her dramas is not seen as crucial" to the interpretation of her plays.[18] On this reading, Hrotswitha turns into an average medieval hagiographer and dramatist treating the conflict of worldly concerns and Christian faith for martyrs, virgins, and Christian heroes.[19] To ignore in this way Hrotswitha's focus on her female characters is to cut out the very heart of her originality.[20]

While the first group of largely male critics tried to change or ignore Hrotswitha's gender, others have gone in another direction and tried to make Hrotswitha into a forerunner of feminist thought. As early as 1913, Paul von Winterfeld, in his study of German poets writing in Latin in the Middle Ages, describes Hrotswitha as a role model and standard-bearer for struggling women of his own time. He sees Hrotswitha's dramas as social documents that show women's struggle for their honor and due in their fight against men's power.[21] But even Winterfeld, who is a sensitive early observer of Hrotswitha's attention to her female characters, seems confused by the many different worlds that Hrotswitha inhabits, and he tries to make sense of her religious asceticism, her "masculine" sense of struggle and aspiration for new rights for women, and her softer, feminine side: "Aber all dieses hohe, fast männliche Streben, zugleich verbunden mit harter, geistlicher Askese, hat doch in Hrotsvit das innige, weibliche Gemüt nicht erstickt" [but all this intense, almost masculine striving linked simultaneously in Hrotswitha's writing with a strict, spiritual asceticism has not stifled her deep feminine nature].[22]

Female readers of Hrotswitha and contemporary feminist critics have taken Hrotswitha to task to an even greater extent than many of her early male readers did. They do not see her as a precursor of feminist thought, as Winterfeld did, but rather blame her for not being feminist enough or for being a nun with repressed sexual fantasies. Some have seen her plays as offensively Christian and patriarchal, the works of an "Uncle Tom trapped by male values."[23] Some of these critics, far from being surprised (as Winterfeld was) by the freedom with which such a female medieval religious figure spoke in her works, have seen her religious identity and her insistence on chastity as a form of oppression that led her to treat her female characters in a sadistic way. In a Freudian vein, Rosamond Gilder in 1931 commented on Hrotswitha's victimization of her female characters in the *Passio ACH* (*Dulcitius*) and *Sapientia*:

> Hrotsvit obtained a certain release for her own emotional suppressions by elaborating these pictures of carnal dangers and the pitfalls of the flesh. These scenes, wherein holy virgins . . . are dragged off to brothels to be "abominably defiled" . . . are the product of a mind that may have denied, but has not forgotten the "sinful lusts of the flesh" . . . [she] gives expression to a vein of sadism which is also associated with certain acts of repression.[24]

It is certainly true that Hrotswitha's double position as a deeply religious canoness and an intellectual with a strong interest in women's roles and reactions frequently led to a bifurcation in her attitudes and that she exhibited an interest in erotic behavior unusual for someone in her position (see section on Hrotswitha's Relationship following); however, Gilder's statement is an oversimplification of Hrotswitha's motives.

Hrotswitha, then, has been placed in an untenable position. She is either portrayed as a woman in man's clothing who "accepts male dominance as a fact of life"[25] and a mediocre hagiographer focusing on the triumphs of the Christian martyrs very like her "male clerkly contemporaries"[26] or as a failed precursor of feminist thought. The first view ignores Hrotswitha's focus on women and the importance to her literary and historical productions of her gender and of the woman-dominated abbey in which she lived. The second recognizes the importance of women to Hrotswitha's life and works but ignores the importance of her historical, religious, and cultural context. To judge her fairly and to reach a balanced assessment of her works, we must ignore neither the religious/historical milieu in which she lived nor her gender and her very obvious interest in her female characters.

Hrotswitha's Self-Definition: The Prefaces

Hrotswitha clearly proclaims a feminine perspective in several different places in her works, both overtly, in a semipersonalized narrative, and indirectly, through identification with the female heroes in her dramas. By creating a three-way link among the presentation of herself, the characters in her dramas, and her female audience, she constructs an ideal feminine self that is slowly revealed through the masks that she creates for herself and for her characters. Indeed, she becomes, in her Prefaces, one of her own characters. This ideal female figure is, in part, a literary construction and is created through language, largely through the verbal links that she creates between herself and her characters (see following discussion). But this figure is also historicized, since Hrotswitha's constructions (both her characters and her self-presentation) reflect the social practices in which they are enmeshed.[27] The characters in her dramas are shown in social and historical contexts that would have resonated with Hrotswitha's female audience, who held beliefs similar to those of her characters. I would maintain that, if we read both the personal narratives and dramas together, we receive from Hrotswitha what might be called an autobiography.

Georges Gusdorf and James Olney, who contributed important formational work on autobiographical theory, have emphasized the significant role that language plays in the formation of self.[28] Building on their work, two recent feminist theorists, Sidonie Smith and Shari Benstock, have applied Gusdorf and Olney's principles to women's autobiographical writing.[29] Smith emphasizes that, unlike male autobiography, which sees the self as isolated, separate, and unitary and focuses on the individuality of self, much of women's autobiographical writing emphasizes the communitarian nature of women's lives and the connectedness of the writer with her family, community, characters, and audience.

While Hrotswitha was writing well before the origins of formal autobiography in fourteenth- and fifteenth-century Europe, her work can certainly be seen to have autobiographical elements and to be a part of the long history of female self-definition through writing in various genres (confessional literature, letters, poetry).[30] Hrotswitha in her self-definition stresses both her individuality and disconnectedness from her literary predecessors and, often ironically, her devotion to and connectedness with her literary community (Terence, the Church Fathers) and her religious community (the nuns, canonesses, and others for whom she wrote). Her fascination with the theater, which has surprised so many of her readers, may well have arisen from a desire to construct herself in new ways and so to create self-definitions in the same way that theatrical masks allow actors to assume new personas. The elements of disguise and role changes that are emphasized in her dramas reinforce similar elements in Hrotswitha's more personal Prefaces. Her use of theater to create characters and her theatrical presentation of herself in her Prefaces are thus mutually determining ways of creating an ideal feminine self.

Throughout the Prefaces and Epistles that introduce the three different sections of Hrotswitha's works (saints' legends, dramas, and historical epics), Hrotswitha reveals a growing self-awareness as an artist.[31] Although the Prefaces are filled with topoi such as the profession of humility, we can gain a sense of how Hrotswitha wants to be remembered if we focus on both her words and her silences. We should pay particular attention to the progression of self-definition in her Prefaces and should compare the language that she uses in her personal narrative with the language used of and by her female characters in a more public and interactive context. The cumulative effect of Hrotswitha's constant use of diminutives, appeals for help from her teachers and patrons, and apologies for trying to write such works in the first place is humorous, and these self-deprecations end up emphasizing the opposite of what she seems to be saying. Hrotswitha is proud of her accomplishments, and she wishes to gain notice for her literary efforts. As Peter Dronke observes, Hrotswitha (in the Preface to her plays) "says little of what she really means and means almost nothing of what she says."[32]

In the Preface to her legends, Hrotswitha begins by referring to her book as *hunc libellum* (1), and she offers it for correction to "the benevolent gaze of all who are wise" [omnium sapientium benignitati]—or at least to those "who take no delight in belittling one who errs" [qui erranti non delectantur derogare]. She disarms her critics by admitting to more than normal numbers of mistakes in prosody and poetic style, but she expects their forgiveness for having admitted her foibles (2). She admits that she came to realize that much of her subject matter was apocryphal but refuses to destroy what she had done, since the false could turn out to be true (3). She apologizes for her immaturity and insufficent knowledge (5), her *rusticitas* (6), for women's frailty (8) (*femineae fragilitati*, a frequently repeated phrase),[33] for having to rely on God's help and not on her own strength (*propriis viribus*, 8), for her *carmina opuscula* (8), for her *talentum ingenioli* (8). Each time she blushes for shame at her inadequacy; however, she assures her audience of her competence, her right to write in whatever style and genre she wishes, and the divine grace that allows her to do all this:

> ne crediti / talentum ingenioli / sub obscuro / torpens pectoris <antro> / rubigine neglegentiae exterminaretur, / sed sedulae malleo devotionis percussum / aliquantulum divinae laudationis referret tinnitum, / quo, si occasio non daretur / negotiando aliud lucrari, ipsum tamen in aliquod saltim extremae utilitatis transformaretur instrumentum. (8)

> [I was eager that the talent given to me by Heaven should not grow rusty from neglect, and remain silent in my heart from apathy, but under the hammer of assiduous devotion should sound a chord of praise. If I have achieved nothing else, this alone should make my work of some value.] (St. John, xxxiii)[34]

Each negative is more than balanced and qualified by a positive (talentum / ingenioli; sub obscuro torpens pectoris <antro>rubigine neglegentiae / sedulae malleo devotionis; aliquantulum / divinae laudationis tinnitum; aliquod, extremae / utilitatis instrumentum).

This wavering between two very different tones and sets of claims prepares us for the many ambiguities we will find in her later Prefaces, her plays, and her life. Some of this, of course, is standard procedure in any literary preface and borrowed from her pagan predecessors; when classical writers undertook to write something substantial in dactylic hexameters, they always provided a *recusatio* or ironic denial of their abilities to undertake such a task or they called on the Muse or Apollo for guidance.[35] But Hrotswitha's pretended (or real) diffidence is not only a literary *topos*; it reveals her very difficult position as a Christian writing in a pagan, classical tradition; a religious figure dealing with themes of passion and eroticism; a woman writing in male-dominated genres; and a portrayer of heroic actions attributed to the female sex.

Hrotswitha's Preface to her dramas provides the clearest statement of her claims and attitudes, and it shows a development in her definition and presentation of self and her willingness to stake out her claim to a place in literary history. She identifies herself here as *clamor validus Gandeshemensis* (3), "the loud shout from Gandersheim," or "strong in fame," using an ironic Latin equivalent of her name, which in Saxon means the same thing as *clamor validus* (*hruot* or *hrôth* = *clamor*; *suid* or *suith* = *validus*) and placing herself firmly in two traditions, classical and Christian.[36] Her self-given name will have reminded her readers of John the Baptist's *ego vox clamantis*, but she is also using *clamor* objectively, calling attention to herself as the "loud shout from Gandersheim," a mocking contrast to her usual self-deprecations.

Having proclaimed her name and place, she uses most of this Preface to place herself within the dramatic tradition that went back to her professed model, Terence. This Preface is also studded with diminutives and self-effacing words and phrases (*ingenioli*, "my poor talent," 3; *huius vilitas dictationis*, "the poorness of this composition," 6; *vel pro mei abiectione vel pro vitiosi sermonis rusticitate*, "if because of my worthlessness or the boorishness of my flawed style," 9; *vilitatem laboris . . . meae inscientiae opusculis*, "while in the other little works that spring from my ignorance, I gathered my poor efforts," 9). They are used, however, in the service of a positive aim: to make clear Hrotswitha's debt to Terence and to justify her depiction of the shameful actions of wanton women in order to highlight more clearly the chastity of holy virgins:

> Unde ego, Clamor Validus Gandeshemensis, non recusavi illum imitari dictando, / dum alii colunt legendo, / quo eodem dictationis genere, / quo turpia lascivarum / incesta feminarum / recitabantur, / laudabilis sacrarum / castimonia virginum / iuxta mei facultatem ingenioli celebraretur. . . . Sed <si> haec erubesco neglegerem, / nec proposito satisfacerem / nec innocentium laudem adeo plene iuxta meum posse exponerem, / quia, quanto blanditiae amentium[37] ad illiciendum promptiores, tanto et superni adiutoris gloria sublimior et triumphantium victoria probatur gloriosior, / praesertim cum feminea fragilitas vinceret / et virilis robur confusioni subiaceret. (3, 5)

> [Wherefore I, the strong voice of Gandersheim, have not hesitated to imitate in my writings a poet whose works are so widely read, my object being to glorify, within the limits of my poor talent, the laudable chastity of Christian virgins in that self-same form of composition which has been used to describe the shameless acts of licentious women. . . . Yet if from modesty I had refrained from treating these subjects I should not have been able to attain my object—to glorify the innocent to the best of my ability. For the more seductive the blandishments of [lovers] who have lost their senses the more wonderful the divine succour and the greater the merit of those who resist, especially when it is fragile woman who is victorious and strong man who is routed with confusion.] (St. John, xxvi–xxvii)

Her earlier tentativeness is gone; she asks help only from God, and any failings are justified by their value in countering pagan lasciviousness:

> Si enim alicui placet mea devotio, / gaudebo; / si autem vel pro mei abiectione / vel pro vitiosi sermonis rusticitate / placet nulli, / memet ipsam tamen iuvat, quod feci, / quia, dum proprii vilitatem laboris, / in aliis meae inscientiae opusculis / heroico ligatam strophio, / in hoc dramatica vinctam serie colo, / perniciosas / gentilium delicias / abstinendo divito. (9)

> [If this pious devotion gives satisfaction, I shall rejoice; if it does not, either on account of my own worthlessness or of the faults of my unpolished style, I shall still be glad that I made the effort. In the humbler works of my salad days I gathered up my poor researches in heroic strophes, but here I have sifted them into a series of dramatic scenes and avoided through omission the pernicious voluptuousness of pagan writers.] (St. John, xxvii-xxviii)

The letter "To Certain Learned Patrons of This Book" [Ad quosdam sapientes huius libri fautores] is more formal, in keeping with the genre of *captationes benevolentiae* (attempts to curry favor with potential patrons). Hrotswitha redoubles her attempts to be groveling and submissive to an almost ridiculous degree; in the first four sections alone, we find "Hrotsvit nesciola" [poor little ignorant Hrotswitha (1)]; "mei opusculum vilis mulierculae" [the paltry work of me, a worthless little woman" (3)]; "arbitrantes mihi inesse aliquantulam scientiam artium, / quarum subtilitas longe praeterit mei muliebre ingenium" [admitting that I possess some little knowledge of those arts the subtleties of which exceed the grasp of my woman's mind (3)]; "rusticitatem meae dictatiunculae" [the unpolished style of my little composition (4)]. She finishes by describing her posture as "bowing low like a reed" [harundineo more inclinata (11)]. Clearly some of her self-deprecation is due to the formality of the genre, but she also writes with a mock humility that is reminiscent of Socratic irony, particularly in Plato's *Apology*: "neque simulando / me nescita scire iacto, / sed, quantum ad me, tantum scio, quod nescio" (10) [At least I do not pretend to have knowledge where I am ignorant. On the contrary, my best claim to indulgence is that I know how much I do not know].

She also offsets any possibility that we might take her exaggerated modesty seriously by including a learned joke with her use of Greek philosophical language drawn from St. Jerome:[38]

Unde non denego praestante gratia creatoris per dynamin me artes
scire, / quia sum animal capax disciplinae, / sed per energian fateor
omnino nescire. (7)

[Hence I do not deny that through the Creator's grace I have knowledge of the arts potentially (*per dynamin*), since I am a living being
with the capacity to learn; yet I confess that I am utterly ignorant
in actuality (*per energian*).] (Dronke, *Women Writers*, p. 74)

Still, despite her self-conscious nods at the tradition of irony established by Socrates and by Hrotswitha herself, she shows quite serious
moments here, admitting confusion over her complex emotions:

Inter haec diversis affectibus, gaudio videlicet et metu, in diversum
trahor; deum namque, cuius solummodo gratia sum id quod sum,
in me laudari cordetenus gaudeo; / sed maior, quam sim, videri
timeo, / quia utrumque nefas esse non ambigo, / et gratuitum dei
donum negare, / et non acceptum accepisse simulare. (6)

[Still I am torn by conflicting feelings. I rejoice from the depths of
my soul that the God through Whose grace alone I am what I am
should be praised in me, but I am afraid of being thought greater
than I am. I know that it is as wrong to deny a divine gift as to
pretend falsely that we have received it.] (St. John, xxix)

As Peter Dronke points out, her allusion to Paul, 1 Corinthians 15:10 ("by
the grace of God I am what I am") will not have escaped her patrons,[39] and
she presents herself as fully aware that she has a divine gift that must be
used wisely and discreetly.

The Preface to her historical epics, addressed to her patron, teacher,
and abbess, Gerberga, was probably written last of her Prefaces after she
had gained a reputation at the Abbey and the court. Here we again find both
a repetition of words and phrases of mock humility and references to what
Dronke calls "the chimera of women's intellectual inferiority,"[40] as well as
elements tailored to the particular genre and audience. She is clearly on
less firm footing writing historical material about Otto and the Abbey than
she was writing saints' lives and plays. She complains that she had no
written records or personal informants about the *res gestae* of Otto and
that she felt like a wanderer through a strange land (4–5).[41] Her words to
Gerberga here—both her appeals to the Abbess ("O mea domna . . . non
pigescat vestri almitiem perlustrare" (2); [O my lady . . . may it not irk your
maternal kindness to read . . .] and her admissions of weakness and per-
plexity ("haut aliter ego regalium multiplicitatem gestorum nutando et

vacillando aegerrime transcurri" (6) [Even so have I traversed the varied path of royal deeds faltering and hesitating, in agony]—show a less self-assured attitude than she reveals in her earlier Prefaces. Oddly, she girds herself in military language at several points. She is a servant "fighting under your ladyship's rule" [sub huiusmodi personae dominio militantium (1)] and a person "defenseless at every point, because I am not supported by an authority" [nunc autem omne latus tanto magis caret defensione, / quanto minus ulla fulcitur auctoritate (8)].

Despite the self-conscious irony, the formalized language, the use of traditional material, and the exaggerations[42] that Hrotswitha employs in all her Prefaces, she gives a clear presentation of her literary, cultural, and personal preoccupations. The picture she gives us is of a woman who is frail in mind and spirit yet strong in her convictions, her natural gifts, and her divine support; a woman who has a straightforward message to convey, yet is a magician of words; a woman who wants to rescue herself and others of her gender from the perdition and obscurity to which they have been confined and to celebrate women's chastity, beauty and worth; and a fighting hero who is a staunch champion of holy virgins.

But, to see beyond the masks and poses that she adopts in her own personal narratives, we must look at a different set of masks, those she creates for the female heroes in her dramas. Hrotswitha often uses the same important thematic words and phrases to describe her characters and herself, and it is in the cross-fertilization of her private and her dramatic works that her self-representation emerges. Each kind of presentation of the female self reveals in a different way the traits, actions, and values that Hrotswitha wanted to promulgate in order to rescue women from the constrictions of the patriarchal tradition by presenting a vision of women triumphant over male power and demonic forces (frequently one and the same thing in Hrotswitha's plays).[43] She does this, not by stripping women of their traditional traits such as frailty and alluring beauty, but by transfiguring these women, making their weaknesses into strengths and showing them resolute in their battles against sin. So, in one of her most famous lines from the Preface to her plays, she says that she uses pagan subject matter and plots of seduction and eroticism precisely to show the strength and glory of those who triumph in such situations:

> quanto blanditiae amentium ad illiciendum promptiores, tanto et superni adiutoris gloria sublimior et triumphantium victoria probatur gloriosior, / praesertim cum feminea fragilitas vinceret et virilis robur confusioni subiaceret. (*Pref.* 5)

> [The more seductive the blandishments of [lovers] who have lost their senses, the more wonderful the divine succour and the greater

the merit of those who resist, especially when it is fragile woman
who is victorious and strong man who is routed with confusion.]
(St. John, xxvii)

The strength and value of women emerge in two ways: through an
interchange between the private narrative and the dramatic characters, and
through the interaction of the characters with each other and with the
audience of the dramas.[44] Hrotswitha uses every means at her disposal to
create interactions and to portray the developing and vibrant female characters who both reflect and help to create Hrotswitha herself.[45] The addition
of dialogue to the legends is important to their transformation.[46] The audience itself, nuns and other canonesses, will also have added a significant
element to this interactive process of the redefinition of women. Just as the
three virgin martyrs in the *Passio ACH (Dulcitius)* watch Dulcitius trying
to deflower the pots and pans in his deluded state and laugh at him, so the
women in Hrotswitha's audience will be able to control the action and the
emotion. The gaze is now theirs; the dramatic perspective has been transferred from male to female, and the women (both inside and outside the
drama) are allowed to dominate.[47]

It is fair to assume that Hrotswitha means to highlight the particular
qualities that she claims to share with her characters by repeating words
and phrases in her Prefaces and her plays. Hrotswitha's constant insistence in her Prefaces on female frailty, weakness, and inferiority (*feminea
fragilitas, vilis muliercula*) is echoed in the *Passio ACH (Dulcitius)* when
Diocletian calls the three sisters (Agape, Chionia, and Irene) "viles
mulierculae" (9). In this scene, the allegedly "shameless little girls" have
successfully defended their honor by deluding, shaming, and tricking
Dulcitius, and Diocletian fears that they are boasting that they have
humiliated the Roman gods. Here the attribution of weakness to these
women by the Roman emperor is contradicted by their past and potential
actions and by his fear of them, just as Hrotswitha's mock-modest professions of inferiority are countered by her accomplishments and her strong
statements of belief in herself.

Another example of such a verbal echo is in the phrase "lascivae feminae"
(licentious women). In her Preface to the dramas Hrotswitha tries to explain her fascination with Terence and to defend herself against the charge
of being *lasciva*. She says that her object is to glorify "the laudable chastity
of Christian virgins in that self-same form of composition which has been
used to describe the shameless acts of licentious women" [quo eodem
dictationis genere, / quo turpia lascivarum incesta feminarum / recitabantur,
/ laudabilis sacrarum castimonia virginum (3)] (i.e., Terence's plays). In the
Passio ACH (Dulcitius), the villain, Dulcitius (whose wife describes him as

non sanae mentis, 7), and his henchman, Sisinnius, call the three sisters *lascivae feminae* (7, 10), exactly the opposite of what these chaste and virginal maidens are and evidence of the deluded state of these men. These virginal characters and others like them are exactly the vehicles through which Hrotswitha counters Terence's licentious women. Hrotswitha has an agonistic relationship with her professed model, Terence, emulating him to surpass and to deny him.[48]

A third link, thematic rather than verbal, can be seen in Hrotswitha's frequent insistence in the *Passio ACH (Dulcitius)* on the power of the three sisters to charm and delude their male antagonists. Twice Dulcitius and then Sisinnius in their deluded states (*non sanae mentis*) claim that the sisters have mocked and tricked them by their witchcraft (*Dulcitius*: "Nunc tandem sentio, me illusum illarum maleficiis," (7); [Now I see—it was their magic that bewitched me]. *Sisinnius*: "pessumdatus sum maleficiis christicolarum," (14) [It is clear that I have been bewitched by the magic of these Christians]).[49] The soldiers echo this with "Miris modis omnes illudimur" [We are all deluded by some strange enchantment (14)]. Hrotswitha's obvious interest in enchantment and illusion is also evident in the way she evokes other worlds through her fictional characters.[50] Like the *maleficia* of the sisters, Hrotswitha's dramatic illusions are put to a good cause but are likely to be misinterpreted by deluded readers/viewers, who level false charges, just as Dulcitius and Sisinnius do in the play. What they see as magic or sorcery is really the power given to the sisters by God to overcome evil and achieve martyrdom. By creating such verbal and thematic links throughout her Prefaces and her plays, Hrotswitha develops and foregrounds a self-defining bond between herself and the female heroes in her dramas.[51]

Hrotswitha's Relationship to Terence and the Hagiographers

Another aspect of Hrotswitha's unique representation of women (including herself) as strong, positive forces for change is seen in her plays' relation to their literary antecedents. Hrotswitha borrows heavily from two different traditions: the classical, and the patristic or hagiographical.[51] I will first briefly examine her debt to Terence[53] and then discuss the legends on which she based her *Passio ACH (Dulcitius)*.

In the beginning of the Preface to her dramas (see foregoing discussion in Hrotswitha's Self-Definition: The Prefaces), Hrotswitha makes clear the extent of her debt to Terence. While some critics have tried to minimize her debt to him,[54] most have taken Hrotswitha's words seriously and seen in her plays a genuine fascination with various aspects of Terentian comedy (style, subject matter, and plot; treatment of female characters). These are the main points that Hrotswitha herself makes in her Preface:

1. She is attracted by Terence's elegant style (*facundia sermonis*, 1)

2. She has not refused (*non recusavi*) to use Terence's plays in composing her own dramas,[55] although it causes her embarrassment to have to think and write about "the dreadful frenzy of those possessed by unlawful love, and the insidious sweetness of passion" [detestabilem inlicite amantium dementiam et male dulcia colloquia eorum, (3–4)].

3. She has used the plots of Terence that portray "the shameless acts of licentious women" [turpia lascivarum incesta feminarum (3)] so as to set off by contrast "the laudable chastity of Christian virgins" [laudabilis sacrarum castimonia virginum (3; cf. 5)].

4. Her poor work (*huius vilitas dictationis*, 6) is inferior to Terence's plays, on a humbler scale (*contractior*) and altogether different from his writing (*penitus . . . dissimilis eius*, 6).

It seems evident that Hrotswitha's fascination with Terence lay largely in his lively dialogue,[56] his stock themes (thwarted marriages, disguised lovers, innocent maidens who are raped), and his subject matter (tales of rape and seduction). There are few real linguistic borrowings from Terence, and Hrotswitha's Latin is mainly Medieval, not classical.[57] Although some critics feel that she overstates the depravity found in Terence's plays to create a pagan, Roman contrast for her Christian characters,[58] it is clear that pagan, Roman drama would not have been the prescribed reading matter for a Medieval religious community and that Hrotswitha might have found more in Terence to upset her (even with the "noble" prostitutes like Bacchis in the *Hecyra*)[59] than many (mostly male) scholars would allow. While Hrotswitha may well have exaggerated the eroticism of Terence's plots the better to highlight the purity of her maidens, she was clearly fascinated by the theme of chastity with its "penumbra of wantonness,"[60] which allowed her heightened dramatic possibilities and an interesting set of conflicts on which to base her dramas.

Hrotswitha used this double perspective to create Christian characters with two dimensions: a goal of Christian chastity, martyrdom, and spiritual love, and an inheritance of secular love and sexual passion. While Carole E. Newlands is right to call Hrotswitha's plays "a strong moral response" to Terence and to say that she tries to redeem the Terentian material,[61] Hrotswitha is keenly aware of both the contrasts already existing in Terence and the potential that her posture opposite Terence creates for her plays. This is not to say that she leaves moral ambiguities in her plays, but the double perspective of Terence/Hrotswitha gives to her plays a complexity that is often denied by her critics. This complexity is evident, for example, in a section of the *Lapsus et Conversio Mariae* (*Abraham*), where the hermit Abraham, disguised as a lover, enters a brothel to rescue his niece, Maria, and kisses her. In this scene, called by a critic "one of the most sensitive and exquisite recognition scenes in any literature," Hrotswitha juxtaposes the religious aspects of the monk's kiss with its profane dimensions to great effect.[62]

Hrotswitha also uses her ambiguous relationship with her pagan/Roman and patristic male predecessors to create active, aggressive female characters, who are the catalysts of her plots. Unlike Terence's women, most of whom are passive, innocent victims and who do not play any active role in their own rescue or even speak on stage (Glycerium in the *Andria*; Pamphila in the *Eunuchus*), Hrotswitha's female characters are the true heroines, while most of her male characters are turned into buffoons (except the religious men). The women in Hrotswitha's plays provide the impulse for the dramatic resolution, and their actions are described in terms of a heroic struggle.[63] But, for all their heroics, they do not simply turn into male characters; rather, Hrotswitha allows her female heroes to exhibit their Christian heroism within their traditional social roles as women (mother in *Sapientia*; wife in *Resuscitatio Drusianae* [*Calimachus*]; sister in *Passio ACH* [*Dulcitius*]; niece in *Lapsus et Conversio Mariae* [*Abraham*]; daughter in *Gallicanus*).[64]

Hrotswitha's use of hagiographical material also reveals the originality she injected into her traditional and largely inherited material, particularly in regards to her representation of women. I will concentrate here on the changes that she wrought in the source for her play, the *Passio ACH* (*Dulcitius*).[65] This play takes place in Thessalonica during the Diocletian persecutions of Christians in the late third and early fourth centuries. It portrays the martyrdom of three sisters, Agape (Love), Chionia (Snow, Purity), and Irene (Peace), the youngest. The emperor offers the girls, who are of noble families, the opportunity to marry members of his nobility, but the girls decline, preferring chastity, spiritual marriage to Christ, and martyrdom to secular marriage. The governor, Dulcitius, and Count Sisinnius are ordered to carry out their examination, punishment, and execution. Dulcitius, however, a philanderer, tries to rape the sisters but, in a state of delusion, mistakes the kitchen utensils for the sisters and attempts to deflower the pots and pans. Many miracles occur to preserve and protect the dignity and integrity of the three sisters: when the soldiers try to strip the clothes off of the women, the clothes stick to their bodies; Dulcitius falls into a deep sleep after his "bewitching"; when Agape and Chionia are burned at the stake, their clothes, hair, and bodies are preserved; two young strangers suddenly appear to take Irene to a mountaintop instead of to the brothel to which she has been consigned by Sisinnius. Sisinnius, also tricked as was Dulcitius by the women's "sorcery" (*maleficia*), finally orders Irene to be shot with arrows. Irene has the last word (see following section on *Passio Sanctarum*).

Hrotswitha retains in her play many elements of the Roman legend, the *Passion of St. Anastasia*,[66] but her changes are fundamental. She drops St. Anastasia, the original protagonist, out of the story altogether, raises the minor figures of the three sisters to hero status, and highlights the buffoonery of the male characters, Dulcitius and Sisinnius. She also emphasizes the very episodes and elements in the Roman legend that an early twentieth-century Bollandist editor of this legend found to be "audacious fiction" that contaminated an otherwise good Greek original.[67]

In the original legend, the women are part of a larger group of six Christians (including one man) who are arrested together; Hrotswitha mentions only the three sisters. Agape and Chionia are questioned briefly along with the other three Christians, and the two sisters are burned at the stake. Irene is kept separate from the group and subjected to a long examination by herself, during which she stands her ground and answers each question put to her firmly and concisely. The focus is mostly on the sacred Christian writings that the sisters were discovered to have had in their possession, an act that contravened an imperial edict (but they are arrested on a separate charge of refusing to eat meat sacrificed to the Roman gods).

Most of the changes that Hrotswitha introduces into the legend strengthen the position of her female characters or reconstitute the social and religious context in an interesting way. Besides eliminating or diminishing the male characters in the legend, Hrotswitha selects, fills out with her dialogue and dramatization, and puts the spotlight on the minor female characters in the original, one of whom (Irene) becomes the driving force of the play. Hrotswitha makes Irene into a strong, aggressive central character who carries on a lively dialogue with Diocletian and Sisinnius, gives lectures on religion, philosophy, and politics, has the last speech in the play, and controls the dramatic action and denouement. She also does not actually die in the play but closes the *Passio ACH* (*Dulcitius*) with a final ringing damnation of Sisinnius and a praise of God. Hrotswitha also introduces an entirely new female character into the play as well, the (unnamed) wife of Dulcitius, who heightens his buffoonery by mocking her husband when he appears disheveled and dirty after his episode with the pots and pans. She thus joins the three sisters, the soldiers, and the palace guards in ridiculing Dulcitius, who is mistaken for the Devil himself and a vile and despicable monster (*daemoniacus . . . diabolus*, 5; *vile ac detestabile monstrum*, 6).

Hrotswitha also adds a new and interesting scene to the s'
lustful antics and delusion in the kitchen. The scene is c
comic and actable scenes in Hrotswitha's dramas, but it also ᴄ..
rious message containing Christian symbolism in its portrayal of the kitchen
as a symbol of Hell and in the analogies it draws between Dulcitius, a cook,
and the Devil.[68] The scene also further strengthens Hrotswitha's representation of women by emphasizing the degradation of men and the heights
to which strong women can and do rise to overcome male force and power
and carnal desire—and to achieve divine bliss and martyrdom.[69]

Thus Hrotswitha uses the complexities that are already present in
her sources and that are produced by the interplay between her works and
their antecedents to create dramas that are full of suspense, interest,
varied tones, and action. These are works of conflict that nevertheless
deliver an unambiguously Christian, moral message. Hrotswitha uses the
ambiguities and tensions in her plays to redefine the role of women in a
difficult time and social milieu and to explore how women could be frail
but heroic; chaste and virginal even when subjected to rape;[70] complex
but morally pure; and objects of men's desire and actions yet active agents
for change. Hrotswitha, unlike many of her male, monastic counterparts,
did not regard the virgin as an ideal form without complexity.[71] Although
she did not expand the idea of virtue to nonreligious women or feature
many unvirtuous women in her stories,[72] she can be credited with expanding the range of possible representations available to religious women
in the tenth century.

Hrotswitha's Audience

We can assume several things about Hrotswitha's audience:

1. They were all, or largely, female and members of a religious
community.[73]
2. They rarely, if ever, saw any other dramatic performances and certainly not dramas written by one of their own community.[74]
3. They identified strongly with Hrotswitha's brave, heroic, chaste,
Christian female martyrs.
4. Hrotswitha developed her characters at least partly in response to
the expectations and attitudes of her female, religious audience.
5. Hrotswitha identified with her audience as she did with her characters, and she set up a complex literary, dramatic, and personal dialogue,
creating lines of communication between herself and her characters, herself and her audience, and her audience and her characters.

In writing for an audience of women and from a woman's perspective, Hrotswitha was engaged in a whole new dramatic dynamic.[75] Her lively dialogues and engaging scenes, such as the comic scene in the *Passio ACH* (*Dulcitius*) where the three sisters are peeking through the door and laughing at the deluded Dulcitius as he embraces the pots and pans, the erotic scenes in the *Lapsus et Conversio Mariae* (*Abraham*),[76] the uplifting scenes throughout the dramas where the heroic women triumph (for example *Passio ACH* [*Dulcitius*] 14)—all must have evoked strong emotional responses from the members of the audience and provided them with unprecedented opportunities to participate in the representation of the actions and triumphs of the Christian virgins and martyrs. As Sandro Sticca points out, the participation of the audience in the telling of a saint's life was an act of faith and constituted a ritual response to an enactment of their deepest beliefs.[77]

Much as the religious women must have enjoyed participation in and viewing of any drama, they would certainly have identified more with Hrotswitha's feminized versions of the saints' lives than with the traditional, male-dominated accounts. For the first time, they saw the dramatic perspective reversed. *The gaze was theirs. They* were the ones watching the powerful Dulcitius, deluded by the innocent *maleficia* of the three sisters and paying amorous attention to the kitchen equipment; *they* could look, spy on him, and laugh along with Agape, Chionia, and Irene. Finally, they could see the rewards of their difficult life and gain reinforcement for their often tested beliefs.

One further question remains to be asked: if these plays were acted or even read aloud dramatically (a hotly contested subject on which there is no agreement), who were the actors? As Pascal points out, those critics who believe that Hrotswitha's plays could not have been staged use as one argument that Hrotswitha would not have found women in her religious community to perform such roles as the prostitute in the *Conversio Thaidis Meretricis* (*Pafnutius*).[78] This criticism is hardly a decisive point against the staging of Hrotswitha's plays. The dramatic quality of the plays and the clear preoccupation with her audience by the playwright are compelling arguments in favor of the position that her plays were acted.

The *Passio Sanctarum Virginum Agapis Chioniae et Hirenae* (*Dulcitius*)

In the *Passio ACH* (*Dulcitius*), Hrotswitha created three women characters with strong resemblances to their creator/author. Like Hrotswitha, they inhabit a patriarchal world of dominance and desire, which becomes literal in the scene where Dulcitius turns into the Devil in Hell's kitchen

(4).[79] Like Hrotswitha, they find ways of turning situations to their advantage, partly through divine aid and partly through their own intelligence and initiative. They move quickly from being objects of trade and barter in the first scene[80]—where Dulcitius tries to arrange noble marriages and convince them to renounce their own Christian identities—to being the primary catalysts and controllers of the dramatic action. Diocletian has the first three and a half lines. They control the rest of the play.

The first scene of the *Passio ACH* (*Dulcitius*) sets the tone and the method of characterization for the rest of the play. Agape immediately establishes her position and the posture that she and her sisters will assume throughout when she uses the formal and authoritative imperative *esto* to answer Diocletian's demand that they deny God. When he accuses her of *fatuitas* ("silliness"), a word designed to mock her intelligence and sense of self and calling attention to her inferior and infantilized position as a woman, she adopts his own word and hurls it back at him in a strong and controlled question that gives the lie to Diocletian's charge of *fatuitas*. After a further mocking remark from Diocletian about her "silly new Christian superstition" [inutilem christianae novitatem . . . superstitionis (1.3)], Agape takes a stern, monitory tone and delivers the first of several lectures on traditionally male topics, this one on politics:

> *Agape*: You are bold to slander the majesty of Almighty God. It is dangerous. . . .
>
> *Diocletian*: Dangerous? To whom?
>
> *Agape*: To you and to the state you rule (*rei publicae*)

Such interference with affairs of state from a woman infuriates Diocletian, who calls Agape *insana* and orders her to be removed.

But no sooner does she leave the stage than Chionia takes her place. In an exchange lasting only three lines, the Agape scene is repeated, with Chionia defending Agape as quite sane and lecturing Diocletian on his stupidity. Diocletian falls back on his only weapon, the traditional charge that had been leveled at women for thousands of years: mental instability. Diocletian in his frustration becomes even more hyperbolic, calling Chionia not merely *insana* but comparing her to a raving Maenad (*ista dementius bachatur*, 1.4). Once she is removed, yet another takes her place. Diocletian hopes that because Irene is the youngest, she will be more malleable, but she turns out to be a match for every man in the play. She adopts all her sisters' ploys, but, in addition, she knows how to take the patriarchal tricks and torments and turn them against the men who control the action.[81] She objectifies herself (before Diocletian can do it), referring to herself in the third person and calling herself by the names that Diocletian wanted to use: "rebellem . . . renitentem" ("rebellious," "a resister," 1.5). She then borrows another leaf from her sister's book, engaging Diocletian in a philosophical debate about the bases of slavery and power until Diocletian, still relying on terms of infantilizing dismissal, tries unsuccessfully yet again to tame Irene ("huius praesumptio verbositatis tollenda est suppliciis," 1.8 [enough of this presumptuous chatter. The rack shall put an end to it. 1.8].

The women continue in this vein, always in control, taking over the directing and appropriating the gaze. They adopt men's roles, performing heroic actions, engaging in political and philosophical debate, and ironically reusing the men's descriptions of them to redefine themselves as the situation develops,[82] offering living proof that the men are just as deluded as they seem to be.

But the male and female roles have not simply been reversed; rather, the women seem to be comfortable in the roles they inhabit, both their traditional and received female roles and their newly adopted masculine aspects, while the men flounder from one posture to another, never successfully locating themselves in a workable discourse.[83] While the women support and reinforce each other, the men become each other's detractors, accusing each other and themselves of madness, delusion, and being bewitched (5, 6, 8, 9, 13, 14). They also admire qualities in the women that they themselves lack: stability, self-confidence, faith, and courage (2,12). They adopt and discard roles aimlessly and unsuccessfully, as Dulcitius does in 2.1–2, where he tries on the role of *amator* with disastrous results.

In her final words, Irene establishes her primacy of place, with Sisinnius having admitted to shameful behavior in the previous line ("quidquid dedecoris accidit, levius tolero, quia te morituram haut dubito", 14 [I accept the shame gladly, since now I am sure of your death]). Irene thunders her curse of damnation for Sisinnius in imperious and authoritative gerundives ("hinc mihi quam maxime gaudendum, / tibi vero dolendum", 14.3 [To me my death means joy, but to you calamity]) and harsh language ("pro tui severitate malignitatis in tartara dampnaberis" 14.3 [For your cruelty you will be damned in Tartarus]) that leave no doubt who is in charge and who has won this contest of wills. Irene's ascent into heaven and reception by Christ is assured; her death remains unmentioned.

Thus ends Hrotswitha's vindication of her female protagonists with whom both she and the audience of her women's community would have identified. Hrotswitha establishes a space to define herself and the women's culture in which she lived by creating a triple subjectivity for herself: as narrator of the lives of others (both fictional and traditional characters who are given life by the identification of her audience with them), narrator of herself in her Prefaces, and protagonist in her own stories by her self-reflexive identification with her characters.[84] She becomes in this process not only a chronicler of women's tales but also a creator of women's history, not only an object of discourse but also the agent of a "conflicted history, inhabiting and transforming a complex social and cultural world."[85] In this way, Hrotswitha, a tenth-century canoness living in the Abbey of Gandersheim, was able to shape and to influence women's ways of knowing.

Notes

1. C. M. Gayley, *Plays of our Forefathers* (New York: Duffield, 1907), p. 2.

2. For background on Hrotswitha, her life and *nachleben*, see Anne Lyon Haight, *Hroswitha of Gandersheim: Her Life, Times and Works, and a Comprehensive Bibliography* (New York: The Hroswitha Club, 1965); Bert Nagel, *Hrotsvit von Gandersheim* (Stuttgart: J. B. Metzler, 1965); Helene Homeyer, *Hrotsvithae Opera* (Munich and Paderborn: Ferdinand Schöningh, 1970); Dieter Schaller, "Hrotsvit von Gandersheim nach Tausend Jahren," *Zeitschrift für die Philologie* 96 (1977): pp. 105–14; Ferruccio Bertini, *Il "teatro" di Rosvita* (Genoa: Tilgher, 1979); Peter Dronke, *Women Writers of the Middle Ages: A Critical Study of Texts from Perpetua (d. 203) to Marguerite Porete (d. 1310)* (Cambridge: Cambridge University Press, 1984), pp. 55–83; Katharina M. Wilson, "The Saxon Canoness: Hrotsvit of Gandersheim," in *Medieval Women Writers*, ed. Wilson (Athens: University of Georgia Press, 1984), pp. 30–63. For discussions of the tenth century, see R. S. Lopez, *The Tenth Century* (New York: Holt, Rinehart, Winston, 1959); E. S. Duckett, *Death and Life in the Tenth Century* (Ann Arbor: University of Michigan Press, 1967).

3. See, most recently, Carole E. Newlands, "Hrotswitha's Debt to Terence," *Transactions of the American Philological Association* 116 (1986): pp. 369–91. See also Cornelia C. Coulter, "The 'Terentian' Comedies of a Tenth-Century Nun," *Classical Journal* 24 (1929): pp. 515–29; Arthur J. Roberts, "Did Hrotswitha Imitate Terence?," *Modern Language Notes* 16 (1901): pp. 478–82; Henry E. Burgess, "Hroswitha and Terence: A Study in Literary Imitation," *Proceedings of the Pacific Northwest Conference on Foreign Languages* (Corvallis: Oregon State University Press, 1968), pp. 23–29; Kenneth DeLuca, "Hrotsvit's 'Imitation' of Terence, " *Classical Folia* 28 (1974), pp 89–102; Dronke, *Women Writers*, pp. 68–73; Katharina M. Wilson, "*Figmenta vs. Veritas*: Dame Alice and the Medieval Literary Depiction of Women by Women," *Tulsa Studies in Women's Literature* 4.1 (1985): pp. 19–21; Judith Tarr, "Terentian Elements in Hrotsvit," in Katharina M. Wilson, ed., *Hrotsvit of Gandersheim: Rara Avis in Saxonia?* (Ann Arbor, MI: MARC Publishing, 1987), pp. 55–62; Katharina M. Wilson, *Hrotsvit of Gandersheim: The Ethics of Authorial Stance* (Leiden: E. J. Brill, 1988), pp. 72–86.

4. Hrotswitha's dates are uncertain, as is most information about her life. Her dates are often given as 935 until perhaps as late as 1002 c.e. See the sources cited

above, n. 2; also A. Daniel Frankforter, "Sexism and the Search for the Thematic Structure of the Plays of Hroswitha of Gandersheim," *International Journal of Women's Studies* 2.3 (1979): p. 222. For information on the history of Saxony and the Abbey of Gandersheim, see G. R. Coffman, " A New Approach to Medieval Latin Drama," *Modern Philology* 22 (1925): pp. 239–71; Coulter, " 'Terentian' Comedies," pp. 515–16; Frankforter, "Sexism," pp. 221–23; Wilson, "Saxon Canoness," pp. 30–31.

5. Hrotswitha was not a nun, as is often erroneously said; see Nagel, *Hrotsvit*, pp. 47–48; Sister Mary Margaret Butler, *Hrotsvitha: The Theatricality of Her Plays* (New York: Philosophical Library, 1960), pp. 52–61. Dronke comments on the mistaken view often held that Hrotswitha's existence was "cloistered" and that she was a nun "immured in her convent, who unaccountably took it into her head to read the plays of Terence and to 'imitate' them by writing edifying Christian counterparts" (*Women Writers*, p. 55).

6. Hrotswitha discusses her education and access to books in the library at Gandersheim in her Preface to the Saints' Lives; see Homeyer, *Hrotsvithae Opera*, pp. 37–38. All references to Hrotswitha's works will be to the Homeyer edition (see n. 2 above).

7. See Wilson, "Saxon Canoness," p. 30.

8. Sandro Sticca, "Sin and Salvation: The Dramatic Context of Hrotswitha's Women," in *The Roles and Images of Women in the Middle Ages and Renaissance*, ed. Douglas Radcliff-Umstead (Pittsburgh: University of Pittsburgh Press, 1975), p. 6.

9. Hrotswitha's plays have traditionally (since Celtis's *editio princeps* of 1501) been entitled *Gallicanus, Dulcitius, Calimachus, Abraham, Pafnutius*, and *Sapientia* by her critics. These are not, however, the titles that Hrotswitha gave to them. Whereas the traditional titles highlight the male characters, the original titles maintain her emphasis on the female protagonists. The second, third, fourth, and fifth plays were originally entitled the *Passio Sanctarum Virginum Agapis Chioniae et Hirenae* (= *Dulcitius*), *Resuscitatio Drusianae et Calimachi* (= *Calimachus*); *Lapsus et Conversio Mariae Neptis Habrahae Heremicolae* (= *Abraham*); *Conversio Thaidis Meretricis* (= *Pafnutius*). (The first play is named after a male character, the sixth after a female character in the original version). Despite the length and awkwardness of Hrotswitha's titles, I shall retain them in order to return to her original intent. For convenience, I shall call the *Dulcitius* (on which I will be focusing) *Passio ACH* (*Dulcitius*).

10. Frankforter, "Sexism," p. 221. Oddly, this comment appears in an article on sexual bias in medieval scholarship. To decribe Hrotswitha in this way robs her of her history and her influence, a fate that so often befalls female writers, composers, and artists. What Frankforter seems to mean is that no female in her culture before Hrotswitha had written the breadth of works she produced or written from this perspective and that, because her works were "lost" for so long, little attention was paid to her until the sixteenth century.

11. Katharina M. Wilson, trans. *The Plays of Hrotsvit of Gandersheim* (New York: Garland Publishing, 1989), p. xiii.

12. Heinrich Bodo, a sixteenth-century German monk and humanist, said of Hrotswitha "Rara avis in Saxonia est" (see Wilson, *Hrotsvit: Rara Avis*, p. ix).

13. For the low regard in which the tenth century has been held, see Lopez, *Tenth Century*,: "Then there was the tenth century, one which in the textbooks disputes with the seventh as the bad eminence, the nadir of the human intellect" (p. 1, quoted by Wilson, *Hrotsvit: Rara Avis*, p. xiv, n. 6). This view has been challenged by many, among them Duckett and Dronke.

14. Wilson, *Hrotsvit: Rara Avis*, p. xii (as part of a discussion of Hrotswitha's reputation).

15. Joseph Aschbach, "Roswitha und Conrad Celtes," *Sitzungsberichte der Kaiserlichen Akademie der Wissenschaften, Philosophisch-Historische Klasse*, vol. 56 (Vienna: Kaiserlich-Konigliche hof-und Staatsdruckerei, 1867), pp. 3–62. See on this A. Daniel Frankforter, "Hroswitha of Gandersheim and the Destiny of Women," *The Historian* 12 (1979): pp. 299–300; Edwin H. Zeydel, "The Authenticity of Hrotsvitha's Works," *Modern Language Notes* 61 (1946): pp. 50–55 (who discusses another attempt in 1945 by Zoltán Haraszti to question the authenticity of all the manuscripts of Hrotswitha, both the one discovered by Celtis in the fifteenth century and all the succeeding ones as well). Zeydel gives an excellent refutation. See Zoltán Haraszti, "The Works of Hroswitha," *More Books: The Bulletin of the Boston Public Library* 20.3 (March 1945): pp. 87–119 and 20.4 (April 1945): pp. 139–73.

16. Zeydel, "Authenticity," pp 50–55.

17. Cf. Frankforter's tongue-in-cheek (?) comment: "And one does not expect such an independent mind to have been nurtured in a medieval female" ("Sexism," p. 223). This bias continues today; even Sticca, who writes sensitively about Hrotswitha's treatment of women, says that Hrotswitha's women, "especially the virgins, are *monsters* of theological stability" ("Sin," p. 8). (My emphasis)

18. Frankforter, "Sexism," p. 225; Sue-Ellen Case, "Re-Viewing Hrotsvit," *Theatre Journal* 35 (1983): p. 535.

19. See Erich Michalka, *Studien über Intention und Gestaltung in den dramatischen Werken Hrotsvits von Gandersheim*, Inaugural dissertation der Ruprecht-Karl-Universität zu Heidelberg (Clausthal-Zellerfeld, Germany: Bönecke-Druck, 1968).

20. Frankforter gives a good example of Hrotswitha's privileging of female over male characters even in her historical epics ("Hroswitha," pp. 300–01, n. 22).

21. Paul von Winterfeld (also de Winterfeld), *Deutsche Dichter des Lateinischen Mittelalters* (Munich: Oskar Beck, 1913), p. 110: "Vor allem aber muss Hrotsvit den emporstrebenden Frauen unserer eigenen Zeit, unseren Gymnasiastinnen, Studentinnen, Lehrerinnen, Dichterrinen als die grosse, um Jahrhunderte voraus geeilte Standartenträgerin erscheinen. Hrotsvit ist sich selbst deutlich bewusst, mit

ihren Schöpfungen für das Recht der Frauen zu streiten und nach Ruhm und Ehre der Männer zu ringen. Ihre Dramen sind in dieser Hinsicht fast soziale Tendenstücke. Überall bleibt in ihnen die Frau Siegerin im Kampf gegen männliche Gewalt und Brütalität" [Especially, however, Hrotswitha must appear to the aspiring women of our own time—to high school students, university students, teachers, poets—as the great standard bearer from the turn of the (tenth) century, ahead of her time. Hrotswitha is very conscious of fighting through her writings for the rights of women and striving for the honor and glory given to men. In that respect her plays are almost social critiques. In all her plays the woman is the victor in her fight against male force and brutality].

22. Winterfeld, *Deutsche Dichter*, p. 110.

23. Quoted by Case, "Re-viewing Hrotsvit," p. 541. Case quotes an interesting reaction recorded at an early London performance of Hrotswitha's *Resuscitatio Drusianae* (*Calimachus*). When Drusiana, the female hero, prayed that she might die rather than yield to her ardent suitor Calimachus, she was greeted by the audience with shouts of laughter. See Christopher St. John, *The Plays of Roswitha* (London: Chatto and Windus, 1923), p. 159. (Christopher St. John is a pseudonym for Christabel Marshall).

24. Rosamond Gilder, "Hrotsvitha, a Tenth-Century Nun—The First Woman Playwright," in *Enter the Actress: The First Women in the Theatre* (London: Harrap and Co, 1931; repr. Freeport, NY, 1971), pp 34–35. See Case's comments on this ("Re-viewing Hrotsvit," p. 538).

25. Frankforter, "Hroswitha," p. 304.

26. Wilson, "Figmenta," p. 21. Wilson says that "Hrotsvit's heroines differ little from the ideal women of man-composed or man-compiled saints' lives and legends." She goes on to say that Hrotswitha is "first a canoness and only secondly a woman. She says little in the praise of women that would not occur in clerkly legends and vitae of female saints; her self-definition is entirely derivative and couched in conventional patristic and hagiographic terms" (p. 30, n.12).

27. See Teresa de Lauretis' discussion of how the term "experience" is used in feminist discourse to describe subjects as they are constructed in language and also as they interact with their social/historical contexts. She defines experience not as the "individual, idiosyncratic sense of something belonging to one and exclusively her own" but rather as a "*process* by which, for all social beings, subjectivity is constructed" (Teresa de Lauretis, *Alice Doesn't: Feminism, Semiotics, Cinema* [Bloomington: Indiana University Press, 1984], p. 159).

28. See Georges Gusdorf, *La découverte de soi* (Paris: Presses universitaires de France, 1948); Gusdorf, "Conditions et limites de l'autobiographie," in Günter Reichenkron and Erich Haase, eds. *Formen der Selbstdarstellung: Analekten zu einer Geschichte des literarischen Selbstportraits. Festgabe für Fritz Neubert* (Berlin: Duncker and Humblot, 1956), pp. 105–23; reprinted in translation in James Olney, ed., *Autobiography: Essays Theoretical and Critical* (Princeton: Princeton University

Press, 1980), pp. 28–48; James Olney, *Metaphors of Self: The Meaning of Autobiography* (Princeton: Princeton University Press, 1972). I would like to thank Diana Robin, whose work on two Renaissance women's autobiographical letters started me thinking about this subject. See her paper in this volume and an unpublished paper entitled "Women's Autobiography and the Letters of Two Fifteenth-Century Italian Women: Theory and Practice" delivered at Hamilton College in March, 1993.

29. See Sidonie Smith, *A Poetics of Women's Autobiography: Marginality and the Fictions of Self-Representation* (Bloomington: University of Indiana Press, 1987), esp. pp. 3–19, 44–62; Sidonie Smith and Julia Watson, eds., *De/Colonizing the Subject: The Politics of Gender in Women's Autobiography* (Minneapolis: University of Minnesota Press, 1992); Shari Benstock, ed., *The Private Self: Theory and Practice of Women's Autobiographical Writings* (Chapel Hill: University of North Carolina Press, 1988); Shari Benstock, *Textualizing the Feminine: On the Limits of Genre* (Norman: University of Oklahoma Press, 1991). See also Domna C. Stanton, "Autogynography: Is the Subject Different?," in Stanton, ed. *The Female Autograph* (New York: New York Literary Forum, 1984), pp. 5–22.

30. Dronke mentions in passing this aspect of Hrotswitha, saying that "aspects of Hrotsvitha's self-awareness become clear if we scan her writings for what I would call *indirectly autobiographic moments*" (*Women Writers*, p. 77). (My emphasis)

31. See Dronke, *Women Writers*, pp. 64 and 65–77 for a good discussion of Hrotswitha's Prefaces. For the Latin text of the Prefaces, see Homeyer, *Hrotsvithae Opera*, pp. 37–39, 233–37, 385–86.

32. Dronke, *Women Writers*, p. 69, cf. p. 82, where he well observes that her insistences on incompetence and submissiveness contain "an element of deliberate over-acting; they can be seen as so many ironic glances at the double standards of the world she knew, and especially of the powerful male-dominated world." Her diminutives he finds "self-assured, even self-assertive, by being self-deprecating."

33. Cf., for example, the Prelude to Hrotswitha's *Basilius*, 9–13 [fragilem vilis sexum . . . mulieris," 10]; Preface to dramas, 5 (*feminea fragilitas*); Hrotswitha's *Epistola Ad Fautores*, 3 [mei opusculum vilis mulierculae].

34. The Latin passages are taken from Homeyer's text; most of the translations from Christopher St. John (= Christabel Marshall) or, occasionally, Dronke. I have printed the Latin text exactly as Homeyer has it; she separates the *clausulae* in Hrotswitha's plays to emphasize the rhythmic and rhyming nature of the prose.

35. Cf. Vergil, *Eclogues* 6.1–12; *Georgics* 3.40–48, 4.559–66; *Aeneid* 1.1–11; 7.37–45; Horace, *Epode* 14; *Satires* 2.1.1–20; *Odes* 1.6, 2.12, 4.2; Propertius 2.1; 2.10; 3.3; 3.9.

36. See Jacob Grimm and Johann Andreas Schmeller, *Lateinische Gedichte des zehnten und elften Jahrhunderts* (Göttingen: Dieterichschen Buchhandlung, 1838), pp. ix–x (note); Dronke, *Women Writers*, p. 70; Wilson, "Saxon," p. 31; Nagel, *Hrotsvit*, pp. 38–39; Coulter, pp. 516–17.

37. The word *amentium*, which most translators take to mean "lovers," in fact means "those who have lost their senses." One editor suggested a possible change to *amantium*, "lovers" (Karolus Strecker, ed. *Hrotsvithae Opera*, 2nd ed. [Leipzig: Teubner, 1930]). I have retained *amentium* but have clarified the problem in my translation.

38. Jerome to Paulinus of Nola *Ep.* 53.2–4, 9.

39. Although, he points out, it has escaped her editors (Dronke, *Women Writers*, p. 74).

40. Dronke, *Women Writers*, p. 75.

41. Homeyer, *Hrotsvithae Opera*, p. 385.

42. See Dronke, *Women Writers*, pp. 69–70, who comments on the opening of Hrotswitha's Preface to her dramas ("Many Catholics can be found who prefer the vanity of pagan books to the utility of holy Scripture"). He says that this is a wild exaggeration and a joke.

43. See Sticca, "Sin," especially pp. 8–9, 18. Sticca says that Hrotswitha's "characterization of her women constitutes a radical departure from medieval tradition, for, transcending the frequent vacuities of antifeminine textual exegesis, she provides . . . a vision of woman triumphant over the demonic forces"(9).

44. See following section on Hrotswitha's Audience.

45. Here, I take issue with critics like Wilson, Sticca, and Frankforter, who see Hrotswitha's characters as one-dimensional (Wilson, "Figmenta," p. 30, n. 12), rigid and lacking in tragic motivation and human sensibility (Sticca, "Sin, " p. 8), and coldly detached (Frankforter, "Hroswitha," p. 313), and Hrotswitha's self-definition as "derivative and couched in conventional patristic and hagiographic terms" (Wilson, "Figmenta," p. 30, n. 12).

46. See Marianne Schütze-Pflugk, *Herrscher- und Märtyrerauffassung bei Hrotsvit von Gandersheim* (Wiesbaden, Germany: Steiner, 1972), who calls Hrotswitha's dramas *"dialogisierte Legenden"* (p. 8).

47. See Case, "Re-viewing Hrotsvit," p. 537, who discusses audience perspective.

48. See following section on Hrotswitha's Relationship.

49. For other allusions to madness and delusion/illusion, see *Passio ACH (Dulcitius)* 1.2–4; 11.5; 12.5; 13.3,4.

50. Cf. Dronke, *Women Writers*, p. 79: "like the girls, she too 'illudes in wondrous ways', by means of her art: in place of *maleficia*, she achieves the innocent magic of dramatic fiction." See also the discussion in Dronke, p. 61.

51. Dronke notes another verbal echo in blushing (*Women Writers*, pp. 77–78).

52. See Homeyer, *Hrotsvithae Opera*, pp. 494–96, for a list of specific borrowings from classical and late-classical authors in Hrotswitha's legends and plays (Prudentius, Sedulius, Terence, and Vergil); Winterfeld's 1902 edition of Hrotswitha's works, especially notes on pp. 119, 122, 130 (P. de Winterfeld, *Hrotsvithae Opera* [Berlin: Weidmann, 1902]).

53. I will not go into detail about Hrotswitha's debt to Terence since this has been amply discussed by many scholars; see bibliography in note 3 above.

54. See, for example, Roberts: "Terence and Hrotswitha both wrote plays, each wrote six, and there the similarity ends" (Arthur J. Roberts, "Did Hrotswitha Imitate Terence?," *Modern Language Notes* 16 [1901]: p. 480).

55. See Wilson, "Ethics," who comments on Hrotswitha's odd phrase *non recusavi* in *Pref.* 3 (p. 77 and n. 72).

56. Coulter, " 'Terentian' Comedies," pp. 528–29.

57. See DeLuca, "Imitation," pp. 89–102, especially pp. 94–99; Coulter, " 'Terentian' Comedies," especially p. 527.

58. See DeLuca's comment that "one has to search far in his [Terence's] plays to find those 'shameless acts of licentious women' that so upset Hrotsvit" (p. 90). Elsewhere he says: "Considering the evidence at hand, why such a howl of moral outrage from Hrotsvit? To speak of the 'wickedness' of Terence's matter seems to stretch even tenth-century morals to the breaking point" ("Imitation," p. 92).

59. Again, DeLuca: "Thais is a wholly likeable and superior type prostitute" ("Imitation," p. 92). Two recent articles on Terence explore audience responses to scenes of rape (often called "seduction") in Terence's plays and emphasize the ways in which classical scholars have excused Terence's young rapists and downplayed the effects of these violent and aggressive acts on their female victims (and audiences). See Zola Marie Packman, "Call It Rape: A Motif in Roman Comedy and Its Suppression in English-Speaking Publications," *Helios* 20.1 (1993): pp. 42–55; Louise Pearson Smith, "Audience Response to Rape: Chaerea in Terence's *Eunuchus*," *Helios* 21.1 (1994): pp. 21–38.

60. Dronke, *Women Writers*, p. 73.

61. Carole E. Newlands, "Hrotswitha's Debt to Terence," pp. 370–71.

62. See Sticca, "Sin," p. 14; also Newlands, "Hrotswitha's Debt," pp. 379–80.

63. See Sticca, "Sin," p. 10, on Constantia's role in the *Gallicanus*; Newlands, "Hrotswitha's Debt," pp. 377, 387–88, n. 53, on heroic language in the *Lapsus et Conversio Mariae* (*Abraham*) and the *Conversio Thaidis Meretricis* (*Pafnutius*).

64. Frankforter, "Sexism," p. 231.

65. See Coulter, " 'Terentian' Comedies," pp. 521–22 for remarks on similar reshaping of an original legend in Hrotswitha's *Gallicanus*.

66. *Bollandi Acta Sanctorum*, vol. 9, Aprilis (Antwerp, 1675), pp. 248–49 (translated in *Butler's Lives of the Saints*, ed. H. J. Thurston, S. J., and Donald Attwater [Westminster, MD: Christian Classics, 1926; rev. 1981], vol. 2, pp. 19–20 [April 3]).

67. See Dronke, *Women Writers*, p. 77; Hippolyte Delehaye, *Etude sur le légendier romain* (Brussels: Société des Bollandistes, 1936), pp. 151–71, especially pp. 163–64, 168–69 (who calls the Latin version of the Greek original "la déplorable version latine," p. 168).

68. See Douglas Cole, "Hrotsvitha's Most 'Comic' Play: *Dulcitius*," *Studies in Philology* 57 (1960): pp. 597–605; Sandro Sticca, "Hrotswitha's 'Dulcitius' and Christian Symbolism," *Medieval Studies* 32 (1970): pp. 108–27; F. W. Locke, "Ganelon and the Cooks," *Symposium* 20 (1966): pp. 141–49; Sandro Sticca, "Sacred Drama and Comic Realism in the Plays of Hrotswitha of Gandersheim," in *Acta VI: The Early Middle Ages*, ed. William Snyder (Binghamton, NY: Center for Medieval and Early Renaissance Studies, 1979), pp. 130–31. Locke discusses a similar scene in *The Song of Roland* that has traditionally been interpreted as merely an instance of *kuchenhumor*, but Locke argues that, when Ganelon is arrested and handed over to the army cooks, he is really being condemned to Hell for treason and that the kitchen here, as in Hrotswitha's *Passio ACH (Dulcitius)* = Hell.

69. This is a good example of Hrotswitha's statement in the Preface to her plays about her use of pagan, sexual themes to better highlight Christian heroism (*Pref.* 5).

70. Hrotswitha seems to believe in "technical virginity," an idea present in St. Augustine. Irene in the *Passio ACH (Dulcitius)* answers Sisinnius's threat to send her to a brothel, saying "Better far that my body should suffer outrage than my soul. . . . If the soul does not consent, there is no guilt" (12.3). See Frankforter, "Hroswitha," pp. 307–08; Newlands, "Hrotswitha's Debt," p. 388, n. 54.

71. See Wilson, "Figmenta," p. 19.

72. Only one female character in Hrotswitha's works is truly bad: the wife of Saint Gongolf in the *Passio Sancti Gongolfi Martiris* (one of the saints' Lives).

73. Case comments that "Given her collective context, Hrotsvit may have been the first woman playwright to write for a community of women" ("Re-viewing Hrotsvit," p. 537).

74. Drama in the medieval church was in its infancy in the tenth century. It is possible that some liturgies were beginning to be performed in Hrotswitha's time; see Karl Young, *The Drama of the Medieval Church* (Oxford: Clarendon Press, 1933); Schütze-Pflugk, *Herrscher- und Martyrerauffassung*, p. 8.

75. Case, "Re-viewing Hrotsvit," p. 537. Case gives an interesting account in her article of her own attempts to stage Hrotswitha's plays for a contemporary audience (pp. 540–42).

76. See especially Hrotswitha, *Lapsus et Conversio Mariae* (*Abraham*) 6.2.

77. Sticca, "Hrotswitha," p. 115.

78. Paul Pascal, *Hrotsvitha, Dulcitius and Paphnutius* (Bryn Mawr, PA: Bryn Mawr Latin Commentaries, 1985), pp. 3–4.

79. See Case, "Re-viewing Hrotsvit," pp. 536–37, for a good discussion of the *Passio ACH* (*Dulcitius*).

80. Case: "Beauty and high station are the trap of objectification" ("Re-viewing Hrotsvit," p. 536).

81. On women's appropriation of men's language, see Alicia Ostriker, "The Thieves of Language: Women Poets and Revisionist Mythmaking," in Elaine Showalter, ed., *The New Feminist Criticism: Essays on Women, Literature, and Theory* (New York: Pantheon Books, 1985), pp. 314–38. The three sisters' appropriation of men's language in Hrotswitha's *Passio ACH* (*Dulcitius*) to fight the patriarchal system is exactly what Hrotswitha herself is doing when she borrows from Terence and the hagiographers to write her own versions of the stories.

82. The male characters use demeaning language and diminutives throughout to define the women (or girls, as they would say). So Dulcitius says "Papae! Quam pulchrae, quam venustae, quam egregiae puellulae!" 2.1 [Ye Gods, but these little girls are beautiful! What grace, what charm!], and he and Sisinnius both call them *lascivae* (wanton, 7, 10). In the last scene, Irene takes over both their authoritative tone and their language, ironically calling herself "tenellae infantiam virgunculae," 14 [a poor, defenseless girl] and again, as in 1.5, distancing herself from the heroic character she has become by using the third person of herself. This phrase is particularly ironic in its context: "You wretched Sisinnius! Do you not blush for your shameful defeat? Are you not ashamed that you could not overcome the resolution of a little child without resorting to force of arms?" [Infelix, erubesce, / Sisinni, erubesce, / teque turpiter victum ingemisce, / quia tenellae infantiam virgunculae / absque armorum apparatu nequivisti superare?].

83. Anthropologists have done interesting work on how women inhabit two traditions at once, the dominant male tradition and a muted female tradition, and thus have an opportunity, which men do not have, to subvert texts and reread them in a different light. See Edwin Ardener, "Belief and the Problem of Women," in Shirley Ardener, ed., *Perceiving Women* (New York: Halsted Press, 1978), pp. 1–17. See also John J. Winkler, "Double Consciousness in Sappho's Lyrics," in *The Constraints of Desire* (New York: Routledge, 1990), pp.162–87, where he talks about the "cultural bi-lingualism" that women are forced to develop (p. 162).

84. Note the verbal echoes discussed above that Hrotswitha creates between herself in her Prefaces and her characters in her plays. See Smith, "Poetics," pp. 3–19, 44–62, for techniques of women's autobiographical writing.

85. Chandra T. Mohanty and Satya P. Mohanty, "Contradictions of Colonialism," *Women's Review of Books* 7.6 (March 1990): p. 19 (there the quote refers to the colonized); Smith and Watson, *De/Colonizing the Subject,* pp. xix–xx.

Gender and Negotiating Discourse
Mediated Autobiography and Female Mystics
of Medieval Italy

Phyllis Culham

Many of the vitae, letters, and literary fragments of female saints[1] in central Italy at the turning of the thirteenth to the fourteenth century have never lent themselves to traditional historicist criticism because of the complexity of the process by which they were constructed. The works for which I wish to suggest a new approach, more conscious of gender, are not a representative sample of the material. They are instead some of the most egregiously problematic texts: the vitae of Margherita of Faenza and Margherita of Cortona, the Sermones of Umiltà of Faenza, and the *Liber* of Angela of Foligno.

The vita of Margherita of Cortona was compiled during her lifetime from her confessions and, probably, read to the public in her presence. It appends letters dictated by the unlettered Margherita to her confessor, Fra Giunta Bevegnati, who claims that she dictated to him for eight days, with others present as witnesses (*Leggenda*, chap. 2). Recent scholars have described how Fra Giunta arranged her "confessions" topically in chapters, each of which served as an exemplum of well-known saintly practices such as conversion, humility, and ecstatic contemplation. Others have noted that Fra Giunta's narrative pattern also permits each chapter to feature a miracle, although a later, unknown editor split Fra Giunta's final, eleventh chapter to form a twelfth, in spite of Fra Giunta's claim in his fourth chapter that God instructed him on how to arrange Margherita's life.[2]

Margherita of Faenza was interviewed by a biographer, Peter of Firenze, chosen by her order shortly before her death. He admits to shortening her narrative and reordering her discussions to make easier reading. Peter says in his prefatory comments that he expected to continue working with Margherita for some time and did not always try to remember each session in detail, with the result that he lost much valuable material when Margherita died suddenly.[3] Umiltà's collection of Sermones claims that another woman took down her talks to her disciples in Latin, but they survive only in a vernacular version edited by a male, who says that he removed excess words.[4]

Angela of Foligno, the most influential of these women for later mystics, began to dictate her spiritual autobiography in the vernacular to her confessor and relative. Arnaldo, who subjected his Latin version of her remarks to her criticism. These memoirs (the *Memoriale*) and the appended letters often refer casually to Angela reading the gospel and missals, so Angela could have understood Arnaldo's Latin. Arnaldo tells us much in his preface and epilogue about how he produced the *Memoriale*. He reordered the material to reflect the chronology of Angela's spiritual journey. He inserted within topical units discussions that resulted from his questioning Angela at a later session either about what she experienced or on the meaning of what she had told him. His notes were initially on scraps, until he realized the significance and scale of their project and bought a large codex just for the purpose of recording Angela's comments. That codex was apparently the basis for the biographical unit known as the *Memoriale*. Arnaldo translated on the spot into Latin as he wrote in the codex. Later he read over his work and brought it back to Angela for correction and clarification.[5]

However, he was not always able to read her what he had written and secure her verification. Hence, he freely admits, he was confused on the sequence and division of the later spiritual steps. He says he could not always keep up with Angela when taking dictation, but, even worse, at the fifth supplementary step he was forced to translate into Latin in his codex the cryptic notes taken by a boy who had attempted to record Angela's vernacular speech. (Apparently Arnaldo's superiors had become uneasy about his contact with Angela and attempted to discourage it, but the text is not explicit on this point.) Arnaldo's principle in general, of which he reminds the reader throughout, was that it was better to lose some of what she had said than for him to pollute the material by adding his own words. But, when Angela told him that his Latin version constructed from the boy's notes was worse than nothing and wanted the fifth supplementary step destroyed, he did not comply. In his preface he describes himself as a mere sifter that let go the fine flour and retained the coarse, a wonderful image that belies his repeated assertion of authorial incompetence.

The *Liber* consists of the *Memoriale* plus the *Instructiones*, letters and sermons by Angela to disciples and friends, not in any chronological order. It is not clear whether one scribe took down all of the *Instructiones*. Some, like instruction 3, have the scribe addressing her as M, probably Mater. Even in instructions in which the scribe injected himself or herself, e.g., the preface to the fourth instruction, the scribe preceded or followed Angela's comments with praise of Angela personally or intellectually, so one may surely assume that someone among her followers was collecting the *Instructiones*, perhaps with help. Angela frequently addressed her comments to *filii mei*. The scribe or scribes of the *Instructiones* often confess to failing to understand the discourse therein recorded.

In his preface to the *Memoriale*, Fra Arnaldo explains the confusing switching between the first and third persons that characterizes that text. He says that Angela spoke in the first person, but he normally turned it into the third when he translated her remarks. He did not, however, always have time to work that out and left some sections in the first person. Hence, for much of the *Memoriale*, Angela is the *fidelis Christi* in the third person, while Arnaldo is the assertive first person *ego frater* or *ego frater scriptor*. Angela's first person narrative is characterized by first person verbs, not by the nominative pronoun, which Arnaldo then had to use to distinguish himself from her.

In these cases, the classic historicist ploys of showing how the text serves the ends of the author or of tracing influences on the author cannot work well. Who are the authors? Mediated autobiography poses a difficult problem for historicists, in particular; but other characteristics of these texts resist the simple application of any interpretative strategy. The women associated with these texts hotly deny any intentionality either as authors or as subjects of their own narratives; all responsibility (both for matter recorded and for the recording) is ascribed to divine will. These texts represent the women as saying that their knowledge of the divine is direct and absolute but that their descriptions of that divine nature, which they claim to understand absolutely, are deceptive. Nonetheless, the larger part of these texts as we have them is devoted to such description. In each case, the text as we see it now has been transformed in some degree by one or more males who claimed no firsthand knowledge (nor understanding, in some cases) of the subject matter transcribed, but the text still explicitly claims the authority of absolute knowledge. Finally, all these texts share the new mendicant orders' insistence on personal responsibility for one's actions and for one's salvation, although this emphasis is undercut by the refusal of subject or speaker to accept any responsibility for the text or for its transcription.[6] Scholars in this century have confronted these difficulties with a variety of techniques.

For the last thirty years, a phenomenological approach has frequently been used to avoid confronting the claim of mystical texts to represent "truth." Phenomenology obviated any need to decide if the narrator was describing paranormal phenomena, recording dreams, wandering in the delusions of advanced psychosis, or devising a literary fable to attract readers or obtain a reputation for sanctity. Bracketing discrete units of description or themes allowed the comparison of mystical texts across gulfs of time and geography without regard for authorial intent or cultural distinctions such as gender. It was considered possible to compare "ineffability," say, or the presence of divinity as darkness in the text of Angela of Foligno and in the writings of her Sufi contemporaries or in the sixth-century A.D. text of Pseudo-Dionysius.[7] Even some of those who used this philosophically oriented approach to these texts, however, began to realize that phenomenology did not necessarily provide the reader with an adequate critical distance from the text or from the reader's own assumptions. "Mysticism" is itself a (common) western phenomenological bracketing of certain experiences and/or ways of making claims about experience.[8] It is hardly surprising that phenomenological bracketing can perpetuate, rather than eliminate, cultural blinders.[9]

More recent, philosophically oriented work on mysticism, clearly influenced by various schools of reader-response and other poststructuralist criticism, have begun to emphasize that we are examining texts rather than historical experience. Nevertheless, many of these contributions slip into viewing these texts as mediated experience rather than as autonomous artifacts and, therefore, bog down in the linguistic problem of talking about mystical descriptions of ineffability that emphasize the inadequacy of their own words for conveying their subject matter. These philosophical discussions, as a result, are attempts to develop tools for dealing with mystical texts rather than offerings of fully developed methods. Many of the scholars involved still seem to be convinced that more sophisticated bracketing and/or better construction of professional lexica are the keys to a better understanding of mystical texts.[10]

Perhaps the single most popular approach to mystical texts, one that has been applied extensively in studying some of these central Italian women, is that offered by psychology. One of the most prominent historians of religion in Medieval culture, Rudolph Bell, discusses these women in a sophisticated and sympathetic manner while relying primarily upon a psychoanalytic approach. Bell, however, has to do all his own bracketing. Neither the female Italian mystics nor their contemporaries in the thirteenth and fourteenth centuries were familiar with modern psychological and psychoanalytic terminology. It is up to Bell to identify textual references to "seeing," "hearing," "understanding," "grace," and "ecstasy" as "anorexic," "psychotic," "schizophrenic," "paranoid," and "hysterical blindness."[11] There may be dangers in such an approach. Bell certainly treats these texts as autonomous artifacts in which he brackets meaning without consideration for authorial intent. Nonetheless, his approach, which denies the self-awareness of either narrator or text, undercuts his own analysis, which depends on the validity of the text as description of experience and behavior. His use of a psychoanalytic model leads him to neglect the impact of social constructions of gender and to rely on relatively ahistorical models of the female psyche.[12]

Other recent efforts to apply the results of psychological research in examining mystical texts exhibit even less self-awareness in their efforts to bracket clinically identifiable symptoms in mystical treatises, while simultaneously assuming the perfect reliability of descriptions originating with (presumably) symptomatic narrators.[13] Neither Bell, a culturally sensitive historian, nor the psychologists attempting to apply clinically derived techniques, are able to handle the problem of the generation of the content and imagery of these mystical texts within their focus on individual psychology. For instance, I have already noted the similarity of the treatment of the Good as Darkness in the text of Angela of Foligno to that in Pseudo-Dionysius. How does psychology deal with this intertextuality? Similarly, I believe that the retreat from Cortona in Margherita's vita is related to Medieval accounts of the Magdalen as anchorite.[14] Yet this interpretation involves the consideration of influences that are beyond psychology's traditionally ego-centered scope.

In these cases, the psychological approach raises more questions than it answers. Both texts, especially that of Angela, are echoed in later works by successors like Gertrude of York and Teresa of Avila. How does an image or topos function both as conceptual coin common to a cultural economy[15] like western mysticism and as a symptom of aberrancy? If the interest for a symptom hunter lies in the idiosyncratic transformation of the common imagery by each saintly psychotic, how can either the clinician or the historian use deviant responses in generalizing about either psychological processes or about a culture at large? If imagery is a symptom, where does the dysfunction lie: in hallucinatory experience? in a false memory of an experience that did not occur in the way described? in a deceptive claim to experiences the speaker never had in an effort to win esteem? The mystical texts provide us with no way of deciding among these possibilities, but selection among these explanations has grave implications for diagnosis or for selection of a clinically derived model.

The problem of causation is especially dicey for the historian. If later symptoms, as reflected in these texts, are "caused" by psychodynamics within the family, as Bell must argue, what can they tell the historian about the contemporary society? If the ultimate cause is some socially structural transformation that is producing dysfunctional families en masse, that may explain the frequently noted geographical and chronological clustering of mystics, as in central Italy in the thirteenth through sixteenth centuries. But it also suggests that historians seeking to understand the generation of these texts should not focus upon transactions within family units, let alone individual psychosis.[16] It hints that considerations of gendered roles in the family and the economy are likely to be more useful.

The manner in which these texts undercut their own statements and authority by insisting on the inadequacy of their own words makes them obvious candidates for deconstructive criticism, but I know of no instance to date in which such criticism has been applied to these or to similar texts. I will not use such an approach because I believe that it would preclude reaching a feminist, gender-aware understanding of these documents. It would treat the extant versions of these texts, all of them pared into their current shape and their units set into their current order by males, as autonomous, self-referential objects not only apart from any authorial intent but even from any historical context, thereby rendering the women who participated in the construction of these texts even less visible.[17] All too often recent poststructuralist criticism has assumed that the spatiotemporal field within which the text was generated is a mere set of historical contingencies without coherent significance, while the verbal epiphenomena, the literary texts, are the intellectually complex developments worthy of critical attention.[18] I shall assume, instead, that the field or cultural economy, including definitions of gender, within which their literary works were shaped is itself a demanding, meaningful text simultaneously requiring explication and supplying tools for the understanding of the verbal texts with which we have been concerned.

I would contend that one can survey these texts again more profitably using the means suggested by Foucault's *Discipline and Punish, The Birth of the Clinic*, and *History of Sexuality*.[19] Considering these mystical texts as discourses within an episteme, in juxtaposition with other discourses, avoids treating either individual or society as a phenomenon of which the other is the epiphenomenon.[20] It considers the interaction of discourses within particular chronological, spatial, and social boundaries without requiring resolution of traditional (but in these cases insoluble) historicist problems revolving around "author" and "intent." The discourse is reduced to an opaque event unassociated with intent; we use only the fact of its existence and its differences from other real or possible discourses in examining its performance.[21] An examination of the process or the negotiation of this discourse replaces the study of author or intent. We do not have to demonstrate, for instance, that Angela read or had read to her Pseudo-Dionysius or, alternatively, that Fra Arnaldo transposed her more mundane discussion into a vocabulary evocative of a learned tradition; nor do we have to decide whether Margherita of Cortona had heard legends of the Magdalen and acted upon them or whether her biographer considered a hermetical interlude a literary sine qua non for a vita he was attempting to place within the holy hooker tradition.

A feminist interest in women's autobiography combined with the Foucauldian study of discourse allows the reintroduction of traditional historicist concern for context, including contemporary constructs of gender, while obviating the questions asked by historicist criticism. Observing the interaction of discourses also facilitates the observation of these mystical texts within several traditional genres at once. Because of the prevailing organization of the scholarly disciplines, these texts have normally been treated exclusively as autobiographical narratives (confessions or exemplary vitae) or simply as philosophical/theological treatises. I have noted earlier the problems that accompany approaches considering these texts exclusively as examples of those genres. The application of a Foucauldian methodology to these texts also serves the purpose of excavating in Foucault's archaeological field to one level below that from which Foucault usually began, namely, the early modern, and allows the use of these texts as a check upon Foucault himself.

In pursuing this investigation, I shall follow recent feminist scholars of biography and autobiography in being alert to gender as an element in discourses about power.[22] As Bartky noted, "if individuals were wholly constituted by the power-knowledge regime Foucault describes, it would make no sense to speak of resistance to discipline at all."[23] A feminist reading of women's texts may offer unique opportunities to study both resistance and subversion. Conversely, Foucault's insistence on the self as process, constantly restructured by and in the dominant discourses of the surrounding culture, is an excellent viewpoint from which to approach women's autobiographies; so Bella Brodzki and Celeste Schenck maintain, "No mirror of her era, the female autobiographer takes as a given that selfhood is mediated . . . the female autobiographer has lacked the sense of radical individuality. . . . "[24] Foucauldian attention to the contemporary discourse of power will elucidate the constraints upon and tools offered to our autobiographers.

Foucault believed that the practice of confession transformed western discourse after penance was regulated and made a sacrament by the Fourth Lateran Council in 1215. He suggested, in summary, that the result was a revolution in where and how people looked for truth. Truth was not discovered by avowals of numerous witnesses or partisans but within a discursive process. The assumption underlying the practice of confession was that truth was inside, held in by shame, fear, threat, or some other form of social power. Most importantly, the power normally held by a speaker was shifted to the listener, who could direct the entire narrative by means of questions. Without the listener, in fact, the speaker had no purpose.[25] The sacramentalization of confession has aptly been called a major appropriation of power by the church hierarchy.[26] At the same time, however, more topics of discourse were permitted. Nothing, no matter how heterodox or aberrant, was excluded in speech with one's confessor.[27]

There is evidence that the new regularization of and emphasis placed on confession at the beginning of the thirteenth century had an impact in Italy in the next hundred years.[28] Nonetheless, the Lateran strictures had to compete with other social and economic developments. Northern and central Italy were, by the standards of that century, heavily populated and economically prosperous. The peninsula north of Rome was the most urbanized area of the western Mediterranean world, whether one measures urbanism by demographic nucleation or by political control of hinterlands by urban centers.[29] In this milieu, the new "third orders," for penitentials who wanted to do holy work in this world rather than retire from it, prospered, as they did in wealthy urban centers in the rest of Europe. As one would expect in an area where Francis had walked, preached, and founded congregations a mere two generations earlier, the Franciscan tertiaries were the most prominent of the new orders.[30] The narratives of the lives of Angela of Foligno and Umiltà of Faenza, especially, supply models for the assumption of religious authority by a prosperous urban elite, especially for the women who had been wives and mothers in that milieu and thereby failed to conform to the prevailing model for the feminine gender, the saintly virgin. This was particularly important in a culture in which marital patterns left many widows who were not expected to remain on their own in widow-headed households but instead to work out their places in other household units.[31]

The new saints were not distinguished by remarkably pious childhoods but, on the contrary, by a conversion experience in adulthood such as that of Francis, i.e., they divested themselves of mercantile and landed wealth. One recent scholar has argued that conversion in texts of this period meant the giving away of one's wealth.[32] Johan Huizinga quoted Pierre d'Ailly's dismay that bourgeois penitentials in France, admired for having chosen their lot, were competing so successfully at begging that they were depriving the truly needy.[33] In short, originally prosperous penitentials were claiming access to religious functions such as organizing and heading charitable foundations and were claiming vocations and religious public identity without submitting themselves to the authority of an order or even, in the case of women, of subjecting themselves to the authority of men.[34] They conceded nothing to the poor, not even their poverty. The ascetic mystics, most of them women, were more publicly and enthusiastically impoverished than were the original poor, to whom charitable help was now supposed to flow through confraternities and hospitals run and founded by the middle-class mendicants. The new female saints secured a double triumph. They gave all they had to the poor and outdid them at poverty, while simultaneously, tacitly criticizing the values of their male relatives who had accumulated the wealth.[35]

It is hardly surprising that some of these new saints, especially the mystics, challenged the church for the power of the confessional. The Fourth Lateran had emphasized that confession had to be made to one's own confessor. In the medical terms used by the Council, he was the physician most familiar with the patient's normal state and most likely to be able to diagnose the cause and comparative severity of the symptoms and to prescribe an appropriate cure, i.e., penance. Margherita of Cortona in her (surely unsolicited) advice to the Bishop of Arezzo said that one must never hide anything from a confessor, just as one must show a physician all one's wounds (*Leggenda*, 8,9). Even the self-effacing and obedient Margherita of Faenza had to be persuaded repeatedly to tell her story to a man carefully chosen by her order. She invoked the relatively new absolute seal of the confessional to retain control of her own narrative after parts of it had been written down by two interviewers, as the preface to her life notes. Angela of Foligno simply left one confessor as inadequate.

Margherita of Cortona reduced her confessor to the role of a secretary and messenger who wrote down for her the letters with which she arbitrated local Guelph-Ghibelline issues in Cortona and offered administrative instructions to the church hierarchy (e.g., *Leggenda*, 8, telling an abbot not to expel a monk).[36] She certainly did not follow her own advice about telling one's confessor everything. Margherita even tantalized hers by refusing to tell him what God had revealed about him, since it would not make him happy (*Leggenda*, 6). Fra Giunta had acquired a supporting role in her narrative but lost his ability to direct it from behind the camera. Even the ability of these confessors to pare and to shape the written text from the confessional narrative was subject to negotiation. All three of those women reviewed the written versions of their comments in one way or another. Umiltà may have reviewed the *Sermones* also; the genre makes it more difficult for the scribe to tell us how she proceeded, and the later editor may have removed prefacing comments as excess words. The freedom to speak of anything, even the depraved, in the confessional enabled the more theologically ambitious Angela of Foligno and the more politically ambitious Margherita of Cortona to be depicted in their texts as heroic sinners of epic stature, while the same texts simultaneously propounded doctrines close to antinomianism, which would have rendered their sins meaningless, and, hence, not occasions for correction. In this way the mediated autobiographies of these women were more startlingly new than the reminiscences that their male bourgeois contemporaries wrote at first in business daybooks and later dictated to scribes writing in special notebooks. Those male contemporaries tended to produce what we would call collective biographies, portraits of a lineage, contexts in which the current writer was subsumed. Gradually, in a way perhaps influenced by the experience of being taken seriously in the first person in the confessional, these male authors moved toward becoming the protagonists of their own autobiographies.[37] In many ways, if less directly and obviously, the female, bourgeois, saintly mystics were already there.

Our mystics' greatest weapon in countering the spiritual power of the confessor, or, indeed, of any theologically trained auditor, was their mysticism itself. By continually asserting the inadequacy of words, they claimed to keep most of the truth locked within themselves, requiring anyone who wanted more of it to petition them repeatedly. The insistence on the superiority of direct mystical knowledge to the mere written text even extended to Angela of Foligno's ubiquitous claim that she understood the scriptures better than Arnaldo or even doctrinal tradition! Margherita of Faenza's insistence that she should not tell anyone all that she had seen appropriated from the confessor the right to own the narrative by taking it and keeping it without divulging it. Umiltà of Faenza was able to speak of her visions and to keep them simultaneously by repeatedly telling her disciples, both men and women, that her revelations were not to be spoken of to those who did not understand. In each case, even that of Umiltà's sermons, these mystics implicitly asserted within the text the right to direct the narrative because a rapture cannot be controlled or directed. They determined the length and the rhythm of the telling. The editor, however, had the effective last word. In short, the texts of the mystical ascetics are the products of negotiations over power between female members of an urban, lay movement and the thirteenth-century bureaucratizing, institutionalizing, male-dominated church.[38]

The sacramentalization of confession and penance tended to make both the discourse and the act of speech itself secret. Earlier Medieval literature is replete with tales of spectacular public penance: barefoot walks to shrines, public self-accusation or even scourging, or lengthy, expensive pilgrimages. The new penitential manuals, however, ordinarily assigned penance to be performed within the household. (e.g., fasting) or within the church (e.g., recitation of prayers). Public ritual had long been a significant element of Medieval urban societies; seasonal ludic activities and church or state processionals were important confirmations of the daily social order.[39] The literal hushing up of confession and penance guaranteed the church's control of the flow of events during mass and attempted to reserve the space outside the church for communal observances or for public liturgy in the form of sermons by members of the teaching orders or public processions to commemorate victory or to seek relief from disease.[40]

The mystic texts transformed the previous liturgy of public confession into another form of discourse. Margherita of Cortona and Angela of Foligno were both described as wanting to arraign themselves publicly for their sins and to suffer public degradation, although they were generally dissuaded by their confessors and other advisors. Earlier, Margherita had confessed from a balcony (*Leggenda*, 2). Arnaldo's methodological preface to the *Memoriale* recounts how Angela shrieked and wailed so much at the great church of Francis at Assisi that she humiliated him in public, and he reacted with anger. In the first instruction, Angela is represented as saying that she wanted to parade naked through public squares with meat and fish around her neck. The eleventh instruction even recommended public penance for all, as long as the motive in undertaking it was not just to be seen. Margherita and Angela's texts recount at length and in repellent detail the scenes of public humiliation they longed for but did not actually experience. The texts suggest a model of internalized piety and self-inflicted humiliation that compromised by leaving public space for the use of church and commune by channeling the desire for public confession and degradation into literature, where fantasy, as well as experience, can be vicariously shared. As Smith comments, "mysticism itself provided a nonscholarly engagement with religious experience to those who were denied access to the realm of formalised theological discourse."[41]

Foucault noted the process by which the public liturgy of the procession to punishment or execution of the early modern criminal was made available to an even larger audience in a purer, distilled form. This represented, he said, an effort to meet two objectives simultaneously: acting appropriately upon the individual perpetrator, and reinforcing good order in the rest of society by means of the spectacle of punishment. Over time, the fate of the perpetrator became less central, and there was more concern for inculcating a belief in punishment and therefore in making current an image of punishment.[42] These mystical texts with their images of depression and degradation consequent on sin reflect a similar process. That is why the confessors and the church preserved and circulated such partially subversive vitae. The earlier theater of confession and public shame was gradually moved out of the squares of the communes into the imaginations of readers to be recalled whenever a sin was contemplated. Women could be protagonists, if not even heroes, while suffering for their communities and while controlling the process of their largely mental suffering.

This negotiation over the control of an important discourse—one which, in the form of the vita, claims to represent a model for life itself—does not simply represent the collision of two historical forces, namely, central, Italian, urban wealth and a church trying to assert authority newly centralized at

Rome. It is also an incipient change in episteme of the sort Foucault assigned to the late eighteenth and early nineteenth centuries. In *Discipline
and Punish*, he described the process by which examining authorities confronted with criminals ceased to ask simply who did what and what the
customary punishment was and asked additionally why something was done:
was the person deranged? under threat? The very language of medical diagnosis used by the Fourth Lateran Council points to the creation of a new
field for expert knowledge and, therefore, an appropriation of the power to
name and to examine.[43] The effects for Medieval religion are much like
those Foucault found for the handling of criminals in the nineteenth century and for the roughly contemporaneous invention of the modern medical preserve of hospitals and illnesses. In neither of Foucault's cases is
severity or consistency of penalties in question; the issue is the orderly
exercise of power under a central authority and appropriation of the instru-
ments of exercising that power.

In this case, gender also fuels the confrontation and influences the
course of the negotiations (e.g., at the simplest level, women claim a share
in the ability to produce knowledge; men shape it into a recognizable contribution to the discourse they maintain). Sidonie Smith noted the "rhetorical utility of self-abnegation for a woman who would dare to speak, even
to instruct . . . " and diagnosed "the self-effacing speaking posture . . . [that]
conceals all faults, including the fault of ambition. . . . "[44] While deeply
engaged in self-abnegation, these privileged, urban women were negotiating the formation of new models of piety that, in time, legitimated a broader
range of female behavior.[45]

In all three of Foucault's topics–punishment, medicine, and confession–the published accounts of individual cases blow the affairs of everyday
life up to epic proportion where they can be easily examined (in all three
cases, poverty, mendicancy, and depression are issues so treated). The trans-
position of these issues into literature enables the middle class to appropriate something that claims to represent these experiences and to claim
knowledge of it even in the case of women, married and within a family. On
each topic, this can be done most effectively by a literature of glorification
that stresses the exceptional nature of the criminal/sick person/sinner and
suggests that the reader of the text can share some of the experiences the
text claims to describe without fearing the same outcome.

There are, then, grounds for suggesting that the epistemic changes in
forms of discourse and organization of knowledge that accompanied the
creation of the state and intellectual disciplines was prefigured by a similar
consolidation and attempt to reorganize power and knowledge on the part
of the Medieval church. Perhaps we can see here the first rumblings of a
process that was temporarily contained within the most pervasive institu-

tion of its day but was eventually to result in the social and institutional effects Foucault placed later. A feminist reading of related texts has highlighted gender as an important element in the negotiations over the form and content of this discourse, suggesting that the transformations that Foucault did discuss should be examined to see if gender played a part in those power struggles, too. While this reading of these mystical texts provides new possibilities for interpretation by highlighting certain features of later Medieval society, an examination of some struggles for power contemporary to the texts illuminates them in turn. A focus upon gender allows us to discover a previously unexplored dimension of the struggle for power, namely, attempts to enter and even to control a dominant discourse. That, in itself, suggests that the historical women behind these texts cannot simply be viewed as psychologically aberrant females.

Notes

1. I shall follow the practice of Caroline Walker Bynum in *Holy Feast and Holy Fast: The Religious Significance of Food to Medieval Women* (Berkeley and Los Angeles: University of California Press, 1987), Michael Goodich in *Vita Perfecta: the Ideal of Sainthood in the Thirteenth Century*, Monographien zur Geschichte des Mittelalters, vol. 25 (Stuttgart: Hiersemann, 1982), and others in referring to all of these women as saints, in spite of the fact that Angela of Foligno and Margherita of Faenza are officially recognized only as *beatae*. As Goodich noted (p. 2), what is significant for the understanding of social history is local or regional reverence; cf. Richard Kieckhefer, *Unquiet Souls: Fourteenth Century Saints and Their Religious Milieu* (Chicago: University of Chicago Press, 1984), p. 17.

2. In addition to *Acta Sanctorum* (hereafter = *AASS*) Feb., vol. 3, there is now Eliodoro Mariani, ed., *Leggenda della Vita e dei Miracoli di Santa Margherita da Cortona* (Vicenza: L.I.E.F., 1978), which offers historical notes. Beatrice Coppini, *La Scrittura e il Percorso Mistico: Il "Liber" di Angela da Foligno* (Rome: Editrice Ianua, 1986), pp. 98–99, resolves the *Leggenda* of Margherita into its constituent *exempla*. Enrico Menestò, "Beate e Sante dell'Umbria tra Duecento e Trecento: Una Ricognizione degli Scritti e delle Fonti Agiografiche," *Sante e Beate Umbre tra il XIII e il XIV Secoli* (Foligno: Edizioni del'Arquata, 1986), p. 72, notes that each chapter also centers upon a miracle.

3. I know of no alternatives to *AASS*, Aug., vol. 5.

4. See *AASS*, May, vol. 5. On the difficulties with the text, see Piero Zama, *Santa Umiltà: La Vita e i "Sermones"* (Faenza: Fratelli, 1974), 18 passim.

5. *AASS*, Jan., vol. 1, is deficient. The best alternative is now Ludger Thier and Abele Calufetti, *Il Libro della Beata Angela da Foligno* (Rome: Grottaferrata, 1985). The identification of the "A" of the text with Angela's relative Arnaldo is not universally

accepted. Mario Sensi, "Angela nel Contesto Religioso Folignate," *Vita e Spiritualità della Beata Angela di Foligno,* Atti del Convegno di Studi per il VII Centenario della Conversione della Beata Angela da Foligno (1285–1985) (Perugia: Schmitt, 1985), p. 43, notes that there was no Arnaldo or Adamus known in Foligno's Franciscan convent. On the other hand a Franciscan Andrea was Foligno's ambassador to Perugia. He had no known connection to Angela. The manuscripts collecting local traditions in which Angela's relative Arnaldo was identified as Brother A are now lost; see Paul LaChance, *Angela of Foligno: Complete Works* (New York: The Paulist Press, 1993), p. 319, n. 4. Either way, the argument above is not materially affected.

6. On the rise of the mendicant orders and the increasing emphasis on works of charity see Bynum, *Holy Feast and Holy Fast,* p. 26, and "The Spirituality of Regular Canons in the Twelfth Century," *Medievalia and Humanistica* 4 (1973): p. 3; Goodich, p. 187; David Herlihy, "Alienation in Medieval Culture and Society," *Social History of Italy and Western Europe 700–1500,* Collected Studies (London: Routledge, 1978), pp. 135–36.

7. For a summary of the central issues and images in the highly influential Pseudo-Dionysius see Thomas Katsaros and Nathanial Kaplan, eds., *The Western Mystical Tradition* (New Haven: College and University Press,1967), pp. 155 ff. On the topos of revelation in darkness in the patristic tradition, see Paul LaChance, *The Spiritual Journey of the Blessed Angela of Foligno According to the "Memorial" of Frater A,* Studia Antoniniana nr. 29 (Rome: Pontificium Athenaeum Antoninianum, 1984), pp. 248–323, especially pp. 296 ff. on the connection with ineffability. LaChance, p. 373, describes the *Memoriale* as "colored by" earlier writers from whom it derived "an atmosphere and a language."

8. Carl A. Keller, "Mystical Literature," in *Mysticism and Philosophy,* ed. Steven T. Katz (Oxford: Oxford University Press, 1978), p.35.

9. Wayne Proudfoot, *Varieties of Religious Experience* (Berkeley and Los Angeles: University of California Press, 1985), p. 135, discusses many older phenomenological treatments of mysticism and notes that they are somewhat circular. They select certain traits as typical of the purest type of mysticism and then find those traits in the texts to which they advised us to attribute the highest value. Proudfoot does not note explicitly that the western bias occurs most obviously in the insistence that texts that speak of "seeing" are usefully analytical, while those which speak of "flying" are fanciful. Nor do phenomenological approaches respect "emotions," such as ecstasy; they prefer texts that "rise above" perceived human limitations. Most western texts meet these standards; many eastern texts do not.

10. The discussions in Steven T. Katz, *Mysticism and Religious Traditions* (Oxford: Oxford University Press, 1983) represent an advance over those in Katz, *Mysticism and Philosophy* in their general admission that they are dealing with texts and not with experience. Nonetheless, even the later essays still tend to lose themselves in the linguistic problems, e.g., H. H. Penner, "The Mystical Illusion," pp. 90 ff., or F. J. Strong, "Language and Mystical Awareness," 152 ff. LaChance, *Spiritual Journey,* p. 9, notes that "one is dealing with interpretation-laden

accounts, a language about the experience and not the experience itself." On the other hand, LaChance, *Complete Works*, p. 47, refers to the "mediated experience."

11. Rudolph Bell, *Holy Anorexia* (Chicago: University of Chicago Press,1985), 42 passim.

12. Bynum, *Holy Feast and Holy Fast*, p. 205, criticizes Bell's approach as "both reductionist and individualistic." Both Bynum (loc. cit.) and Proudfoot, p. 121, disapprove of dismissing the participant's own understanding or interpretation of an experience as an epiphenomenon. Bynum argues that the meaning of any image must be culturally construed to some extent, and Proudfoot notes that the mystic's understanding of the experience is an essential part of the experience. Joan Jacobs Brumberg, *Fasting Girls: The History of Anorexia Nervosa* (New York: Plume, 1989), pp. 43–46 and pp. 294–96, offers a critique of synchronic psychological models of anorexia-like, generally ascetic behavior and of Bell in particular. She cites additional studies of Medieval women that claim to diagnose anorexia. Susan Mosher Stuard, "The Sociobiological Model and the Medieval Evidence," *American Anthropologist* 86 (1984), pp. 410–12, provides more traditional, historically oriented criticism of the general application of models derived from the modern west.

13. Especially egregious examples are the essays in Dean, *Psychiatry and Mysticism* (New York: Humanities Press, 1976), many of which attempt cross-cultural study of mysticism.

14. Examples collected in the basic Victor Saxer, *Le culte de Marie Madeleine en occident* (Paris: Presses Universitaires, 1959), 14 passim. On the resemblance of the narrative structure of the *Leggenda* to the standard Medieval stories about the Magdalene, see Coppini, p. 99.

15. I am using the term *economy* as Foucault uses it to refer to a system of exchange in which different sorts of incentives function and am invoking his implied model in which incentives like those supplied by market mechanisms compete with traditionally assigned values. On the influence of Angela of Foligno, see Decima L. Douie, "A Franciscan Mystic of the 13th Century," *Franciscan Essays* 1 (1932), pp. 120 ff; John Moorman, *A History of the Franciscan Order from Its Origins to the Year 1517* (Oxford: Clarendon Press, 1968), pp. 89 ff.and 103 ff.; Mario Sensi, "Il Movimento Francescano della Penitenza a Foligno, " in *Il Movimento Francescano della Penitenza nella Società Medioevale*, Atti del 3 Convegno di Studi Francescani a Padova, ed. Mariano D'Alatri (Rome: Istituto Storico dei Cappuccini, 1980), pp. 399 ff; Peter Dronke, *Women Writers of the Middle Ages* (Cambridge: Cambridge University Press, 1984), pp. 207 ff. Proudfoot, pp. 122–23, notes that mystics often try to place themselves within a tradition to establish their bona fides, given the intrinsic difficulty of verifying mystical claims.

16. For compilations illustrating this clustering, see Rudolph Bell, *Holy Anorexia*, pp. 216–30; Donald Weinstein and Rudolph Bell, *Saints and Society* (Chicago: University of Chicago Press, 1982), pp. 252–71; Goodich, *Vita Perfecta*, passim. Economically and demographically driven changes in relationships between

individuals and families in northern Europe in the later Medieval period are dis-
cussed in Michael Mitterauer and Reinhard Sieder, *The European Family* (Chicago:
University of Chicago Press, 1982), pp. 77 ff., and for Italy in James B. Ross, "The
Middle Class Child in Urban Italy Fourteenth to Early Sixteenth Centuries," in *The
History of Childhood*, ed. Lloyd de Maus (New York: Atcon, 1974), pp. 199ff.

17. The difficulty of reconciling deconstructionist criticism and feminist approaches is discussed by Phyllis Culham in "Decentering the Text," *Helios* 17 (1990):
pp. 161–70. Bynum, *Holy Feast and Holy Fast*, p. 83, makes the point that women's
vitae were even more subject to being reduced to a stereotype than were men's,
presumably because there was even less publicly attested data on them.

18. Some instances cited in Phyllis Culham, "Ten Years After Pomeroy," *Helios*
13 (1987): pp. 18 ff. Ironically, the Foucauldian/feminist approach suggested here
would legitimate the study of "images of women" in author X, Y, or Z with attention
to the author as participant in a dominant cultural discourse or to the contribution
of a normative discourse to a woman's definition of herself, her horizons, or her
body, cf. the "self-policing subject" of Sandra Lee Bartky, "Foucault, Femininity and
Patriarchal Power," in *Feminism and Foucault: Reflections on Resistance*, ed. Irene
Diamond and Lee Quinby (Boston: Northeastern University Press, 1988), pp. 61–86.

19. Michel Foucault, *Discipline and Punish: The Birth of the Prison*, trans.
Alan Sheridan (New York: Vintage, 1979), *The Birth of the Clinic: An Archaeology
of Medical Perception*, trans. A. M. Sheridan (New York: Vintage, 1974), *History of
Sexuality*, vol. 1, trans. Robert Hurley (New York: Random House, 1980).

20. Cf. Norbert Elias, *The Civilizing Process*, vol. 1 of *The History of Manners*
(New York: Harper, 1978), p. xv, xvii.

21. Foucault, *Birth of the Clinic*, pp. xvii–xix.

22. For additional discussions of feminism's compatibility or lack thereof with
Foucault, see Jana Sawicki, "Feminism and the Power of Foucauldian Discourse,"
in *After Foucault: Humanistic Knowledge, Postmodern Challenges*, ed. Jonathan
Arac (New Brunswick, NJ: Rutgers University Press, 1988), pp. 161–78; Diamond
and Quinby, p.xiv. This is not to deny the danger that Foucauldian approaches could
result in "a return to female anonymity," the warning issued by Domna C. Stanton,
ed., *The Female Autograph: Theory and Practice of Autobiography from the Tenth
to the Twentieth Century* (New York: New York Literary Forum, 1984), p. 16, citing
other cautionaries. Nonetheless, her own discussion of competing discourses and
female participants demonstrates that a feminist approach can avoid this problem.
For more on women's autobiography, see Barbara K. Gold's paper in this volume.

23. Bartky, "Foucault, Femininity and Patriarchal Power," p. 82.

24. Bella Brodzki and Celeste Schenck, eds., *Lifelines: Theorizing Women's
Autobiography* (Ithaca, NY: Cornell University Press,1988), p. 8.

25. J. D. Mansi, *Sacrorum Conciliorum Nova et Amplissima Collectio*, p. xxii.;
Mary Lydon, "Foucault and Feminism," in *Feminism and Foucault*, ed. Irene

Diamond and Lee Quinby (Boston: Northeastern University Press, 1988), pp. 137–39, offers an informative discussion of the unique historical resonance of the French *aveu*, which "has the positive value of guaranteeing the speaker a place in the scheme of things."

26. Kieckhefer, "Unquiet Souls," p. 135.

27. Foucault, *History of Sexuality*, pp. 60–102.

28. E.g., perhaps, the copying of the "Laurentian Penitential"; see J. T. McNeill and H. M. Gamer, *Medieval Handbooks of Penance* (New York: Columbia University Press, 1938), p. 352.

29. Herlihy, "Alienation," pp. 135–36.

30. Moorman, pp. 216 ff; Mario Sensi, "Incarcerate e Penitenti a Foligno nella Prima etá del Trecento," in *I Frati Penitenti di San Francesco nella Società del Due e Trecento*, ed. Mariano D'Alatri (Rome: Istituto dei Cappuccini, 1977), pp. 37 ff. On the ironically symbiotic relationship of Francis' successors and the urban bourgeois, Lester K. Little, *Religious Poverty and the Profit Economy* (Ithaca, NY: Cornell University Press, 1978), pp. 203–05.

31. Charles de la Roncière, "Tuscan Notables on the Eve of the Renaissance," in *A History of Private Life*, vol. 2 *Revelations of the Medieval World*, ed. Georges Duby (Cambridge, MA: Belknap, 1988), p. 229, is admittedly discussing Tuscany, but there is little reason to think things much different in these closely neighboring cities. Jean Delumeau, *Sin and Fear: The Emergence of A Western Guilt Culture 13th to 18th Century* (New York: St. Martin's, 1990), pp. 450–51, traces the rising concern from the fifteenth through the eighteenth centuries about widows and their sexuality. Umiltà and Margherita of Faenza were Vallombrosans, neither Franciscans nor tertiaries; their careers, however, took them to Florence, where there was a special interest in these kinds of activities and where they were highly admired. On the differences between the old and the new types of saints, see Kieckhefer, "Unquiet Souls," pp. 144 ff and Rudolph Bell, *Holy Anorexia*, pp. 84 ff. Margherita of Cortona does not quite fit this model of urban wealth, since she was born to a family of peasants. But she became the mistress of a wealthy man (perhaps a noble) in her midteens and, after his death when she was about thirty, went to the city of Cortona, where she was taken up by women who would meet these criteria.

32. Weinstein and Bell, *Saints and Society*, p. 216.

33. Johan Huizinga, *The Waning of the Middle Ages* (London: E. Arnold and Co., 1924), p. 153.

34. See note 31 and Little, pp. 173; de la Roncière, "Tuscan Notables," pp. 165–66.

35. On the dramatic increase in the number of women among the new saints and their disproportionate association with mysticism and asceticism, see Bynum, *Holy Feast and Holy Fast*, 21 ff. (and on their charitable acts as implicit criticism of male kin); Weinstein and Bell, *Saints*, pp. 233 ff.; Kieckhefer, "Unquiet Souls," pp. 150 ff.

36. On the local arbitration, see Goodich, *Vita Perfecta*, p. 168, and on the identification of these local Cortonese Ghibellines with the Fraticelli, Giovanna Casagrande "Realità Storica e Movimenti Religiosi in Umbria nel Secolo XIII e nella Prima Età del XIV," in *Sante e Beate Umbre tra il XIII e il XIV* (Foligno, Italy: Arquata, 1986), p. 27.

37. Philippe Braunstein, "Toward Intimacy: The Fourteenth and Fifteenth Centuries," in *History of Private Life*, ed. Georges Duby (Cambridge, MA: Belknap, 1988) pp. 54–42. Male clerics who shared some of the mystical tendencies of our women (e.g., Jacopone da Todi) tended either to do their own writing or to rely on scribes who were subordinate to them in some way. Their works are more monographic in nature, offering material more impersonally and with less revelation of the individual spiritual search.

38. On the efforts to standardize canonization procedures and control them from Rome, see Goodich, *Vita Perfecta*, passim; on pp. 31, 55, he discusses the process of constructing vitae from confessions to serve as the dossiers to support canonization. On the relationship of the saint and the biographer/confessor, see Kieckhefer, "Unquiet Souls," p. 7.

39. On the transition, see McNeill and Gamer, *Medieval Handbooks*, pp. 28 ff.

40. E.g., Edward Muir, *Civic Ritual in Renaissance Venice* (Princeton: Princeton University Press, 1981), pp. 187, 231, 250. The attempt to reserve the public spaces takes effect slowly, of course, and is never absolute in its effect. Crises such as the Black Death evoke a return to public penance, but that tends to be publicly sanctioned and enacted by the community en masse (Marvin B. Becker, *Medieval Italy: Constraints and Creativity* [Bloomington: Indiana University Press, 1981], pp. 138 ff). Weinstein and Bell, in fact, describe the new saints as expiators for the community rather than heroic individuals, *Saints and Society*, p. 177.

41. Sidonie Smith, *A Poetics of Women's Autobiography: Marginality and the Fictions of Self-Representation* (Bloomington: Indiana University Press, 1987), p. 10. The claim of desire for humiliation presented in vivid language is especially interesting given Delumeau's claim (pp. 470–74) that women's modesty hindered them in confession and made public confession especially difficult. This account, which stresses the negotiation among individual, culture and institution, and the subversive nature of the texts, as well as the fact that they are texts rather than immediate experience, differs from the explicitly Foucauldian and feminist treatment of Susan Bordo, "Anorexia Nervosa: Psychopathology as the Crystalization of Culture," Diamond and Quinby, pp. 87–117, whose thesis is readily apparent from her title. The extravagance of the language of guilt and expiation in the *Memoriale* is presumably what led LaChance to assume that there must have been a proportionate cause in Angela's life, e.g., *Complete Works*, p.17.

42. Foucault, *Discipline and Punish*, pp. 93 f.

43. Ibid., and Foucault, *Birth of the Clinic*, pp. 60 ff.

44. Sidonic Smith, *Women's Autobiography*, pp. 4 and 54, respectively.

45. Cf. Carolyn G. Heilbrun, "Non-Autobiographies of 'Privileged' Women: England and America," Brodzki and Schenck, *Lifelines*, p. 70, and Personal Narrative Group, eds. *Interpreting Women's Lives: Feminist Theory and Personal Narratives* (Bloomington: Indiana University Press, 1989), p. 102, a lucid and accessible discussion seemingly Foucauldian in method.

The Saint of the Womanly Body:
Raimon de Cornet's Fourteenth-Century Male Poetics

St. John E. Flynn

It has to be admitted that the name of Raimon de Cornet is not one that immediately springs to mind when one reflects on the history and development of the European lyric tradition.[1] He is, by anyone's standards, even a Medievalist's, an obscure literary figure.[2] This, however, should not deter us from examining, or perhaps I should say reexamining, his work. Current critical trends within general literary studies, and within Medieval studies, in particular, encourage us to break new ground. New Medievalism, which Stephen G. Nichols contends "denotes a revisionist movement in Romance Medieval studies that is resolutely eclectic yet relatively consistent in its concerns and presuppositions,"[3] seeks to relegitimize Medieval studies through the convergence of contemporary critical theory, Medieval history, and textuality, while current debates about canon formation urge us as scholars to broaden our horizons and incorporate writers whom tradition has consigned to that limbic space known as "the margins."

This new force in Medieval studies is the rationale for what I plan to do in this article. My enterprise is to evaluate in the light of recent feminist criticism two Latin lyrics written by Raimon de Cornet sometime around the middle of the fourteenth century. My approach will not be original. The same sort of thing has already been done with respect to early vernacular lyric poets such as Petrarch and Sidney.[4] Where I hope to do something different is in my use of feminist critics such as Hélène Cixous and Luce Irigaray to analyze the modus operandi of two fourteenth-century Latin religious lyrics. These pieces are different from other works previously analyzed using feminist criticism in two ways: they are sacred, and they are not written in the vernacular. There is a relative paucity of contemporary critical studies in the area of Medieval Latin religious poetry; this body of literature exists in that limbic space already named. I seek here to contribute to its demarginalization.

Before beginning, I want briefly to introduce our poet, Raimon de Cornet. The biographical information culled from his works and those of his contemporaries is scant but suggests that his life was marked by a varied clerical career.[5] Born around the year 1300 in the small town of Saint-Antonin in the Rouergue region of Provence, he was, by 1324, *capela ordenat*, that is, a member of the secular clergy. For eight months and nine days he belonged to the Order of St. Francis and, as a *frayre menor* (friar minor), identified himself with the Spirituals and the doctrines of Peter John Olivi. The Spirituals were an ascetic faction within the Franciscan Order who, troubled by what they saw as a progressive tendency toward worldliness in the Order, developed a very rigid, narrowly defined concept known as the *usus pauper* or "poor use"; this was based on the belief that Christ and the Apostles owned no material possessions, save what they wore, and held all monies in a common purse. This idea of Christ as the perfect model for true poverty was the basis for the Spirituals' vociferous criticism of the Order. In his decretal of 1323, *Cum Inter Nonnullos*, Pope John XXII declared the Spirituals to be heretics. In 1326 at Avignon, Peter John Olivi and several of his followers were accused of heresy. Several of the Spirituals were burnt at the stake. Raimon, as a fellow poet, Guilhem Alaman, informs us,[6] was almost among this unlucky number and was lucky to escape with his life.

Raimon subsequently left the Franciscan Order. He continued for a time as a member of the secular clergy. However, sometime after 1340 he joined the Cistercian Order, becoming a *monge blanch* (white monk). He seems to have spent an indeterminable period in the Cistercian monastery at Pontaut in the diocese of Aire, in what today is the Landes region of France, and may, indeed, have died there sometime after the midpoint of the century.

As well as living a life that would have fitted him for a part in *The Name of the Rose*, Raimon was also a troubadour. Fifty-four of his pieces survive; these poems are generically varied and include works both lyrical and nonlyrical, religious and profane. He was at the forefront of the new poetry that emerged at the beginning of the fourteenth century and sought to continue the classical troubadour tradition. Raimon was the leading light of the *Ecole Toulousaine*, the Toulouse School of poetry that formed at this time and was allied to the poetry competition begun in Toulouse in 1323 by the *Consistoire de la Gaie Science*. This annual contest, aimed at perpetuating and renewing the poetic traditions of the classical troubadour era, awarded prizes to the best poems of a religious nature. Raimon won one of the prizes in 1333. Of the fifty-four extant pieces left by our poet, fifty-two are in Medieval Occitan; the remaining two are in Latin, and it is upon these that I wish to focus our attention.[7]

Raimon was one of only two Medieval Occitan poets to write both vernacular and Latin lyrics. The only other troubadour to do so, as far as we know, is Cavalier Lunel de Monteg who, interestingly enough, also belonged to the *Ecole Toulousaine* and was writing circa 1330.[8] It is my contention that Raimon's two poems were written after he had rejected vernacular Franciscanism and had embraced the Latin monastic tradition of the Cistercian Order. His two extant Latin pieces, one a litany to the Virgin Mary, the other a eulogy of the life of the great Cistercian founding father, Bernard of Clairvaux, are testimony to his Cistercian vocation; both are suffused with Cistercian spirituality, and both were probably written to form part of the daily divine offices of the monastery.[9]

The second poem is a *proza* (prose) as the manuscript title informs us. The *proza*, sometimes called the *sequentia*, had its origins in the eighth-century monastic liturgy. During the Mass of the Roman rite, between the Epistle and the Gospel, there were two chants, the Gradual and the Alleluia, which were linked with the verse of a psalm. In plainchant convention, it became traditional to prolong the singing of the final *-a* of the Alleluia, and the melody that was thus produced was known as the *Jubilus* or, more correctly, a *sequentia*. In the eighth century the custom developed of adapting a text of prose, that is *prosa*, to fit the *sequentia*. This became known as a *sequentia cum prosa*.

Raimon's first piece might also have been composed for one of the daily offices of the monastery. In fact, it may even be that both pieces were written to celebrate the Feast of St. Bernard on August 20th, a day of special significance for a Cistercian community. I would even like to suggest a specific year of composition for these pieces; 1353 was the two-hundredth anniversary of the death of Bernard, and this year would coincide with the time that Raimon was in the monastery at Pontaut. These two poems may have formed part of the monastic liturgical celebration of the anniversary of St. Bernard's death.

Both pieces are also fine examples of male sexual poetics borne of patriarchal discourses. The following evaluation will seek to show how, through the figure of the Virgin, Raimon de Cornet sings the praises of Bernard of Clairvaux in a strategy that, by means of the objectification and reification of the Virgin's body, denies her autonomous existence. She functions, therefore, uniquely as a means for the poet to express his own desires. Her body is appropriated and transformed by the male poet, and she becomes "Other," what Hélène Cixous describes, in "The Laugh of the Medusa," as "the uncanny stranger on display,"[10] nothing more than a male poetic construct, devoid of any sense of female subjective reality.

In theorizing the role and function of Woman within the symbolic order, Luce Irigaray speaks of the dichotomy between female eroticism and the phallomorphic "system of representation and desire"[11] that denies Woman any voice, any substance, any subjectivity, due to her imperfection, her lack[12] of the "only definable form"[13] accorded any value: the penis. Within the symbolic, female sexuality "has always been theorized within masculine parameters,"[14] and Woman has always been defined in terms of her difference; hence, she becomes Other, or what Hélène Cixous defines as "uncanny." She is the silent object of male desire, delineated by what Luce Irigaray terms a male "sexual imaginary" that renders her "a more or less complacent facilitator for the working of man's fantasies."[15] The result is the symbolic construction of the passive female Other. As Laura Mulvey comments, "[t]he determining male gaze projects its fantasy onto the female figure, which is styled accordingly."[16] This "prevalence of the gaze" creates what Irigaray calls the "dominant scopic economy," which signifies Woman's "relegation to passivity: she will be the beautiful object."[17]

It is Hélène Cixous who articulates Irigaray's dominant scopic economy within the realm of the literary. In "The Laugh of the Medusa" she makes the observation that:

> writing has been run by a libidinal and cultural—hence political, typically masculine—economy: that this is a locus where the repression of women has been perpetrated, over and over, more or less consciously, and in a manner that's frightening since it's often hidden or adorned with the mystifying charms of fiction.[18]

Within this libidinal, cultural, and scopic economy, Woman's body has, she further contends, "been more than confiscated from her."[19]

It is at this point that we can turn to the first of Raimon's poems, the litany, the archetypal prayer of supplication to the Blessed Virgin that Rémy de Gourmont rather poetically (and inaccurately) calls "le registre des grâces de la femme, des symboles par quoi se désigne la créature d'essence unique"[20] ["the register of the graces of woman, the symbols by which the creature of unique essence represents herself"].[21]

This litany describes the Virgin with forty-four different epithets, which define her in forty-four different ways. The piece gives no real material presence to the Virgin; she is designated primarily by abstractions that bear no relation to her subjective being. She is "mare benignitatis" [sea of kindness] in verse (v.) 4, "speculum regalis curie" [mirror of the royal court] in v. 7, and "lumen Eclesie" [light of the Church] in v. 13. Through such a procedure, the Woman is deprived of a subjective existence within the poem; she is reified in the extreme, reduced to an agglomeration of inhuman metaphors that together construct a body that is in no way her own.

The rare epithets that do acknowledge her physical being exemplify the patriarchal system, insisting upon bodily states and functions defined for her by what Hélène Cixous calls "parental-conjugal phallocentrism,"[22] glossed in this case by the pronouncements of Christian theology. Hence, in v. 1 the Virgin is "Mater Jesu, castrum virginitatis," [Mother of Jesus, fortress of virginity], in v. 2 she is "vas integrum," [Unspoiled vessel] and, perhaps most tellingly, in v. 11 she is "Sancticimum corpus humilitatis" [Most holy body of humility]. Her material being, when acknowledged, is appropriated by the male so that, when he insists upon her virginity and her motherhood, she is forced to play the theological and doctrinal roles assigned her by the signifying male; her body has, indeed, been confiscated from her and reconfigured according to a male perception of her Otherness, that is, her motherhood. We shall have cause to return to this later.

What Raimon does do for the Virgin, however, is to give her a textual body; he constructs her for his own purposes and according to his own desires. But where does the "body of the text" come from, and what desires does it express? The epithets used by Raimon to construct the Virgin in his litany show an obvious indebtedness to the writings of St. Bernard of Clairvaux; some are drawn from biblical sources upon which the Cistercian Father expounded in copious sermons (for example, his eighty-six *Sermones in Cantica Canticorum*, based on the Old Testament Song of Songs). Others, however, are culled from certain of his homilies, in particular, his four homilies *In Laudibus Virginis Matris* [*On the Praises of the Virgin Mother*], written in contemplation of the Annunciation as contained in the first chapter of the Gospel of Luke. Although the litany is ostensibly and superficially in praise of the Virgin, a study of these intertextual elements confirms that what Raimon really seeks to do, his desire, if you will, is to extol the greatness of St. Bernard on the occasion of the two-hundredth anniversary of his death, by recreating, through the figure of the Virgin, Bernard's own texts, which were familiar to any Medieval Cistercian monk.

In v. 2, Raimon describes Mary as "vas integrum," combining "vas," a commonplace biblical invocation of the Virgin,[23] and a reference to her perpetual virginity, "integrum"; Bernard's phrase in the homilies *In Laudibus Virginis Matris* is "mater intacta" [unspoiled mother] (2.8.24).[24] When in v. 5 Mary is given the epithet "lux omnibus," Raimon recalls a sentence from the second homily, "Ipsa ergo est nobilis illa stella ex Iacob orta, cuius radius universum orbem illuminat" [She is therefore the noble star sprung from Jacob, whose beam lights up the whole world] (2.17.20–21). "Sancticimum corpus humilitatis" [Most holy body of humility] of v. 11 takes its inspiration from paragraphs 5–9 of Bernard's first homily *In Laudibus* in which he insists on the essential humility of the Virgin in accepting the divine role given her by God. As St. Bernard writes:

Pulchra permixtio virginitatis et humilitatis, nec mediocriter placet
Deo illa anima, in qua et humilitas commendat virginitatem, et
virginitas exornat humilitatem. (1.5.19–21)

[A beautiful mixture of virginity and humility, that soul is pleasing
to God in no unexceptional way, a soul in which both humility
commends virginity, and virginity adorns humility.]

It was, above all else, Mary's humility and virginity that impressed the saint;
she possessed both virtues completely: "felix Maria, cui nec humilitas defuit,
nec virginitas" ["Happy Mary, in whom neither humility nor virginity were
lacking"] (1.9.16).

Two of the epithets used in Raimon's litany are to be found in Bernard's
four homilies *In Laudibus*, but not in reference to the Virgin. "Concilium
cecretum dietatis" [Secret council of God] of v. 19 seems to be a
reconfiguration of a phrase from the second homily: "Uno tali consilio
secretis caelestibus et admittitur testis, et excluditur hostis, et integra
servatur fama Virginis Matris" [And the witness is admitted to one such
council of heavenly secrets, and the enemy is excluded, and the pure reputation of the Virgin Mother is preserved] (2.13.8–10). The "odor suavitatis"
[fragrance of sweetness] of v. 33 reproduces another phrase of Bernard from
the third homily:

Solent angeli adstare orantibus et delectari in his quos vident levare
puras manus in oratione: holocaustum sanctae devotionis gaudent
se offerre Deo in odorem suavitatis. (3.1.14)

[The angels are accustomed to assisting with their prayers and take
delight in those whom they see raising pure hands in prayer: they
rejoice to offer themselves to God in the fragrance of sweetness as
a sacrifice of holy devotion]

This phrase was not Bernard's own; it appears four times in the Vulgate:
Genesis 8: 21, Ecclesiasticus 24: 20, 23, and Ephesians 5: 2.

Other metaphors chosen by Raimon to adorn his own private Virgin
show an indebtedness to the Song of Songs expounded in the *Sermones
super Cantica Canticorum*[25] already mentioned. Raimon would undoubtedly have been acquainted, not only with the Vulgate text, but also with
Bernard's exposition of it.[26] This Old Testament work was one of the most
critical to the development of Catholic theology during the Middle Ages,
particularly mariology.[27] The Shulamite bride of the Song of Songs was
interpreted as a figure, not only of the Church, but also of Mary. Christ

became identified with the lover/bridegroom.[28] Mary was thus seen as both the bride and the Mother of Christ, and furthermore as his daughter, an interesting configuration indeed.

Bernard's interpretation of the Song of Songs is tropological rather than mariological; the bride is not necessarily interpreted as a figure of the Virgin, but is seen in a more general spiritual way.[29] However, the allegorical interpretation that took the Shulamite bride as a figure for the Virgin had already been established by Honorius Augustodunensis (Honorius of Autus), whose treatise *Sigillum Beatae Mariae* was the "first systematic mariological exposition of the Song of Songs"[30] and is dated to c. 1100,[31] some thirty-five years before the first of Bernard's sermons on the book. And yet, on account of Bernard's eighty-six sermons on the Song of Songs and his pivotal role in the development of mariology, no Cistercian could read the Song of Songs without seeing in it myriad mariological references, It was Bernard's various sermons celebrating the Virgin that, according to Marina Warner, "mark the fulcrum of devotion to the Virgin in the west."[32] Bernard had tied the tropological (that is, the personal, that which pertains to the individual soul) to the mariological elsewhere in his sermons concerning Mary's *compassio* (compassion) as she stood in front of the cross. This marian development is commented on by Sandro Sticco:

> [I]t is above all in the mysticism of Bernard that the theme of the compassion acquires a particular and exceptional distinction thanks to his refined and exquisite sensitivity. He emphasizes the element that is decisively human and personal in the sublime emotion felt by the Virgin at the moment of her Son's sufferings.[33]

Bernard, Mary, and the Song of Songs were part of the same associational matrix from the perspective of a white monk such as Raimon. For the medieval period, the Cistercian order, and Raimon de Cornet, the Virgin and the Song of Songs blossomed "[in]to full glory in the impassioned love and language of St. Bernard."[34] Likewise, the Virgin, the Song of Songs, and Bernard of Clairvaux "open to full glory" in Raimon's litany.

The "Mons lilium" [Mountain lily] of v. 3 and the "Florumque flos" [Flower of flowers] of v. 32 echo verses from chapter 2 of the Song of Songs in which the *sponsa* (bride) speaks of herself: "Ego flos campi, et lilium convallium" [I am the flower of the field and the lily of the valleys]. Her husband continues, "Sicut lilium inter spinas, sic amica mea inter filias" [Just as the lily among thorns, so is my beloved among the daughters] (Song 2: 1–2). The lily is a favorite symbol of Mary's purity and of her beauty. In an attempt to rework the traditional expression, Raimon adds a different emphasis to the image of the lily. "Mons lilium" replaces "lilium convallium"; Raimon simply moves his lily out of the valley and onto the mountainside, creating a variation on the traditional image.

The Virgin is "turris David" [tower of David] in Song 4: 4, and she is "turris fiducie" [tower of faithfulness] for Raimon (v. 3). This epithet is linked closely to "castrum virginitatis" in v. 1. Mary is associated with these fortifications because of her fortitude and her inviolable chastity. Raimon maintains the tower but changes the modifier to attribute her strength to her faith, moving away from consideration of her royal heritage.

The "Vivusque fons" [living spring] of v. 4 recollects Song 4: 15[35] in which the *sponsa* is described by her husband as "Fons hortorum, puteus aquarum viventium" [Fountain of gardens, well of living waters]. Mary is seen as the living fountain: she gave birth to the Redeemer who brought life to humanity.

In v. 8, Raimon resorts to a standard epithet for the Virgin, "Virga Jesse" [Rod of Jesse]. *Virga* meaning "rod" forms a pun in conjunction with *virgo* meaning "virgin." In his *Speculum Ecclesiae* (*Mirror of the Church*), Honorius Augustodunensis (whose treatise *Sigillum Beatae Mariae* [*The Seal of Blessed Mary*] was the "first systematic mariological exposition of the Song of Songs"[26]) explains the attribution of this metaphor to the Virgin:

> Jesse fuit pater David regis, qui erat radix hujus sacrae stirpis. De hac radice David ut arbor succreverat, de qua nobilis virga pullulaverat, quia virgo Maria de ejus progenie originem duxerat. Haec virga florem protulit, dum virgo Maria Christum genuit. Ipse enim dicit: *Ego flos campi et lilium convallium* (*Cant*. 2). Campus est terra inarata, et est virgo inmaritata. Hic campus preciosum florem produxit, cum Christus de Virgine natus mundo illuxit.[36]

> [Jesse was the father of King David, who was the root of this holy shoot. From this root David had grown up like a tree, from this root the noble rod had sprouted, because the Virgin Mary had brought forth the source of this by her offspring. This rod produced a flower, while the Virgin Mary bore Christ. He says indeed: *I am the flower of the field and the lily of the valleys* (Song of Songs 2). The field is unploughed earth, and is the unmarried virgin. This field produced a precious flower, when Christ, born of the Virgin, began to shine on the world.]

Honorius links the "virga Jesse" explicitly with the "flos campi et lilium convallium" of Song of Songs 2: 1; the unploughed earth of the field is the body of the Virgin who produced the flower that was Christ. Yet again Raimon's epithet is tied to Bernard through the Song of Songs.

In constructing the textual Virgin of his litany, Raimon resurrects the memory of St. Bernard. The Virgin thus has no subjective qualities but serves only to reflect the greatness of the Abbot of Clairvaux, dead for two hundred years. The textual body is essentially fragmented, composed of forty-four short epithets; there is no sense of wholeness or unity in a body so constituted and no identity, which would seem to be indicative of the symbolic inability to define Woman other than by indirect references to what she is not. As Luce Irigaray states, "*She is neither one nor two.*" She cannot, strictly speaking, be determined either as one person or as two. She renders any definition inadequate. Moreover she has no "proper name."[37] This litany bears testimony to the lack of the symbolic order; the Virgin Mary cannot be adequately defined, since, as we have seen, she is at once mother, bride, and daughter of Christ, what Robert Magliola calls a "triple paradox."[38]

In the second piece, a verse biography of the Cistercian saint, Raimon again forms a strong identification between the Virgin and the saint.[39] In v. 26, "Mimmus et dulcis Marie," Raimon tells of the literary ties between Mary and Bernard; he sang of her greatness in his sermons (just as she sings of his greatness in Raimon's litany), so she was his subject—or is that his object? He loved her and sought her goodness for himself: "Hic amator Jesu matris / Sueque bona quesivit" (vv. 29–30).

However, the link between the Virgin and the saint is established explicitly from the first strophe: "Hodorem puerque cepit / Bonum dare plus quam nardus" (vv. 3–4). Why should Bernard, in his youth, have begun to smell sweeter than nard? The answer lies in the comparison with the Virgin. Again the Song of Songs becomes the intermediary, this time between Bernard and the Virgin. Song 1: 12 says "cum esset rex in accubitu suo, nardus sponsae dedit odorem suum"; the nard offered by the bride to the groom becomes, for Bernard, in his *Sermones in Cantica Canticorum*, a symbol of Mary's humility.[40] This was made manifest at the Annunciation where, in the *Magnificat*, the Virgin attributes her selection to what she believes God saw in her, her humility. As she says, "respexit Deus humilitatem ancillae suae" (Luke 1: 48). Thus, in making reference to "nardus" in v. 4, Raimon compares the humility of Bernard, who accepted the monk's habit from God while still a boy—"puer" v. 3—to that of Mary who became the handmaid of the Lord while still a girl.

This marian bond is further strengthened in the sixth strophe with the reference to the Medieval legend of the lactation of St. Bernard by the Virgin; the saint was infused with spirituality through receiving the Virgin's milk from her breasts.[41] She serves as a mother figure from whom Bernard gleans his virtue through this mystical union. This correspondence between the two saintly figures, Mary and Bernard, invests the latter with the

same spiritual authority and affectivity as the former; Mary's spiritual qualities are passed to Bernard through the mystical suckling. Raimon again
seeks to define Bernard through the figure of the Virgin, a figure assembled
by patriarchal tradition and legend.

The ultimate identification between the Virgin and the saint is confirmed in the motif of the Mother. In the litany, Mary is rarely described in
physical terms. When mention of her physical existence is made, it is pos-
ited in terms of motherhood: the first strophe begins "Mater Jesu." In the
second piece, Mary, in suckling Bernard, is again defined by motherhood.
Furthermore, in mariological terms, Mary is Mother of God, Mother of the
Redeemer, and Mother of the Church.

This same definition by motherhood may also be attributed to Bernard. He was one of a small number of influential Churchmen who often,
in their writings, used maternal imagery in reference to themselves. Bernard saw himself as a nurturing mother to his monks. As Caroline Walker
Bynum explains:

> Bernard of Clairvaux, whose use of maternal imagery for male
> figures is more extensive and complex than that of any other twelfth-
> century figure, uses "mother" to describe Jesus, Moses, Peter, Paul,
> prelates in general, abbots in general, and, more frequently, him-
> self as abbot. To Bernard, the maternal image is almost without
> exception elaborated not as giving birth or even as conceiving or
> sheltering in a womb but as nurturing, particularly suckling.
> Breasts, to Bernard, are a symbol of the pouring out towards oth-
> ers of affectivity or of instruction and almost invariably suggest to
> him a discussion of the duties of prelates or abbots.[42]

Thus, from Raimon's point of view, both the Virgin and Bernard of Clairvaux
are maternal figures. Julia Kristeva, in her essay "Stabat Mater," contends
that the maternal is the only identification that the symbolic order can
bestow on Woman:

> If it is not possible to say of *woman* what she *is* (without running
> the risk of abolishing her difference), would it perhaps be different
> concerning the *mother*, since that is the only function of the "other
> sex" to which we can definitely attribute existence?[43]

As she goes on to show, the association of Woman with motherhood reaches
its apogee with Christianity, which, Kristeva reflects, "is doubtless the most
refined symbolic construct in which femininity, to the extent that it tran-
spires through it—and it does so incessantly—is focused on *Maternality*."[44]

The Virgin Mary is, then, the archetypal Christian fabrication. But to what end does St. Bernard, and subsequently Raimon, identify the masculine with the Maternal? For the Abbot of Clairvaux, the motivation is humility as displayed by the Virgin at the Annuciation: Bernard sees in Mary the virtues for which he strives. For Raimon, the end, the desire, is the exultation of St. Bernard; through his two poems, Raimon affirms the similarities between the Virgin and the saint. She is the means to legitimize the life of St. Bernard, since, as Julie Kristeva notes, "the most intense revelation of God, which occurs in mysticism, is given only to a person who assumes himself as 'maternal'" through complete humility, as Mary did.[45] The ultimate example of Raimon's male poetics is, therefore, his use of the only aspect of Woman that can be specified within the symbolic order to venerate St. Bernard—that is, the maternal.

Each poem thus compliments the other as each seeks to establish a link between the figure of the Virgin and the Cistercian saint; in the litany Bernard provides a textual model for the Virgin, and in the eulogy the Virgin serves as a model for the life of Bernard. In both cases, the figure of the Virgin is a male poetic construct used as a means of defining the saint and of expressing Raimon's admiration for him. As in secular poetry from the Medieval Occitan troubadours to the present day, Raimon de Cornet uses the same symbolic strategies to present an idealized female who reflects the male's desires. The Virgin in her imagined state is not real in any subjective, autonomous sense, but she becomes a figure for Bernard himself—his womanly body.

Appendix

The following are the complete Latin texts of Raimon de Cornet's pieces and an English translation of each.[46]

1. A 17
   Le digz frayre R. Canso en lati.

1. Mater Jesu, castrum virginitatis,
   Vas integrum, plenum sciencie,
   Mons lilium, turris fiducie,
   Vivusque fons, mare benignitatis,
5 Lux omnibus sis bone voluntatis.

2. Maria, sol, lux omnis claritatis,
   O speculum regalis curie,

Virga Jesse, dans fructum gracie,
Jerusalem tutela civitatis
10 Custodi nos amore caritatis.

3. Sancticimum corpus humilitatis,
..... cathedra misericordie,
...........lumen Eclesie,
...........randis potestatis
15 ....tatis.

4. Pax gencium, liberque veritatis,
Mors demonis atque superbie,
Radix Syon, arbor pudicie,
Concilium cecretum deitatis,
20 Da gaudium nobis eternitatis.

5. Ars arsium summe suptilitatis,
Benivolens virgo prudencie,
Graticima gaudens justicie,
Peccatibus succurre, Trinitatis
25 Solacium, regina pietatis.

6. Refugium nostre fragilitatis,
Devocio cordis mundicie,
Honor et laus Deo cotidie
Tibique sit, rosa, flos onestatis,
30 Et omnibus in celis coronatis.

7. Rosarum rosa leticie,
Florumque flos magne ressencitatis,
33 Visita nos, odor suavitatis.

[1. Mother of Jesus, fortress of virginity,
Unspoiled vessel, full of knowledge,
Mountain lily, tower of faithfulness,
And living spring, sea of kindness,
5 Light of all, may you be of good will.

2. Mary, sun, light of all brightness,
O mirror of the royal court,
Rod of Jesse, giving the fruit of grace,

Protector of the city of Jerusalem,
10 Guard us with love of charity.

3. Most holy body of humility,
    .... seat of mercy,
    .... light of the Church,
    .... of power,
15 ....

4. Peace of nations, and book of truth,
    Death of evil and of pride,
    Root of Zion, tree of modesty,
    Secret council of God,
20 Give us the joy of eternity.

5. Art of arts of supreme subtlety,
    Well-wishing virgin of discretion,
    Rejoicing in welcome justice,
    Help of sinners, consolation of the Trinity,
25 Queen of devotion.

6. Refuge of our weakness,
    Prayer of the untainted heart,
    Let there be honour and glory to God everyday,
    And to you, rose, flower of honesty,
30 And to all those crowned in heaven.

7. Rose of roses of joy,
    And flower of flowers (of great consent?),
33 Visit us, fragrance of sweetness.]

2. A 33
    proza. Le digz frayres Ramons

1. Amore Dei Bernardus
    Habitum sanctus accepit,
    Hodorem puerque cepit
  4 Bonum dare plus quam nardus.

2. Bernardus, lux monacorum,
    Sascer fuit doctor legis,

Ex virtute summi regis,
8 Vir sascerdos plenus morum.

3. Clare Vallis abbas iste
Primus castam deferebat;
In mente sepe lugebat
12 Passionem Jesu triste.

4. Deo vovit quod de selo
Viveret pauper et castus,
Obediens egit pastus
16 Sic mansitque bono zelo.

5. Exilium vanis dictis
Mitis dabat fructuosus,
Promtusque religiosus
20 Bonis stetit, non delictis.

6. Frati bono Dei mater
Sui lactis dedit potum,
Nam vidit eum devotum
24 Talis erat iste frater.

7. Graticimus predicator,
Mimmus et dulcis Marie,
Confessor hic muse vie
28 Rate fuit conservator.

8. Hic amator Jesu matris
Sueque bona quesivit
Ex hoc in au letus ivit
32 Ad gloriam Dei patris.

9. Jesu sit omneque bonum
Rose sue matri rite;
Sancti nam Bernardi vite
36 Monachis fescerunt donum.

[1. St. Bernard, through the love of God
Received the habit,
And, while still a boy, began to give off
4 A fragrance better than nard.

2. Bernard, light of monks,
   Was a holy doctor of the law,
   By virtue of the highest king,
 8 He was a man and priest full of moral character.

3. That first abbot of Clairvaux
   Was an example of chastity;
   He would often, in his mind,
12 Sadly mourn the suffering of Jesus.

4. He vowed to God in heaven
   That he would live pure and chaste,
   He lived as an obedient shepherd
16 And thus he remained filled with good zeal.

5. Mild and fruitful,
   He imposed exile on empty talk,
   A zealous man of religion,
20 He always upheld the good, not the bad.

6. The mother of God gave a drink
   Of her milk to the good brother,
   For she saw him to be devoted.
24 Such a man was that brother.

7. He was a most agreeable preacher,
   And singer of sweet Mary,
   (_____
28 _____?)

8. This man was a lover of the mother of Jesus
   And he sought his own salvation
   Hence he has gone into the court (of heaven)
        rejoicing
32 To the glory of God the father.

9. To Jesus and to the rose his mother
   Be all glory as is due
   For, of the life of St. Bernard,
36 They made a present to his monks.]

Notes

1. I owe a debt of gratitude to Dr. Sarah Spence whose influence and example provide the subtexts to this essay, and to Chuck Platter for pestering me for a vaguely promised abstract. I cannot begin to thank Kyle Shaddix.

2. There are only three critical works that deal in any significant way with Raimon de Cornet: Camille Chabaneau and J.-B. Noulet, *Deux manuscrits provençaux du XIVe siècle* (Montpellier, France: Au bureau des publications de la société pour l'étude des langues Romanes, 1888); Alfred Jeanroy, "Raimon de Cornet, troubadour," *Histoire littéraire de la France* 38 (1949): pp. 31–65; St. John E. Flynn, "The Last Troubadour: Raimon de Cornet and the Survival of Occitan Lyric" (master's thesis, University of Georgia, 1989). The Chabaneau and Noulet text is an edition of the two manuscripts, together known as "le Registre de Cornet," that contains all but two of Raimon's fifty-four extant poems. This edition will henceforth be abbreviated to *Deux mss.*

3. Stephen G. Nichols, "The New Medievalism: Tradition and Discontinuity in Medieval Culture," in *The New Medievalism*, ed. Marina S. Brownlee, Kevin Brownlee and Stephen G. Nichols (Baltimore, MD: Johns Hopkins University Press, 1991), p. 1.

4. See, for example: Nancy J. Vickers, "Diana Described: Scattered Woman and Scattered Rhyme," *Critical Inquiry* 8.2 (1981): pp. 265–79, and Moira P. Baker, "*The Uncanny Stranger on Display*: The Female Body in Sixteenth- and Seventeenth-Century Love Poetry," *South Atlantic Review* 56.2 (1991): pp. 7–25.

5. See Chabaneau and Noulet's introduction to Raimon, *Deux mss.* 29–46.

6. He does this in a *tenso* that Raimon initiates with him. See A 30 in Chabaneau and Noulet, *Deux mss.,* pp. 63–65.

7. Both of these Latin pieces occur in ms. A of the "Registre de Cornet" and are numbered A 17 (the litany to the Virgin) and A 33 (the eulogy of Bernard of Clairvaux).

8. What little is known about Lunel de Monteg is gathered by Edouard Forestié, who also edited the troubadour's poems, in his *P. de Lunel, dit Cavalier Lunel de Monteg, troubadour du XIVe siècle, mainteneur des jeux floraux de Toulouse* (Montauban, France: Imp. Forestié, 1891). The text of Lunel's Latin litany to the Virgin is given in an edition by Camille Chabaneau, "Poésies inédites de divers troubadours (G. d'Anduze, Raimon de Salas, G. d'Hautpoul, Joyos, Cavalier Lunel de Montech)," *Revue des langues romanes* 4e sér. 33 (1889): pp. 117–21.

9. The texts of these poems can be found in the appendix to this chapter.

10. Hélène Cixous, "The Laugh of the Medusa," in *New French Feminisms*, ed. Elaine Marks and Isabelle de Courtivron, trans. Keith Cohen and Paula Cohen (New York: Schocken Books, 1981), pp. 245–64.

11. Luce Irigaray, "This Sex Which Is Not One," trans. Claudia Reeder, in Elaine Marks and Isabelle de Courtivron, eds. *New French Feminisms* (New York: Schocken Books, 1981), pp. 101.

12. Irigaray, "This Sex," p. 99.

13. Irigaray, "This Sex," p. 101.

14. Irigaray, "This Sex," p. 99.

15. Irigaray, "This Sex," p. 100.

16. Laura Mulvey, "Visual Pleasure and Narrative Cinema," in *Visual and Other Pleasures* (Bloomington: Indiana University Press, 1989), p. 19.

17. Irigaray, "This Sex," p. 101.

18. Cixous, "Laugh of the Medusa," p. 249.

19. Cixous, "Laugh of the Medusa, p. 250.

20. Rémy de Gourmont, *Le latin mystique* (Paris: Editions Crès, 1922), p. 143.

21. All translations throughout this essay are my own.

22. Cixous, "Laugh of the Medusa," p. 246.

23. See Albert Blaise, *Le vocabulaire latin des principaux thèmes liturgiques* (Turnhout: Brepols, 1966), p. 243.

24. All references to the homilies *In Laudibus Virginis Matris* are taken from vol. 4 of Bernard of Clairvaux, *Sancti Bernardi Opera*, ed. Jean Leclercq and Henri Rochais (Rome: Editiones Cistercienses, 1966).

25. For the Latin test of these sermons, see Bernard of Clairvaux *Sancti Bernardi Opera*, vols. 1–2.

26. As E. Ann Matter comments, "Bernard's homilies [on the Song of Songs] were inspired by and intended for the devotional life of the Cistercian movement" (*The Voice of My Beloved: the Song of Songs in Western Medieval Christianity* [Philadelphia: University of Pennsylvania Press, 1990], p. 39).

27. For detailed discussions of the development of marian theology in the Christian tradition, see Sandro Sticca, *The "Planctus Mariae" in the Dramatic Tradition of the Middle Ages*, trans. Joseph R. Berrigan (Athens: University of Georgia Press, 1988) especially chapters 2, 4, and 5. The role of the Song of Songs in the growth of mariology is elaborated by E. Ann Matter, *Voice of My Beloved*, especially chap. 6, "The Woman Who is the All: The Virgin Mary and the Song of Songs."

28. As F. J. E. Raby comments in his *A History of Christian-Latin Poetry from the Beginnings to the Close of the Middle Ages*, 2d ed. (Oxford: Clarendon, 1953), p. 365: "It was impossible that the Medieval imagination should fail to see on many pages of the Old Testament prophecies and symbols of the Virgin and of the

miraculous birth by which she became the mother of Christ. It was in the Song of Songs, so full of rich colour and sensuous beauty, that the most fascinating and mystical prefigurations were found. The Shulamite, interpreted also as the Church, became now the Mother of Christ, and Christ himself the lover, the *dilectus meus*."

29. See Ann W. Astell, *The Song of Songs in the Middle Ages* (Ithaca, NY: Cornell University Press, 1990), pp. 75–77.

30. See Matter, *Voice of My Beloved*, p. 155.

31. See Matter, *Voice of My Beloved*, pp. 155 and 172 n. 18.

32. Marina Warner, *Alone of All Her Sex: the Myth and the Cult of the Virgin Mary* (New York: Vintage Books, 1983), p. 130.

33. Sticca, *"Planctus Mariae,"* p. 107.

34. Warner, *Alone of All Her Sex*, p. 128.

35. Neither of the two verses from chapter 4 of the Song of Songs that I highlight here is covered by any of Bernard's sermons on the book. Upon his death in August 1153, Bernard had only reached the very beginning of chapter 3 in his commentary. Nevertheless, as I have already stated, it seems clear that, in this litany, Raimon wishes to recall both the Song of Songs and Bernard's glorification of it in his sermons, indicating both as subtexts to his own litany.

36. J.-P. Migne, *Patrologia Latina*, 221 vols., 2d ser. (Paris: J.-P. Migne, 1844–1864) vol. 172, col. 904–05 (hereafter referred to as *PL*).

37. Luce Irigaray, "The Sex Which is Not One," p. 101.

38. Robert Magliola, "Sexual Rogations, Mystical Abrogations: Some Données of Buddhist Tantra and the Catholic Renaissance," in Clayton Koelb and Susan Noakes, eds., *The Comparative Perspective on Literature* (Ithaca, NY: Cornell University Press, 1988), p. 197.

39. Raimon does not seem to have had specific subtexts for his *Proza* as he did for his litany to the Virgin. Two sequences in honor of St. Bernard, one from a fourteenth-century manuscript and one from a fifteenth-century manuscript, are to be found in the Clemens Blume, ed., *Analecta Hymnica Medii Aevi*, 55 vols. (Leipzig: O.R. Reisland, 1886–1922), vol. 55 (1922), pp. 110–112.

40. Migne, *PL*, vol. 183, col. 992.

41. For discussions of this legend see Caroline Walker Bynum, *Jesus as Mother: Studies in the Spirituality of the High Middle Ages* (Berkeley and Los Angeles: University of California Press, 1982) p. 132, and n. 76; Brian Patrick McGuire, in "Bernard and Mary's Milk: A Northern Contribution," *The Difficult Saint: Bernard of Clairvaux and His Tradition* (Cistercian Studies Series 126. Kalamazoo, MI: Cistercian Publications, 1991).

42. Bynum, *Jesus as Mother*, p. 115.

43. Julia Kristeva, "Stabat Mater," in *Tales of Love*, trans. Léon S. Roudiez (New York: Columbia University Press, 1987), pp. 234–63.

44. Kristeva, "Stabat Mater," p. 234.

45. Kristeva, "Stabat Mater," p. 235.

46. The translations are my own. I wish to express my thanks to Dr. Robert R. Harris of the Classics Department at the University of Georgia for his help with and suggestions for some of the more difficult lines. For a full description of the "Registre de Cornet" from which these two Latin pieces are taken, see Chabaneau and Noulet, *Deux mss.*, V–IX, and also François Zufferey, *Bibliographie des poètes provençaux des XIVe et XVe siècles* (Genève: Droz, 1981) XVIII–XXI. See also my "Last Troubadour," pp. 3–4, and nn. 1 and 2.

Petrarch's Sophonisba: Seduction, Sacrifice, and Patriarchal Politics

Donald Gilman

In Petrarch's unfinished Latin epic the *Africa* (1339–43), the character of Sophonisba is ambiguous and perplexing. Through her overpowering sensuality, deceitful devices, and adulterous transgressions, she embodies attributes of the stereotypical seductress. Like such biblical, mythological, and classical temptresses as Delilah, Circe, and Cleopatra, she ensnares men, leading her husband Syphax to "a shameful imprisonment and death"[1] and inducing her lover Massinissa to question his commitment to Scipio Africanus and the Roman cause. Craig Kallendorf has recently described her as "an evil character."[2] Certainly, the narrative of her suicide, her banishment to the circle of unrequited lovers, and her condemnation as a seditionist supports this view. Even her posthumous cries in the *Triumph of Love* confirm this blame: Africa, she proclaims, may have suffered, but Italy did not rejoice.[3]

Any absolute classification invites questions, and Petrarch's thoughts on the expected probity of women elude clear and categorical interpretation.[4] Laura's allurements in the *Rime Sparse*, for example, instill within the poet-lover moral misdirection and emotional paralysis. Ultimately, though, she assumes a place in paradise (*Rime* 266)[5] and, in the *Triumphs*, celebrates chastity and overcomes oblivion. Similarly, in the *Africa*, Petrarch praises Dido's virtue (4.5–6),[6] and commends Lucretia, who, after incurring the shame of rape, commits suicide and precipitates the overthrow of tyranny (3.652–772). In both cases, the pain resulting from immoral love leads to a metaphorical parturition: Aeneas' founding of Rome; the emergence of the Republic. Suffering, then, is limited neither to the heroic struggles of Scipio nor to the valiant deeds of Roman legions. Birth results in a death that sustains life, and the maternal figure is central to this cycle.

Initially, Sophonisba does not appear morally exemplary. However, in experiencing unrequited love and the disgrace of possible Roman servitude, she confronts a crisis that recalls the conflicts of Dido and Lucretia. Further, by remaining loyal to her father and the Carthaginian cause, she demonstrates an inner resolve and defiant courage that characterize Scipio. In spite of these complexities, critics have largely seen her as integral to the narrative but incidental to the anguish of a moral dilemma that confronted by a "man" ends in his glory or damnation.[7] Like Vergil's representation of Aeneas and Dido, and like Petrarch's historical-fictive love for Laura, the Massinissa-Sophonisba episode details a battle between virtue and vice. It complements Scipio's struggles to establish Roman rule in North Africa, and it is integral to the events that culminate in the political, thematic apotheosis of Rome that celebrates the victory of reason over emotion, justice and peace over impiety and contention, and Christian providence over pagan self-interests.[8] A focus on Scipio or Massinissa, however, overlooks the significance of Sophonisba, in particular, and of woman, in general, in the determination of male redemption or retribution. As a woman who seduces but suffers, Sophonisba is a problematic character who may elucidate Petrarch's view of the nature and role of the feminine figure in man's anguish and actualization of moral purpose. Thus, through an examination of the figure of Sophonisba within the contexts of patriarchal prerogatives and the limitations of liberty, I will attempt in this essay to describe Petrarch's view of woman as a being who, entrapped by her physical nature and societal expectations, enables man to select a course of action leading to salvation or ending in retribution.

Neither Sinner nor Saint

Upon returning to Vaucluse on Good Friday, 1333, Petrarch was inspired "to write something poetic in heroic verse about Scipio Africanus."[9] Ennius, Vergil, Lucan, and Silius Italicus had established the Roman precedent of poeticizing legend and history. Employing Livy's accounts of Rome's conquest of Carthage, he discovered the narrative of his epic. History, however, is not poetry. Unlike a chronicler who attempts to report events fully and accurately, Petrarch defined poetic creativity as a process of eclectic imitation. By blending the ideas and images of previous poets, he aspired to compose a poem historically true but stylistically original. Vergil's *Aeneid* becomes the structural model of the *Africa*. But moral philosophy cannot be discounted, for, from a late Medieval perspective, the thought and wisdom of Plato and Cicero endow the epic verse of Homer and Vergil, respectively. History verifies Scipio's political greatness, but philosophy explains the dynamics of these attainments. Thus, in adapting Livy's history to Vergil's epic form, Petrarch creates a text that accommodates verifiable facts to fourteenth-century notions of poetic mimesis and moral teachings.[10]

The Massinissa-Sophonisba episode that appears in book 5 of the nine-book epic is central to the narrative and thematic development of the text. Structurally, the *Africa* may be divided into two parts: books 1–4 describe Scipio's growth of historical consciousness and moral responsibility, and books 6–9 detail the fulfillment of prophecy and the consequences of the hero's devotion to family, state, and political cause. In the first two books Petrarch relates a dream in which Scipio's father, Publius Cornelius Scipio, tells his son to avenge his death and to avert Carthage's conquest of Rome. Like any good hero in a revenge drama, Scipio discharges his duties. A successful campaign against Hannibal's Carthage, though, depends upon the assistance of the Numidian king, Syphax. In books 3 and 4, Scipio's friend, Laelius, succeeds in winning Syphax's alliance through a description of Rome's virtuous leaders past and present. But Syphax betrays his word through his marriage to Sophonisba, daughter of the Carthaginian leader, Hasdrubal, son of Gisgo. Massinissa, a Numidian friendly to Scipio, defeats Syphax's army; upon entering the Numidian city of Cirta, he encounters Sophonisba and, like Syphax, becomes enchanted by her. Massinissa vacillates in his allegiance to Scipio. Recognizing the importance of Massinissa's aid, Scipio intervenes and reminds the Numidian of his commitment. Through Massinissa's renewed resolve, Scipio succeeds, in books 6–8, in defeating Hannibal's Carthage and in extending Roman rule to North Africa. Book 9 is a praise of Scipio's compassion in sparing Carthage from destruction and his glorious return to Rome. Virtuous actions prevail over immoral intentions.

The encounter between Sophonisba and Massinissa in book 5 plays a crucial role in the success or failure of Scipio's campaign. Narratively, the tale recounts the meeting of boy and girl. Upon passing through the shattered walls of Cirta, Massinissa is overpowered by Sophonisba's seductive beauty and ethereal sensuality. Sophonisba is aware of the consequences of defeat, and she plays upon his emotions. A captive, she seizes his right hand and acknowledges his prerogative to determine her destiny of death or imprisonment. Death, she asserts, is preferred to the shame of slavery. Tears of distress moisten the earth, and profuse kisses of his feet entrap the conquering general. Massinissa is sensitive to her laments and offers to protect her position as queen. Tormented by the dilemma of his pledge to Scipio and his promise to Sophonisba, he undergoes a psychomachia. His eventual decision to marry her creates problems. Syphax remains alive; Sophonisba has clearly committed adultery; and Scipio now suffers the deep disappointment of disloyalty from both Syphax and Massinissa.

The second half of the tale centers attention upon Scipio's reproach of Syphax and his attempts to convince Massinissa of his errors. In a series of vitriolic attacks against Sophonisba, Syphax reinforces the portrait of her as a scheming seductress. Undoubtedly, his wife's relationship with Massinissa has incited jealousies within him; but Scipio recognizes the dangers of her wiles in stirring Syphax to sedition and in possibly persuading Massinissa to shift sides. Virtue triumphs as Scipio's will or *imperium* rules. Challenged by a dilemma, Massinissa utters, "What am I to do?" (5.766) [Quid agam? (5.583)]. But in sensing shame, he complies with Scipio's command. Like a Corneillian hero, he exercises a superhuman determination to follow the path of virtue, renouncing his love, regretting his disloyalty, and resolving to respect his pledge to Sophonisba that will assure her a dignified death.

Sophonisba, like a criminal marked for condemnation, is sentenced to a situation that defines the pain, remorse, and anguish of war. A passion overtakes her, and she emits a venomous anger against the Roman leaders and their followers. Her frustrations are real: her family is losing its ancestral claim and country, and she has been deprived of liberty and her love for Massinissa. In spite of a succession of imprecations that damn Scipio to disgrace and Massinissa to defamation and censure, reason controls passion at the end. She recognizes the meaningless battle that she has waged. With an apparent quiet, she swallows the poison and commits a suicide that resembles the tragic plights of Shakespeare's Cleopatra and Racine's Phèdre:

> "Sol alme" inquit "superique, valete,
> Massinissa, vale, nostri memor."
> (5.770–71)

> ["Sweet sun, farewell; farewell, ye gods:
> farewell, my Massinissa; think of me!"
> (5.1007–08)]

All players in this drama, then, are reduced to two denominators: suffering and sacrifice.

Clearly, Sophonisba is a sinner. Her entrapment of Syphax, her enticement of Massinissa, and her frenzied curses on Syphax and Massinissa reflect the image of woman as an instrument of evil. As an African, she must have had, in reality, a dark complexion. But in his fictive description of her voluptuous beauty, Petrarch depicts her in ethnocentric terms that recall Laura's ethereal sensuality: a facial beauty excelling the brilliance of the stars; a forehead as white as snow; a graceful neck and slender shoulders; flowing flaxen hair; captivating eyes; a lilylike complexion embellished by roselike cheeks and rubylike lips; a curvaceous bosom; shapely hands and fingers; soft, sensuous hips; and dainty, divine feet. Art adorns nature. Besides having the attractions of a "purple bodice graced with divers jewels [that] swathe her heaving breast" (5.88–89),[11] she plays upon Massinissa's sympathy by yielding to his authority, praising his heroism, and crying for pity. The reality of race or historical accuracy becomes therefore subordinate to the blason of a seductress. Her beauty and sympathy combine to produce an attraction that resembles a fire devouring Massinissa's marrow. And Massinissa becomes a "captive prey of a captive foe, a haughty conqueror subdued by conquered victim" (5.97–99).[12]

The passion for Sophonisba's beauty that momentarily diverts Massinissa's attention away from his commitment to Scipio explains Syphax's downfall. In confessing his betrayal of Scipio, Syphax notes that unwarranted and uncontrolled desires for Sophonisba led to his marriage and his subsequent shame. As a Carthaginian, she was an alien entering the Numidian capital. Through her seductions and "artful plaints" (5.467) [lacrimisque malignis (5.354)], she employed charms that undermined his capacity to govern. Lust's "hidden flame" (5.465) [tacitis . . . flammis (5.352)] induced him to disclaim loyalties to friends and cause, and the fires of passion emerge as an incendiary of a war waged and won by Scipio. Morally and militarily subdued, Syphax sees Sophonisba as the source of his sin and suffering:

> Illa,
> illa suis manibus misero tulit arma marito,
> Induit illa latus, capiti tum cassida caro,
> Tum gladium dextre, clipeum dedit illa sinistre
>   (5.356–59).

> [To her wretched spouse
> with her own hands she brought the arms of war,
> arrayed him for the field, placed on his head
> the helmet, thrust the sword in his right hand,
> bound to his left the shield
>   (5.470–74).]

Syphax's repetition of *illa* suggests rancor and resentment in his accusations, but his admission of misjudgments does not prevent him from remembering his pleasure in her sensuousness and his love for a "savage wife" (5.482) [coniugioque . . . fero (5.366)].

After her suicide, Sophonisba descends to her place in Hades and joins the company of disappointed lovers: Orpheus and Eurydice, Achilles, Oenone,

Lavinia, and Pyramis and Thisbe. Her punishment fits the crime; for, like the other suffering souls, she must endure a "self-hatred" and "disgrace" (6.57) [odiumque . . . ruborque (6.46)] that have evolved from "misguided passion, folly, crime, deceit, and thieving plots by adulation cloaked" (6.58–59).[13] Petrarch's allusion to a misguided passion or *malesuadus amor* is significant, and it suggests his condemnation of her actions. In a study of the *amor stultus* of mythological lovers, Katherine Heinrichs has traced their transgressions as recorded in Ovid's *Heroides* and has explained the reasons for their condemnation as presented in Medieval glosses of the text. According to Heinrichs, each anecdote is an indictment against carnal love and thereby "serves as an exemplum to abhor evil and imitate the good."[14] Such a fate is "monitory, intended to illustrate the danger of pursuing *temporalia* and the superiority of pursuing higher goals."[15] Orpheus, with whom Sophonisba shares a place in the third circle in Hades, may have sought a *summum bonum* and have charmed the gods through his music. But Petrarch, like Medieval glossators,[16] depicts him as

> iterum spoliator Averni
> Orpheus Euridien frustra revocare parabat
> (6.55–56).

> [the ravager of Hell,
> still bent on his vain purpose to retrieve
> Eurydice
> (6.70–72).]

Thus, in yielding to concupiscence, he perceives the consequences of misdirected intention and, like Sophonisba, endures the pain of a destructive love.

Boccaccio, in his *Filocolo* (4.44) describes the stages of the *amor stultus* that begin with fear, evolve into sin, and culminate in grief and sorrow. Certainly, the "grief and tears and sighs" (6.55)[17] of these loves in the *Africa* depict Sophonisba's lamentable situation as a sinner. But, if Sophonisba is hardly a saint, her actions do not deserve total rebuke. Instinctive anxieties account for her initial responses to Massinissa who, upon entering Cirta, is a "prowling wolf"(5.7) [lupus nactus (5.6)] seeking to plunder and devour. Her sensual beauty, though adorned by elegant dress and jewels, forms part of her nature. Her use of rhetoric that plays upon Massinissa's emotions may suggest dissimulation and manipulation. But Sophonisba remains true to her commitment: a preference for the freedom of death over servitude to Roman soldiers. Her suicide actualizes and validates her words, fills her people with grief, and enables her to confront her destiny in Hades with resignation and dignity. Both in this world and the next, she suffers the distress of a troubled soul [violentus spiritus (5.773)]. However, in spite of the initial judgment of Minos and Rhadamanthus who ascribe to her the guilt of shirking human responsibilities, the supreme arbiter Aeacus over-rules and seems compassionate in his sentence:

> Mortis amor causa est, lucemque coacta reliquit.
> Tertia claustra sibi sunt, legibus abdita nostris:
> Huc eat, immerite neque hec iniuria nostra
> Accedat nunc voce recens: satis aspera vite
> Mansit apud superos fortuna et mortis acerbe
> (6.20–24).

> [She died for love; she was cast forth from light
> by force; the third precinct of my domain
> claims her by right. And thither let her go
> and suffer at our hands no further hurt
> that she has not deserved. Her lot in life
> and manner of her death were harsh enough
> (6.25–30).]

The pain of separation characterizes Sophonisba's state; for, as a victim of suicide or prisoner of Rome, she is destined to long for Massinissa vainly and eternally. Sophonisba, then, emerges as a problematic character who reflects Petrarch's view of the feminine figure. In accepting the poison that Massinissa has had prepared for her, she recognizes her fate and responds instinctively and humanly.

Passion possesses her, and, unlike the exemplary, transcendent natures of Massinissa and Scipio, her emotions prompt her to damn Scipio to exile and to pray for Massinissa's censure. Such a revenge, according to Petrarch, is consistent with the feminine personality and recalls for him a small, weak, womanly mind (*Familiares* 9.5).[18] Sentiments overpower reason and explain, in part, the reasons for women weeping at funerals (*Seniles* 14.1; see also *Seniles* 10.4). In *Seniles* 15.3, Petrarch continues to generalize about female characteristics. Servants, he writes, may be irritations and inconveniences, but "woman for the most part is a real devil, an enemy of peace, a fountain of impatience, a subject for quarrels—to be without her is certain tranquillity"[19] (*Seniles* 15.3). In brief, wives are "for those who enjoy endless female company, nightly embraces and squabbles, babies' wailing and sleepless bother" (*Seniles* 15.3).[20] Procreation of the race requires woman—a *malum necessarium*. But even as a necessary evil, woman may not enable man to attain distinctions. A family, he notes, produces "cares and labors"[21] (*Seniles* 15.3), whereas glory is attained through individual talent, strength of resolve, and divine assistance.

In spite of these misogynistic attitudes toward women, Petrarch presents in Sophonisba a character who practices courage and fortitude at the end. Just as virtue and reason had enabled Massinissa to avoid Syphax's errors, Sophonisba overcomes fear and affirms the credibility of her decision to die. She accepts Massinissa's gift "willingly" (5.949) [*libens* (5.727)]; and, with lucid reasoning and unflinching forthrightness, she proclaims an honorable death to be preferred to a senseless marriage. For Petrarch, woman is not invariably evil. He acknowledges the accomplishment of great women (*Familiares* 21.8), extols Griselda's patience and perseverance (*Seniles* 17.3), and affirms the moral distinctions of Porcia, Hypsicratea, and Alcestis (*Seniles* 17.4). Gender may predispose particular thoughts and actions, but intelligence, integrity, and intention determine the redemption or retribution of man and woman alike.

In the opening verses of the epic, Petrarch describes Scipio Africanus as "the man renowned for his great deeds, redoubtable in war" (1.1–2).[22] Combat delineates unequivocal lines of demarcation between the forces of good and the powers of evil. As a Carthaginian, Sophonisba is situated outside the parameters defined by Scipio and the codes of virtuous conduct: she must be subdued. In her marriage to Syphax, she has demonstrated her capabilities as a seditionist who has persuaded her husband to defect from the Roman cause. In her encounter with Massinissa, she captivates a Numidian general whose allegiance to Rome is crucial to Scipio's success. Massinissa must choose between the virtue represented by Scipio and the vice symbolized by Sophonisba. Feminine wiles have induced Syphax to betray his loyalties to Rome, and they threaten to corrupt Massinissa's morality and to disrupt Scipio's campaign. Sophonisba, then, employs the art of seduction and emerges as a sinner in this moral play.

As we have seen, however, Sophonisba's actions are ambivalent. Unlike Lucretia who is an innocent victim of rape, Sophonisba invades a public arena that is reserved for military exploits and male ethics. A Carthaginian woman residing in a Numidian city conquered by the Romans, she is sexually, ethnically, and politically marked as an outsider. As made known in Scipio's dream in book 1, providence assures Scipio's victory and Sophonisba's defeat. In recognizing her situation outside the boundaries of conventional codes of conduct, she commits a suicide that recalls Lucretia's noble resolve to restore her integrity as a wife and mother. According to Massinissa, Sophonisba is a tragic heroine who, like Phaedra and Dido, struggles against, and eventually succumbs to, a divine design. Undoubtedly, she is not the faithful wife or conscientious mother pictured in Petrarch's portrayal of

Lucretia or in his praise of Griselda (*Seniles* 17.3). And the fulfillment of
Roman destiny requires her death and relegation to silence in an isolated
corner in Hades. But if Sophonisba is not a saint, she deserves, nevertheless, understanding and compassion. In his farewell to her, Massinissa extols her as a "mirror and model of all excellence" (5.828) [exemplum
specimenque decoris (5.631)]. Infatuation and regret may have incited his
words. But Sophonisba's moral ambiguities that end in her death and disgrace call for an examination of the dynamics that account for Petrarch's
view of the role and actions of woman.

From Marginalization to Legitimacy

Livy identifies Sophonisba succinctly as "the wife of Syphax, the daughter of Hasdrubal the Carthaginian."[23] Petrarch does not diverge from this
historical fact. However, in shaping history to the form of Vergilian epic and
the moral philosophy of Cicero and the Stoics, he defines Sophonisba's dual
roles of daughter and wife as an axis that ends inevitably in her downfall.
As the daughter of Hasdrubal, she conforms to the expected patterns and
accepted behavior of fourteenth-century woman: passive, compliant, docile,
and obedient to patriarchal and political authorities. But she also confronts
the conflict of adhering to the altered alliances of her husband Syphax. By
remaining loyal to her father and the Carthaginian cause, she maintains a
marginalized existence that cannot be reconciled with Syphax and
Massinissa's allegiance to Scipio. A private duty becomes entangled with
public commitment. As a faithful daughter, she becomes an unfaithful wife.
Her gender becomes, therefore, a source of her sin, and it compels her to
cross a border that distinguishes the domestic domain delegated to women
from the political arena assigned to men. By intruding upon patriarchal
territories Sophonisba articulates a self-authority that leads to her downfall
and death and, conversely, to the reestablishment of an accepted order.[24]

Neither Livy nor Petrarch explicitly describes Sophonisba's qualities as
Hasdrubal's daughter. Nevertheless, according to Petrarch's interpretation
of her relationship with Massinissa, she appears, as the wife of Syphax, to
be disloyal to her husband. But, as the daughter of Hasdrubal, she seems
to emerge as an agent of the Carthaginian cause; for, by inducing Syphax
to renounce his allegiance to Rome, she acknowledges her heritage and
thereby announces her political affiliation. Syphax's betrayal of Scipio, then,
is not Sophonisba's sin against Carthage. Certainly, Scipio, in exacting
Syphax's enslavement, recognizes the place for blame and, as a military
leader tempered by battles against the Carthaginians, is aware of their
strengths and strategies. Sophonisba must be contained. By persuading

Syphax to shift sides, Sophonisba may have employed deceits, but she also demonstrates a commitment to her father and the Carthaginian cause. Tenaciousness and trickery seem to identify her, and these attributes also denote qualities for success in war. Further, as Livy tells us, these traits characterize Sophonisba's father, Hasdrubal.

Petrarch refers to Hasdrubal as cowardly and wicked (1.122–26; 6.774–75). These qualities identify the trepidation of the Carthaginians and the inequity of their campaign. Hasdrubal is guilty by association. Livy, on the other hand, emphasizes Hasdrubal's integrity in his struggles for Carthaginian supremacy and his use of intelligence in devising strategy. Two incidents seem especially relevant.

Early in the epic, when Scipio Africanus listens to his father's plea to avenge his death, he learns of the Carthaginians' panicked withdrawal from Spain. Petrarch is following the facts that he learned from Livy. But, in his efforts to differentiate the forces of good from the powers of evil, he is employing half-truths that distort the bravery of Hasdrubal and his troops. According to Livy (28.1.2–28.3.16), Hasdrubal, along with Mago, commanded an army that occupied Spain during Hannibal's invasion of the Italian peninsula. Scipio Africanus's uncle, Gnaeus, opposed Hasdrubal and, in 217 B.C., is joined by his brother Publius Cornelius, Scipio's father. The superior strength of the Romans compelled Hasdrubal to employ intelligence and subterfuge. Hasdrubal commands his men to feign flight, and the extension of the flanks of his army results in a diffusion of the Roman attacks. The Romans eventually encircle the Carthaginians in Orongis, which Hasdrubal and his men refuse to surrender. A fierce battle ensues, and the Carthaginians flee in fear only after their recognition of death and destruction.

Besides the courage and prowess that Hasdrubal and his army demonstrated until their awareness of inevitable defeat, strategy is an essential element in war. Petrarch's accusation of Hasdrubal's perfidiousness [perfidus . . . Hasdrubal (1.123)] denotes a characteristic of battle that Livy confirms but contextualizes. According to Livy (25.32.1–25.36.16), when Hasdrubal defeated Publius Cornelius and his brother Gnaeus in 211 B.C., he "was well acquainted with every form of treachery practiced by barbarians" (6.465) [peritus omnis barbaricae (25.33.2)]. But in practicing realism, he perceived the need to weaken the Roman forces by convincing the Spanish armies to defect. Assisted by the Numidian calvary led by Massinissa, Hasdrubal's army slays Scipio's father and uncle. Through strategy and strength, Hasdrubal experiences the exhilaration of victory. And like the Carthaginians previously overtaken by fear, the Romans retreat, with "more slain in flight than in battle (6.471)."[25]

Hasdrubal's use of stratagem, moreover, extends to the use of his daughter. According to Livy, Hasdrubal "gave him [i.e., Syphax] his daughter in marriage" (8.413)."[26] Sophonisba complies with his wishes and therefore becomes a political pawn.[27] Hasdrubal, like Scipio, recognizes the crucial importance of Syphax's allegiance. After Scipio Africanus's victory over his army in Spain, Hasdrubal continues the war against the Romans in Africa. In a series of events curiously omitted by Petrarch,[28] Livy tells of the almost simultaneous arrival of Hasdrubal and Scipio in Cirta. Both present their respective arguments to Syphax in order to win his support. Perceiving Scipio's mastery of persuasion, Hasdrubal foresees the conclusion of a treaty between the Numidian and Roman generals. Again, he has lost a battle, but he continues the war with Sophonisba who, as Syphax's wife, now becomes a principal player.

Faithful to her father and cause, Sophonisba becomes entwined in a web of relationships that will inevitably end in self-destruction.[29] Employing intelligence and intention in a politically expedient but morally questionable effort, she emerges again as an enigmatic character. As a dutiful daughter, she does not deviate from the expectations of silent subordination. But, in adhering to her father's will, she is compelled to challenge patriarchal authorities. Her quiet compliance becomes paradoxically a defiant cry: by accepting and actualizing her legitimacy as Hasdrubal's daughter, she assumes political roles that are illegitimate for a woman. As an "insider" in her family, she becomes an "outsider" to the Romans. Carthaginian heritage and female gender support Syphax's claims of the differences that define her identity. The oppositions inherent in her place as the daughter of a Carthaginian general and as the wife of a Numidian ally of Rome cannot be reconciled. The unquestioning obedience that has marginalized her to the enclosure of family and state becomes the shrieking curse against Rome that proclaims her legitimacy as a Carthaginian seductress and seditionist (5.727–66).

Sophonisba's birth as a Carthaginian woman is, therefore, the source of her sin and suffering. Gender reinforces the battle lines: Roman/Carthaginian; male/female; reason/passion; virtue/vice. Within this plan, Sophonisba is clearly at a disadvantage. By exercising loyalty and courage, she practices qualities associated with Scipio and, in Livy's account, virtues demonstrated by her father. But in a culture defined by absolute values, she defies conventional codes, transgresses the restrictions of passivity and silence imposed upon women, and participates in activities reserved for men. These infractions of expected conduct disturb a sociopolitical order, and, as Hasdrubal's daughter, she bears the stigma of subversion that must be corrected. Death neutralizes and naturalizes her actions, consigning her to silence, separation from Massinissa, and eternal closure. Her suicide, then, expiates her from her sin of birth. But, in undergoing the suffering that Hasdrubal indirectly inflicts upon her, she becomes a sacrificial victim who advances the justice and peace prophesied in Scipio's dream.

Through her sacrifice, then, Sophonisba emerges as a maternal figure. At first glance, the political culpability and seditious activity of a seductive Sophonisba contrast with Laelius's earlier description of the domestic passivity and brutal assaults of a raped Lucretia (3.684–732).[30] But silencing and sacrifice link these two feminine figures who, as victims of circumstances, engender the restoration of moral and political norms. In spite of their respective innocence or blame, both are expelled from patriarchal enclosures: Lucretia's rape by Tarquinius Superbus isolates her morally and psychologically from her husband and family; and Sophonisba's betrothal by her father to Syphax throws her onto a political battleground outside the limits of her family. Admittedly, Lucretia struggles against Tarquin's advances, whereas Sophonisba acquiesces to her father's wishes. However, both suffer a suicide that restores a natural order. In yielding to a subservience enforced by death, they endure a sacrifice that assures the actualization of destiny: the birth of the Republic; the conquest of Carthage. Their respective deaths, then, assume a meaning, but this significance surfaces through the actions of men. Through the suicide of his wife, Lucretia, Brutus discovers the resolve to pursue Tarquin, to avenge his wife's rape, and to establish his identity as the leader of society. Similarly, after Sophonisba's suicide, Massinissa receives rewards from Scipio, witnesses the shameful entry of Syphax into Rome, and shares in Scipio's glory. As sacrificial victims, Lucretia and Sophonisba enable men to fulfill their patriarchal roles as agents of providence.

Toward the end of book 3, Petrarch likens Lucretia's suicide to the anguish and despair of a "mother-bird" [parentem . . . volucrem (3.732–33)] who, upon discovering her nestlings stung by a serpent, is destined to lead a life of mourning (3.732–35). Through use of the recurrent image of a grieving, violated, or terrorized mother-bird,[31] Petrarch conveys an unequivocal stance on the place and role of woman. Unlike Sophonisba, Lucretia, who longs for her lost chastity, is hardly a stereotypical seductress. But in admitting Tarquin, Lucretia unknowingly oversteps bounds. Tarquin's rape becomes Lucretia's sin of adultery; and, in legitimizing her identity as a "woman" (3.878) [Femina (3.693)], she suffers a shame that is expiated only through self-annihilation. Similarly, Sophonisba plays the role of Hasdrubal's daughter and Syphax's wife. Situated on a fulcrum that requires the impossible balancing of two contradictory forces, she cannot remain oblivious to, and anonymous in, a world that requires active participation. Her actions author her identity that results in Syphax's calumny of her actions, and her legitimacy as Hasdrubal's virtuous daughter and loyal compatriot coincides and clashes with her roles as immoral seductress and dangerous seditionist.

Everywoman

Through this portrayal of Sophonisba, Petrarch constructs a paradigm of the feminine figure. Codes of conventional conduct require passivity, but circumstances compel a participation in patriarchal politics. Cries of pain ensue and result in a self-sacrifice that leads to both a personal isolation and public restoration of order. Sophonisba crosses the River Lethe and, like Lucretia, enters the enclosure of Hades. As historical personages, they become in death "supernumeraries in history."[32] However, as we have seen, their suicides produce consequences that enable men to vindicate crime and to renew society with justice and order. For Petrarch, history verifies this thought, but myth, legend, and biblical scripture validate and artistically amplify its significance. In particular, the images of Medusa and Dido in the text elaborate Petrarch's view of woman and, through their parallels with Eve, relate Petrarch's perceptions to historical happenings and what was perceived as universal truth.

In mythology, Medusa continues the tradition of other temptresses who, like Circe and Calypso, transform virtuous heroes into concupiscent idlers. Narratively, the parallels between Sophonisba and Medusa as seducers of masculine virtue are evident, and Petrarch reinforces this relationship in the portrait that describes Sophonisba's allurements.[33] Her eyes exert the same petrifying powers of Medusa's glare that

> . . . pectora posset
> Flectere quo vellet, mentesque auferre tuendo,
> Inque Meduseum precordia vertere marmor
> (5.37–39).

> [. . . could rouse
> desire or bend a will however firm
> or to Medusan marble change the heart
> of an admirer
> (5.51–54).]

Like Medusa, Sophonisba is a monster (5.40), lulling her prey into transfixed passivity and insinuating the soul with venomous vileness. Medusa's serpentlike locks may affect more terror than attraction. But the serpent as the seductive agent attracts and attacks; and Sophonisba's flowing flaxen hair (5.45) and Medusa's sensuous appearance blind, confuse, and paralyze.

Medusa, though, does not deserve complete condemnation. Through her captivating charms, she attracts a crowd of jealous rivals and incites lust.[34] Neptune, upon seeing her, is overtaken by an uncontrollable passion, and he seizes her in the temple of Minerva. Violated, Medusa is no longer a follower of the goddess of wisdom and chastity; expelled from the temple, she is denounced and separated from society. Like Sophonisba, then, she embodies an evil that is inflicted upon her by a situation outside her powers. In corrupting male virtue through her petrifying glance, she invades a territory that extends beyond female limits designated by Minerva and her followers. Medusa must be restrained, and her actions must be directed. As the mythographers tell us, Perseus follows the advice of Minerva and, retaining reason and practicing fortitude, decapitates her.[35] In many respects, Medusa's plight, like Sophonisba's, is one of sacrifice; for, after emblazoning the image of Medusa's head on his shield, Perseus deploys this weapon and, like Massinissa and Scipio, restores justice and peace. Consigned to a proper place, Medusa becomes an instrument of good that, controlled by Perseus, results from pain and death, and that testifies to the strength of the forces of masculine virtue to resist the temptations of feminine dissolution.

The defining of a historical Sophonisba in terms of a mythological Medusa changes registers in the text and thereby presents a more universal picture of woman. The associations between the factually verifiable and the imaginatively conceived come together in the legendary figure of Dido. In his parting words with Sophonisba, Massinissa enumerates women who have suffered unrequited love and have descended to Hades. Sophonisba will join a company that includes Dido (6.62–63). The allusion to Dido is not surprising, for, as we have noted, Petrarch's *Africa* reflects an attempt to accommodate the substance of Livy's history to the structure of Vergil's epic poetry. Scipio's heroic campaign to actualize a glory promised to Rome continues the tradition of Aeneas' trials to found Rome. Aldo S. Bernardo and Craig Kallendorf,[36] moreover, have identified parallels between the Massinissa-Sophonisba episode and the Aeneas-Dido encounter. Like Sophonisba and Medusa, Dido engages in an illicit love that threatens Aeneas's destiny and thereby encroaches upon male prerogatives. But unlike her historical and mythological counterparts, she is extolled for her chastity and righteousness.

After hearing Laelius's description of Rome's attainments and destiny, Syphax likens Lucretia to Dido:

Sentio preterea quid femina vestra pudica
Morte velit: ne cuncta sibi iam candida Dido
Arroget

(4.4–6).

[I can see
likewise what your chaste matron sought of death:
that our fair Dido might not claim alone
such honor

(4.5–8).]

Syphax is obviously recalling the minstrel's earlier words (3.418–36), which praise Dido's contributions to Africa. As a fugitive from Tyre, she built the prosperous, powerful city of Carthage; and, remaining loyal to her dead husband, Sychaeus, she declined marriage proposals from Iarbas that the Carthaginians approved. The minstrel alludes to her shameless passion for Aeneas (3.427), and he believes that her suicide affirms her fidelity and attests to her probity.

In his *Triumph of Chastity* (10–18, 154–59), Petrarch praises Dido's chastity and, in his *Seniles* 4.5, defends her efforts to build Carthage. This representation of Dido as a model of chastity conforms to Medieval interpretations of Vergil's text.[37] But Dido is also a problematic character.[38] Like Sophonisba, she endures the same fate: relegation to the third circle of disappointed lovers. At first, she remains, as Syphax notes, faithful to Sychaeus. However, in submitting to a love for Aeneas that Venus inflicts upon her, she breaks her marriage vows. This transgression prompts Dante to assign her to the circle of the Lustful,[39] and it justifies other Medieval thinkers to see her as impure.

In many respects though, the story of Dido is the tale of Sophonisba.[40] Fleeing Tyre, Dido is a widow expelled from a domestic enclosure. Adjusting to the demands of exile and the chastity of widowhood, she undertakes a task associated with masculine talents: the building of a city that rivals the dominance of Rome. Circumstances have forced her to undertake this task and therefore to subvert the subordinate status that women must occupy. Like Sophonisba and Medusa, she articulates, through her actions, a personal identity and acquired authority. In a world defined by absolute values, she transgresses patriarchal boundaries; and, as Jupiter had already determined in the first book, Dido is destined to be controlled. Her suicide actualizes this design, silencing and enclosing her in Hades. As a follower of Juno, she impedes the advancement of Roman destiny decided by Jupiter and to be executed by Aeneas. In order to protect Aeneas, Venus induces Dido to confuse Cupid for Aeneas's son, Ascanius, and thereby exploits the

Carthaginian queen's maternal instincts. Cupid's kiss kindles Dido's passion and incites her to meet with Aeneas, a situation that ends in his call to virtue and in her shame, suffering, and suicide. Understandably, as a player in a tragic, patriarchal play, she curses Aeneas and his descendants and foreshadows Sophonisba's cries of contempt against Scipio and Rome.

The comparisons that Petrarch draws between Sophonisba and her counterparts in myth and legend expand and establish a consistent view of the feminine figure. Narratively and thematically, moreover, Sophonisba recalls the purpose and role of Eve.[41] Petrarch does not create a vision of the prelapsarian state. But Sophonisba's resistance to Roman rule reminds the reader of Eve's disobedience that results in the Fall and in man's separation from God. Further, like the author of Genesis, Petrarch describes a transgression that ends in the pain of fragmentation and contention. The expulsion of Adam and Eve may not initially seem to parallel the torments of Syphax and Sophonisba. But Syphax's shameful entry into Rome and Sophonisba's descent to Hades depict a depravity and death that recall the wretched and forlorn state of Adam and Eve outside the walls of Eden.

Through their respective transgressions, both Sophonisba and Eve effect, in different ways, a fall from grace. As Dora and Erwin Panofsky have noted, the early Church Fathers link Eve with Pandora, both of whom introduce corruption and discontent into this world.[42] For Gregory of Nazianzus, Eve is the scriptural counterpart of the pagan Pandora: a "deadly delight" solely responsible for the Fall of Man.[43] Ian Maclean and Diane Kelsey McColley have, in their survey of Medieval and Renaissance accounts of human physiology and psychology, documented the tendancy to attribute differences in behavior to differences in gender.[44] Sexual distinctions become physiological defects. In commenting on passages in Genesis (1.26–27; 2.2–3), Thomas Aquinas, for example, sees man as tending to produce an offspring "perfect in masculinity."[45] The "debility" or "unsuitability" of woman in the process of procreation results, he believes, from physical conditions that, as Aristotle and Galen had earlier stated, related female imperfections to the humors.[46] Medieval theologians applied these observations to moral judgments. Man emerges as representative of the masculine, more active nature of God. Conversely, woman must be viewed as an instrument of death and vileness. Destined by the curse of the Fall to be subordinate to man, she is commanded, according to Alexander of Hales, to nurture her offspring. Passivity and domesticity, then, define her status, and thus an active role and physical and spiritual superiority are ascribed to man.[47]

Eve, though, is also one of the three players in the *felix culpa* and, as the Church Fathers saw her, a precursor of Mary.[48] The redemption of Adam's sin necessitated Christ's crucifixion; and, according to an analogy by Justin Martyr and Tertullian, Eve's adherence to the word conceived by

the serpent is offset by the Virgin's acceptance of the angel Gabriel's an-
nouncement.[49] Sin precedes and prescribes salvation; for, as Irenaeus wrote,
"Adam had necessarily to be restored in Christ . . . and Eve in Mary, that a
virgin become the advocate of a virgin, should undo and destroy virginal
disobedience by virginal obedience."[50] Thus, whether in the ninth-century
hymn, "Ave maris stella," where the name Eve (*Eva*) is inverted with Gabriel's
salutary word, "Ave," to the Virgin, or in Milton's *Paradise Lost*, where
Jesus is the "son of *Mary*, second *Eve*,"[51] a pattern emerges: Eve's sin and
suffering require the Virgin's sacrifice and intercession in the divine design
of humankind's fall and redemption (emphasis added).

In the *Confessions* (5.9), Augustine personalizes the consequences of the
Fall.[52] Becoming ill in Rome, he fears death. But physical expiration is less
terrifying to him than the spiritual condemnation that he has inherited from
Adam. The torments of the fever extend to spiritual struggles. Through the
contrite prayers of his mother, St. Monica, he is spared two deaths. Neither
Eve nor Mary is mentioned. But in referring to Adam and the curse of original sin, and in describing his mother as a "chaste, sober widow,"[53] Augustine
sets forth oppositions between virtue and vice, passion and reason, and carnal
appetite and spiritual redemption. Eve, Augustine writes elsewhere,[54] is a
reflection of *concupiscentia*. Like the serpent who represents the senses, she
tempts the higher faculty of reason possessed by Adam. "Our flesh is an Eve
within us,"[55] and these inner contentions that afflict Augustine in Rome
become metaphorically the source of his sin and suffering.

In this anecdote, Augustine does not rebuke the nature of woman, for
St. Monica represents the opposing force that enables him to recover. Rather,
he denounces indirectly the *sensualitas* of woman who diverts man's attention away from the spiritual.[56] In his *City of God* (14.11), he elaborates on
the role of Eve in human affairs. Although she has infected the world with
moral disease, he does not accuse her of seduction. In accepting the serpent's
words as truth, she unknowingly leads Adam astray. Adam, however, is in
a more privileged and culpable position; and, in refusing "to be separated
from his companion,"[57] he disregards the truth that God has revealed to
him personally and directly. Like Sophonisba and Syphax, Adam and Eve
"were not both deceived by believing, yet both were taken captive by sin-
ning and ensnared in the devil's toils" (14.11).[58] If, moreover, Eve's decep-
tions induce disorder, decay, and death, a therapeutic shame results. For
Augustine, the words of the Psalmist become relevant: "Fill their faces with
shame, and they will seek your name, Lord" (*Ps.* 83.16).[59] Toward the end
of the work, Augustine sees woman's gender not as a defect but as a natural
condition for procreation (22.17). And born from the rib of a sleeping
Adam, she prefigures, and becomes representative of, the Church that develops from the blood and water flowing from the wounds of the crucified

Christ. Thus, the physical union of Adam and Eve adumbrates and signifies the spiritual marriage of Christ and the Church.

Eve enacts, therefore, the meaning of her name and defines the nature of woman. Like Sophonisba, Medusa, and Dido, she violates the limits of a natural order and thereby assumes an identity. Sin disrupts order; and, through suffering and sacrifice, she submits to a subjugation that expiates her transgression and enables humankind to seek rest and peace. Eve, the mother of man, dies and, at the same time, foreshadows the coming of Mary, the mother of God. Pain characterizes this parturition. The decapitation of Medusa enables Perseus to exercise virtue that, according to Boccaccio, affords him the means to conquer evil and to resemble Christ in his defeat of Satan.[60] Aeneas's abandonment of a dying Dido is, according to Petrarch, the necessary response of a virtuous man destined to found Rome.[61] And just as Eve's transgression and expulsion presage and necessitate Mary's birth of Christ and the establishment of the Church in Rome, Sophonisba's sin and self-sacrifice are integral to Scipio's actualization of justice and law assured by Roman rule.

Conclusion

Toward the end of the epic, Petrarch presents one final glimpse of the female figure. Before the battle of Zama, two allegorical matrons, Rome and Carthage, present the merits of their respective cases before Jupiter (7.500–658). Virtue, Jupiter declares, must prevail. As we know, Scipio defeats Hannibal. But Rome, according to Jupiter, will neglect the principle of virtue, allowing ambition to obscure the piety and heroism of Scipio. In language suggestive of the Apocalypse, he tells of the coming of a "Maid" [virgine (7.723)] who will give birth to a redeemer. Rome is destined to pass away, but the pain and sacrifice derived from unconditional love will assure a renewal of justice and peace. The allusion to the Incarnation defines indirectly the role of woman. The milk from the Virgin will nurture Christ (7.724). The blood flowing from Lucretia's breasts incites the rise of the Republic. The image of the vanquished Medusa strengthens Perseus' armor, which, in turn, foreshadows Rome's strong, secure protection in the person of Scipio, conqueror of Sophonisba. Dido's tears and laments that are consumed by the fire of the funeral pyre presage the cries and wails of the Carthaginians who witness their city torched by the Romans and "burning in those soaring crimson flames" (8.1541).[62]

In spite of her moral imperfections, Sophonisba reflects characteristics of this paradigm. Like her biblical, mythological, and classical counterparts, she yields to destiny, complying with Hasdrubal's desires. However, through her participation in the Carthaginian campaign, she blurs sexual roles. As a political pawn, she is led to commit suicide, which, like Dido's, assumes tragic dimensions. But Sophonisba's intrusion upon patriarchal territories and her subsequent silencing in Hades explain the pain of birth. In a classic study on the notion of human will, Theodor Mommsen describes Petrarch's portrayal of the dilemma of man in terms of Hercules' choice between virtue and vice.[63] Massinissa is situated at a similar crossroads, and, by adhering to Scipio's counsel, he follows the path of virtue. But, if Massinissa is a player in this moral drama, Sophonisba is hardly a passive locus of feminine beauty. Rather, through her charm endowed by nature and her circumstances determined by birth, she stimulates Massinissa to perceive and pursue a good that is identified with Scipio and ordained by providence. Scipio's Rome rises to glory, and Sophonisba, as a subdued member of the body politic, has played her part. In struggling to establish peace and order, Scipio will suffer the wounds of battle that will recall Petrarch's allusions to Christ's "gaping wounds" (1.18) [larga . . . vulnera (1.13)]. But as we have seen, Sophonisba's role as woman reenacts Eve's disgrace in the *felix culpa* and thereby activates man's aspiration to exercise virtue in his search for harmony. Petrarch's unfinished epic, then, poeticizes Livy's narrative and validates salvation history; for, as a daughter of Hasdrubal and Adam, Sophonisba submits to a suffering and sacrifice required in the rebirth of temporal and divine patriarchal order.

Notes

1. Aldo S. Bernardo, *Petrarch, Scipio and the "Africa": The Birth of Humanism's Dream* (Baltimore: Johns Hopkins University Press, 1962), p. 105.

2. Craig Kallendorf, *In Praise of Aeneas: Virgil and Epideictic Rhetoric in the Early Italian Renaissance* (Hanover, NH: University Press of New England, 1989), p. 40.

3. 's Africa pianse, Italia non se rise, "Triumphus Cupidinis" 2.83, in Francesco Petrarca, *Rime e Trionfi*, ed. Ferdinando Neri (Turin: Unione Tipografico-Edizione Torinese, 1966), p. 525. All subsequent references to verses in the *Triumphs* will correspond to this edition.

4. Studies on Petrarch's view of woman concentrate on Laura. Attention centers on the anguish of the persona in the respective works and on how the female figure impels Petrarch to decide between virtue and vice, reason and passion. Aldo S. Bernardo in *Petrarch, Laura, and the "Triumphs"* (Albany: State University of New York Press, 1974), chap. 1 reviews past approaches. In later chapters, he examines the feminine

throughout Petrarch's writings and concludes that Petrarch describes the ambiguity of Laura in terms of the poet's self-reflections. Giuseppe Mazzotta, "The *Canzoniere* and the Language of Self," *Studies in Philology* 75 (1978): pp. 271–96, describes Petrarch's expression of personal conflict and, in his *The Worlds of Petrarch* (Durham, NC: Duke University Press, 1993), examines the mythological structures and intellectual assumptions that explain the conflict. Other studies confirm the ambiguity of woman as depicted by Petrarch: Robert M. Durling, "Petrarch's 'Giovene donna sotto un verde lauro,'" *Modern Language Notes* 86 (1971): pp. 1–20; John Brenkman, "Writing, Desire, Dialectic in Petrarch's *Rime* 23," *Pacific Coast Philology* 9 (1974): pp. 12–19; John Freccero, "The Fig Tree and the Laurel," *Diacritics* 5 (1975): pp. 24–40; Thomas M. Greene, *The Light in Troy: Imitation and Discovery in Renaissance Poetry* (New Haven, CT: Yale University Press, 1982), chaps. 5–7; Sara Sturm-Maddox, "The Poet-Persona in the *Canzoniere*," *Francis Petrarch, Six Centuries Later: A Symposium*, ed. Aldo Scaglione (Chapel Hill and Chicago: University of North Carolina Press and the Newberry Library, 1975), pp. 192–212; Sara Sturm-Maddox *Petrarch's Metamorphoses: Text and Subtext in the "Rime Sparse"* (Columbia: University of Missouri Press, 1985); Sara Sturm-Maddox *Petrarch's Laurels* (University Park: Pennsylvania State University Press, 1992); Nancy J. Vickers, "Widowed Words: Dante, Petrarch, and the Metaphors of Mourning," in *Discourses of Authority in Medieval and Renaissance Literature*, ed. Kevin Brownlee and Walter Stephens (Hanover, NH: University Press of New England, 1989), pp. 97–108; and Thomas P. Roche, *Petrarch and the English Sonnet Sequences* (New York: AMS Press, 1989), chap. 1. More recently, Barbara L. Estrin, *Laura: Uncovering Gender and Genre in Wyatt, Donne, and Marvell* (Durham, NC: Duke University Press, 1994), 1–90, discusses the mutable, multivalent meanings that Laura, or Petrarch's model of woman, assumes and conveys. For more on this topic, see Paul Allen Miller's essay in this volume.

5. All citations of the respective poem and verse numbers of the *Rime* correspond to Francesco Petrarca, *Canzoniere*, ed. Gianfranco Contini (Turin: G. Einaudi, 1964).

6. All references to the book and line numbers of the *Africa* correspond to Francesco Petrarca, *Africa*, Edizione nazionale delle opere di Francesco Petrarca, ed. Nicola Festa (Florence: Sansoni, 1926). All English translations are taken from Francesco Petrarca, *Petrarch's "Africa,"* ed. and trans. Thomas G. Bergin and Alice S. Wilson (New Haven, CT: Yale University Press, 1977); book and line numbers in English correspond to this edition.

7. Critics have generally seen Sophonisba in terms of Petrarch's other feminine figures, especially Laura. See Umberto Bosco, *Francesco Petrarca* (Bari: Laterza, 1961), p. 45; Adelia Noferi, *L'esperienza poetica del Petrarca* (Florence: Le Monnier, 1962), pp. 41–42, 215–21; and Thomas G. Bergin, *Petrarch* (New York: Twayne, 1970), pp. 163–64. More recently, Ezio Raimondi, *Metafora e storia: Studi su Dante e Petrarca* (Turin: G. Einaudi, 1970), pp 180–87, and Sturm-Maddox, *Petrarch's Metamorphoses*, p. 30, and *Petrarch's Laurels*, p. 288, see Sophonisba in terms of the mythological figure of Medusa. Charles Ricci, *Sophonisbe dans la tragédie*

classique italienne et française (Grenoble: Allier Frères, 1904), chap. 1, sees the ambiguities of Sophonisba's situation in the *Africa* as the basis for subsequent tragic representations. In his *Petrarch, Scipio and the "Africa"*, pp. 149–56, Bernardo analyzes the narrative in terms of Massinissa's conflict between loyalty to Scipio and lust for Sophonisba. In an earlier study, "Dramatic Dialogue and Monologue in Petrarch's Works," *Symposium* 7 (1953): pp. 92–119, Bernardo sees this conflict as reflective of the images of the sun and shade which, suggestive of the moral states of Scipio and Sophonisba, express poetically the persona's anguish. More recently, Kallendorf, *In Praise of Aeneas*, pp. 40–41, 46–49, corroborates this thought, seeing Sophonisba as a representation of Vergil's Dido who threatens to foil Aeneas's destiny to found Rome. For both Bernardo and Kallendorf Sophonisba is important, but secondary to, Massinissa in Petrarch's description of the agony of moral conflict.

8. Robert Bolgar, *The Classical Heritage and Its Beneficiaries* (Cambridge: Cambridge University Press, 1954), p. 255; Bernardo, *Petrarch, Scipio and the "Africa,"* p. 206.

9. "Letter to Posterity," *Seniles* 18.1, in Francis Petrarch, *Letters of Old Age*, 2 vols., ed. A. Bernardo, Saul Levin, and Reta A. Bernardo (Baltimore, MD: Johns Hopkins University Press, 1992), vol. 2, p. 676. All references to the *Seniles* correspond to this edition.

10. Numerous studies detail the interrelationship of history, epic, and moral philosophy in Petrarch's *Africa*. See especially Pierre de Nolhac, *Pétrarque et l'humanisme*, 2 vols. (1907; rev. ed., Paris: Champion, 1965), vol. 1, pp. 123, 211, vol. 2, pp.1–65, 127; Bernardo, *Petrarch, Scipio and the "Africa,"* p. 5; Richard T. Bruère, "Lucan and Petrarch's *Africa*," *Classical Philology* 56 (1961): pp. 83–99; Nicholas Mann, *Petrarch* (Oxford: Oxford University Press, 1984), pp. 16–17, 50–51. Giuseppe Billanovich, "Petrarch and the Textual Tradition of Livy," *Journal of the Warburg and Courtauld Institutes* 14 (1951): pp. 137–208, traces Petrarch's reconstruction and emendation of the fragments of Livy's history available in the early fourteenth century. For more recent and relatively comprehensive treatments of Petrarch's use and artistic adaptations of history, see Eckhard Keller, *Petrarca und die Geschichte* (Munich: Wilhelm Fink Verlag, 1978); Guido Martellotti, "Storiografia del Petrarca," in *Scritti petrarcheschi*, ed. Michele Feo and Silvia Rizzo (Padua: Antenore, 1983), pp 474–86; and Mazzotta, *Worlds of Petrarch*, chap. 5.

11. variis nam purpura gemmis / Intertexta tegit regine pectora meste (5.66–67).

12. captiva captus ab hoste, / Victaque victorem potuit domuisse superbum (5.73–74).

13. Et malesuadus amor, scelus, ira, fidesque dolique, / Furtaque blanditiis immixta (6.47–48).

14. Katherine Heinrichs, *The Myths of Love: Classical Lovers in Medieval Literature* (University Park: The Pennsylvania State University Press, 1990), p. 63; Katherine Heinrichs "Mythological Lovers in Chaucer's *Troilus and Criseyde*,"

Journal of the Rocky Mountain Medieval and Renaissance Association 12 (1991): p. 15.

15. Heinrichs, "Mythological Lovers," p. 35, lists such glossators as Rémi d'Auxerre, Arnulf of Orleans, Bernard Silvestris, Coluccio Salutati, and Boccaccio.

16. For a fuller treatment of Orpheus and his interpretation in Medieval literature, see John B. Friedman, *Orpheus in the Middle Ages* (Cambridge: Harvard University Press, 1970). The use of allegory in Medieval and Renaissance literature has been expansively studied. However, several studies treating narratives as *exempla* should be noted: Douglas Bush, *Mythology and the Renaissance Tradition in English Poetry* (Minneapolis: University of Minnesota Press, 1932); Jean Seznec, *The Survival of the Pagan Gods*, trans. Barbara Sessions (New York: Harper and Row, 1953); J. B. Allen, *The Ethical Poetic of the Later Middle Ages* (Toronto: University of Toronto Press, 1982) and *The Friar as Critic: Literary Attitudes in the Later Middle Ages* (Nashville: Vanderbilt University Press, 1971). Petrarch sees an interrelation between poetry and theology (*Familiares* 10.4; *Seniles* 4.5), noting as well in these letters the importance of allegory in the poetic process. For a more extensive examination of Petrarch's theories of poetic creativity, see Concetta Greenfield, Studies in Fourteenth and Fifteenth Century Poetics (Ph.D. diss., University of North Carolina, Chapel Hill, 1971), chap. 5.

17. labor et lacrime et longo suspiria tractu (6.45).

18. Petrarch repeats this idea in *Africa*, 8.830–34.

19. Femina ut in plurimis verus est diabolus hostis pacis: fons impatientiae: materia iurgiorum: et insomni negotio delectantur, (390r): Francesco Petrarca, *Opera latina* (Venice: n.p.,1501). All subsequent Latin quotations from the *Seniles* and their respective folio pages correspond to this edition.

20. uxorea habeant: muliebri sine fine consortio et nocturnis amplexibus atque conuitiis, vagituque infanium: et insomni negotio delectantur, (390r).

21. curas . . . et labores, (390r).

22. conspicuum meritis belloque tremendum (1.1).

23. uxor Syphacis, filia Hasdrubalis Poeni, vol. 8, p. 406: Livy, *Ab urba condita* 30.12.11, 14 vols., trans. and ed. Frank Gardner Moore, Loeb Classical Library (Cambridge: Harvard University Press, 1940). All references to the book, chapter, and section number in Livy's history correspond to this edition. Livy provides additional details of Sophonisba at 29.23.3–10, 30.12.11–22, 30.13.9–14, 30.15.1. Petrarch probably did not know other ancient commentaries on Sophonisba.

Shelley P. Haley, "Livy's Sophonisba," *Classica et Mediaevalia* 40 (1989): pp. 171–81, presents an excellent description and critical interpretation of Livy's portrait of Sophonisba and of subsequent representations by Polybius, Appian, Diodorus Siculus, Dio Cassius, and Zenoras. She concludes that Livy's representation of her is stereotypical and literary rather than historical. As a temptress, Livy's Sophonisba resembles Vergil's Dido and Horace's and Propertius's Cleopatra.

24. In Margaret W. Ferguson, Maureen Quilligan, and Nancy J. Vickers, eds., *Rewriting the Renaissance: The Discourses of Sexual Difference in Early Modern Europe* (Chicago: University of Chicago Press, 1986), the editors examine in their introduction a similar idea. Employing Jacob Burckhardt's thought on the equality of man and woman as one of their major premises, they note that such a balance exists only when women are enclosed, silenced, or "marginalized" (pp. xxviii–xxix). Such presumptions "naturalize" their subordinate status in a patriarchal society (p. xxix). Although no essay in this collection treats Petrarch's view of woman, Peter Stallybrass, "Patriarchal Territories: The Body Enclosed," pp. 123–42, demonstrates that any transgression of status boundaries defined by gender results in a restoration of order or a "subservience enforced by death" (p. 132).

25. caesique prope plures in fuga quam in pugna sunt (25.34.14) vol. 6, p. 470.

26. filiam ei numptum dederit (30.13.5) vol 8, p. 412. See also Livy, *Ab urbe condita*, 29.23.3–5.

27. As Haley, "Livy's Sophonisba" points out (p. 174), Livy, *Ab urbe condita*, (29.23) makes this point clear and is following Polybius (14.1.4) as his principal source.

28. The lacuna that occurs between books 4 and 5 includes the coincidental arrivals of Hasdrubal and Scipio at Cirta and their respective arguments to gain Syphax's assistance. Petrarch also excludes Syphax's marriage to Sophonisba, his change of alliance from Scipio to Hasdrubal, and Massinissa's victory over Syphax. For these accounts, see Livy, *Ab urbe condita*, 27–29. Thomas G. Bergin and Alice S. Wilson, *Petrarch's "Africa,"* pp. 255–56, summarize the narrative that Petrarch excludes. For a critical examination of the possible reasons for these omissions, see Bernardo, *Petrarch, Scipio and the "Africa,"* pp. 142–51, especially pp. 149–51.

29. Haley, "Livy, Passion, and Cultural Stereotypes," *Historia* 39.3 (1990): pp. 375–81, demonstrates that Livy's description of Massinissa, Syphax, and the Numidians is one of concupiscence that contrasts with the *temperantia* of Scipio and the Romans. Such a stereotypification, that Petrarch may have detected from his reading of Livy, supports the idea of the exploitation of Sophonisba who, as a Carthaginian, becomes the victim of Numidian libido or passion.

It should be noted that many classical historians did not view Sophonisba as a traitorous temptress. In particular, Polybius, Diodorus Siculus, and Dio Cassius all agree on her charms and sensuousness, but they extol her loyalties to family and cause. Diodorus Siculus, in a brief but illuminating passage (27.6.7), corroborates Livy's narrative. But, in adding that Sophonisba was at first married to Massinissa, he discounts the charges of her lasciviousness. Dio Cassius (17.57.51) confirms Massinissa's attractions to her beauty and cultural interests. According to Zenoras (9.11), moreover, Sophonisba originally complied with her father's wishes to marry Massinissa. Unfortunately for Hasdrubal and Sophonisba, Syphax changes his allegiance to Scipio. As Livy has told us, Hasdrubal then gives his daughter to Syphax, who subsequently renounces the Roman cause. Hurt and vindictive, Massinissa defects from the Carthaginians and wins numerous victories for Scipio (Dio Cassius

17.57.53; Zenoras 9.13). In this reconstruction of history, Sophonisba remains obedient to her father and is seen even more emphatically as a political pawn who also
renounces a passionate love for a more reasoned, filial duty.

30. My reading of Petrarch's use of the rape of Lucretia parallels in many ways
the interpretation of Livy's account by Sandra R. Joshel, "The Body Female and the
Body Politic: Livy's Lucretia and Verginia," in *Pornography and Representation in
Greece and Rome*, ed. Amy Richlin (New York: Oxford University Press, 1992), pp.
112–30. The rape of Lucretia has incited considerable critical interest. Hans Galinsky,
Der Lucretia-Stoff in der Weltliteratur (Breslau: Priebatsch, 1932), surveys the history of this theme. More recently, Ian Donaldson, *The Rapes of Lucretia: A Myth
and Its Transformations* (Oxford: Oxford University Press, 1982) critically examined
the passage and its varying interpretations. See also Patricia K. Joplin, "Ritual Work
on Human Flesh: Livy's Lucretia and the Rape of the Body Politic," *Helios* 17
(1990): pp. 51–70. In her study of Shakespeare's *Rape of Lucrece*, Heather Dubrow,
Captive Victors: Shakespeare's Narrative Poems and Sonnets (Ithaca, NY: Cornell
University Press, 1987), chap. 2, examines Livy's accounts of the rape, its transmission into Elizabethan England, and its portrayal of the status of women in Roman
and Renaissance cultures.

31. See, in particular, Francesco Petrarca, *Africa*, 7.15–19, 8.409–11 and 678–81.

32. I am borrowing this term from Heather Dubrow, *Captive Victors*, p. 157
n.16, who, in turn, is expressing an idea formulated by Linda Bamber, *Comic Women,
Tragic Men: A Study of Gender and Genre in Shakespeare* (Stanford, CA: Stanford
University Press, 1982), chap. 6.

33. In sonnets 179 and 197 of his *Rime sparse*, Petrarch describes Laura's
beauty in terms of Medusa's magic. By extension, since we have noticed parallels in
the portraits of Sophonisba and Laura (5.18–64), Petrarch's description of Medusa
in the *Rime* becomes relevant for our understanding of her role in the *Africa*.
Conforming to images of the stereotypical seductress, Laura as a representation of
Medusa entangles the persona in her blond hair (197.5–8). Further, in the final
canzone (*Rime sparse* 366), the poet prays to the Virgin for intercession, but, in
visualizing Medusa, he becomes petrified as he remembers his lust for Laura (366.111–
12). For a more complete examination of the role of Medusa in the *Rime*, see
Kenelm Foster, "Beatrice or Medusa: The Penitential Element in Petrarch's
Canzoniere," in *Italian Studies Presented to E. R. Vincent*, ed. Charles Peter Brand,
Kenelm Foster, and Uberto Limentani (Cambridge: Cambridge University Press,
1962), pp. 41–56.

34. For summaries of the myth, see Ovid, *Metamorphoses*, 2 vols., ed. and
trans. Frank Justus Miller. Loeb Classical Library (Cambridge: Harvard University
Press, 1966), 4.743–803; Lucan, *The Civil War*, ed. and trans. J. D. Duff. Loeb
Classical Library (Cambridge: Harvard University Press, 1962), 9.626–699; Hyginus,
The Myths of Hyginus, Poetica Astronomica, 22.12, ed. and trans. Mary Grant,
University of Kansas Humanistic Studies 34 (Lawrence: University of Kansas Press,
1960), p. 195; Fulgentius, *The Mythologies. Fulgentius the Mythographer*, 1.21,

trans. Leslie George Whitbread (Columbus: Ohio State University Press, 1971), pp. 61–63.

35. Allegorical readings of the relationship between Medusa and Perseus interpret Medusa's decapitation as the victory of reason over passion. As one of the three Gorgons, Medusa's charms result in man's decay and death. Fulgentius, *Mythologies*, 1.21, and Pierre Bersuire, *Metamorphoses ovidiana moraliter . . . explanata* (1509; repr. New York: Garland, 1959), 41v, see Sthenno as a force awakening the mind, Euryale as a strength filling the mind with terror, and Medusa as a power that induces despair. In elucidating Dante's *Inferno* (9.52–63), the fourteenth-century commentators, Graziolo de' Bambaglioli, Jacopo della Lara, and Pietro di Dante, understand the three Gorgons as representative of forces that capture the imagination (Sthenno), devastate reason (Euryale), and lead man to self-annihilation (Medusa). In his *Commento sopra la "Divina Commedia,"* Boccaccio sees Medusa as the capacity that overtakes human will and intellect; and, by inciting concupiscence in man, she destroys and annihilates. Texts of these commentaries on Dante are presented in *Divina Commedia nella figurazione artistica e nel seculare commento*, vol. 1 of *Inferno*, ed. Guido Biagi (Turin: Unione Tipografico-Editrice Torinese, 1921), p. 248.

36. Bernardo, *Petrarch, Scipio and the "Africa,"* pp. 141–43, 150; Kallendorf, *In Praise of Aeneas*, pp. 40–41, 46–49.

37. Kallendorf, *In Praise of Aeneas* pp. 41–43, points out that Dido was a model of chastity. Seneca, in commenting on *Aeneid* 4.3, notes that the Aeneas-Dido episode reflects a movement from erotic love to virtuous admiration (Kallendorf, p. 42). This idea was, according to Kallendorf (p. 43), continued by Macrobius, Jerome, Augustine, Justin. See also Mary Louise Pratt, "Dido as an Example of Chastity: The Influence of Literature," *Harvard Library Bulletin* 17 (1969): pp. 216–39. For the parallels between Vergil's *Aeneid* and Petrarch's *Africa*, see Richard Seagraves, "The Influence of Vergil on Petrarch's *Africa*," (Ph.D. diss., Columbia University, 1977).

38. Kallendorf, *In Praise of Aeneas*, p. 43, and Robert Hollander, *Boccaccio's Two Venuses* (New York: Columbia University Press, 1977), pp. 48, 171–72, 216, examine Medieval commentaries that describe Dido as impure. The examples cited by Kallendorf include Tertullian (*De exhortatione castitatis*, chap. 13; *De monogamia* 17; *Ad martyres* 4, *Apologia* 50), Servius's *Commentary on the "Aeneid"* 1.340, 4.36, 4.335, and 4.674; Priscian, *Perigesis* 5.184–86. Hollander, pp. 171–73, discusses Boccaccio's ambiguous portrait of Dido, noting the complications of determining her moral rectitude as presented by several recent critics (Giorgio Padoan, A. E. Quaglio, and Vittore Branca). See also Carlo Pascal, "Didone nella letteratura d'Africa," *Athenaeum* 5 (1917): pp. 285–93.

39. *Inferno* 5.61–62. Dante Alighieri, *The Divine Comedy*, 6 vols, ed., trans., and annotated by Charles Singleton (Princeton: Princeton University Press, 1970–76), vol. 1, p. 50. This and all subsequent references to the canto and verse number in the *Divina Commedia* correspond to this edition. It should be noted that Dante places Dido in the circle with other seductresses, including Cleopatra (*Inferno* 5.63) and Helen of Troy (*Inferno* 5.64–65).

40. Both the text and secondary studies establish Dido's tragic dilemma and downfall. However, Barbara Bono, *Literary Transvaluation: From Vergilian Epic to Shakespearean Tragicomedy* (Berkeley and Los Angeles: University of California Press, 1984), chap. 1, presents an insightful reading of Dido's tragedy as part of an epic where men assume active roles and where women must remain passive.

41. Sturm-Maddox, *Petrarch's Metamorphoses*, pp. 113–17, 121–22, describes Laura as suggestive of Eve in Petrarch's personal conflict that recalls the Fall. Carlo Calcaterra, *Nella selva del Petrarca* (Bologna: Cappelli, 1942), pp. 225–28; Durling, "Petrarch's 'Giovene donna,'" p. 18; Bortolo Martinelli, *"Feria sexta aprilis*: la data sacra nel canzoniere del Petrarca," *Rivista di storia e letteratura religiosa* 8 (1972), pp. 449–84; and Thomas P. Roche, "The Calendrical Structure of Petrarch's *Canzoniere*," *Studies in Philology* 71 (1974): pp. 152–72, have suggested that Petrarch is recreating the Fall in the *Rime sparse*.

42. In Dora Panofsky and Erwin Panofsky, *Pandora's Box: The Changing Aspects of a Mythical Symbol* (New York: Pantheon, 1962), pp. 11–13. The Panofskys cite, in particular, such theologians as Tertullian, Irenaeus, Gregory of Nazianzus, and Origen, all of whom take as their point of departure Hesiod's description of Pandora in his *Works and Days*, vv. 53–82, 90–97.

43. Gregory of Nazianzus, *Adversus mulieris se nimis ornantes*, 115ff, as cited by Dora and Erwin Panofsky, *Pandora's Box*, p. 12.

44. Ian Maclean, *The Renaissance Notion of Woman* (Cambridge: Cambridge University Press, 1980), especially chaps. 2 and 3, and Diane Kelsey McColley, *Milton's Eve* (Urbana: University of Illinois Press, 1983), chaps. 1 and 2.

45. perfectum secundum masculinum sexum, *Summa Theologia* 1 *a* 92, 1, quoted by Maclean, *Renaissance Notion of Woman*, p. 93.

46. propter virtutis activae debilitatem, vel propter aliquam materiae indispositionem, *Summa Theologia* 1 *a* 92, 1; quoted by Maclean, *Renaissance Notion of Woman*, p. 93. According to Maclean (pp. 8, 28), Aquinas derives this idea from several passages in Aristotle (*De Generatione animalium* 2.1–3, 20; *Physics* 1.9; *Historia animalium* 9.1) and in Galen (*De usu parium corporis* 14). Maclean (p. 8) also notes that Albertus Magnus concurred with Aristotle in this thought.

47. See Maclean, *Renaissance Notion of Woman*, pp. 10–11, for Alexander of Hales thoughts expressed in *Summa*, as well as for similar statements by Augustine, *De Genesi ad litteram* 12.16, Aquinas, *Summa Theologia* 1 *a* 92, 1, St. Bonaventura, *In libros Sententiarum expositiones* 3.12 art 39.1, and Peter Lombard, *Sententiae* 3.12. For a survey and examination of misogyny in the Middle Ages, see R. Howard Bloch, "Medieval Misogyny," in *Misogyny, Misandry, and Misanthropy*, ed. R. Howard Bloch and Frances Ferguson (Berkeley and Los Angeles: University of California Press, 1989), pp. 1–25, and *Medieval Misogyny and the Invention of Western Romantic Love* (Chicago: University of Chicago Press, 1991).

48. This theme has been extensively examined. Several studies that seem especially useful in recording Medieval and Renaissance interpretations of Eve as a

player in the Redemption include Arnold Williams, *The Common Expositor* (Chapel Hill: University of North Carolina Press, 1948); J. M. Evans, *"Paradise Lost" and the Genesis Tradition* (Oxford: Clarendon, 1968); and J. B. Trapp, "The Iconography of the Fall of Man," in *Approaches to "Paradise Lost,"* ed. C. A. Patrides (Toronto: University of Toronto Press, 1968), pp. 223–65.

49. Evans, *"Paradise Lost,"* pp. 100–01, documents this idea as related by Justin Martyr (*Dialogue of Justin and Trypho* 100) and Tertullian (*De carne Christi* 17), and he identifies the source of the relationship between Adam's sin and Christ's sacrifice in Paul, Rom. 5:19 and 1 Cor. 21–22. He also notes that Paul, in Eph. 5:31–32, sees Eve's union with Adam as analogous to Christ's establishment of the Church. See also Trapp, "Iconography," pp. 226 and 258, as well as studies by Ernst Guldan, *Eva und Maria: eine Antithese als Bildmotiv* (Graz-Cologne: Böhlau, 1966) and Lino Cignelli, *Maria, nuova Eva nella patristrica greca* (Assisi: Porziuncola, 1966).

50. Irenaeus, *Demonstration of the Apostolic Teaching* 33, as quoted by Evans, *"Paradise Lost,"* p. 102. For a similar idea, see Hrotswitha's use of Terence as discussed by Barbara K. Gold in this volume.

51. John Milton, *Paradise Lost* 10.183, ed. Merritt Y. Hughes (Indianapolis: Bobbs-Merrill, 1962), p. 240. See also *Paradise Lost* 5.387 and 12.327.

52. Petrarch's reading of Augustine is well established. See, in particular, Pierre de Nolhac, *Pétrarque et l'humanisme*, vol. 2, chap. 9; Ugo Mariani, *Il Petrarca e gli Agostiniani*, 2nd ed. (Rome: Edizioni di storia e letteratura, 1959); Nicolae Iliescu, *Il "Canzoniere" petrarchesco e Sant'Agostino* (Rome: Società Accademica Romana, 1962); P. P. Gerosa, *Umanesimo cristiano del Petrarca: Influenza agostiniana, attinenze medievali* (Turin: Bottega d'Erasmo, 1966); Bortolo Martinelli, *Petrarca e il Ventoso* (Bergamo: Minerva italica, 1977); and Sturm-Maddox, *Petrarch's Metamorphoses*, chap. 5.

53. viduae castae ac sobriae, Augustine, *Confessions*, 2 vols., ed. and trans. William Watts, Loeb Classical Library (Cambridge: Harvard University Press 1977), vol. 1 p. 240. For a fuller examination of this passage, see Nancy Jones, "By Woman's Tears Redeemed: Female Lament in St. Augustine's *Confessions* and the Correspondence of Abelard and Heloise," in this volume.

54. Larry S. Crist, "Le *Jeu d'Adam* et l'exégèse de la chute," *Etudes de civilisation médiévale (Mélanges E.-R. Labande)* (Poitiers: C.E.S.C.M., 1974), p. 181; and Sturm-Maddox, *Petrarch's Metamorphoses*, p. 160 n. 59, cite two passages from Augustine that equate concupiscence with Eve: *De sermone Domini in monte secundum Matthaeum* (*PL* 34.1246) and *Liber de paradiso* (*PL* 14.329). See also D. W. Robertson, *Preface to Chaucer* (Princeton: Princeton University Press, 1962), p. 75; and Evans, pp. 74–76.

55. Augustine, *On the Psalms*, cited by McColley, *Milton's Eve*, p. 11.

56. See Robertson, *Preface to Chaucer* pp. 69–75; A. Kent Hieatt, "Eve as Reason in a Tradition of the Allegorical Interpretation of the Fall," *Journal of the*

Warburg and Courtauld Institutes 43 (1980): pp. 221–26; and Sturm-Maddox, *Petrarch's Metamorphoses*, p. 117.

57. ille autem ab unico noluit consortio dirimi, Augustine, *City of God*, 7 vols., ed. and trans. Philip Levine, Loeb Classical Library (Cambridge, MA: Harvard University Press, 1966), vol. 4, p. 330. All subsequent references and quotations correspond to this edition. This thought seems to have originated with 1 Timothy 2:14: "Et Adam non est seductus, mulier autem seducta in praevaricatione fuit." [Adam was not deceived, but the woman was deceived and was in transgression.] For an examination of Cornelius Agrippa's later use of this same argument, see Diane S. Wood, "In Praise of Woman's Superiority: Heinrich Cornelius Agrippa's *De nobilitate* (1529)," in this volume.

58. non sunt ambo decepti, peccando tamen ambo sunt capti et diaboli laqueis implicati, Augustine, *City of God*, vol. 4, p. 332.

59. Imple facies eorum ignominia, / Et quaerent nomen tuum, Domine! (*Ps.* 83.16), Augustine, *City of God*, vol. 4, p. 342.

60. Boccaccio, *De genealogia deorum* 1.3, ed. Vincenzo Romano (Bari: Laterza, 1951); cited by Bernardo, *Petrarch, Scipio and the "Africa,"* p. 139.

61. *Seniles* 4.5; *Letters of Old Age*, vol. 1, p. 141.

62. Carthago flammis arderet in illis (8.1084).

63. Theodor Mommsen, "Petrarch and the Story of the Choice of Hercules," *Journal of the Warburg and Courtauld Institutes* 16 (1953): pp. 178–92. See also Charles Trinkaus, *The Poet as Philosopher: Petrarch and the Formation of Renaissance Consciousness* (New Haven, CT: Yale University Press, 1979).

Laurel as the Sign of Sin:
Laura's Textual Body in Petrarch's *Secretum*

Paul Allen Miller

The disquiet stemming from the historicity of the signifier adumbrates a pathos that is translinguistic, that embraces "mores et habitus," the historicity of culture. For Petrarch, a generation after Dante, the intuition of this pathos was no longer redeemable; it was tragic. . . . [1]

Misogyny in our culture consists of a series of specific associations between the esthetic and the feminine, which in essence turns women into a text to be read and thus to be appropriated.[2]

In book 3 of Petrarch's *Secretum*, a Latin dialogue on the poet's sins, Augustinus, a fictional representation of Saint Augustine, tells Franciscus, the poet's persona, that Franciscus is bound by two chains that prevent him from contemplating his own mortality and assure his damnation: his love for Laura, and his pursuit of poetic glory.[3] In this paper, I will argue that Petrarch's collocation of woman and text is neither arbitrary nor reducible to the formula that Laura as the poet's beloved is the cause of his fame.[4] Rather, this linkage of Laura to the pursuit of poetry's laurels is the product of a series of deeper epistemic, ideological, and sexual tensions that determine its necessity. The problem, then, is more complex than a simple identification of beloved with text would allow.

Nonetheless, it is clear that *one* of Laura's functions in Petrarch's work is to stand as a symbol for his poetic ambition. Indeed, in Petrarch's own time the identification of Laura with his poetry was suggested by both Boccaccio and Giacomo Colonna, and it was only ambiguously refuted by the poet himself.[5] Likewise, the numerous puns on the relation between Laura's name and the laurels of Apollo show that, at times, Petrarch himself deliberately exploited this symbolic function.[6] All the same, such an understanding of Laura's role both within the *Secretum* and throughout the Petrarchan corpus, while certainly not incorrect, represents a substantial oversimplification. A wider optic is needed.

My contention will be that Laura functions in the *Secretum*'s textual economy as a signifying body per se. Her role is that of the material signifier, as opposed to the logically intelligible signified. As such, she is implicated in a complex series of substitutive relations in which she becomes successively identified with the letter rather than the spirit in Petrarch's text and with the sensible as opposed to the intelligible.[7] In short, Laura comes to function, not as that which transcends the material, but as the substance that potentially makes the re-presentation of the transcendental possible. As I shall argue later, this identification of the female body with the materiality of the signifier is hardly an innovation on Petrarch's part, but rather is part of a sexual/textual strategy that subtends the whole of the Western tradition.

Clearly, Laura's role as a material signifier does not exclude her from being identified with Petrarch's poetic text and the glory associated with it, but the implications of this role do not stop there. It brings with it the more basic problem of the status of the sign itself in late Medieval and early Renaissance culture. That is to say, it forces us to pose the problem of the period's changing cultural understanding of the relations that were thought to obtain between signifier and signified.[8] This problem of the sign, moreover, is indissociably linked with the function of the feminine in the symbolic economy of this crucially liminal period situated between a Medieval *épistémê* dominated by the concept of *auctoritas*[9] and the subsequent Renaissance humanists' openness to history. The nature of this link between the semiotic and the sexual becomes clearer when the question is posed: what is the role of the feminine in the salvational history of the individual, masculine spirit at the birth of the European Renaissance, or what does the feminine signify? As we shall see, women and signs constitute two of the primary moments in a larger dialectic that ultimately determines the roles of poetry, antiquity, humanist studies, sexuality, and salvation in the Petrarchan and early Renaissance *épistémê*. For the question that Augustinus forces Franciscus to ask in the *Secretum* is: does Laura truly aid the poet in his quest for the transcendence of this world and ascension to the next; or does the very materiality, which allows her to function as a signifying substance, forever obscure the ideal essence of the divine signified?[10] In short, is the figure of the feminine readable, and does the text we call Laura yield an intelligible meaning? As Victoria Kahn has put it, "The problem under discussion [in book 3 of the *Secretum*], then, is not simply Franciscus's psychological resistance [to giving up the pursuit of love and fame] but also the resistance of . . . texts to yield[ing] up their secrets. . . . The psychological dilemma is finally an interpreter's dilemma."[11] It is as much an episte-mological and ideological problem as it is a personal or literary one. In this paper I seek to follow the complex ways in which this equation of Laura with the signifier plays itself out in the *Secretum* and to situate this moment of semiotic instability in a larger historical context.

The question of the role of women in the symbolic economy is one whose roots run deep within the Italian poetic tradition and the Christian west and one that frequently evokes what at first seem to be contradictory responses. On the one hand, Petrarch's great predecessor, Dante, established the model whereby a real, physically embodied woman becomes the mediator between her God and her lover. Indeed, Dante in the *Paradiso* can only look upon the divine light to the extent that it is reflected in the eyes of Beatrice (*Paradiso*, 1.43–69, 2.22–36, and 3.1). She is the material vehicle for the manifestation of the transcendent.[12] Dante is drawing upon the preexisting tradition of the *dolce stil nuovo's* neo-Platonic conception of woman, the roots of which can be traced to Saint Bernard and Saint Bonaventure's visions of the Blessed Virgin as mediator between God and Man.[13] Indeed, in the official ideology of the High Middle Ages, the figure of the feminine has no autonomous, positive value aside from its instrumental subordination to man's salvation. Women exist as part of a seamless web of signs and their referents, which, properly read, can lead men to the divine. In this semiotic world, all is unity. There are no unbridgeable gaps. The whole world exists to be recuperated by a single divine plan. Woman as part of that plan, though fallen, is yet one more signifying substance that reveals God to man.[14]

On the other hand, however, the same fetishization of woman that allows her to function as a moment in the revelation of the divine also pictures her as the "devil's gateway."[15] For her very status as sign labeled her as a potential road to perdition. Woman, according to this view, is never a primary substance but is always, at best, a secondary reflection of that substance, just as she is second in the order of creation in the most commonly cited story from Genesis (2.21–24). Her status as a belated intermediary emphasizes her nature as a material surface, the sensual beauty of which may well serve as a distraction that prevents the beholder from directly intuiting the divine logos, instead of as a mediator that re-presents the always already absent divine.[16] Tertullian, in fact, links woman directly with the concepts of "dress and ornament."[17] As a superficial adornment or decorative embellishment, she may serve, not only as the mirror reflecting divine beauty, but also as the veil that prevents its direct intuition. Consequently, the suspicion under which the rhetorical and poetic arts were held by the early Church Fathers and the learned culture of the Middle Ages was applied to women as well. As R. Howard Bloch writes:

we cannot separate the concept of woman as it was formed in the
early centuries of Christianity from a metaphysics that abhorred
embodiment . . . woman's supervenient nature is, according to such
a mode of thought, indistinguishable from the acute suspicion of
embodied signs.[18]

Thus, while the material world of both women and signs could serve as a
tropological vehicle to reflect the glory of their divine origin, this model of
reading functioned only so long as the letter remained clearly and unambiguously subordinated to the spirit and the sensible to the intelligible, as
in Dante's *Paradiso*. The moment the signifier is granted the least measure
of autonomy from the transcendental signified, it ceases to function as a
vehicle for salvation and transforms itself into the road to damnation.[19]

The problem is that Petrarch's world, however, is no longer that of
Dante and the High Middle Ages.[20] As Thomas Greene and others have
observed, it is precisely Petrarch's rediscovery of the centrality of difference
that marks him as the first poet of the Renaissance. This fact is seen most
clearly in Petrarch's conception of his relation to the ancients. Whereas
Dante and his predecessors saw the ancient world as continuous with their
own, the later Renaissance humanists, in their recognition that the ancient
world was a lost reality that had to be recovered, admitted that their own
world was discontinuous from both that of the ancients and the Middle
Ages. When Politian, a century after Petrarch, announces that there is not
one text of the ancients that we really understand, he affirms the presence
of a new conception of intertextuality that differs radically from that of the
vast majority of his predecessors and many of his contemporaries, men
who, with a clear conscience, could and did transcribe Ovid's *Remedia
Amoris* as "ad laudem et gloriam Virginis Mariae" [for the praise and glory
of the Virgin Mary].[21]

Petrarch's semiotic universe and its vision of its own genealogy is no
longer isomorphic with that of his predecessors. He is caught in the gap
between two different conceptions of intertextuality: one, humanistic and
historical; the other, ecclesiastical and centripetal, consisting of a series of
allegories and moralizing commentaries. Where Dante in the *Commedia* is
invited to join the community of ancient poets and led to the very threshold
of paradise by Vergil, Petrarch in the *Rime sparse* faces a constant combat
against imminent personal dispersion, in which pagan and Christian allusions are, at turns, complementary to and in conflict with one another.[22] At
the center of this conflict is Petrarch's relationship with Laura and the
system of ambivalent connotations and cross-determinations that constitute the Laura/*lauro* figure. Petrarch's work is marked by a new understanding of the historical and rhetorical nature of human discourse—its

material otherness—and, in turn, this understanding itself constitutes a new barrier to the traditional power of the Christian logos to illuminate the individual soul.[23] In this regard, Robert Durling's commentary on Petrarch's choice of the word *fragmenta* to characterize his collection is exemplary:

> For Petrarch the term expresses the intensely self-critical aware-
> ness that all integration of texts and selves is relative, temporary,
> threatened. They flow into multiplicity at the touch of time, their
> inconsistencies juxtaposed as the successive traces of a subject
> who dissolves and leaves only words behind.[24]

Thus Petrarch, in his increased awareness of the materiality and thus historicity of the sign, marks a point in the history of European thought at which both textuality per se and the figure of the feminine as text begin to float free of the integrated system of subordinations that governed their behavior in the symbolic economies of the Middle Ages.[25] The syntax that allowed these subaltern terms (i.e., textuality and the feminine) to function as tropes of the divine begins to disintegrate. The world of Petrarch and his humanist successors is no longer a seamless web of signs and their referents but a brave new world of signifiers that are ever in danger of coming unmoored from their signifieds. Hence the humanists' task is, not only to recover the "true" meaning of ancient texts, long since allegorized in works such as the *Ovide Moralisé* to conform to a Christian teleology, but also implicitly to renegotiate the full realm of signifiers and signifieds, including those connected with the feminine.[26]

One way of doing this was through classical imitation, bringing the fallen world of the present back into conformity with the golden age of its classical past. Yet, as Christians, the humanists were nonetheless forced to confront the radical alterity of their beloved ancients. How were these material signifiers with their various possible signifieds (divine allegories, pagan myths, historical reconstructions, contemporary poetic practices) to be used in ways that did not allow pagan meanings to subvert the divine truth? For the recognition of historical difference, which allows the recuperation of an authentic past, is also that which precludes the process from ever reaching closure.[27] The gap between signifier and signified can never be fully bridged. Thus, as Thomas Greene notes, in the most sophisticated form of *imitatio* practiced by Petrarch, there is always a never fully resolved "conflict between two *mundi significantes*," the polytheist past and the Christian present.[28]

From this perspective, Petrarch's love for Laura and his pursuit of poetic glory through imitation of the ancients can be said to be two parts of the same semiotic matrix. For, when Augustinus links Laura with

Petrarch's literary passion and cites both as distractions from the poet's contemplation of his own salvation, he both questions the signifying function of the feminine, which Dante took for granted, and signals a more general epistemological break. Laura, in fact, is never treated as an autonomous subject but always as a text, both in the *Secretum* and in Petrarch's poetry. As Nicholas Mann observes, her "real substance . . . is her role in the *Canzoniere* and the *Trionfi*: as figure of poetic inspiration, rhetorical ornament and finally moral improvement."[29] Like Beatrice, hers is a signifying body, yet Laura's ability to mediate between the poet and his god is undercut by that very material surface that makes her part of this world rather than the next.[30]

Thus, Augustinus in the *Secretum* charges that Laura's physical beauty has actually changed the nature of Franciscus's immaterial soul and so perverted the natural semiotic order by allowing the material vehicle of signification, the signifier, to alter the spiritual essence of signification, the signified. The problem is then further compounded by Petrarch's seeking an artistic representation of that beauty and so creating a representation of a representation, or the signifier of a signifier, and opening the possibility of an infinite regression:

> Illius mutata frons tibi animum mutavit; letus et mestus pro illius varietate factus es. . . . Quid autem insanius quam, non contentum presenti illius vultus effigie, unde hec cuncta tibi provenerant, aliam fictam illustris artificis ingenio quesivisse, quam tecum ubique circumferens haberes materiam semper immortalium lacrimarum? (156)

> [When she changed her face it changed your soul; you were made happy or sad by her vicissitudes. . . . What however was more insane than when, not content with the image of that face when it was present, from which all these evils sprang, you sought another made by a famous artist, so that carrying it with you everywhere you might always have material for immortal tears?]

The diction in the last part of the passage, where Augustinus refers to Petrarch's commissioning the portrait of Laura, is telling. The representation of Laura by the Sienese painter, Simon, is said to provide a cause (*materia*) for immortal tears. The juxtaposition of *materia* with *immortalis* shows once again how the order of signification, which allowed the medieval *épistémê* to function and women and signs to remain in their places, had been subverted. For that which is material, and hence finite or mortal, is provoking tears that are, not only constant (*semper*), but specifically immortal, thus referring to the sorrows of Petrarch's soul. As Augustinus cries out, earlier in the dialogue, "O cece, necdum intelligis quanta dementia est sic animum rebus subiecisse mortalibus?" [*Aug.* O blind man, do you not yet see how great a madness it is to have subjected your soul to mortal things in this way?] (140).

The appropriateness of such a reading of this passage is confirmed by the two sonnets from the *Rime sparse* in which the problem of the portrait is specifically depicted. Thus, in poem 77, Petrarch remarks:

> L'opra fu ben di quelle che nel cielo
> si ponno imaginar, non qui tra noi,
> ove le membra fanno a l'alma velo. . . .

> [The work is one of those which can be imagined only in Heaven, not here among us, where the body is a veil to the soul. . . .]

Here we find four crucial terms: the body, the soul, the veil, and the true depiction. The representation of Laura is pictured as one that captures the nature of her soul through an earthly rendering. Thus, the immaterial signified appears to be fully captured by its material signifier, the portrait. The paradoxical status of this statement is made clear both by the reference to the body as the veil of the soul,[31] wherein the material world is conceived of as a screen that prevents the intuition of the transcendental rather than as the medium that makes it possible, and by the limits of artistic representation as depicted in the final tercet of the following poem (78.12–14). There Petrarch laments that, however wondrous the portrait might be, unlike Pygmalion's statue in Ovid's *Metamorphoses*, it cannot come to life. It cannot speak. This reference to the world of antiquity is, in turn, paralleled by a similar reference to the Greek sculptor, Polyclitus, in the opening lines of poem 77. Not only do these two allusions constitute an aesthetic framing device tying the sonnets to one another, but also they clearly link the problematic of the status of classical antiquity, and hence of humanist studies in general, to that of Laura, the poet's beloved. Together they form a single meditation on the status of poetry, antiquity, the sign, and representation in relation to the logos at the opening of the Renaissance.

This meditation as described in the *Secretum*, however, produces no easy answers. Indeed, Petrarch's real contribution is not so much that of offering solutions to the problem of representation as it presented itself to his epoch, as it is the production of a series of fruitful and historically significant contradictions and aporias.[32] Thus at times in the *Secretum*, Petrarch goes so far as to deny Laura's manifestly fallen, material nature.

The women of the ancient world were mortal, "mulier mortalis erat Thais et Livia" [Thais was a mortal women, as was Livia], he says. His beloved is a reflection of the divine:

> Ceterum scis ne de ea muliere mentionem tibi exortam, cuius mens terrenarum nescia curarum celestibus desideriis ardet; in cuius aspectu si quid usquam veri est, divini specimen decoris effulget; cuius mores consumate honestatis exemplar sunt; cuius nec vox, nec oculorum vigor mortale aliquid, nec incessus hominem representat? (136)

> [But do you know that you are talking about a woman whose mind, not knowing worldly care, burns with heavenly desire, in whose face, if anything true truly exists, shines a vision of divine beauty; whose habits are a model of absolute probity, of whom neither the voice, nor the liveliness of her eyes are in anyway mortal, nor does her gait seem human?]

At the same time, the uneasy pairing of terms such as *celestis* (heavenly) with *desiderium* (desire) and *ardere* (to burn) with *divinus* (divine), like that we saw earlier between *materia* and *immortalis*, reveals the presence of an unrecuperable terrestrial remainder—an element of purely mortal desire—that will constantly subvert Petrarch's attempts throughout the dialogue to defend the incorporeal nature of his love.

All the same, he argues, Augustinus is mistaken. Laura is the cause of his virtue rather than his fall:

> me, quantulumcunque conspicis, per illam esse; nec unquam ad hoc, si quid est, nominis aut glorie fuisse venturum, nisi virtutum tenuissimam sementem, quam pectore in hoc natura locaverat, nobilissimis hec affectibus coluisset. (144)

> [Whatever little you see me to be, I am through her, nor would I ever have come to this point in my reputation and renown, if she had not cultivated with the most noble sentiments the ever so slight seed of virtue which nature had placed in my breast.]

She is not only a reflection of the divine but the active cause of his nobler pursuits. She does not divert him from the road to salvation but leads him to it. For he has loved only her soul, not her body:

> neque enim, ut tu putas, mortali rei animum addixi; nec me tam corpus noveris amasse quam animam, moribus humana

transcendentibus delectatum, quorum exemplo qualiter inter celicolas vivatur, admoneor. (140)

[For neither, as you think, have I devoted my soul to a mortal affair; nor will you have known me to have loved the body as the soul, since I was attracted by her morals which transcend the merely human. I am instructed by their example as though by one who lives among the heavenly hosts.]

Her body, the mortal signifier of the immortal soul, has been but the necessary vehicle for leading him to the transcendental signified, the divine logos. It is her inner spiritual nature he has loved, not her outer mortal beauty.

Augustinus, however, rejects this neo-Platonic and courtly argument that the love of Laura has led the poet to the love of God.[33] Franciscus, he says, has the order reversed: he should not love the creator because of the creature, but the creature because of the creator. As in the example cited earlier, where a change of Laura's facial expression had changed the nature of Petrarch's soul, Franciscus has perverted the divine semiotic order:

Aug. ab amore celestium elongavit animum et a Creatore ad creaturam desiderium inclinavit. Que una quidem ad mortem pronior fuit via.

Fr. Noli, queso, precipitare sententiam: Deum profecto ut amarem, illius amor prestitit.

Aug. At pervertit ordinem.

Fr. Quonam modo?

Aug. Quia cum creatum omne Creatoris amore diligendum sit, tu contra, creature captus illecebris, Creatorem non qua decuit amasti, sed miratus artificem fuisti quasi nichil ex omnibus formosius creasset, cum tamen ultima pulcritudinum sit forma corporea. (146–48)[34]

[*Aug.* She led your soul away from the love of heavenly things and from the creator she turned your desire toward the one created. Indeed she alone was the speedier route toward death.

Fr. Do not hasten to pass sentence, I beg of you: the love of her has made me truly love God.

Aug. But that perverts the order.

Fr. How so?

Aug. For while each created thing ought to give pleasure through our love of the Creator, you however, captured by the allurements of the creature, have not loved the Creator as was fitting, but you wondered at the craftsman as though he had created nothing at all more beautiful than her, though bodily form is the least of all beauties.]

In the end, after close questioning and frequent admonitions, Petrarch is forced to admit that Laura's physical beauty is what makes her signifying function possible. He loved the signifier before the signified. "*Aug.* Me ne ludis? An si idem animus in squalido et nodoso corpore habitaret, similiter placuisset? *Fr.* Non audeo quidem id dicere" [*Aug.* Are you joking with me? Or if the same soul had inhabited a filthy and misshapen body, would it have pleased you just the same? *Fr.* No, indeed, I do not dare to say it] (148). Thus agreeing with Augustinus, he concedes both her mortality and the priority of her material surface over her signifying function.

Nonetheless, Petrarch responds that, while what Augustinus says may be true in principle—that he loved Laura first for her body, and that in doing so he has perverted the divine semiotic order by placing the signifier before the signified and the creature before the creator–all the same, Petrarch argues, human beings achieve knowledge through the senses and so must rise from the material to the spiritual. For these are the epistemological shackles in which we are born:

Fr. neque enim animus cerni potest, nec imago corporis talem spopondisset; at si oculis appareret, amarem profecto pulcritudinem animi deforme licet habentis habitaculum.

Aug. . . . . si . . . nonnisi quod oculis apparet amare potes, corpus igitur amasti. (148)

[*Fr.* For neither is the soul able to be seen, nor could the appearance of the body guarantee a corresponding soul, but if it did appear to my eyes, truly I would love the beauty of the soul even if it had an ugly home.

Aug. . . . . If . . . you are only able to love what appears to your eyes, then you loved her body.]

We can only know what we can perceive, Petrarch contends, and thus we reason from appearances to that which transcends them. Consequently, the material must precede the eternal in this epistemological order of things.

This argument is analogous to the whole humanist problematic. The meaning of the text can only be established through an understanding of its historical and material specificity, through the evidence gathered by our perceptions. This is what makes the recovery of antiquity possible. But, to base our readings on our perceptions of the text's historical determinations is ultimately to deny the presence of a divine logos, in the Platonic sense, that anchors and guarantees all meaning. For the concrete, material specificity of the letter may never be completely subordinated to the spirit. It always leaves a trace or remainder.[35]

Here we have arrived at the root epistemological question that governs the structure of book 3 of the *Secretum* from beginning to end and thus its dual problematization of women and signs. The medieval *épistémê* was ruled by the presence of a sovereign signified ruthlessly subordinating all texts to a preexisting meaning. Yet, for Petrarch, it is no longer clear that meaning can be separated from the means of transmitting it.[36] The order of the divine may require the signified to precede the signifier, but human perception necessarily proceeds in inverse order.

Indeed, other analogous statements from Franciscus on the necessity of mortals using the means available to them can be found throughout the *Secretum*. Thus, later in the third book when the discussion shifts away from Laura to the second of the two adamantine chains binding Petrarch, his desire for poetic glory, Franciscus defends his pursuit of mortal glory as that which is fitting for the merely human:

> *Fr.* Neque enim deus fieri cogito, qui vel eternitatem habeam vel celum terrrasque complectar. Humana michi satis est gloria; ad illam suspiro, et mortalis nonnisi mortalia concupisco.

> *Aug.* O te, si vera memoras, infelicem! si non cupis immortalia, si eterna non respicis, totus es terreus. . . .

> *Fr.* . . . istum esse ordinem, ut mortalium rerum inter mortales prima sit cura; transitoriis eterna succedant, quod ex his ad illa sit ordinatissimus progressus. (194–98)

> [*Fr.* For I do not desire to become a god, so that I might possess eternity or embrace heaven and earth. Human glory is enough for me; I aspire to that, and as a mortal I only desire mortal things.

> *Aug.* Oh you unhappy man, if you speak truly. If you do not desire immortal things, if you do not look for the eternal, you are completely terrestial. . . .

> *Fr.* . . . . this is the [proper] order, that among mortals the first care
> should be for mortal affairs; then let eternal things come after
> transitory ones, because from these affairs to those is the most
> orderly progression.]

Thus Franciscus implicitly proposes what might be called an inductive strategy of reading, as opposed to Augustinus' deductive strategy. Nor is there any mean point between them, as Franciscus says later "sedes vestra celum est, michi autem terrena nondum finitur habitatio" [your seat is heaven, my earthly stay however is not yet finished] (212). In short, they live in separate realms and therefore do not possess the same set of epistemological constraints.

The problem, then, from Petrarch's perspective (and he inhabits both voices in this dialogue) is strictly insoluble.[37] How is one to know the meaning produced by a given signifier, if the only way to be sure is to possess that meaning before the act of interpretation begins? How can one possess the signified without moving through the material medium that makes meaning in the world possible? The problem recurs throughout the dialogue. Augustinus, for example, eventually persuades Franciscus that his love for Laura is sinful, and Petrarch asks him how he may escape it. Augustinus replies that he must first stop desiring her. Petrarch retorts that if he did not desire her, he would not love her (160–66). As Victoria Kahn writes, "The problem is that to use the text correctly, one already has to have the rectified will that the text is supposed to educate, just as in order to flee Laura, Franciscus must have the resolution that he can only acquire by having already fled."[38] Similarly, Augustinus later argues that Petrarch should not seek glory, the worldly manifestation of success, but should pursue virtue—the reality behind that manifestation. Glory will then devolve to him of its own accord (204–06).

In each of these cases, Augustinus argues that men must pursue the transcendent (i.e., the divine, freedom from desire, and virtue) while letting the material take care of itself. Nonetheless, Petrarch each time responds that human beings exist in the world of the sensible and can only perceive the transcendent through its mediation. They are always caught up in a world of interpretation. If signifiers possessed a necessary link with their signifieds, this problem would not occur and meaning would be self-evident. But, in the fallen historical world of the humanists, meaning is contingent and historically variable. There are no unmediated truths.[39] Our meanings are not only in this world, but of this world.

To recapitulate, the debate between Petrarch and Augustine centers around Laura's function as a signifier in both Petrarch's life and work. Does she make the transcendental signified, God's logos, manifest to the senses, or does she deflect the poet's thoughts from the eternal to the merely temporal? Does Laura as a signifier possess a natural and necessary relationship to the signified, or does she merely lead to an infinite chain of other signifiers, forever deferring the moment of ultimate revelation and conversion?[40] The Augustinian moment of conversion, it should be remembered, is instantaneous and absolute. It is an end point that manifests a significance present from its very origin, and hence it constitutes a new beginning or rebirth of the self.[41] The signified, in fact, produces the signifier and controls it at its own discretion. Thus, in opposition to Petrarch, there is no inductive, tropological process, no need for the externalities of rhetoric.

In this light, the relationship between Petrarch's love of Laura and his pursuit of poetic glory comes into sharper focus. For poetry, like Laura, is a text that seduces by the beauty of its signifying surface, while, at the same time, promising its lover the possibility of a transcendental signified, if only he is patient enough to delve deeper. But here, too, in the *Secretum* as in life, it is an unresolved question whether poetry's many tropological turnings ever produce the desired moment of revelation.[42] Thus, at one point in the dialogue, when Augustinus has convinced Franciscus of the immoral nature of his love for Laura, the poet asks him how he might free himself from this first of the two adamantine chains that bind him. Augustinus responds by citing a passage from Ovid's *Remedia Amoris*, which advises, "successore novo vincitur omnis amor" [every love is conquered by its new successor] (162). Franciscus rejects this option on the grounds that it will lead merely to an infinite series of substitutive relationships, an endless chain of signifiers with no final redeeming signified, "Ereptum vero uni iugo collum per infinita sordidorum servitiorum genera circumferre non laudo" [Truly I do not approve of carrying my neck around through an endless series of filthy servile relationships, once I have freed it from one yoke] (162). This passage not only enacts the association of Laura with poetry, through the citation of Ovid, but also demonstrates an implied semiotic equivalence between Laura and the poetic text, in their mutual ability to serve as signifiers that promise a full plenitude of meaning yet often lead merely to a chain of still more signifiers. Neither poetry nor love, in the end, can guarantee closure. Love, poetry, and the world of the literary text become interchangeable, at this level.

This notion of the dangerous creation of a beautiful surface that promises meaningful depths is, of course, familiar from Tertullian, who, as we noted earlier, defined dress and ornament as two of women's essential traits in their function as the devil's gateway. In a similar vein, Petrarch in book 3 of the *Secretum* must defend, not only his love for Laura and his pursuit of poetic glory, but also his fondness for garnishing his works with quotations from ancient authors (178–80)[43] and his use of stylistic ornament

(204). In the case of both women and texts, the problem is essentially the same: what are we to make of the erotics of reading? Do the pleasures of love and the text lead us on to deeper meanings, or do they seduce us into remaining on the surface and reveling in merely sensual delights? Is rhetoric merely a form of harlotry, a seduction of the flesh that ultimately denies the possibility of transcending the world of the merely material for that of the eternal and spiritual? As Augustinus in book 2 asks in regard to Franciscus's humanistic studies, "Lectio autèm ista quid profuit?" [What moreover has that reading accomplished?] (72). For, to receive pleasure from words, he says, is to be like birds who sing themselves to death, delighting in the sweetness of their own songs (74).[44] It is a self-destructive fetishization of the signifier to the detriment of what is really important, the transcendental signified.

Augustinus only approves of literary texts to the extent that they can be subordinated to the ruling Christian logos, even if this involves doing damage to the philological integrity of the text. Thus, at the end of book 2, Franciscus cites Vergil's description of the storm loosed by Aeolus on Aeneas's fleet in book 1 of the *Aeneid* as an allegory of how the body and its associated passions must be ruled by reason (Aeolus) or they will lead men to destruction (the storm). Augustinus replies that he approves of this reading, even if Vergil never intended such a meaning:

> Laudo hec, quibus abundare te video, poetice narrationis archana. Sive enim id Vergilius ipse sensit, dum scriberet, sive ab omni tali consideratione remotissimus, maritimam his versibus et nil aliud describere voluit tempestatem; hoc tamen, quod de irarum impetu et rationis imperio dixisti, facete satis et proprie dictum puto. (124–26)[45]

> [I praise these hidden parts of the poetic narrative of which I see you find so many. For whether Vergil himself understood it, while he was writing, or any such consideration was the furthest thing from his mind and he wished to describe nothing other than a storm at sea with his verses; nonetheless what you said about the onset of anger and the rule of reason, I think has been said with due elegance and propriety.]

The passage reveals a kind of historical schizophrenia at work in Petrarch's text. On the one hand, Augustinus praises Franciscus's subjection of this complex and multivalent scene from the *Aeneid* to a reductive and anachronistic reading that rigorously asserts the hegemony of the Christian transcendental signified. On the other, he readily admits the possibility that such a reading may be false from the perspective of authorial intent and that the transcendental signified cannot completely account for the historical specificity of the signifier.[46] The letter must be subordinated to the spirit, but, in the brave new world of the Renaissance, it is not clear that the spirit is up to the task.

The pleasures of the text, then, are those of the flesh; and the body, as Augustinus never ceases to remind us, is unclean. We should contemplate only its ultimate putrefaction, so as to keep our minds fixed on death and the world beyond the senses (46, 54, 168). This is especially true of the female body, he notes, which is particularly fetid, but carries within it a poison that causes men to forget its transitory nature:

> Pauci enim sunt qui, ex quo semel virus illud illecebrose voluptatis imbiberint, femenei corporis feditatem, de qua loquor, sat viriliter, ne dicam satis constanter, examinerint. (188)

> [For few are those who, after having once drunk in the poison of seductive pleasure, examine with sufficient masculine vigor (*viriliter*), not to say constancy, the putridness of the female body.]

Thus, Laura's body is a sign that succeeds only in obscuring its own corruption. It is a beautiful surface that blocks the poet's vision of his own mortality in the same way that his pursuit of poetic glory gives him delusions of secular immortality.[47] It is no coincidence, then, that it is on this very page that Augustinus begins his assault on the second adamantine chain binding the poet, the desire for poetic glory:

> Sed quoniam, tametsi pro necessitate tua pauca quidem, pro brevitate autem temporis satis multa de uno morbo dicta sunt, ad alia transeamus. Restat ultimum malum quod in te curare nunc aggrediar. . . . Gloriam hominum et immortalitem nominis plus debito cupis.

> [But since, although with respect to your needs it has been very little, yet with respect to the brevity of time sufficiently much has been said about one malady, let us move on to other things. There remains one final evil in you which I shall try to cure now. . . . You desire the glory of men and the immortality of your name more than you should.]

The use of the word *cupio* (desire) here clearly reveals that, from Augustinus's perspective, poetic and carnal desire are two different examples of a single phenomenon. Nonetheless, even his own discourse—or that of Petrarch speaking through him—does not completely escape the snares of this carnal knowledge, as when he recommends that the "putridness of the female body" be examined "with sufficiently masculine vigor." For the adverb *viriliter*, derived from the word for man, or even husband, *vir*, genders this act of examination in such a fashion that, in any other context, one might easily read this sentence as advocating exactly the opposite of what we are meant to believe Augustinus intends. A virile examination of the female body might lead to results other than what the saint seems to be recommending. The affective and titillating language suggests a fascination with the very act he is forbidding.[48] Indeed, by itself, the sentence seems more fitted to the language of the bawdy comedy of the double entendre than to a rigorous interrogation of conscience and the pursuit of sin. Nor is this aspect of Augustinus's diction the result of a single, isolated slip, for in the sentence immediately preceding the passage quoted, Augustinus says, "Verum hoc acriter viriliterque cogitandum est" [But this should be thought about with acute masculine vigor]. Thus, even for Augustinus, it seems, the letter is never fully subordinated to the spirit.[49]

All the same, his consciously articulated position is clear. The poet must abandon both love and fame (206).[50] Indeed, the two are causally connected:

> Ista quoque, quam tuam predicas ducem a multis te obscenis abstrahens in splendidum impulit baratrum. . . . Iam quod innumeris illam te laboribus implicuisse commemoras, hoc unum verum predicas. Quid autem hic tam magni muneris invenias, cogita. Cum multiformes enim sint labores, quos declinare non licet, quanta dementia est novos sponte sectari! At quod fame clarioris avidum per illam te factum esse gloriaris, compatior errori tuo. (146, see also 182)[51]

> [She too, whom you call your leader, while pulling you away from filthy deeds, pushed you into a splendid abyss. . . . When now you say that she involved you in countless (poetic) labors, this is true. Think, however, of what kind of reward you will receive for this. For when there are so many tasks which it is not permitted to decline, how great a madness it is to seek new ones of your own volition. And because you revel in having been made hungry for greater fame through her, I pity your error.]

It is the poet's love for Laura that has driven him to seek poetic fame. On this level, the laurels and Laura are one. Neither exists without the other. Petrarch, moreover, by concentrating on the things of this world, is forfeiting the next: "Nichil est quod eque oblivionem Dei contemptum ve pariat atque amor rerum temporalium" [Nothing else equally produces the forgetting or even contempt of God as does the love of temporal affairs] (154).[52] "Amor rerum temporalium" [love of temporal affairs], of course, applies equally well to Laura and poetry. Laura, thus, according to Augustinus, does not represent a mediation between God and the poet, but an idol or fetish.[53] The sign is not transparent but opaque. Where Beatrice was a "mediatrix," Laura, in John Freccero's words, is "a brilliant surface, a pure signifier."[54]

Augustinus further solidifies the link between Laura and the poet's pursuit of glory by asserting that ultimately Petrarch loved her name as much as or more than he loved her (42, 158, 186). In doing so, Augustinus alludes to Petrarch's use throughout the *Canzoniere* of Ovid's retelling of the Apollo and Daphne myth as a metaphor for his own pursuit of love, glory, and transcendent metamorphosis. Laura thus stands, not only for poetry and the laurel that crowns the poet's success, but also for the rhetoric of classical imitation that allows him to achieve it. She becomes one with the signifying body, par excellence, the literature of the ancients (see for example *Rime Sparse* 5 and 6). Again, the essential problem with Petrarch's fixation on Laura's name is his excessive focus on the signifier rather than the signified, on surface rather than depth, while the polyvalent nature of Laura's name (denoting a woman, the myth, poetry, and Petrarch's status as laureate) is precisely an illustration of that very sense of semiotic instability that we earlier noted as defining the Renaissance.[55]

Finally, Petrarch's identification of the feminine body with the materiality of the signifier is at one with a consistent trend not only in the Middle Ages but throughout western thought in which women are associated with the body rather than the spirit, with the signifier rather than the signified.[56] They represent the world of matter, men the realm of the spirit. Accordingly, women are inextricably linked to the damnation inherent in fixating on the merely material. The ultimate aporia of this line of thought, though, is found in Petrarch's initial response to Augustinus: men live in the world of the material and can only rise through it to the ideal. In this way, the inferior and subjugated terms in this series of binary oppositions— the feminine, the material, the signifier—always threaten to reassert their presence. The historical threatens to undo the eternal. By the same token, while Petrarch never denies the validity of Augustinus's arguments, he also never agrees to abandon his love for Laura nor his pursuit of poetic glory (212–14).[57] In so doing, he helps create a new poetic space that opens the way for the next two centuries of secular verse through his ultimate refusal to deny himself the seductions of the signifying surface.[58]

To conclude, the unstable position of the figure of the feminine and the sign in Petrarch's text, as we have just outlined it, is important for two reasons. First, as we have seen, the position of the beloved in Petrarch is different from that found in the late Medieval tradition, where women, though seen as related to the fallen and the material, were also viewed as possible vehicles for men's salvation.[59] They were part of the divine plan. But, with Petrarch's heightened sense of historical difference, the role of the beloved in the lover's salvation, just as the role of ancient and poetic texts in the revelation of the divine logos, is radically questioned. In this new *épistémê*, the figure of the feminine has more autonomy and therefore becomes more dangerous.

The second and more important thing our examination has shown is that the figure of the feminine in Petrarch does not exist as a value in itself. Rather, gender, I would assert, is always just one element in the complex ideological and epistemic structures that constitute the belief system of a given society.[60] And thus, while certain elements in gender relations remain constant over long periods of time, such as the tendency to link the feminine with the material and the masculine with the spiritual, the way those constants play themselves out and the precise effects those processes generate thereby depend upon the nature and positioning of their implication in the larger structures of discourse and power that govern the social whole. It is only by following these figures of gender and gendered figures throughout the complex turnings of their textual and ideological existences that it is possible to speak meaningfully about the issues they raise and see those issues as part of a larger, totalizing structure, rather than as uncomplicated ends in themselves. For then those figures are ever left open to new strategies of appropriation.

Notes

I would like to thank Professors Barbara K. Gold, Charles Platter, and Edward V. George for their invaluable suggestions in revising this essay.

1. Thomas Greene, *The Light in Troy: Imitation and Discovery in Renaissance Poetry* (New Haven, CT: Yale University Press, 1982), p. 8.

2. R. Howard Bloch, *Medieval Misogyny and the Invention of Western Romantic Love* (Chicago: University of Chicago Press, 1991), p. 46.

3. Francesco Petrarca, *Secretum*, ed. Enrico Carara, *Prose* (Milano: Riccardo Ricciardi, 1955), p. 130: "*Aug.* Duabus adhuc adamantinis dextra levaque premeris cathenis, que nec de morte neque de vita sinunt cogitare." [You are held down by two adamantine chains which allow you to think about neither life nor death.] All

further citations will be from this volume and given in the text. For a similar image, see *Rime sparse* 264, "I'vo pensando," lines 81–83, where the poet describes his raft as being held among the rocks by two knots. The text and translation of this and all other passages from the *Rime Sparse* are from Robert M. Durling, ed. and trans., *Petrarch's Lyric Poems: The Rime Sparse and Other Lyrics* (Cambridge: Harvard Universiy Press, 1976). On 264, as a vernacular and poetic version of book 3 of the *Secretum*, see Giles Constable, "Petrarch and Monasticism," in *Francesco Petrarca Citizen of the World: Proceedings of the World Petrarch Congress, Washington D. C., April 6–13, 1974*, ed. Aldo S. Bernardo (Albany: State University Press of New York, 1980), pp. 58–59 and 77–76; and Hans Baron, *Petrarch's "Secretum": Its Making and Its Meaning* (Cambridge, MA: The Medieval Academy of America, 1985), pp. 47 and 55–56.

4. For an example of this formula, see David A. Carozza and H. James Shey, *Petrarch's "Secretum": With Introduction, Notes and Critical Anthology* (New York: Peter Lang, 1989), p. 16.

5. For a good analysis of this problem and a survey of the relevant bibliography, see Sara Sturm-Maddox, *Petrarch's Laurels* (University Park: Pennsylvania State University Press, 1992), pp. 1–3.

6. See, for example, *Rime sparse* 5, 22.34, 23.39–40.

7. See Richard Waswo, *Language and Meaning in the Renaissance* (Princeton: Princeton University Press, 1987), p. 36, on how, in Renaissance and Medieval rhetoric, "Beside the linguistic dichotomy of word/thing or sign/signified stands the rhetorical one of style/thought or manner/matter, neatly lined up with other dualisms that constitute the theoretical frameworks of ontology (human/divine, flesh/spirit), epistemology (sensible/intelligible), and moral psychology (passion/reason)."

8. Jean-Joseph Goux, *Symbolic Economies*, trans. Jennifer Curtiss Gage (Ithaca, NY: Cornell University Press, 1990), pp. 171 and 174–75; Greene, *Light in Troy*, p. 30.

9. Greene, *Light in Troy*, p. 12.

10. Baron, *Petrarch's "Secretum,"* pp. 5–6.

11. Victoria Kahn, "The Figure of the Reader in Petrarch's *Secretum*," *PMLA* 100.2 (1985): p. 156, see also p. 164.

12. Joan Ferrante, *Woman as Image in Medieval Literature: From the Twelfth Century to Dante* (New York: Columbia University Press, 1975), pp. 129–31, 141 and 152.

13. Ferrante, *Women as Image*, pp. 3, 100, 122–23, and 127.

14. Greene, *Light in Troy*, pp 85–86; Paul Zumthor, *Essai de poétique médiévale* (Paris: Seuil, 1972), pp. 34–35; Thomas H. Greer, *A Brief History of the Western World* (New York: Harcourt, Brace, Jovanovich, 1987), p. 238, cited in Kim Robertson,

"Heteroglossia, History, and Humanism: Bakhtin's Novel Perspective on the Renaissance," *Recapturing the Renaissance: New Perspectives on Humanism, Dialogue, and Texts*, eds. Diane S. Wood and Paul Allen Miller, (Knoxville, TN: New Paradigm Press, 1996).

On woman as both *res* and *signum*, see Ferrante, *Women as Image*, pp. 1 and 61. See also Umberto Eco et al., "On Animal Language," in *On the Medieval Theory of Signs*, eds. Umberto Eco and Constantino Marmo (Philadelphia: John Benjamins Publishing Company, 1989), p. 4, on Saint Augustine's collapsing of the ancient world's distinction between natural signs (such as symptoms that are the signs of a disease) and conventional signs (i.e., language), thus creating a unified semiotic network.

15. R. Howard Bloch, *Medieval Misogyny*, pp. 11 and 90.

16. R. Howard Bloch, *Medieval Misogyny*, p. 29, "The patristic articulation of gender assumes a relationship of male to female built upon the analogy of the world of intelligence to that of the senses. Such an idea has, of course, deep roots in Platonic tradition. Yet it was Philo Judaeus (c. 20 B.C.–c. A.D. 50) who, under the influence of models of interpretation of Alexandrian Middle Platonism of the first century B.C., transformed the Genesis story into an 'allegory of the soul in which man is mind and woman sense perception.'" See also p. 25.

17. "De Cultu," 16 cited in R. Howard Bloch, *Medieval Misogyny*, p. 41.

18. R. Howard Bloch, *Medieval Misogyny*, p. 37, see also pp. 31–33, 40, 44–47.

19. R. Howard Bloch, *Medieval Misogyny*, p. 32, "The 'genderized opposition' of the letter to the spirit can also be seen to participate in . . . [the] radical privileging of the signified over the signifier in the Christianized Platonism of the West."

20. On the collapse of the ontological link between words and things, as exhibited by Dante, in the linguistic assumptions of the Renaissance, see Waswo, *Language and Meaning*, pp. 59–60, including n. 59, and 70.

21. Politian, *Prosatori latini del Quattrocento*, ed. Eugenio Garin (Milan: R. Ricciardi, 1952), p. 598, cited in Greene, *Light in Troy*, p. 9. For an illustrative distinction between Medieval and Renaissance readings of Vergil, including the contrasting interpretive strategies of Dante and Petrarch, see Craig Kallendorf, *In Praise of Aeneas: Virgil and Epideictic Rhetoric in the Early Italian Renaissance* (Hanover, NH: University Press of New England, 1989), pp. 1–8 and 14. On the *Remedia*, see Pierre Nolhac, *Pétrarque et l'humanisme* (Paris: Librairie Honoré Champion, 1965, first printed in 1907), second edition, vol. 1, p. 178. See also Robertson, "Heteroglossia," pp. 1–5.

22. Greene, *Light in Troy*, pp. 17, 29–30. For Dante's *Commedia* as a pivotal work in the shift between a Medieval concept of a vertical unity of discourses and the Renaissance's increased awareness of the horizontal plane of historicity, see Mikhail Bakhtin, "Forms of Time and Chronotope in the Novel," in *The Dialogic Imagination*, ed. Michael Holquist, trans. Caryl Emerson and Holquist (Austin: University of Texas Press, 1981), pp. 156–58. For the significance of Petrarch's title, *Rime sparse*, see Durling, *Petrarch's Lyric Poems*, p. 26. On the theme of personal

dispersion, see Nancy J. Vickers, "Diana Described: Scattered Woman and Scattered Rhyme," *Critical Inquiry*, 8.2 (Winter 1981): p. 277.

For Petrarch's desire to create a new unity between rhetoric and poetry on the one hand, and philosophy and theology on the other, the effect of which would be to neutralize the material specificity of the sign, see Charles Trinkaus, "Petrarch and the Tradition of a Double Consciousness," *The Poet as Philosopher: Petrarch and the Formation of Renaissance Consciousness* (New Haven, CT: Yale University Press, 1979), in particular p. 41.

23. See Greene, *Light in Troy*, pp. 81–126; Durling, *Petrarch's Lyric Poems*, pp. 32–33; and Kahn, "Figure of the Reader," pp. 154–66, where she shows that, for Petrarch, citations from ancient sources were no longer automatically neutralized in their rhetorical otherness by the medieval concept of *auctoritas*.

24. Durling, *Petrarch's Lyric Poems*, p. 26.

25. See Ernst Cassirer on the related contradiction between Petrarch's new, humanist curiosity about the external and natural world and the contrary need to retreat into Augustinian inwardness as exemplified in the "Ascent of Mount Ventoux," when Cassirer writes: "He sees nature and man, the world and history in a new splendour; but time and again this splendour itself seems blinding and seductive" (*The Individual and the Cosmos in Renaissance Philosophy*, trans. Mario Domandi [Philadelphia: University of Pennsylvania Press, 1972], p. 144). Lyell Asher, "Petrarch at the Peak of Fame," *PMLA* 108.5 (1993): pp. 1051–52, sees the "Ascent of Mount Ventoux" as traversed by a "tension" between "reverent forms" and "irreverent aims."

26. Goux, *Symbolic Economics*, p. 174; Gerald Bruns, "What Is Tradition?" *New Literary History* 22 (1991): pp. 4 and 7–9; Glenda McLeod, *Virtue and Venom: Catalogs of Women from Antiquity to the Renaissance* (Ann Arbor: University of Michigan Press, 1991): pp. 61–62; Greene, *Light of Troy*, pp. 16–17, 29–30. It should be noted that Greene does not deny Dante a historical consciousness but sees it as partial and fragmentary compared to Petrarch's. For Petrarch's own statements on the dangers of reading and the polysemous nature of texts, see *Familiares* 2.8.822 and Kahn, "Figure of the Reader," p. 154.

27. Greene, *Light in Troy*, pp. 98 and 195; Margaret McGowan, *Ideal Forms in the Age of Ronsard* (Berkeley and Los Angeles: University of California Press, 1985), p. 6. See also Enrico Carrara, *Francesco Petrarca*, *"Il mio segreto"* (Florence: Sansoni, 1943), translated and reprinted in Carozza and Shey, *Petrarch's "Secretum,"* p. 249.

28. Greene, *Light in Troy*, p. 46. In Petrarch, this problem is ultimately left unresolved. For many of the later poetic humanists, the balance shifts decisively toward history, the secular, and woman as object of erotic rather than spiritual desire. See, for example, the sonnets of Ronsard, the late Du Bellay, Sidney, and Shakespeare; Paul Allen Miller, "Sidney, Petrarch, and Ovid, or Imitation as Subversion," *ELH* 58 (1991): pp. 499–522.

29. Nicholas Mann, *Petrarch* (Oxford: Oxford University Press, 1984), p. 95; on Laura as displaced by the desire for writing, see also Kahn, "Figure of the Reader," p. 162.

30. Sturm-Maddox, *Petrarch's Laurels*, p. 61: "In the Laura of the *Rime* the roles of Beatrice and the siren, the positive and the negative are combined."

31. This image recurs at line 114 of *Rime sparse* 264.

32. On the integral nature of oxymoron and contradiction to Petrarchan thought, see Greene, *Light in Troy*, p. 118.

33. Rocco Montano, "La prese di conscienza: Il *Secretum*," *Lo spirito e le lettere* (Milano: Mazorati, 1970), vol. 1, translated and reprinted in Carozza and Shey, *Petrarch's "Secretum,"* p. 215.

34. See also ibid., pp. 144–46; and G. A. Levi, "Pensiero classico e pensiero cristiano nel *Secretum* et nelle *Familiari* del Petrarca," *Atene e Roma* 35 (1933), translated and reprinted in Carozza and Shey, *Petrarch's "Secretum,"* p. 234.

35. Jacques Derrida, *Of Grammatology*, trans. Gayatri Chakravorty Spivak (Baltimore: Johns Hopkins University Press, 1976), pp. 61–73.

36. In Derridean terms, Augustinus consistently privileges *phoné*, the immediate presence of meaning to the soul, while Petrarch sees meaning for human beings as indistinguishable from *écriture*, a signification that is ultimately fallen, external, and corporeal. See *Of Grammatology*, p. 17. On the pertinence of this distinction to Petrarch and Medieval theology, see Asher, "Petrarch," pp. 1053–54.

37. As Durling poses the question: how does the trope or the figure reveal the real without also revealing its imposition on it? See "The Ascent of Mont Ventoux and the Crisis of Allegory," *Italian Quarterly*, 18 (1974): p. 8: "A preliminary formulation of what Petrarch is developing in the ascent of Ventoux would be as follows: for experience to be valid, it must conform to the pre-established patterns provided by the religious tradition: the traditional analysis of the transition from old to new (conversion), and the examples of successful embodiment of the paradigms. But if one's experience does conform, it is suspect: it is subject to the experience of having been pre-arranged."

38. Kahn, "Figure of the Reader," p. 162.

39. John Freccero, "The Fig Tree and the Laurel: Petrarch's Poetics," *Diacritics* 5 (1975): p. 36; Kahn, "Figure of the Reader," pp. 163–64.

40. Greene, *Light in Troy*, pp. 110–11; Kahn, "Figure of the Reader," p. 163.

41. See *Confessions*, 8.12, where Augustine reads the famed passage from Paul's *Letter to the Romans*, "nec ultra volui legere, nec opus erat. statim quippe cum fine huiusce sententiae, quasi *luce* securitatis infusa cordi meo, omnes dubitationis *tenebrae* diffugerent," emphasis added [Neither did I want to read more, nor was it necessary. Indeed immediately at the end of this very sentence all shadows of doubt

fled, as if the light of certitude had flooded into my heart], vol. 1, p. 464, Loeb Classical Library (Cambridge: Harvard University Press, 1977); Freccero, "Fig Tree and Laurel," p. 36; Francis X. Murphy, "Petrarch and the Christian Philosophy," in *Francesco Petrarca Citizen of the World*, ed. Aldo S. Bernardo (Albany: State University of New York Press, 1980), p. 239; Kahn, "Figure of the Reader," pp. 156–57.

42. Bloch, *Medieval Misogyny*, p. 58, "The danger of the feminine . . . is that of the undecideability of poetry itself."

43. Kahn, "Figure of the Reader," p. 160.

44. Kahn, "Figure of the Reader," pp. 160 and 163. For a comparison with Boethius's having been misled by the surface beauty of the Muses, see Ferrante, *Woman as Image*, p. 48.

45. For another example of Petrarch endorsing an allegorical strategy of reading, see letter 10.4 to his brother Gherardo, in which he provides a key to decoding his first *Eclogue*. The central conflicts in this poem, according to Petrarch's own reading, revolve around the questions of whether or not he should enter a monastery as his brother did, and of whether it is better to write religious poetry, as represented by the Psalms, or secular poetry, as embodied by Vergil and Homer. Once again, the value of the ancients, of poetry, and of secular life are inextricably tied to the possibility of a reading that privileges a preexisting, transcendental signified and seeks to nullify the aleatory specificity of the material text. Yet, the very fact that Petrarch must provide his brother with such specific instructions, in the context of a letter that seeks to defend poetry as "not in the least contrary to theology" reveals that the danger of an "errant" reading always lies just beneath the surface. Thus, while the letter says that in the poem, "Apollo" stands for "Jesus"— an interpretation that makes possible a salvational reading of the Daphne and Apollo subtext surrounding Laura in the *Rime sparse*—nonetheless, if the assimilation of the pagan deity by his Christian "counterpart" were as complete as Petrarch pretends, then there would be no need to defend his pursuit of Laura and poetic glory in the *Secretum*, nor for the opening sonnet of the *Rime sparse*, in which he terms both his love and his poetry a "juvenile error," while still publishing the collection. See Francesco Petrarca, *Letters on Familiar Matters, Rerum familiarum libri IX–XVI*, trans. Aldo S. Bernardo (Baltimore, MD: Johns Hopkins University Press, 1982), pp. 69–75; Petrarca, *Poesie Latine*, ed. Guido Martellotti and Enrico Bianchi (Torino: Giulio Einaudi, 1976), pp. 186–95; Constable, "Petrarch and Monasticism," p. 77.

46. As Craig Kallendorf notes, "the increasing historical sophistication that Petrarch and his followers brought to their scholarship made the vision of Virgil as prophet of a divinely ordained Roman Empire look increasingly naive. As the Renaissance humanists became more self-conscious about their renewed interest in antiquity, they became increasingly aware of how different pagan culture was from that of Charlemagne, for example, and how difficult it was to make Virgil into a prophet of Christ" (*In Praise of Aeneas*, p. 8). This same allegory of the winds of Aeolus is also discussed later (pp. 28–30) in reference to its appearance in *Seniles* 4.5. Here Kallendorf lucidly contrasts this example of Petrarch's Christianizing

revision of Vergil with passages found elsewhere that express the poet's profound uneasiness with his model's paganism (*Familiares* 22.10) and with Aeneas's "sacrifices to demons . . . (Francesco Petrarca, *Opere latine*, p. 740)." Thus, the kind of historical schizophrenia that we detect in the passage just cited from the *Secretum* is hardly an isolated incident, but rather appears to be constitutive of the poet's often complex and conflicted relation to antiquity. On the continued existence of this "reading of the *Aeneid* as a Neoplatonic allegory . . . in the early Renaissance," see Diana Robin, *Filelfo in Milan* (Princeton: Princeton University Press, 1991), p. 155.

47. Mann, *Petrarch*, p. 92.

48. I owe this particular formulation to Barbara K. Gold.

49. For another example of Petrarch's rhetoric undercutting the position his characters are ostensibly advocating, see Carrara, *Francesco Petrarca*, p. 247.

50. Carozza and Shey, *Petrarch's "Secretum,"* p. 12.

51. Compare *Rime sparse* 360.84–135, where Love defends his actions to Reason by claiming that he has kept Petrarch "pure and clean," while restraining him from "a thousand vicious acts." On 360's relation to the *Secretum*, see Francesco Tateo, *Dialogo interiore e polemica ideologica nel "Secretum" de Petrarca* (Florence: Le Monnier, 1965), translated and reprinted in Carroza and Shey, *Petrarch's "Secretum,"* p. 266.

52. Mann, *Petrarch*, pp. 93–94.

53. Ferrante, *Woman as Image*, pp. 21–22.

54. Freccero, "Fig Tree and Laurel," pp. 39–40; see also Greene's important corrections, *Light in Troy*, pp. 114–15.

55. Freccero, "Fig Tree and Laurel," pp. 37–38; Carrara, *Francesco Petrarca*, pp. 246–47; Greene, *Light in Troy*, pp. 113–14 and 126; Margo Cottino-Jones, "The Myth of Apollo and Daphne in Petrarch's *Canzoniere*: The Dynamics and Literary Function of Transformation," in *Francis Petrarch, Six Centuries Later: A Symposium*, ed. Aldo Scaglione, North Carolina Studies in the Romance Languages and Literatures: Symposia, vol. 3 (Chapel Hill and Chicago: Department of Romance Languages, University of North Carolina and the Newberry Library, 1975), pp. 152–57; and Durling, "Petrarch's 'Giovene donna sotto un verde lauro,'" *Modern Language Notes* 86.1 (1971): p. 11, n. 14.

56. For the Middle Ages, see Ferrante, *Woman as Image*, pp. 6, 8, 19, and 40–41; and Bloch, *Medieval Misogyny*, pp. 26–29. More generally, see Goux, *Symbolic Economics*, pp. 5, 90, 136–37, 146, 222–23, and 231; Hélène Cixous and Cathérine Clément, *The Newly Born Woman*, trans. Betsy Wing (Minneapolis: University of Minnesota Press, 1986), pp. 50, 95, and 100; Julia Kristeva, "About Chinese Women," in *The Kristeva Reader*, ed. Toril Moi, trans. Seán Hand (New York: Columbia

University Press, 1986), pp. 141 and 151; and Luce Irigaray, *This Sex Which is Not One*, trans. Catherine Porter with Carolyn Burke (Ithaca, NY: Cornell University Press, 1985), pp. 26, 36, and 84.

57. See *Rime sparse* 264.136; and Carozza and Shey, *Petrarch's "Secretum,"* pp. 20 and 22; Mann, *Petrarch*, p. 93; Montano, "La prese di conscienza," p. 215; and Morris Bishop, *Petrarch and His World* (Bloomington: Indiana University Press, 1963), p. 214.

Similarly, at the end of *Rime sparse* 360, when Reason is called upon to judge the debate between Love and Petrarch over whether the poet's devotion to Laura has been an elevating or degrading passion, the poet ultimately has Reason defer, citing the need for more time in "so great a lawsuit." See Sturm-Maddox, *Petrarch's Laurels*, p. 61. On how this essentially contradictory stance pervades the whole of Petrarch's poetry, see Durling, "Petrarch's 'Giovene Donna,' " p. 20.

58. Levi, "Pensiero classico," pp. 235–36.

59. See also Nancy Jones' paper in this volume.

60. See, for example, Paul Allen Miller, "Sive Deae Seu Sint Dirae Obscenaeque Volucres," *Arethusa* 22 (1989): pp. 47–80.

Woman, Space, and Renaissance Discourse

Diana Robin

The house, an *opus operatum*, lends itself as such to a deciphering which does not forget that the "book" from which the children learn their vision of the world is read with the body, in and through the movements and displacements which make the space within which they are enacted as much as they are made by it.

Pierre Bourdieu

A whole history remains to be written of *spaces*—which would at the same time be the history of *powers* (both of these terms in the plural)—from the great strategies of geopolitics to the little tactics of the habitat.

Michel Foucault

It has now become a commonplace among feminist historians that women's experience of the Renaissance—if they had one at all—differed from men's substantially.[1] As Juliana Schiesari has written:

If the Renaissance once meant the flowering of great works by great men in the expression of a *Geistesgeschichte*, Marxism and feminism have taught us that individual freedom and self-expression were not available to all subjects at the time. And while the Renaissance once meant the advent of the "individual," feminism and psychoanalysis now require that we question how individuality has been predicated on an unspoken hierarchy of differences. Such theoretical and political discourses have recast our understanding of Renaissance culture and civilization in ways that are as irrevocable as they are provocative of further debate.[2]

Similarly, women's experience of space—always a metaphor for subjectivity—differed from men's in the culture of early modern Italy. Images of

165

space and spatial plenitude were metonymic in humanist thought for the notion of the expanding consciousness of "man." But the new humanist ideology of space and spatial expansiveness that was so decisively expressed in fifteenth- and sixteenth-century painting, architecture, city planning, and literature also reinforced a consciousness that was increasingly narrow and exclusionary in its social and sexual dimensions. It was grounded, as Lauro Martines has argued, in upper-class demand. "The drive for grandeur and for more ample living spaces sprang from the new needs and wishes of the commanding social groups . . . and the rising awareness that [male, upper-class] elites could reapportion or remake the urban space if they so willed."[3] Nowhere was the ideal of spatial expansiveness more clearly enunciated as the exclusive prerogative of the male than by the architect and theorist, Leon Battista Alberti (1404–72). In the following passage, Alberti stresses throughout the point that the generous dimensions of the houses he would design would provide windows with broad vistas, areas outdoors for the taking of exercise, and social spaces suitable for the staging of conversations of a philosophical nature—all for the men of the family:

> I would prefer to locate the house of a gentleman somewhere dignified . . . where it could enjoy all the benefit and delight of breeze, sun, and view. It should have easy access from the fields, and a generous reception area for the arrival of guests; it should be in view, and have itself a view of some city, town, stretch of coast, or plain, or it should have within sight the peaks of some notable hills or mountains, delightful gardens, and attractive haunts for fishing and hunting. . . . There should be a large open area in front of the gates for chariot and horse races, its dimensions greater than the distance a young man could hurl a javelin or fire an arrow. Likewise within the gates there should be no shortage of semiprivate spaces, walkways, promenades, swimming pools, areas both grassed and paved over, porticoes, and semicircular loggias, where old men may, meet for discussion in the welcome winter sun. . . .[4]

As for the women of the family, Alberti was just as firm in his views about the necessity for their confinement to carefully circumscribed spaces within the house as he was about the appropriateness of the grandiose proportions he recommended for the men's living areas:

> I recall reading in the historian Aemilius Probo that it was the custom in Greece for women not to be admitted to table except

for meals with relatives. . . . And certainly to my mind, any place reserved for women ought to be treated as though dedicated to religion and chastity; also I would have the young girls and maidens allocated comfortable apartments, to relieve their delicate minds from the tedium of confinement. . . . The husband and wife must have separate bedrooms . . . to ensure that the husband not be disturbed by his wife when she is about to give birth or is ill.[5]

While upper- and middle-class women were being enclosed in more confining domestic spaces by fifteenth-century architectural theorists and planners than they had been in the walled castles, country villas, and urban dwellings they had inhabited in previous centuries, an analogous pattern of exclusion could be observed in the literary production of gender. From the end of the fourteenth century on, interest in typologies of gender were evident in two cultural phenomena in early modern Europe. The one was the so-called *querelle des femmes*, the theoretical debate on woman's versus man's nature.[6] The other phenomenon, closely related to the *querelle*, was the sudden proliferation of catalogues and encyclopedias of women's lives.[7] These biographical catalogues, which featured the lives of ancient, modern, and sometimes mythological women, were alike in their homogenization of their female subjects into a set of stock types. Content not to have to alter an already successful formula, the compilers of these catalogues produced and reproduced distorted images of historical women that remained virtually unchanged over a period of almost three hundred years. The Renaissance typing of intellectually and artistically gifted women as exceptions to the rule of women's inferiority, or simply as men trapped in women's bodies, and the reduction of such women to a set of stereotypes, to a list of familiar exempla, in the catalogues, encyclopedias, and biographical dictionaries of the early modern period functioned to create a mystique about women that supported their exclusion from the schools and academies, and from the professions and the guilds, as well as from the spaces of their own cities and houses.[8]

Woman, Sex, and the Boccaccian Space

Of these early biographical catalogues, Boccaccio's exaggeratedly misogynistic Latin catalogue of 104 women's lives, *De claris mulieribus (Concerning Famous Women)*, published in 1355,[9] was perhaps the single most important influence in the subsequent stereotyping of women in European literature.[10] By 1500, the *De claris mulieribus* was out in several different Latin editions; it had also been translated into five languages and was widely known in France, Italy, Spain, England, and Germany.

Boccaccio's misogyny operates primarily on a genital level.[11] The 104 women in his catalogue of famous women fall neatly into eight stock types classifiable by status or occupation: goddesses; queens, empresses, or heads of state; military women; craftswomen, painters, sculptresses, and other artists; prostitutes and courtesans; witches, seers, and prophets; scholars and literary women; and wives, sisters, and daughters. The real distinction he makes among women, however, is sexual. The danger to men from border-crossing women is pollution (from women's impure bodies) not job loss or demotion. The good woman is pure in body (that is, nonsexual); the bad, impure (that is, sexual). There is no middle ground. If a famous woman scholar, poet, or artist has a celibate life, she receives praise as an exception among women, but, if a gifted woman is sexually promiscuous, she is simply judged true to her race (*genus mulierum*). Working from a synthesis of classical, patristic, and medieval literary traditions in misogyny, Boccaccio is more blatantly derisive of his female characters than his ancient sources Livy, Ovid, Pliny, and Valerius Maximus. In Boccaccio, for example, the future mother of Romulus and Remus, Rhea Silvia, becomes pregnant after deciding to take a lover "as many modern nuns do." His classical sources, on the other hand, make it clear that Rhea Silvia's pregnancy is the consequence of a rape and that the raped woman is the victim in the story, not the agent.[12] And, while Boccaccio's Artemisia and Hortensia are successful because they display qualities that are perceived as essentially male (the warrior queen Artemisia shows "a man's courage," and the orator Hortensia "has the skills of a man"), this kind of editorializing is absent from Boccaccio's classical sources for these two women's stories, Pliny and Valerius Maximus, where, although derogatory judgments of women may be suggested— by, for example, the mere mention of such women's names—they are not explicitly expressed.[13]

His exceptional women, as Valerie Wayne has argued, serve to control and stabilize received boundaries between the genders, so that, far from challenging the norms about women, the concept of exceptionality actually reinforces societal norms.[14] And, since exceptionality demonstrates aberration, the exceptional woman serves as an exemplum of what is to be avoided, of what is "not natural."[15] Each of Boccaccio's portraits of women constitutes a negative example, "one that discourages rather than encourages emulation. Considered as a totality the text functions as a refutation of its apparent thesis."[16]

Early modern catalogues of women after Boccaccio produce and replicate stereotypes that resemble Boccaccio's, particularly those of his learned women. By the middle of the sixteenth century in European catalogues of women, the intellectual/literary woman has hardened into a distinct type. The emergent stereotype exhibits a number of stock characteristics, representing a composite of at least four different learned women from Boccaccio's catalogue: Sappho, Cornificia, Proba, and Hortensia. The principal themes that characterize the learned woman of the catalogues are:

1. her debt to a paternal figure (a father or older brother) for her intellectual and/or artistic gifts;
2. her rejection of gender-specific work roles; she refuses women's work (needlework, spinning) so that she can take up men's work (writing, scholarship);
3. her renunciation of sex; she is a virgin if unmarried, a chaste wife if married; the learned woman often rejects marriage so that she can immerse herself in her studies, writing, or creative development.
4. her transsexuality or even masculinity; she is a woman who who is said to act more like a man than a woman; typically she is a transgressor of prescribed sex/gender boundaries. (The poet Cornificia and the orator Hortensia stepped outside the limits for their sex *[foemineum superasse sexum]*).

Battista Fregosa published a historical encyclopedia, *De factis dictisque memorabilibus*, that included biographical entries for both ancient and modern learned women in 1483.[17] His modern list included only five women: the tenth-century nun and dramatist, Hrotswitha of Gandersheim; the thirteenth-century scholar and abbess, Elizabeth of Thuringia; and the fifteenth-century Italian humanists Isotta Nogarola, Battista Malatesta, and Cassandra Fedele. In 1487 Jacopo Filippo da Bergamo published his Latin catalogue, *De claris scelestisque mulieribus*, the largest collection of women's lives yet to be published. Bergamo's *Lives*, some of them lifted word for word from Boccaccio, included over eighty female saints and a short list of modern learned women. Among these were Cassandra Fedele, Battista Malatesta, Isotta Nogarola, her sister Ginevra Nogarola, and her aunt Angela Nogarola.[18]

One of the most interesting books in the catalogue tradition is an unfinished, anonymous catalogue that appeared in a 1521 anthology of women's lives compiled by Jean Tixier de Ravisi. This work consists almost solely of captions without lives. Clearly, the anonymous author intended first to slot all known women into one type or another and then to add the names and vitae later. Among the author's captions are "Poetesses," "Virgins and Martyrs," "Common Whores," "Prostitutes Converted to Virtue," and "Illustrious Queens"; also listed under separate headings are "Women who Wore Men's Clothes" and "Women who were sometimes Men and Sometimes Women."

Another catalogue of distinguished modern women by Giuseppe Betussi came out in 1545, as a supplement to his Italian translation of Boccaccio's *De claris mulieribus*. Betussi's work featured fifty modern women's lives, including the then canonical group of women in Fregosa, Bergamo, and Ravisi, with two new additions: a Nogarola granddaughter, Veronica da Gambara, and a Malatesta great-granddaughter, Vittoria Colonna. Giovanni Battista Ignazi published a Latin catalogue of lives of famous Venetian men and women in 1554, which again included the same list of learned women in Fregosa's catalogue. By the beginning of the seventeenth century, in Giacomo Alberici's *Catalogo breve degli illustri et famosi scrittori venetiani* (1605), only Cassandra Fedele had survived from the old canon, and five new sixteenth-century women writers were added to the canon: Lucretia Marinelli, Moderata Fonte, Foscarina Giulia da Ponte, and Olimpia Malipieri. Some forty years later, Jacopo Filippo Tomasini published the first modern, heavily annotated catalogue of learned men and women's lives, *Elogia literis et sapientia illustrium* (1644), which included not only a long entry on Fedele but one on a woman not previously in the canon, the Brescian humanist, Laura Cereta.

With the exception of the Tomasini vitae, the catalogue versions of learned women's lives were transmitted almost without alteration, from compiler to compiler, over a period that spanned nearly 250 years. The canonical biographies of Cassandra Fedele provide an example of the distortions in women's individual and collective histories that survived via the catalogue tradition. The biographical tradition that was perpetuated about Fedele for over two centuries contains all four themes that I describe above as characteristic of the learned woman of the catalogues. According to the catalogues, Fedele owes her greatest intellectual debt to her learned father; she takes up the pen after relinquishing her needles and loom; she remains a lifelong virgin, prefering a life of study and solitude to marriage and familial obligations; and her scholarly career is described in the catalogue vitae as like a man's—as Julius Caesar Scaliger had put it in an epigram addressed to Fedele, one might think she was a man.[19]

But what was the truth about Fedele's life? It is instructive to compare the myth with archival sources and other records of her life.[20] Taught Greek and Latin grammar at an early age by a Servite monk, Fedele cannot have been intellectually influenced by her father, since he seems not to have had formal schooling of any sort, or a career, nor did he leave writings of his own. Her career was nothing like that of her humanist peers. She was never admitted to university, never held an academic post, and, because she was a woman, her works—collected letters and several orations—remained unpublished until the seventeenth century, when there was a revival of interest in women writers and artists. And far from being a virgin, Fedele was married for twenty-three years, and quite openly so, to Gian-Maria Mappelli, a physician from Vicenza. In other words, the catalogues misrepresented the facts of Fedele's life, and they left no space for the fictions of her own making (her essays and letters).

Christine's Use of the Metaphor of Urban Space

The only woman to produce a work in the tradition of the early modern catalogue of women was Christine de Pizan (1363–1431). Unlike Boccaccio's popular catalogue of women, Christine's *Cité des dames* remained virtually unknown in Europe until the end of the eighteenth century. Though she thoroughly mined Boccaccio's *De claris mulieribus* for its wealth of stories, the genre of the catalogue and of the collected lives of women suggested to her a completely different kind of space for the representation of women's lives and works. To Christine, the writing of the history of women was like the clearing of a site and the laying of a foundation for the building of a city; it entailed the manipulation of space, building materials, and lives. The framework she chose for her history was an allegory in which three female elders and mentors (the Ladies Reason, Rectitude, and Justice) appear to her in a dream. Christine's moral guides instruct her in the life stories of great women and commission her to build an allegorical city—a cluster of palaces, houses, public buildings, temples, streets, and squares surrounded by high walls, towers, bastions, and moats—made of the histories of women (1.4.3; 1.5.1). Her pen, according to the instructions of Lady Reason, will serve as her trowel, her ink as the mortar. The foundation of the city will consist of the lives of the most powerful women in the world—queens, empresses, and goddesses; the walls and towers of the city will be made of the lives of women famous for their loyalty to parents and husbands; and the city roofs will be constructed from the lives of female saints and martyrs.

Christine rejects Boccaccio's genitally oriented paradigm of femininity. In her revision of his catalogue of women, she deletes his running commentaries on the sexual histories of his subjects and locates women, instead, as excavators, planners, architects, and builders in the metaphysical plains and spaces of history; the edifice she erects is a city not simply of memory but of meaning and purpose in the world. Mothers and the mother/daughter bond are central, as Maureen Quilligan has recently shown, to Christine's project.[21] Two events set the stage for the picture of the matriarchal city to be revealed: the framing of the allegory with three maternal figures—Reason, Rectitude, and Justice—and Christine's insertion of her own mother into the work, whom she depicts on the opening page of the

Cité in a characteristic maternal pose: Christine's mother is calling her daughter to put down her writing and come to supper (1.1.1). The Ladies Reason, Rectitude, and Justice, each of whom addresses Christine as daughter, represent not a simple replication but a tripling or perhaps even a trinity, of mother figures. The story of one pair of mothers, in particular, is pivotal to Christine's project of rewriting Boccaccio and patriarchal history. Boccaccio tells the story of an anonymous Roman mother who breast-feeds her own mother so that she can rescue her from starvation so as to illustrate the principle that there is no greater virtue than the loyalty of children—sons *and* daughters—to their parents.[22] But, in Christine's retelling of the story (unlike the Boccaccio tale), she stresses the singularity of the mother/daughter bond. And it is significant that both in this tale and the larger work itself (which opens, as I have noted, with the author's mother calling her to supper), the figure of the nurturant mother is foregrounded. In Christine's text, breast-feeding, because of its reversibility for daughters and mothers, becomes emblematic for the priority of the mother-daughter love bond over all other ties. Only a daughter can return to her mother the quality of love that she once received. "In this way the daughter gave back to her mother in old age what she had taken from her mother as an infant."[23]

Building a City of the Self in the Pastoral

Laura Cereta, born a century after Christine de Pizan, in Brescia in 1469, seems to take up the challenge implicit in the *Cité*; it is time for women to respond to their attackers, to create a place—a new city—for themselves in the world, and to build it through the writing of a history of their own. In Cereta's case, it is an archaeology of the self that is undertaken: an autobiography, in the form of a book of personal letters.[24] Like Christine's *Cité*, where mothers and foremothers occupy a pivotal place, Cereta's letterbook is a woman-centered text. These two works are unparalleled in fifteenth-century European literature in their emphasis on the female.

In two of Cereta's most autobiographical letters, she builds her city of self, not among the walls and cramped streets of the town, but in the pastoral, a likely starting place, since the identification of nature with the female, and with the maternal body, is a standard trope in the Renaissance.[25] In the first of these letters, she reminds her mother of the day the two of them spent together in the country after their long separation; here Cereta's reconciliation with her mother is presented as analogous to her return to a utopic space in nature, after the dystopic loneliness of the city. In the second letter, the figure of the maternal body reappears in a scene of a Saturnian age pastoral, in which nature is spontaneously fertile and nurturant without the intervention of man.

In Cereta's autobiographical letters, her earliest memories are of abandonment and separation from her mother. She is sent away from home to a convent at the age of 7, when her mother is no longer able to care for the several children she has at home. Two years later, when Cereta is sent home from the convent, she recalls that her mother followed her around the house as though she was fearful of losing her again. This may be a case of projection or conscious reversal; perhaps it is Cereta, the child, who fears abandonment. Later she remembers being handed over to a strange, Dickensian figure, whose appearance frightened and alarmed her: "Montana fovit altera a matre nutrix, quae tumida guttur enode rugabat ora lurida" (I was taken care of by another nurse after my mother, Montana, whose wrinkled features had a yellowish pallor and whose throat was swollen with a goiter).[26]

In a letter to her mother dated September 9, 1485, nine months after her marriage, Cereta recalls the events and sensations she experiences on the day she and her mother spent walking together in the country:

That day should be marked with a white stone because it was so happy. Filled with a sense of gladness, we surveyed the lovely meadows, blooming with flowers, glistening with stones and winding streams. Noisy birds were singing in the morning sun. The local people, who were singing and playing on double-mouthed oaten pipes and reed flutes . . . came to meet us when we stepped down from our wagon. Some were herding sheep, while others were pressing milk from the swollen udders of ewes. Now and then the cattle would fill the valley with the sounds of their lowing as they drew nearer to us. But there were tents that had been erected; and there a humpbacked girl was soothing our ears with local ballads to the accompaniment of sweet melodies. And when the rhythms of the song were in tune with the strings of her lute, her fingers strummed out harmonies with a Thracian quill. Thus, the beating feet of that little farm girl yielded to the group of dancers, whom the boxwood pipes and tambourines called as they danced. There a pleasant wooded glen, thick with white willows, offers deep shade. In that place there is a grove that belongs to Idalian Venus, and there both the Naiads and the Napean nymphs can revel in the afternoon shadows. For greenness, my dear one, enfolded us on all sides. Thus, with charm and freshness, the sensations aroused by the land filled full our city-bred minds. It would have filled them still more elegantly if you had come during the time of the Saturnalia, when your presence was requested and sought so many times.

[Foelix nimium ad limites, atque albo lapillo numeranda lux, qua perfusae gaudio pulchrescentia illa floribus prata, et glareis, circumlabentibusque rivis ornata lustravimus. Concinebant illic sub radiis matutini solis aves garrulae. Venere vel obviam cantilantes biforis avenis atque arundinibus agrestes, qui innexi vincula scripea, ut primum curru, cogebant oves alii, atque alii ubera distenta premebant. Tunc passim venientis armenti mugitibus arva replentur. Stabant autem horto medio tenta tentoria, gibbosa puella patriis quibusdam fabulis dulci cantu aures mulcebant, et ubi canoris mox respondebant fidibus numeri, Threicio et digiti pulsabant pectine voces. Sic indulgebant choreis plaudentes illius plebesculae pedes, quos vel saltuantes, timpana buxusque vocabant. Ibi salicum albicantium nemorosa sylvula amoena densius sub opacitate frondebat. Idaliae ibi Cytheraeque lucus, sub quo non Dryades solum gratis umbris, sed volupe vel ipsae possint Nayades, Napeaeque fruisci. Visebatur enim quaquaversum, deliciae meae, viriditas. Sic lepide atque laute civiles animos ruralis affectus implebat. Implesset tamen urbanius, si totiens in Saturnalibus perquisita, conclamataque venisses. Vale.][27]

Julia Kristeva's analyses of representations of the maternal body in the paintings of Cereta's Venetian contemporary, Giovanni Bellini, open up a space for the rereading of this and others of Cereta's letters.[28] Kristeva rejects Lacan's theory that the infant first enters into the realm of the symbolic (that is, language) at "the mirror stage": when, on glimpsing its reflected image, it apprehends, for the first time, distinctions—between the "I" and the "other" (or mother), between the subject and the object—that enable language. Kristeva posits an earlier threshold, prior to the "mirror stage," for the child's entrance into the arbitrary system of signs we call language: the semiotic stage, which begins in utero and marks the early weeks and months of the infant's life. She envisions this stage as a space of womblike enclosure and engulfment that she calls the *chora*, which, in Greek, denotes a space in which a thing is contained, as opposed to the term *topos*, which refers to a place or spot which may or may not be empty. Her use of the term *chora*, she says, comes from Plato's image of the "chora" in the *Timaeus* as the maternal "receptacle" out of which all being is generated.[29] In more concrete terms, Kristeva describes the *chora* as a place of sounds, pulsions, drives, and musical rhythms like that of the womb: a system of signs prior to language in which mother and child constitute a unity.

Cereta's letter to her mother suggests fantasies of return to a Kristevan *chora* of rhythms, pulsions, and music; it also suggests a reversal of mother-daughter roles similar to the one in Christine's tale in which the daughter breast-feeds her mother. In Cereta's letter, it is the daughter who desires the mother, and the daughter who reproaches the mother for her absence. And, as in the Kristevan *chora*, there is in Cereta's valley a sense of enclosure and engulfment; here the space is full of pastoral sounds and mother and daughter are sheltered in a valley by the mountains rising in the distance. Images of full udders, blooming meadows, ears filled with melodies, and minds and hearts filled with pleasurable sounds, sights, and smells convey a sense of utopic plenitude and bliss. On that day, only sensory, nonverbal signs and sounds exchanged are remembered: the smell of cattle and wild flowers, the lingering phrases of a child's song, the rhythms of the dance, the feel of the deep shade in the copse, and the nearness of her mother. If there had been conversation, it was not remembered, as were the visual, aural, olfactory and tactile pleasures of the day. In the middle of the day, as Cereta and her mother approach a garden, they encounter a group of local people who are making music under a canopy or a tent. Among them is a young girl who sings songs that tell stories (*fabulis*) to them, evoking in this utopic scene childhood memories of the maternal voice.[30] Moreover, the interweaving of bird songs, the sounds of the girl's voice and lute, the oaten pipes, the tambourines, the rhythmic beating of feet, and, above all, the laughter of mother and daughter all suggest what Kristeva calls the "riant" space of the *chora*:[31]

> Voice, hearing, and sight are the archaic dispositions where the earliest forms of discreteness emerge. The breast, given and withdrawn; lamplight capturing the gaze; intermittent sounds of voice or music—all these meet with anaclisis. . . . At that point, breast, light, and sound become a *there*: a place, a spot, a marker. The effect, which is dramatic, is no longer quiet but laughter. . . .[32]

Cereta's positioning of the story of the humpbacked girl who sings tales at the center of a letter in which she reproaches her mother for her long absence suggests a relationship between Cereta and the child, between poetry and lack, and between writing and wounding. A constant tension is also set up here between the themes of human loss and lack and the repeated evocations of the bounty of nature. As in another letter, where Cereta describes the dream she has of a glittering ship that disappears under the waves before she can board it, her letter to her mother depicts a longing that cannot be fulfilled and a fulfillment—as in the Demeter myth—that can only signify the coming of fresh loss.[33]

Painting Spaces for the Self

Images of the maternal body are equally imbedded in the pastoral in a letter that Cereta addresses to her father's attorney, Sigismondo de Bucci, in the *Epistolae*.[34] In this letter, she explains the two-track strategy that she has quite consciously developed for the expanding of her space, in and through both her writings and the linen canvases she fills with the embroidered pictures she crafts with needle and thread, an art she says she learned during the two years she spent in the convent.[35] The subjectivity and spaces Cereta builds, and enters into, in her letter to Bucci place her in conflict with her own sense of obligation. She views herself first reluctantly as a daughter and wife, whose primary duties are to care for her father and husband. As a woman responsible for the lives of others, she must do her own work invisibly, when she can no longer be seen: at night, when the rest of the household sleeps and, in the early mornings, before they awaken. Thus, the kind of work she describes here is doubly framed and boxed as feminine: her night writing, because night is the time when women do their writing; her embroidery, because needlework is women's work.[36] Still, in the natural landscape of the scene she has embroidered, Cereta reaches again for the space of the *chora*, in presenting a picture of nature even less cultivated than she did in her letter to her mother. Here are strange, primordial fields, valleys, mountains, and rivers and a kingdom of beasts: a scene before man, before cultivation, and before the city:

> I still don't have any time that is unoccupied, not even to catch my breath; it is as though I am being pulled in two different directions—by meeting my father's demands and, at the same time, the needs of my husband. The one situation, because of the present circumstances, demands that I be here continuously; the other pulls me away from here. And so I am harried by the desire to be alternately in two places. I have no free time at all to spend on my books unless I work productively during the nights and sleep very little. Such is the scarcity of time for those who expend both their talents and energy for the sake of their families and themselves equally. But wakefulness—that thief of time—finds a period of time to sequester from the rest of the day. During that time, after

working by lamplight for much of the night; and again, when the sun sets, the onset of darkness never keeps me away from my books. But as soon as the sun rises again, I spend the hours right after dawn working a piece of linen with a painted needle. And so my relentless regime of work at forbidden hours has resulted in this canvas, painted with a web of different colored threads. The work has taken three months of sleepless nights. But it has none of Alchimedon's genius; and such a loss of time is wasteful when time, the necklace of life, is spent on pointless work. . . . Anyhow, the work is a rectangular shawl for a woman; displayed in the middle of the shawl is a savage leopard with a vast variety of spots. A writhing, crested dragon dominates the left side of the shawl, its quivering forked tongue, its fiery eyes, and its painted scales enno-bling the creature and suggesting its cruelty. Opposite these beasts, a lion with flowing mane and savage aspect stretches wide its gaping jaws toward the right; it is as though all the creatures on the earth were menacing and growling at one another, first one, then an-other. Higher up, an eagle swoops down through the air to attack a hawk; the eagle's wings cast a shadow over the smaller bird, while he, bent backwards, fights back with his beak and talons. Golden Phoebus, high above all, illuminates a silvery, crescent moon with his streaming beams of light. Beyond the beasts, the lofty face of a mountain with twin peaks rises in the distance, and from it a river flows down in the opposite direction, coursing down through the valley that lies in between. . . . Bare overhanging rocks frame the plain on one side, and some of these rocks are piled one over another; from the rugged summit of this promontory, smoke and flames erupt in fiery billows. Meadows blooming with flowers and every herb, on hillock after hillock, clothe the plain on the other side. A wooded glade with shade-bearing cover shelters both sides of the mountain, where first edible fruits ripen in their boughs and then olive trees droop under the gentle burden of their berries. A field surrounds them; and vines are stretched and linked to one another all around, curling upwards and downwards with graceful-ness. Among these, the creeping tendrils of the vine contain in their leaves darkening grapes. . . . At this point I need not mention that the silkworm of Arabia is introduced for smooth, elegant, and even thread or how the hemp is carded for a long time with a spiny comb and the precious cloth of fine linen is gently and carefully spread out for the one who will lay the warp, lest I be said to be a resurrected Pamphile of Greece, or Arachne of Colophon. . . .

[Nulla tamen unquam, vel parva respiratio, vacuum mihi tempus exhibuit; velut quae paternae rei familiaris indulgentia non minus, quam maritali cura distringar. Illa nanquam iugiter, pro existentium opportunitate me invocat, haec avocat. Alterno utrinque studio sollicitor. Nullum a me dari potest omnino litteris ocium, nisi sub vegetissimo somno, dormiam minimum. Tanta est parsimonia temporis apud eos qui suis aeque ac sibi solertiae non minus, quam laboris impendunt. Sed furatrix horarum vigilantia divisum die toto spatium invenit, in quo, post noctis multae lucernam, rursus matutina me agam; nunquam enim primae labentis diei tenebrae litteras fallunt. Redeunitis autem orientis prima fax, illuso acu picta veliculo, datur. Sic tenax laboris improbi ratio telam hanc interfilari colorum reciprocatione distinxit. Opus trimestris lucubrationis hoc fuit, sed non aliqua tamen Alchimedontis divinitate, permixtum. Prodiga sane iactura, qua vitae monile tempus tam inani labore profunditur.... Oblongus igitur cohoperturae paniculus torvam in medio Pantheram, et conspicua satis macularum varietate distinctam, ostendit. At levam tenet intortus, cristatusque Draco, quem lingua divisim tremula et pictaturae squammae, radiantesque oculi, parata crudelitate nobilitant. Has contra bestias iubatus et feritatis aspectu febriens leo propatulas in dexteram hiatu fauces adaperit: quasi subvivi omnes irritatim secum infremant, minitenturque vicissim. Altius in resupinum, et rostro atque unguibus propugnantem per inane milvum nigricans pennis Aquila devolat. Sed aureus in summo Phoebus argenteam corniculatamque Lunam intercursantibus radiis illustrat. Ultra feras celsitudo bicipitis montis ascendit: ab cuius interiacente valle emissus amnis adverso curso defertur.... Sed alterum nuda solum et prominentia saxa, saxis aliis, atque aliis super imposita, compingunt, e quorum proscisso vertice flammigerum, interfumansque globatim eructatur incendium. Alterum circunvestiunt prata florea et viridius monticulatim omni herba virentia. Montis utrunque latus, umbrosis operculis nemus opacat, ubi pomantes hinc suos inter ramos esculi, inde vero leniter dependulae baccis olivae, confruticant. Hic, quacunque ambit campus, obtenduntur, adalliganturque circum propagines, praelonga sursum, deorsum gracilitate curvatae. Has inter pampini reptatu sequaci circunflui, nigrantes in palmite sustinent uvas.... Nunc tereti aequalique filo bombyx Arabiae deductus, praeteriri fas est; nunc spinoso pectine carminatum diu stuparium, et lini byssini precia orditurae lenius, blandiusque fusa posthabeo, ne altera Pamphile Graeca, vel Arachne Colophonia ... dicar insurgere....][37]

This passage suggests an interesting opposition between Cereta's and the Renaissance architect, Alberti's, treatments of space. Leon Battista Alberti proposes that spaciousness, amplitude, and harmony are realizable ideals in the planning of both public and private space:

> The principal ornament to any city [and private residence, as we have seen above] lies in the siting, layout, composition, and arrangement of [its parts]—its roads, squares, and individual works: each must be properly planned and distributed according to use, importance, and convenience. For without order there can be nothing commodious, graceful, or noble.[38]

Cereta, on the other hand, is obsessed with her sense of the exiguousness of space/time—*spatium*, which, like the Greek word *chora*, suggests an enclosed area that has something in it, but which, unlike the Greek term, can also connote the temporal. She longs for *spatium*, a place and time free of housework and household accounts so that she can read, write, and study, and at last finds this *spatium* during the hours of the night when her husband and the rest of the household are asleep. Her insomnia, her nightly vigils (*vigilantiae*) are a double-edged thing: they are thieves of time (*furatrices horarum*) that give her a few extra hours for her work while they transgress, at the same time, the mores of the family. Above all, she savors the nights as islands of creativity and peace and as the time when she is most productive. Time, she writes, is the "necklace of life that is wasted in meaningless work" (qua vitae monile tempus tam inani labore profunditur).[39] But this time-necklace is not only an adornment; she imagines it also as a tight chain that constrains the days of one's life from birth to death:

> This living of ours is so uncertain and aimless that time, speeding onward, tightly binds the day of our birth to that of our death.
>
> [Est enim vagum adeo et instabile hoc vivere nostrum ut natalem extremumque diem velox hora perstringat.][40]

Cereta's letter to Bucci is also marked by an ambivalence about her own work, about how she chooses to fill space and what constitutes wasted space, and wasted lives. She explains that she has chosen to express herself with both a pen *and* a needle—the standard emblems that separate male from female space in the Renaissance ideology of gender—thus intimating that she may mean to throw out the conventions of gender or at least confound them.[41] The rest of the letter demonstrates, in effect, a superimposition or double exposure of the products of her pen and needle in an *ekphrasis* that describes the scene she has designed and embroidered with silk thread on a linen shawl meant for a woman (perhaps her mother or sister), which has taken her months to complete. The scene on the shawl is a landscape that reveals a conception of the nature and the world very different from the scenes of walled towns and tilled fields crowded with men, women, and domestic animals in the illuminated manuscripts and paintings of the fourteenth through the sixteenth centuries.

Claudia Lazzaro has recently argued that, although landscape painting in the Renaissance represents an imaginary relationship between culture and nature in which nature is always identified with the female, the model of human dominance over nature is a relatively recent paradigm, not appearing at least until the end of the seventeenth century or even later.[42] The dominant paradigm in early modern Italy is a pairing of man and nature (or art and nature) in a "mutually enhancing dialectic."[43] This pairing can be seen in seventeenth-century horticultural manuals. Giovanni Ferrari's *Flora* (1633) and Paolo Clarici's *Istoria e coltura delle piante* still treat the garden within the Renaissance paradigm of the reciprocity of art and nature, rather than the domination of one over the other.[44] "Gardens were not described in the military language of domination, conquest, and victory," writes Lazzaro. "In the Renaissance view one of the principal actions that art, culture, man, or the gardener performs on nature is not subduing but rather unveiling the order inherent there."[45] The idea of this pairing is well articulated in Leon Battista Alberti's *De architectura*:

> The pleasure to be found in objects of great beauty and ornament is produced either by invention and the working of the intellect, or by the hand of the craftsman, or it is imbued naturally in the objects themselves. The intellect is responsible for choice, distribution, arrangement, and so on, which give the work dignity; the hand is responsible for laying, joining, cutting, trimming, polishing, and such like, which give the work grace; the properties derived from Nature are weight, density, purity, durability, and the like, which bring the work admiration. These three must be applied to each part of the building, according to its respective use and role.[46]

In Cereta's painting of the world, there is no pairing of man and nature because man has been deleted from the world. Absent from her canvas are human figures, domestic animals, houses, buildings, walls, roads, paths. The objects she depicts can be divided into two categories: the feral and the vegetative. The peculiar feature of Cereta's scene is the contrast between a nature that is benign and nurturant and an animal kingdom that is hostile and menacing. The foreground of the canvas features an arrangement of wild beasts roaring at one another and positioned as if ready to attack. In the center of the long shawl is a spotted leopard, flanked on the left by a dragon and on the right by a roaring lion; above these figures an eagle and a hawk struggle in midair. In the background, illuminated by a gilded sun and a crescent moon sewn in silver thread, are twin peaks of a mountain, a river that flows down into the valley from the mountains, and a volcano that emits a plume of smoke. Beneath overhanging rocks, there is a meadow blooming with flowers, vines laden with ripe grapes, and stands of shade and other trees laden with berries, nuts, and winter apples.

As in the letter to her mother, Cereta reveals in this letter to Bucci her distance from nature. Again a painter of landscapes, she portrays herself in this letter as an alien—a sojourner—in nature. In the letterbook, a genre that, in the Renaissance, is almost solely occupied with urban concerns as separate from nature, Cereta has already marked herself as an other by inserting the pastoral into her book.[47] Are the wild animals, squawking and growling in her canvas, analogues to the men and women with whom she frequently quarrels in her letters? Certainly, the choric, fecund image of nature in this landscape resembles the space to which she returns in her mother's letter.

Pressing home the point that women have not always been confined to the spaces to which they are restricted in her time, Cereta ends the letter by identifying herself as author, weaver, and woman, not an isolated or exceptional woman, but as a continuation of Christine's "city"—of Christine's history of women. Cereta reminds Bucci that she belongs to a long tradition of gifted women, which includes two figures from her *Cité*: Arachne, a spinner and dyer, who was the first to invent "weaving art works into cloth like a painter"; and Pamphile, a colorist also, weaver, and inventor, who discovered the art of spinning silk from observing silk worms (I.39.1—I.40.1).[48] Cereta's references to Arachne and Pamphile also suggest the close relation women have had to nature as harvesters and cultivators, though she herself, as we have said, remains distant from that frame. Still, the main questions remain for Cereta. How should the *spatium* of a life be used? And what is the function of the writer/painter and her canvas? Is what she makes, in the end, just an empty simulacrum, as she complains in another letter?

> When this piece was done and complete, as though it were the empty simulacrum of my long wakeful nights, I withdrew my idle hands from the vanity of this preoccupation.
>
> [Hac arte iam plena, iamque facta velut vigiliarum inane simulacrum, ociosas a pompa huius implicamenti manus abduxi.][49]

Notes

1. If women had a Renaissance at all is still a matter of debate; Joan Kelly-Gadol in her 1977 article, "Did Woman Have a Renaissance?" reprinted in *Women, History, and Theory* (Chicago: University of Chicago Press, 1984), pp. 19–50, was the first to pose the question (her answer was no). Following her were: Merry Wiesner, "Spinsters and Seamstresses: Women in Clothing Production," in *Rewriting the Renaissance, The Discourses of Sexual Difference in Early Modern Europe*, ed. M. W. Ferguson, Maureen Quilligan, and Nancy J. Vickers (Chicago: University of Chicago Press, 1986), pp. 191–205; Judith Brown, "A Woman's Place was in the Home," in *Rewriting the Renaissance*, pp. 206–26; Juliana Schiesari, "In Praise of Virtuous Women? For a Genealogy of Gender Morals in Renaissance Italy," *Annali d'italianistica* 7 (1989): pp. 66–87; Schiesari and Marilyn Migiel, eds., *Refiguring Woman: Perspectives on Gender and the Italian Renaissance* (Ithaca, NY: Cornell University Press, 1991), pp. 1–15; Margaret King, *Women of the Renaissance* (Chicago: University of Chicago Press, 1991); Gerda Lerner, *The Creation of Feminist Consciousness: From the Middle Ages to the Seventeenth Century* (New York: Oxford University Press, 1993), esp. pp. 3–20; Christine Klapisch-Zuber, ed. *A History of Women in the West. Vol. 2: Silences of the Middle Ages* (Cambridge: Harvard University Press, 1992), pp. 1–10, et al.

2. Schiesari and Migiel, *Refiguring Woman*, pp. 2–3.

3. Lauro Martines, *Power and Imagination: City States in Renaissance Italy* (New York: Random House, 1980), p. 272.

4. Leon Battista Alberti, *Ten Books on Architecture*, ed. Joseph Ryckwert, trans. James Leoni (London: Alec Tiranti, 1955), p. 145.

5. Ibid., p. 149.

6. See Linda Woodbridge, *Women and the English Renaissance: Literature and the Nature of Womankind, 1540–1620* (Urbana: University of Illinois Press, 1986), chapter 1; and Constance Jordan, *Renaissance Feminism: Literary Texts and Political Models* (Ithaca, NY: Cornell University Press, 1990), pp. 11–64, for a description of the debate.

7. Giacomo Alberici, *Catalogo breve degli illustri et famosi scrittori venetiani* (Bologna, 1605); Jacopo Filippo Bergamo (alias J. F. Foresti), *Liber de claris scelestisque mulieribus* (Ferrara, 1497); Giuseppe Betussi, *Libro di M. Gio. Boccaccio delle Donne Illustri Tradotto per Messer Giuseppe Betussi* (Venice, 1545); Giovanni Boccaccio, *De claris mulieribus* (Venice, 1480); Ioannis Baptista Egnatius, *De Exemplis Illustrium Virorum Venetae Civitatis atque aliarum gentium* (Venice, 1554); Battista Fregosa, (alias Campofregosa, alias Baptista Fulgosius), *Factorum Dictorumque Memorabilium Libri* 9 (Venice, 1483; repr. with a supplement by Justo Gaillardo Campo, Paris, 1578); Jean Tixier de Ravisius, *De memorabilibus et claris mulieribus aliquot diversorum scriptorum opera* (Paris: Simon Colinaci, 1521); Iacopo Filippo Tomasini, *Elogia Literis et Sapientia Illustrium ad vivum expressis*

imaginibus exornata (Padua, 1644). In addition, Margaret King, in *Women of the Renaissance* cites a number of early modern catalogues I have not seen myself: Brantome, *The Lives of Illustrious Women*; Pierre Le Moyne, *The Gallerie of Heroic Women*; Pietro Paolo de Ribera, *The Immortal Triumphs and Heroic Enterprises of Eight Hundred and Forty-Five Women*; and Bartolomeo Goggio, *In Praise of Women*.

    8. On the function of gender stereotypes, see esp. Hazel Carby, *Reconstructing Womanhood: The Emergence of the Afro-American Woman Novelist* (New York: Oxford University Press, 1987); Carby argues that stereotyping works to justify exclusionary policies and practices, and it functions also "as a disguise, or mystification, of objective social relations" (p. 22). On the squeezing of working women out of the work place in Renaissance Italy and Germany, see esp. Judith Brown, "A Woman's Place," pp. 206–26; Merry Wiesner, "Spinsters and Seamstresses," pp. 191–205; Merry Wiesner, *Working Women in Renaissance Germany* (New Brunswick, NJ: Rutgers University Press, 1986); and Margaret King, *Women of the Renaissance*, pp. 62–80. After having worked in a great variety of roles and occupations in the twelfth, thirteenth, and fourteenth centuries, around 1350–80 women began to be prohibited by guild rules and city statutes from working in the higher-skilled trades. Between the fifteenth and sixteenth centuries, ordinances governing women's participation in the labor force multiplied, and what began as restrictions on the roles working women could play in the guilds in fifteenth-century Italy resulted in their total exclusion from those guilds by the sixteenth century.

    9. Boccaccio, *Concerning Famous Women*, trans. Guarino A. Guarino (New Brunswick, NJ: Rutgers University Press, 1963) is the edition to which I refer throughout this article.

    10. Woodbridge, *Women and the English Renaissance*, chap. 1.

    11. R. Howard Bloch, *Medieval Misogyny and the Invention of Western Romantic Love* (Chicago: University of Chicago Press, 1991) is careful to point out that misogyny was not peculiar to Boccaccio or the Middle Ages: "The denunciation of women . . . constitutes something of a cultural constant. Reaching back to the old testament and to ancient Greece and extending though classical, Hellenic, Judaic, and Roman traditions all the way to the fifteenth century, it dominates ecclesiastical writing, letters, sermons, theological tracts, and discussions and compilations of canon law; scientific works, as part of biological, gynecological, and medieval knowledge; and folklore and philosophy. The discourse of misogyny runs like a vein . . . throughout medieval literature" (p. 7).

    12. Boccaccio, *Concerning Famous Women*, chap. 55, pp. 123–27; chap. 82, p 185; For example, in Bocc. 43, Rhea Ilia is a Vestal Virgin who betrays her vow because she lusts for sex; Livy (1.3.4) *Ab urbe condita*, 14 vols., ed. and trans. Frank Gardner Moore. Loeb Classical Library. (Cambridge: Harvard University Press, 1940), on the contrary, says that Rhea Silvia was violently raped (vi compressa); no "culpa" is explicitly attributed to her (as it is in Boccaccio). In Ovid (*Fasti* 4.54), the rape/pregrancy sequence is compressed in a euphemism: "Mars was attracted to Ilia, and

she bore you, Romulus" [Ilia placet Marti teque parit]. The stress on pure versus dirty women is medieval and Boccaccian, not classical.

13. Pliny 36.4.30–32, Val. Max. 4.6. ext. 1; and Val. Max. 8.3.3.

14. Valerie Wayne, "Zenobia in Medieval and Renaissance Literature," in *Ambiguous Realities: Women in the Middle Ages and Renaissance,* ed. Carole Levin and Jeanie Watson (Detroit: Wayne State University Press, 1987), pp. 48–65.

15. Ibid., p. 61.

16. Constance Jordan, "Boccaccio's In-Famous Women," in *Ambiguous Realities: Women in the Middle Ages and Renaissance,* ed. Carol Levin and Jeanie Watson (Detroit: Wayne State University Press, 1987), pp. 28–29.

17. On the catalogues from Fregosa to Tomasini, see n. 10.

18. For more on Angela and Isotta Nogarola, see Holt Parker's paper in this volume.

19. Cassandra Fedele, *Epistolae et orationes,* ed. Iacopo Filippo Tomasini (Padua: F. Bolezetta, 1636), p. i: Indagere valet nullum si foemina verum / quod lateat gremio, consilioque Dei, / Nec Genium celso naturae educere caeli: / Nunquam tu fueris foemina, sed vir eras.

20. Cassandra Fedele's collected letters are extant in an early printed edition only: *Epistolae et Orationes,* ed. Iacopo Filippo Tomasini (Padua: F. Bolozettta, 1636). On the archival sources on Fedele, see esp. Cesira Cavazzana, "Cassandra Fedele erudita Veneziana del rinascimento," *Ateneo Veneto* 29 (1906): vol. 2, pp. 73–91, 249–75, 361–97; and Diana Robin, "Cassandra Fedele's *Epistolae* (1488–1521): Biography as Effacement," in *The Rhetoric of Life-Writing in the Renaissance,* ed. Thomas Mayer and Daniel Woolf (Ann Arbor: University of Michigan Press, 1995); and Diana Robin, "Cassandra Fedele," in *Italian Women Writers: A Biographical Sourcebook,* ed. Rinaldina Russell (New York: Greenwood Press, 1994).

21. Maureen Quilligan, *The Allegory of Female Authority: Christine de Pizan's Cité des dames* (Ithaca, NY: Cornell University Press, 1991).

22. Boccaccio, *Concerning Famous Women,* chap. 63, pp. 142–43.

23. Ibid., 2.11.1; p. 115; I am very much indebted here to the analysis of this episode in relation to Nancy Chodorow's theories of mothering in Maureen Quilligan, *The Allegory of Female Authority,* pp. 121–23.

24. Cereta's bound book of letters survives in two manuscripts: the Ven. Marc. 4186 (late fifteenth century); Vat. lat. 3176 (sixteenth century). Her letter-book was printed posthumously and only once: *Epistolae,* ed. Iacopo Filippo Tomasini (Padua: Sebastiano Sardi, 1640); her editor, Tomasini, whose catalogue of men and women's lives, *Elogia Literis et Sapientia Illustrium* (Padua: ex Typographia Sebastiani Sardi, 1644), I cite above, includes a vita of Cereta in both his *Elogia Literis* and his edition of her letters. On Cereta, the essential work is Albert Rabil, Jr., *Laura*

Cereta: Quattrocento Humanist (Binghamton, NY: Medieval and Renaissance Texts and Studies, 1981); see also Marco Palma, "Laura Cereta," in *Dizionario biografico degli italiani* (Rome: Istituto della Enciclopedia italiana, 1960), pp. 726–30; and Ettore Caccia, "Cultura e letturatura nei secoli XV e XVI," in *Storia di Brescia* (Brescia, 1963), *II. La Dominazione Veneta* (1426–1574). Ed. Giovanni Treccani degli Alfieri. Brescia: Morcelliana, 1963, pp. 474–535, 2.486, 494–96. I am, at present, preparing an edition of her collected letters in translation.

25. On Renaissance gardens and the symbolism of the female body, see esp. Claudia Lazzaro, "The Visual Language of Gender in Sixteenth-Century Garden Sculpture" in *Refiguring Woman: Perspectives on Gender and the Italian Renaissance*, ed. Juliana Schiesari and Marilyn Migiel (Ithaca, NY: Cornell University Press, 1991), pp. 71–113.

26. Tomasini, *Elogia Literis,* Letter 59, p. 147.

27. Ibid., letter 11, pp. 27–28. This and all subsequent translations of Cereta are mine.

28. Julia Kristeva, "Motherhood According to Giovanni Bellini," in *Desire in Language: A Semiotic Approach to Literature and Art*, trans. Thomas Gora, Alice Jardine, and Léon S. Roudiez (New York: Columbia University Press, 1980), pp. 237–70; see also Kristeva's other essays in *Desire in Language* and in *The Kristeva Reader*, ed. Toril Moi (New York: Columbia University Press, 1986); see critical essays on Kristeva in Toril Moi, *Sexual/Textual Politics: Feminist Literary Theory* (New York and London: Routledge, 1988), pp. 161–73; Kelly Oliver, *Reading Kristeva: Unraveling the Double-Bind* (Bloomington: Indiana University Press, 1993); Elizabeth Grosz, *Sexual Subversions* (Boston: Allen and Unwin).

29. Kristeva, "From One Identity To An Other," in *Desire in Language*, p. 133. Plato defines the *chora* in the *Timaeus* (5la–b) as "the mother and receptacle of all created and visible and in any way sensible things [which itself] . . . is an invisible and formless being which receives all things and in some mysterious way partakes of the intelligible, and is [itself] most incomprehensible" (in *The Collected Dialogues of Plato*, ed. Edith Hamilton and Huntington Cairns, trans. Benjamin Jowett [Princeton: Princeton University Press, 1961], p. 1178).

30. On fantasies of the maternal voice, see Toril Moi, *Sexual/Textual Politics*, p. 114, quoting Hélène Cixous in *La Jeune Née* (Paris: UGE, 1975); and Kaja Silverman, *The Acoustic Mirror: The Female Voice in Psychoanalysis and Cinema* (Bloomington: Indiana University Press, 1988), esp. pp. 72–140.

31. On the "riant spaciousness" of the *chora*, see Kristeva, "Motherhood" in *Desire in Language,* pp. 237–70, and "Place Names" in *Desire in Language*, p. 283. Kristeva also suggests provocatively (in "Stabat Mater" pp. 180–81, *Kristeva Reader*, ed. Toril Moi), that mothers and daughters "reproduce among themselves the strange gamut of forgotten body relationships with their mothers. Complicity in the unspoken, connivance of the inexpressible, of a wink, a tone of voice, a gesture, a tinge, a scent . . ."

32. Kristeva, "Place Names," in *Desire in Language*, p. 283.

33. I am much indebted to Marianne Hirsch's discussion of the theme of the mother-daughter bond and the Demeter/Persephone myth in her *The Mother/Daughter Plot. Narrative, Psychoanalysis, Feminism* (Bloomington: Indiana University Press, 1989), esp. pp. 1–27. Hirsch argues that the mother/daughter love bond has been excluded from the major traditions of the family in western literature (p. 43); certainly this is true in Greek tragedy, where mother/daughter and sister/sister relations are marked by intense hostility, distance, and lack of relationship.

34. Tomasini, letter 2, *Elogia Literis*, pp. 12–17.

35. Ibid.; and Tomasini, Letter 59, to Nazaria Olympia, on learning to embroider: *Elogia Literis*, pp. 145–54. According to Vasari, both embroidery *and* painting were more acceptable avenues than writing for female self-expression in fifteenth-century Italy; Whitney Chadwick, *Women, Art, and Society* (London: Thames and Hudson, 1991) notes that the second edition of Vasari's *Vite* included the following well-known Renaissance women painters: "Suor Plautilla, a nun and the daughter of the painter Luca Nelli, who painted a *Last Supper* (now in the refectory of Santa Maria Novella in Florence); Lucretia Quistelli della Mirandola, a pupil of Alessandro Allori; Irene di Spilimbergo, who studied with Titian but who died at eighteen having completed only three paintings; Barbara Longhi; five female miniaturists; Sophonisba Anguissola, the best known woman painter of sixteenth-century Italy, and her sisters; and three Bolognese women: Properzia de' Rossi, Lavinia Fontana, and Elisabetta Sirani—as proof that Renaissance Italy could claim its own women of learning and achievement" (p. 27).

36. For the notion of "framing and boxing" in the providing of rituals that reinforce societal norms, I am indebted to Mary Douglas, *Purity and Danger. An Analysis of Concepts of Pollution and Taboo* (London: Routledge and Kegan Paul, 1966), esp. pp. 58–72.

37. Tomasini, letter 2, *Elogia Literis*, pp. 12–17.

38. Alberti, *Ten Books on Architecture*, p. 191.

39. Tomasini, letter 2, *Elogia Literis*, p. 13.

40. Tomasini, letter 63, to Deodata Leone, *Elogia Literis*, p. 176.

41. On sex roles, work roles, and symbolism, see King, *Women of the Renaissance*, esp. pp. 190–218: the representation of women writers as females who abandoned the spindle and distaff to do men's work is standard from Boccaccio on. The identification, however, of the female needle (or spindle) with the male pen is highly unusual in the Renaissance; the only other humanist woman I know of who boasts that she both writes and sews is Catherine des Roches (1545–87); see Tilde Sankovitch, *French Women Writers and the Book: Myths of Access and Desire* (Syracuse, NY: Syracuse University Press, 1988), pp. 50–53.

42. Claudia Lazzaro, "Visual Language," pp. 74 ff.; cf. Keith Thomas, *Man and the Natural World: A History of the Modern Sensibility* (New York: Pantheon, 1983), chap. 1.

43. Lazzaro, "Visual Language," p. 74.

44. Ibid., pp. 74–75.

45. Ibid., p. 77.

46. Alberti, *Ten Books on Architecture,* p. 159.

47. The fifteenth-century humanist letterbook is an urban genre; the insertion of depictions of the pastoral in humanist epistles is practically unknown in the period.

48. Both women weavers are also in Boccaccio, though not in contiguous passages as they are in Christine, which makes it all the more likely that Cereta was using the *Cité* as her source; see Boccaccio, *Concerning Famous Women*, chap. 17, pp. 38–39, and chap. 42, pp. 95–96.

49. Tomasini, letter 59, *Elogia Literis,* p. 49. So much more than vanity is suggested by the Latin word *pompa*–ostentatiousness, selfishness, self-centeredness, superficiality, frivolousness, and more. *Implicamentum* (a word unattested in the *Oxford Latin Dictionary* but related to *implicatio*) is another difficult image to capture in translation; in any case the image connotes something intricate, interwoven, complicated, involved, difficult, and (by extension) time consuming and distracting.

In Praise of Woman's Superiority: Heinrich Cornelius Agrippa's *De nobilitate* (1529)

Diane S. Wood

Heinrich Cornelius Agrippa von Nettescheim's youthful polemic, the *De nobilitate et praecellentia foeminei sexus,* was one of the most important texts concerning the role and status of women in the French Renaissance. Written in 1509, but not published until 1529, this treatise encapsulates the principal arguments used by all the major defenders of womankind in sixteenth-century France. In the Latin original and its French translation (c. 1530), this work propelled the ongoing debate concerning woman's role, the *querelle des femmes,* which had begun with Christine de Pizan a century earlier.[1] In fact, in its various reeditions, Agrippa's text continued to be read well into the eighteenth century.[2] Agrippa's refutation of traditional misogynist thinking by means of Biblical and canonical texts, as well as classical literature, was never surpassed in its completeness and clarity of expression. The arguments Agrippa formulated were used and reused, making an understanding of his approach vital to those interested in women's status in early modern France.

Agrippa argues that the contemporary treatment of women is contrary to both divine and natural laws. According to him, laws, customs, and education all contribute to the suppression of women. Changing such human constructs is his implicit goal. Using both logic and hyperbole, his arguments subvert the traditional rationale for misogynistic practices that had been developed from the writings of the early Church Fathers. The rhetorical effectiveness of his strategy reveals why this work came to be one of the central texts in the *querelle.* Not content with proving that women are equal, he enthusiastically sets out to prove their inherent superiority to men and thereby ensures, through the novelty of his approach and his rhetorical exuberance, the great popularity of this treatise. His proof of female superiority challenged those misogynist arguments dear to the traditional patriarchal social order, suggesting the need for a new respect for women.

189

A youthful Agrippa wrote the *De nobilitate* in 1509 but did not publish it until twenty years later. This slender work has a four-part structure. First, Agrippa reinterprets the so-called Yahwist or second creation story from Genesis 2–3, which served as the basis of Christian misogyny. He then enumerates the God-given, superior qualities of women. This is followed by a catalogue of famous women from antiquity and the Bible who exemplified these qualities. In the final, and perhaps most interesting, section of the treatise, Agrippa reflects on the reasons for the relative scarcity of important and influential women in his own era, attributing contemporary women's low status and lack of achievement to the tyranny of men, who restrict their freedom and opportunities.

His radical stance in proclaiming the superiority of women doubtlessly enhanced the *De nobilitate's* popularity with the partisans of the *querelle des femmes*,[3] but the extreme nature of his views has led to debate over the interpretation of the declamation. Whereas some scholars of rhetoric have suggested that the treatise be read ironically, because of its strategy of inversion, feminist readers beginning with Lula Richardson have generally taken Agrippa seriously and do not consider this treatise to be a paradox, a rhetorical exercise that, in Marc van der Poel's words, defends a thesis "against the common opinion"[4] in the tradition of Erasmus's *Praise of Folly*, but rather a document that demonstrates the irrationality of Renaissance misogyny's traditional argumentative substructure. Far from being a literary trifle the *De nobilitate* is consistent with Agrippa's other declamations and, like them, presents serious theological arguments of a persuasive nature.[5] By substituting a female-dominated structure, Agrippa systematically inverts the male/female oppositions that traditionally served to subordinate women. I first examine the hyperbolic techniques used by Agrippa, as well as his insistent vocabulary, which undercuts traditional misogynist views. I then evaluate the impact of his polemical writings on the *querelle*, especially on Hélisenne de Crenne, whose thinking is shaped by the *De nobilitate* and whose writing reflects how female readers of the 1530s and 1540s received Agrippa's major theses. I trace the arguments of the treatise from the scriptural position of parity between the genders to the conclusion of the superiority of one over the other, to reveal the development of Agrippa's logic. Using the same techniques as sixteenth-century misogynists, he manipulates the traditional sources to prove the opposite thesis.

Agrippa's treatise is full of passion and a sense of moral outrage, especially in the strident passages that depict the injustices of the social order of his time. Here, as in his other treatises, Agrippa is concerned with Christian values on the level of practical morality.[6] The restraints on women, he argues, are human constructs that may be changed, and his implicit goal in writing the *De nobilitate* is to bring these changes about. First, however, he must establish that woman is not inherently inferior in God's plan and then offer examples of women from the past who have been given the opportunity to develop their talents. He emphasizes that duty to the love of truth motivates him (89). In fact, he explains that remaining silent would have been sacrilege, considering how divine law had been subverted:

> Tamen non tam multa diximus, quam plurima adhuc dicenda reliquerimus quia non ambitione commotus, aut meae commendationis causa ueni ad scribendum, sed officio et ueritate, ne tanquam sacrilegus tam deuoto sexui debitas sibi laudes (ut talentum mihi creditum suffodiendo) impia quadam taciturnitate surripere uidear si silerem (89).[7]

> [However numerous were my arguments, I left many points to be treated because I came to write not from ambition or to advance myself but out of duty to truth so that I might not, if I kept silent, appear to commit a sort of sacrilege, hiding by means of an impious silence the praise that such a pious sex merits, as though burying in the earth a treasure which had been given to me.]

Claiming to speak out strongly and truthfully, Agrippa makes no pretense of offering a value-neutral set of arguments. Indeed, his description of his own interest in these questions personalizes the account and explains his vehement tone. He remarks on the audacious novelty of his project:

> Certauit fateor intra me saepius audacia cum pudore. Nam ut innumeras mulierum laudes, virtutes, summamque praestantiam oratione velle complecti, plenum ambitionis et audaciae putabam, sic foeminas maribus praeferre, tamquam euirati ingenii plenum pudoris videbatur. Hinc forte causans cur quum pauci admodum de mulierum laudibus scribere tentarunt, nullus hactenus quod certo sciam earum supra viros eminentiam adserere ausus est. (48)

> [I confess that more than once, inside myself, my audacity had to combat my scruples. For wanting to embrace in one discourse the countless merits of women, their virtues, their absolute superiority was, I thought, totally audacious, although to grant them pre-eminence over men appeared to indicate an emasculated mind and the height of shame. This would explain, perhaps, why since few authors have attempted to write praising women, not a single one, until now, has dared to affirm their superiority over men.]

Agrippa's use of the expression "an emasculated mind" [evirati ingenii] is
especially interesting. It suggests that defending womankind would leave a
writer open to charges that he did not have a mind that was characteristic
of, or in the service of, *viri* (men). The youthful and presumably virile
Agrippa overcomes his scruples concerning the possible castrating effect of
defending women.[8] He approaches his task with humility, commenting that
his style might not be equal to the nobility of his subject matter: "vt vix me
escusatum iri fidam, qui rem adeo sublimem humiliori quam par est dicendi
forma complexus sum" (48) [I can barely hope to be pardoned who have
embraced such a noble subject with a more modest style than is fitting].
The tentative nature of his preliminary remarks fades when he launches
into his arguments.[9]

In the *De nobilitate,* Agrippa declares that the women of his age have
greatly reduced opportunities to participate actively in life outside the home,
and, unable to keep silent, he feels impelled to offer an impassioned description of their pitiful state. Anticipating feminists of our own times, he
blames social and institutional factors for the subordination of women.[10]
Arguing that the treatment of women in his day is contrary to both divine
and natural laws, he questions the traditional, Biblical justifications for
women's inferior status. Laws, custom, and education all contribute to
suppressing women: "data mulieribus libertas iam iniquis legibus interdicitur,
consuetudine usuque aboletur, educatione extinguitur" (87) [the liberty
which was once granted to women is forbidden to them today by unjust
laws, is abolished by custom and tradition, and is extinguished by educa-
tion]. This tyrannical repression by men goes against divine law (87). He
repeatedly underscores his belief that the sources of the violation and subversion of laws concerning woman's dignity are man-made. Great evil is
perpetrated by those who do not heed God's word. These misdeeds are overt
and demonstrate bad faith: "Sed tanta est recentium legislatorum improbitas,
qui irritum fecerunt mandatum Dei" (88) [But our new lawmakers have
such bad faith that they do not take into consideration the commandment
of God]. Some men even tyrannically misuse scripture as a justification for
oppressing women: "Sunt praeterea qui ex religione autoritatem sibi arro-
gant in mulieres, et ex sacris litteris suam probant tyrannidem" (88) [There
are some as well who use religion to authorize themselves to exercise their
authority over women and who found their tyranny on Holy Scripture].
Indeed, most of the restrictions placed on women during the Middle Ages
and through the sixteenth century are based on misogynist interpretations
of scriptures and canon law.[11]

Agrippa observes that injustice towards women is widespread in the
society around him. He feels that the freedom once enjoyed by women in

ancient Rome, and which is their natural heritage, has been usurped.[12] Laws preclude women from acting in certain legal capacities:

> Publica quaeque officia legibus sibi interdicta sunt. Postulare in iudicio licet prudentissimae non permittitur. Repelluntur praeterea in iurisdictione, in arbitrio, in adoptione, in intercessione, in procuratione, in tutela, in cura, in testamentaria et criminali causa. (87)
>
> [Public office is forbidden to them by law. It is not permitted, even for the wisest of them, to start legal action against someone. They are excluded as well from legal action about judgments, adoptions, the right to bring suits, administration, guardianship, matters of inheritance, and criminal trials.]

Women lack not only legal opportunities but also, contrary to scripture,[13] they are barred from religious functions that were open to them in the early Church (87). Fallible human beings, not the divine plan, oppress women (88). By stressing the culturally determined nature of the oppression, he implies that such restrictions can be changed.

The restrictions that Agrippa has in mind concern the public arena. He observes that women's activities are strictly limited to the domestic sphere, portraying the opportunities open to women as limited to needlework:[14] "Mulier namque mox ut nata est, a primis annis domi detinetur in desidia, ac uelut altioris prouinciae incapax, nihil praeter acus et filum concipere permittitur" (87) [When scarcely born, in fact, woman is kept idle at home from her earliest years and, as though she were incapable of more important functions, she has no other perspective than needles and thread]. This idleness is especially distressing to Agrippa.[15] He believes that women have many inherent but hitherto undeveloped abilities that remain dormant. Unfortunately, women do not fare better when they reach puberty. He sees only two options for women at that point in their lives, neither of which includes self-determination: "Ubi exinde pubertatis annos attigerit, in mariti traditur zelotypum imperium, aut uestalium ergastulo perpetuo recluditur" (87) [Then, when she arrives at puberty, they hand her over to the jealous power of a husband or they lock her up forever in a religious convent]. Agrippa's word choice conveys his disdain for these "opportunities."[16]

Agrippa portrays male/female power relations by means of a vivid simile of victor/vanquished. He contends that enforcing submission to male authority by means of legal prescriptions is tyrannical: "His itaque legibus mulieres uiris tanquam bello uictae uictoribus cedere coguntur, non naturali, non diuina aliqua necessitate aut ratione, sed consuetudine, educatione, fortuna et tyrannica quadam occasione id agente" (88). [Thus these laws constrain women to submit to men like the vanquished before the victors and all that without reason or divine or natural necessity but under the pressure of custom, of their education, of chance, or of some tyrannical circumstance]. The arbitrariness of the constraints suffered by women are especially obvious in this passage. The powerless vanquished have no choice but to submit to their oppressors.

While he was very concerned with the legal and educational status of women, Agrippa primarily grappled with theological questions in the *De nobilitate*. The first (or priestly) creation story of Genesis 1.26–27 establishes that both men and women are created in the image of God, a passage that caused great trouble to the Church Fathers who tried to reconcile it with Paul's statements concerning the subordination of women to men in 1 Corinthians 11.7–9.[17] Unlike Augustine and Aquinas, who differentiated between the body and the soul, for Agrippa the concept of parity regarding the souls of men and women is extended to all their qualities. He boldly contrasts female refinement with male coarseness (49, 96). According to him, the only differences between the sexes lie in their reproductive organs:

> Deus Optimus Maximus, cunctorum genitor, Pater, ac bonum utriusque sexus foecunditate plenissimus, hominem sibi similem creavit, masculum et foeminam creauit illos: quorum quidem sexuum discretio non nisi situ partium corporis differente constat, in quibus vsus generandi diuersitatem necessariam requirebat. . . .(49)

> [God, the very good and very great Father and creator of all beings, who alone possesses the fecundity of both sexes, created humans in his own image and created them male and female: indeed, there is no distinction of the sexes except where it separately concerns the parts of the body in which the action of procreating demands a necessary diversity.]

All other qualities of men and women are equal, a belief underscored by his use of the adjective *idem*:

> Eandem vero et masculo et foeminae, ac omnino indifferentem animae formam tribuit, inter quas nulla prorus sexus est distantia, eandem ipsa mulier cum viro sortita est mentem, rationem atque sermonem, ad eundem tendit beatitudinis finem, vbi sexus nulla erit exceptio. (49)

[But he gave to man and to woman absolutely the same identical type of soul where there are no differences between the sexes. Woman received as her share the same intelligence as man, the same reasoning ability, the same language; she aims for the same end as he does, beatitude, which will not exclude either sex.]

Agrippa interprets scripture to say that each sex has the same opportunity for eternal salvation. He refers to passages in the Gospels to emphasize that after the Resurrection the distinctions between the sexes will be further reduced, since there will be no expression of sexuality:[18]

Nam iuxta euangelicam veritatem, resurgentes in proprio sexu, sexus, non fungentur officio, sed angelorum illis promittitur similitudo. Nulla itaque est ab essentia animae inter virum et mulierem, alterius super alterum nobilitatis praeeminentia: sed vtriusque par dignitatis innata libertas. (49)

[For, according to the truth of the Gospel: "While they will rise as their own sex, they will no longer acquit themselves of the functions of their sex but it has been promised to them that they will be likened to angels." Thus, because of the essence of their souls, there is no preeminence of nobility of one sex over the other and, by birth, they are equal in dignity and liberty the one to the other.]

Thus, as regards the soul, there is perfect equality between man and woman, since the divine essence of the genders is equal. Agrippa repeats the same idea at the end of the treatise, paraphrasing 2 Corinthians 5.17: "non tamen est acceptor personarum Deus: in Christo enim nec mas, nec foemina, sed noua creatura" (88) [Thus God has no preference for any person, for in Christ there is neither male nor female but a new creature]. The new creature of the Gospels has the promise of salvation through Christ regardless of his or her gender.

While Agrippa begins with the concept of the parity between the genders as defined in scripture, he soon moves on to a reversal of hierarchies. With a sweeping generalization antithetical to Augustine and Aquinas, who found woman to be inferior in all other aspects besides her soul, Agrippa posits that she is superior: "Quae autem praeter animae diuinam essentiam in homine reliqua sunt, in iis muliebris inclyta stirps durum virorum genus in infinitum pene excellit" (49) [But, apart from the divine essence of the soul, over all things that constitute the human being, the illustrious female sex is almost infinitely superior to the harsh male sex]. With this statement, he begins to dismantle the accepted hierarchical truth concerning men and women.

The traditional justification for the subordinate status of women is the biblical creation story. Agrippa's most outstanding contribution to the *querelle* is his recasting of the story of Eve in terms favorable to women. He provides a progression of arguments to prove the superiority of women, and he thereby overturns the usual justifications for their subordination. This reasoning is all the more effective because he uses familiar, biblical sources in a way directly contrary to that of the misogynists.[19] Eve's superiority is evidenced in four different ways. She is superior by virtue of her name *(a nomine)*, the order of her creation *(ab ordine)*, the place of her creation *(a loco)*, and the material from which she is formed *(a materia)*. Agrippa contrasts these four aspects of Eve's origin with Adam in a series of oppositions. First, Eve's name is superior, since it means "life" whereas Adam's name means "earth." Second, Eve is superior in the order of her creation. She is created second and, as such, reflects improvement over Adam who serves as her prototype. Third, Eve is created in the Garden of Eden, which is preferable to being created outside of it like Adam. Finally, God makes Eve from bone, a more refined material than the earth out of which he formed Adam (50–55).

By means of these juxtapositions, Agrippa shows that God's plan culminated in the creation of woman. His presentation underscores that the divine plan accords womankind a special consideration that is denied to her in the sixteenth century. He associates Adam with earth, materiality, and the natural world, whereas Eve represents a higher level of abstraction— life, refinement, and civilization.[20] By twice identifying Adam with the earth *(a nomine* and *a materia)* and by elevating Eve's place and order of creation *(a loco* and *ab ordine)*, Agrippa erodes the traditional scriptural interpretation that undergirds Christian misogyny.

In the *De nobilitate,* Agrippa also rejects the standard argument that Eve is the source of all humankind's woes, attributing them instead to Adam. He emphasizes her innocence, since she had not yet been created when the fruit was forbidden to Adam: "viro namque interdictus erat fructus ligni, mulieri non item, quae neque dum creata erat" (65) [the fruit of the tree was forbidden to man not to woman who had not yet been created]. With emphatic redundancy he places the guilt on Adam, inserting his name in the place usually occupied by Eve's in the traditional explanations of the consequences of the Fall:

> illa enim Deus ab initio liberam esse voluit, vir itaque comedendo peccavit, non mulier, vir mortem dedit, non mulier. Et nos omnes peccavimus in Adam, non in Eva, ipsumque originale peccatum non a matre foemina, sed a patre masculo contrahimus. (65–66)

[God wanted her to be free from the beginning. It is thus man who committed sin by eating, not woman; man who brought about death not woman. And we have all sinned through Adam not Eve, and we are burdened with original sin not because of our mother who is a woman, but because of our father who is a man.]

Blaming the fall on Adam, Agrippa absolves Eve and all subsequent women from the guilt of original sin.

Those who have perpetuated the denigration of Eve are special targets in the *De nobilitate*. Agrippa speaks directly to the men who would use scholastic arguments to prove the opposite contentions about women. Pushing to the limit the implications of their arguments, he charges them with trying to prove the absurd proposition that the wickedness of men is better than the goodness of women: "Ite nunc viri fortes et robusti, et vos praegnantia Pallade, ligata tot fasciis scholastica capita, et totidem exemplis contrariam illam probate sententiam, quod melior sit iniquitas viri quam mulier benefaciens" (70) [Go ahead now, you strong and robust men, and you, disciples of scholasticism, pregnant with Athena. Prove by as many examples the opposing thesis that the wickedness of man is better than the good actions of woman]. This willful caricature and distortion of his opponents' goals conveys a total lack of respect. He derides their abilities, suggesting they could only win by using tactics that would ultimately please him: "Certe non poteritis illam tueri, ni recurratis ad allegorias, ubi tunc aequalis cum viro mulieris erit authoritas" (70) [Without a doubt you cannot prove it without having recourse to allegories where the prestige of woman will equal that of man].

Whereas he accords flimsy allegorical proof of women's inferiority to his opponents, Agrippa implies that his views are strongly supported. He defends the soundness and straightforwardness of his argumentation and sources:

Ideoque non tam studium fuit rhetoricis figmentis officiosisque mendaciis verba in laudes ornare quam rem ipsam ratione, authoritate, exemplis, ipsisque sacrarum litterarum, et vtriusque iuris testimoniis commenstrare. (48)

[I am less concerned with adorning with clever images or charming fictions that praise than with presenting my own thesis and founding it on reason, authority, and witness drawn from Holy Scriptures and the two laws.]

Agrippa endeavors to expose fallacious reasoning, basing his arguments on
scripture and canon law, the same sources regularly used by detractors to
disprove the worth of women. He chooses these sources because they offer,
following the standards of his era, undisputable proof for his arguments
through reason, authority, example, and witness and, above all, because his
opponents use them.

Despite the youthful aggressiveness of his antischolastic rhetoric
and his inflammatory tone, Agrippa's own arguments come from a traditional mold that he modifies for his own purpose.[21] He freely uses
proofs taken from Aristotle for purposes of which the Stagirite would
have never dreamed. He founds his argument on the Aristotelian logic
of the group: "Est etenim Aristotelis validum hoc argumentum: cuius
generis optimum est nobilius optime alterius generis, hoc genus esse
altero nobilius" (70) [One finds in Aristotle the following argument which
is weighty: when the best element in one group is nobler than the best
in another, then the first group is nobler than the second]. By this logic,
women as a group are superior, since their sex includes the Virgin Mary.
Likewise, "Similiter argumentari licebit, cujus generis pessimum pejus
est pessimo alterius, id genus esse illo quoque inferius" (71) [One can
argue in a similar manner saying that when what is the worst in one
group is poorer than what is worst in another, this group is also inferior
to the other]. For this reason Judas, the worst of all humans, taints his
entire gender, since he is a man.

Agrippa singles out beauty, chastity, modesty, invention, courage, and
honor as the special female virtues that elevate woman's dignity. His defense of chastity is especially important, since misogynists traditionally stress
the notion that women have insatiable sexual appetites.[22] Agrippa suggests
the contrary. The bulk of the *De nobilitate* catalogues the female virtues
and lists the names of women who exemplified these abstractions. His catalogue includes famous women from antiquity and from the Bible, as well
as the fifteenth-century heroine, Joan of Arc. The meritorious lives of these
women serve, by example, as proof that their gender is superior. This method
of argumentation is typical of early treatises supporting women.[23] Rather
than structuring arguments in a logical progression, Agrippa strengthens
his case by the sheer number of examples he cites.[24]

While there are many women who are mentioned in Agrippa's list, the
Virgin Mary and Margaret of Austria, his patroness, occupy the highest
places among them. He stresses the Virgin Mary's role as redemptress of
humanity. In his view, Jesus is the son not of man but of woman (107).
Mary embodies the Church, which she faithfully kept alive at the time of
the crucifixion when Jesus' male followers were in despair: "Accedit huc
quod tota ferme theologorum scola, asserit, Ecclesiam tunc non nisi apud

solam mulierem, puta Virginem Mariam mansisse, atque, ob id, et merito religiosus ac sacer faemineus sexus appellatur" (67) [Let's add to this, according to the affirmation of almost the entire school of theologians that the Church only remained (at the time of the crucifixion) embodied in a single woman, the Virgin Mary, which causes the female sex rightly to be called religious and sacred]. References to the Virgin Mary occur several times in *De nobilitate*. An especially long reference to her is placed between the discussion of courage and chastity. God chose her, a woman, to be the most exalted of all humans, "quod dignissima omnium creaturarum, qua nec unquam dignior fuit, nec futura est" (70) [the noblest of all creatures, the one that no one surpasses and will never surpass in dignity]. In his enthusiasm for her greatness and for the doctrine of her Immaculate Conception,[25] Agrippa elevates her to the level of Christ, himself: "ipsa inquam beatissima virgo Maria qua siquidem praeter originale peccatum concepta sit, ne Christus quidem, quod ad eius humanitatem attinet, maior erit" (70) [if it is true that the Blessed Virgin Mary was conceived outside of original sin, in what concerns his humanity not even Christ will be greater]. Keeping within orthodoxy concerning her humanity and that of her Son, he erases all notion of Mary as a subordinate.

Margaret of Austria likewise receives the highest status. At the conclusion of the liminary dedication of the *De nobilitate*, Agrippa praises her as the embodiment of all virtues and of feminine superiority. He extols her not only for her high birth and personal qualities, but also for her deeds. In his opinion, as "praesentaneo exemplo" [a present example] she is without peer in demonstrating female merit and represents irrefutable proof of the worth of womankind. When Agrippa praises Margaret's character, he makes a particularly interesting use of the metaphor of the sun:

Tibi . . . serenissima Margareta . . . hanc operam nostram ideo devotam dedicatamque constituto . . . vt te (quae ad id virtutum fastigium ascendisti, quod, cuncta quae de foeminei sexus laudibus praedicantur, vita et moribus superasti), praesentaneo exemplo, ac teste fidissima, eiusdem sexus vestri decus, et gloria, quasi sole quodam splendidius elucescat. (48)

[most serene Margaret . . . I deem this work of ours consecrated and dedicated to you, in order that with you (who have attained such a height of virtues that you surpass by your life and moral standards all the praise addressed to the female sex) as the present example and the irrefutable witness, the honor and the glory of this sex that is your own may shine forth more brilliantly, as if in the presence of the sun.]

The sun is usually associated with males. Agrippa's choice of image embodies a sense of Margaret's active nature, as well as connotations of her power and patronage.[26] When Agrippa focuses exclusively on Margaret, he leaves out several other noteworthy contemporary women who are probably excluded for personal and political reasons.[27]

The *De nobilitate* was widely disseminated both in the 1529 Anvers Latin edition and in five editions of the French translation.[28] While traces of Agrippa's influence may be seen in several French authors,[29] the mark of Agrippa's treatise is most clearly seen in the writing of Hélisenne de Crenne, the author of the first French sentimental novel, *Les angoysses douloureuses qui procèdent d'amour* (1538). She followed the success of this bestseller with two polemical works that borrow from the *De nobilitate*, *Les épistres familieres et invectives* (1539) and *Le songe* (1540). Her Fourth Invective Letter catalogues famous women writers and is patterned after Agrippa's. She even modeled an encomium to Marguerite de Navarre after Agrippa's praise of his patroness:

> ie n'estime point, qu'au preterit iamais fut, ne pour le futur peult estre personne de plus preclaire & altissime esperit, que tresillustre & magnanime princesse, ma dame la royne de Nauarre, c'est vne chose toute notoire, qu'en sa reginale excellente & sublime personne, reside la diuinité Platonicque, la prudence de Caton, l'eloquence de Cicero, & la Socratique raison: & à brief parler sa sincerité est tant accomplie, que la splendeur d'icelle à la condition femenine donne lustre. . . .

> [I believe that never was there in the past, nor will there ever be in the future, a loftier or more brilliant spirit than the most illustrious and distinguished princess, the queen of Navarre. It is a fact widely acclaimed that her royal and lofty person combines Plato's godlike wisdom, Cato's prudence, Cicero's eloquence, and Socrates' wisdom. Her sincerity is so accomplished, in short, that her brilliance enhances all of womankind; her example alone is enough to refute your vain and futile opinions.][30]

In this passage she borrows not only the technique of focusing on a single contemporary woman to prove the worth of women of her times, she also uses his imagery of the sun.

Le songe draws on Agrippa's discussion of Genesis, repeating his presentation of Eve's superiority over Adam in the four categories of name, origin, place, and matter. She freely adapts his arguments concerning the concept of the parity of the male and female soul, but she fleshes out his abstractions and incorporates them into a worldview consistent with her other texts. Her entire corpus is didactic, founded on the belief that women are capable of rational persuasion and that they may, therefore, be encouraged to develop their noblest selves. This didacticism was all the more vital, since, as her novel illustrates, sensuality is an ever tempting lure away from virtue. Because women have immortal souls equal to men's, it is important to win these souls for God.[31] De Crenne invents none of her arguments praising her sex but takes them straight from the translation of the *De nobilitate*.[32] She reads widely in French, especially works dealing with the *querelle,* and her subsequent writings reflect the interests of the readership of popular fiction in Paris in the 1530s and 1540s. While Agrippa furnishes de Crenne with learned arguments that probably would have been beyond her ability to formulate due to the limits of a sixteenth-century woman's education, she supplements them with a moral indignation growing out of personal experience as a woman in a society controlled by men. By her own example, she illustrates the potential of the female mind.

De Crenne is not the only author to follow Agrippa's lead in denouncing limits placed on women. Louise Labé, her contemporary from Lyon, likewise urges women to "eslever un peu leurs esprits par-dessus leurs quenoilles et fuseaus" [raise their minds a bit above their spindles and distaffs].[33] Regardless of their zeal, however, these women did not have the resources of Agrippa's erudition in formulating a defense of woman. The *De nobilitate* provided the theoretical arguments for the *querelle* in an easily accessible format. The women who read him in Latin and, especially, in the French translations provided the passionate zeal to keep the debate going. This zeal stemmed from their own lived experience in a society in which they were stifled by reduced possibilities. In a day when most women could only dream of being accepted as equals by men, Agrippa proclaimed they were superior.[34] His highly influential Latin treatise carried the prestige of that language in a century of biliteracy, but its dissemination in the vernacular allowed women to appropriate it for their own use.[35]

Agrippa's subversive reversal of traditional hierarchies won wide acceptance by the partisans of the *querelle des femmes*. Using formal rhetorical proof and traditional sources, he arrived at very new conclusions. The *De nobilitate* set the standard for learned discourse about women in the period, meriting the title "le *Talmud,* la *Confession d'Augsbourg* de la secte féministe," bestowed on it by Théodore Joran.[36] By presenting the extreme notion that women are superior to men, Agrippa seriously undermined established notions about the relationship between the sexes. While it would be anachronistic to attribute twentieth-century views to a sixteenth-century scholar, Agrippa's strong support of women and his belief in their inherent abilities makes him a kindred spirit to those of our own era who continue to struggle against the forces that suppress women.

Notes

1, Lula M. Richardson's *The Forerunners of Feminism in French Literature of the Renaissance from Christine of Pisa to Marie de Gournay*, Johns Hopkins Studies in Romance Literatures and Languages 12 (Baltimore, MD: Johns Hopkins University Press, and Paris: PUF, 1929); Marc Angenot's *Les Champions des Femmes* (Montreal: Quebec University Press, 1977); and Joan Kelly's "Early Feminist Theory and the *Querelle des Femmes*, 1400–1789," *Signs* 8 (1982): pp. 4–28 outline the major aspects of the *querelle*. I am very grateful to Paul Allen Miller for the generous help in conceptualizing this article and with the translations from the *De nobilitate*, to Barbara K. Gold, whose insightful comments sparked significant improvements in my article, to Marc van der Poel for bibliographical aid, and to Edward V. George, whose enthusiasm for Renaissance Latin rhetoric is contagious.

2. See Marc van der Poel's "Review of Henri Corneille Agrippa's *De nobilitate*," *Rhetorica* 10 (1992): pp. 303–11. My paper also incorporates material Professor van der Poel presented in his unpublished paper "Cornelius Agrippa's *Treatise on the Excellence of Women*: Feminist Encominum or Rhetorical Paradox?" at Texas Tech University, 14 Apr. 1994, as well as other very helpful suggestions. Van der Poel stresses that the enthusiasm for the *De nobilitate* lasted into the eighteenth century ("Review of *De nobilitate*," p. 303). Charles G. Nauert Jr.'s biography, *Agrippa and the Crisis of Renaissance Thought*, Illinois Studies in the Social Sciences 55 (Urbana: Illinois University Press, 1965), is helpful concerning Agrippa's life and his long association with Margaret of Austria and her father, the Emperor Maximillian I.

3. In his review of the *De nobilitate*, van der Poel discusses questions concerning the interpretation of the text: "One of the problems these scholars are confronted with is the fact that it has not yet been firmly established whether the treatise is a serious writing or not" (p. 303). Van der Poel's forthcoming book unambiguously takes the position that Agrippa's work is serious. He sees the *De nobilitate* as somber indictment of sixteenth-century society: "This radical criticism of society ought to be read as a polemical thesis, intended to provoke discussion, especially among theologians, in an academic setting or otherwise" (p. 310).

4. Van der Poel, personal interview, 20 Apr. 1994. Van der Poel bases his definition on Charles Etienne's "contraires a l'opinion de la pluspart des hommes". See Warner G. Rice's "The *Paradossi* of Ortensio Lando," *Language and Literature* 8 (1932): p. 67.

5. Van der Poel's article on another of Agrippa's declamations is also pertinent for the *De nobilitate*. See his "Agrippa von Nettesheim and Rhetoric: An Examination of the *Declamatio de Originali Peccato*," *Humanistica Lovaniensia* 39 (1990): pp. 179–180.

6. See van der Poel's "Agrippa and Rhetoric," p. 199, for an explanation of the connection between these values and the study of rhetoric in the sixteenth century.

7. All references are to the edition of the *De nobilitate et praecellentia foeminei sexus*, ed. Roland Antonioli, Charles Béné and Odette Sauvage (Geneva: Droz, 1990), p. 89. Please note that this edition is inconsistent in its usage of consonantal and vocalic *u* and *v*. See Marc van der Poel's review for comments on the edition's irregularities in punctuation and mistakes in spelling. While the spelling of the edition has been retained, I have, on occasion, emended the punctuation of the Antonioli edition.

8. In point of fact, most of the defenders of women in the *querelle* were men who, like Agrippa, faced derision for their stance. See Angenot, *Champions des Femmes*, p. 4.

9. Agrippa appears to be using *humilitas* as a mask. See Ernst Robert Curtius's discussion of the medieval topos of *humilitas* and its use as a literary convention in his *European Literature and the Latin Middle Ages*, trans. Willard R. Trask (New York: Pantheon, 1953), pp. 411–12.

10. Feminists are increasingly focusing on questions of power in society. Gayle Rubin "places the oppression of women within social systems, rather than in biology" in her article "The Traffic in Women: Notes on the 'Political Economy' of Sex" in *Toward an Anthropology of Women*, ed. Rayna R. Rester (New York: Monthly Review Press, 1975), p. 175. Gayle Green and Coppélia Kahn begin their discussion of "the social construction of woman" with the premise "that the inequality of the sexes is neither a biological given nor a divine mandate, but a cultural construct" ("Feminist Scholarship and the Social Construction of Woman," in *Making a Difference: Feminist Literary Criticism*, ed. Gayle Green and Coppélia Kahn [London and New York: Methuen, 1985], p. 1). Chris Weedon devotes a chapter to the discussion of power in *Feminist Practice and Poststructuralist Theory* (Oxford: Basil Blackwell, 1987), pp. 107–135: "For feminists, the attempt to understand power in all its forms is of central importance. The failure to understand the multiplicity of power relations focused in sexuality will render an analysis blind to the range of points of resistance inherent in the network of power relations, a blindness which impedes political resistance" (p. 124). Weedon views Foucault as a groundbreaker in this area. In her *Gender Trouble: Feminism and the Subversion of Identity* (New York and London: Routledge, 1990), Judith Butler exposes "the foundational categories of sex, gender, and desire as effects of a specific formation of power" (p. x).

11. Inter alia, see Rosemary Radford Ruether's "Misogynism and Virginal Feminism in the Fathers of the Church," in *Religion and Sexism: Images of Woman in the Jewish and Christian Traditions*, ed. Rosemary Radford Ruether (New York: Simon and Schuster, 1974).

12. Roland Antonioli discusses Agrippa's views of Roman legal egalitarianism in his "L'Image de la femme dans le *De nobilitate et praecellentia foeminei sexus de H. C. Agrippa*," *Acta Universitatis Lodziensis, Folia Litteraria* 14 (1985): p. 36.

13. Joel 2.28 and Acts 2.17.

14. See Michelle Z. Rosaldo's discussion of the domestic versus the public orientations of gender roles in "Women, Culture, and Society: A Theoretical Overview," in *Women, Culture, and Society*, ed. Michelle Z. Rosaldo and Louise Lamphere (Stanford, CA: Stanford University Press, 1974), pp.19–24 *et passim*. Until recently, women have been associated solely with household duties. See Michel Foucault in his *The Use of Pleasure, The History of Sexuality*, vol. 2, trans. Robert Hurley (New York: Vintage, 1990), p. 157. Medieval instructions typically confine women to the home. See Eleanor Commo McLaughlin's "Equality of Souls, Inequality of Sexes: Women in Medieval Theology" in *Religion and Sexism. Images of Woman in the Jewish and Christian Traditions*, ed. Rosemary Radford Ruether (New York: Simon and Schuster, 1974), p. 231. In her article in this volume, Diana Robin states that the rejection of this kind of female work in favor of masculine occupations was used to characterize the writers included in the catalogues of women after Boccaccio's *De claris mulieribus* (1355). In contrast, Patricia Klindienst Joplin celebrates "the voice of the shuttle" as resistance to oppression. See her "The Voice of the Shuttle is Ours," *Stanford Literature Review* 1 (1984): pp. 25–53.

15. Idleness was also anathema to Hélisenne de Crenne, for whom writing becomes the antidote to boredom. In an invective, she portrays it as a sort of lifesaving device to keep her from the fear of "going under and drowning in the perilous sea of inactivity." See Hélisenne de Crenne, *A Renaissance Woman: Helisenne's Personal and Invective Letters*, ed. and trans. Marianna M. Mustacchi and Paul J. Archambault (Syracuse, NY: Syracuse University Press, 1986), p. 102. Diana Robin's paper in this volume shows how exceptional Laura Cereta was in choosing "to express herself with both a pen *and* a needle."

16. Convent life was not always considered a bad alternative. See Mary Kinnear's *Daughters of Time. Women in the Western Tradition* (Ann Arbor: Michigan University Press, 1982), p. 66, on the partial autonomy offered to women by the religious life. In her first personal letter, Hélisenne de Crenne relates how she would have preferred to remain in the convent where she was educated, but familial considerations caused her to leave. She evokes convent life as a rich intellectual experience. See de Crenne, *A Renaissance Woman*, pp. 39–40.

17. See Kari Elisabeth Børresen's *Subordination and Equivalence. The Nature and Rôle of Woman in Augustine and Thomas Aquinas* (Washington, DC: University Press of America, 1981) for the views of SS. Augustine (pp. 29–30) and Thomas Aquinas (pp. 170–71) concerning the souls of women. For Aquinas, a woman's body was always a bar to holiness. See Kinnear, *Daughters of Time*, p. 63.

18. Luke 20, Mark 12, and Matthew 22.

19. His logical presentation will repeatedly be reused by others like de Crenne in succeeding eras who are less schooled in formal dialectics and canon law.

20. Hélène Cixous and Catherine Clément present these oppositions in their *The Newly Born Woman*, trans. Betsy Wing (Minneapolis: University of Minnesota

Press, 1975), p. 61. Many other critics have pointed out these traditional male/ female oppositions including Kinnear, *Daughters of Time*, 58–59, Foucault, *Use of Pleasure*, 46, and Sherry Ortner in her article "Is Female to Male as Nature is to Culture?" in *Women, Culture, and Society*, ed. Michelle Z. Rosaldo and Louise Lamphere (Stanford, CA: Stanford University Press, 1974), pp. 72–83. For Aristotle's comments and his series of oppositions equating females with the earth in *On the Generation of Animals*, see Mary R. Lefkowitz and Maureen B. Fant's *Women's Life in Greece and Rome* (Baltimore, MD: Johns Hopkins University Press, 1982), p. 82.

21. Agrippa's statements concerning Eve conform with ideas expressed in the sermons of Humbert de Romans, Master-General of the Dominican Order (1194–1277). See the discussion of Romans' widely disseminated views in Bede Jarrett's *Social Theories of the Middle Ages, 1200–1500* (1926; repr., New York: Frederick Ungar, 1966), pp. 69–72.

22. See Kinnear, *Daughters of Time*, p. 64, and McLaughlin, "Equality of Souls," p. 225. R. Howard Bloch discusses what he calls the "feminization of the flesh" and the strength of female desire in his *Medieval Misogyny and the Invention of Western Romantic Love* (Chicago: University of Chicago Press, 1991), pp. 9, 27, *et passim*.

23. See, for example, Christine de Pizan's *The Book of the City of Ladies*, trans. Earl Jeffrey Richards (New York: Persea, 1982), an English translation of the 1405 text, de Crenne's *A Renaissance Woman*, and François de Billon's *Le fort inexpugnable de l'honneur du sexe feminin* (1555; repr., East Ardsley, England: S. R. Publishers, New York: Johnson Reprints, and The Hague: Mouton, 1970). This cataloguing of famous women was also prevalent in Italy. See Diana Robin's article in this volume for a list of Italian catalogues.

24. Susan Suleiman discusses the effect of redundancy in didactic texts, including exempla and paraboles, in her article "Le récit exemplaire. Parabole, fable, roman à thèse," *Poétique* 32 (1977): pp. 479–80.

25. Agrippa's earliest theological polemic concerns the monogamy of Saint Anne where he supported the views of the great humanist reformer, Jacques Lefèvre d'Etaples. See Nauert, *Agrippa and the Crisis*, pp. 61–65, 183–84.

26. For Aristotle's comments on the sun as a masculine image, see his *Generation of Animals*, trans. A. L. Peck, (Cambridge: Harvard University Press, 1953), p. 11.

27. Louise de Savoie and her daughter, Marguerite de Navarre, occupied prominent positions in catalogues of French women of the period, but they were Margaret of Austria's great rivals. They, along with Margaret of Austria, negotiated the "Paix des dames" in 1529. In 1526 Agrippa dedicated his *De sacramento matrimonii* to Marguerite de Navarre, then Duchess of Alençon. He received twenty gold pieces for the dedication but was never "in her inner circle." See Nauert, *Agrippa and the Crisis*, p. 90. This work was printed in the same volume of Agrippa's short works along with the *De nobilitate*. Nauert also discusses the unpleasant experiences Agrippa

had while court physician to Louise de Savoie, pp. 85–103. He would later have difficulties with Margaret of Austria. See Nauert, pp. 216–17.

28. Stephen Rawles lists two printings of the translation (c. 1530) in his dissertation "Denys Janot, Parisian Printer and Bookseller (fl. 1529–1544): A Bibliographical Study" (University of Warwick, 1976), nos. 227 and 228. The French translation also appears in a 1530 edition by Galliot Du Pré (Paris), a 1530 edition by Martin de Keyser (Antwerp), and a 1537 edition by François Juste. This proliferation of editions testifies to the wide interest in the treatise.

29. Antonioli sees the influence on Louise Labé and on Antoine Du Moulin who prefaced Pernette du Guillet's *Rymes*. See Antonioli's "L'image," p. 38.

30. De Crenne, *Les épistres*, f. K7r–v. and *A Renaissance Woman*, p. 101.

31. De Crenne, *Le songe* (Paris: Denis Janot, 1540), f. 14v.

32. See Mustacchi and Archambault's notes 64 and 74 crediting Agrippa as a major source for de Crenne's invectives in *A Renaissance Woman*. While she probably read some Latin, de Crenne was more likely to have read the translation, probably in a Denis Janot edition.

33. Louise Labé, *Oeuvres complètes*, ed. François Rigolot (Paris: Flammarion, 1986), p. 42.

34. Angenot explains this hierarchical thinking as an integral part of the thinking pattern of the era and views it as an extension of the ancient topos of *mundus inversus, Champions des Femmes*, p. 163. Madeleine Lazard likewise sees this claim to female superiority as a typical sixteenth-century intellectual stance that excludes concepts of parity in her *Images littéraires de la femme à la Renaissance* (Paris: PUF, 1985), p.12. Angenot points out, however, that, in contrast to male authors, the women authors he studied are content to prove parity. See his p. 5.

35. Dorothy Gabe Coleman treats the question of the biliterary in her *The Gallo-Roman Muse* (Cambridge: Cambridge University Press, 1979), p. 183.

36. Théodore Joran, *Les féministes avant le féminisme* (Paris: Arthur Savaète, 1911), p. 35.

The Artificial Whore: George Buchanan's *Apologia pro Lena*

Charles Platter

 Sometime in the 1540s the Scottish humanist, George Buchanan, a teacher of Latin at the College de Guyenne in Bordeaux (where the young Montaigne was among his pupils), composed a mock defense of prostitution for his friend, Briand de Valleé, *conseiller* in the Bordeaux parliament for 18 years, distinguished lawyer, and friend of Rabelais.[1] The poem, which appears fourth among the elegies in Buchanan's collected works, is titled *Apologia pro lena* (*Defense of the Procuress*) and purports to be an outraged response to a *bordelais* decree outlawing brothels.[2] Its most intense affiliations, however, are neither contemporary nor political but with the tradition of Latin poetry and, particularly, of Augustan elegy. One result of this interaction with antiquity is that the heavily textured aesthetic surface that Buchanan creates to argue the question of the *lena* and of prostitution has much less to do with women than it does with poetry and the art of imitation.[3] The procuress herself is spoken for by the poet/advocate, to be judged by the male tribunal (represented by Briand de Valée); she never speaks on her own behalf.[4] Further, the elegiac background of the poem gives Buchanan the opportunity to emulate his predecessors by taking an apparently frivolous theme (in their case erotic poetry) and using it as the medium for a complex consideration of poetry and the principles surrounding its production. The result, as I will suggest, is an innovative artistic use of imitation, but one that approaches the feminine only by creating a procuress with no personal desires or attributes of her own and who is controlled and altogether obscured by the associations of the poetic tradition that Buchanan uses to construct her.

 I will first attempt to summarize the relation between the *pro lena* and its sources, to show how Buchanan's imitative practice is an active and creative continuation of his elegiac models, who likewise used erotic poetry as a vehicle for discussions about poetics.[5] A particularly significant feature of the practice of the Augustan elegists was the construction of an erotic world where love replaced politics as the proper business of a man and in which traditional gender roles were reversed. In it the lover represents himself as entirely at the mercy of the mistress (*domina*), who regularly rejects him but who provides a point of departure for the composition of his poetry.[6] Catullus's Lesbia, Tibullus's Delia, and Propertius's Cynthia are given a textual power and autonomy that allow them to dominate the poet and his poetry and to form the background for the poet's complaint.

Buchanan's reconstitution of the *lena* departs distinctly from his models in this respect. By focusing on an intermediary figure, the procuress, instead of the desirable beloved, Buchanan directs his male addressee's attention away from the beguiling figure of the courtesan to that of the *lena* (procuress), a far less sympathetic figure from the point of view of the male gaze.[7] He refigures her in such a way that she both possesses a highly textured aesthetic surface that invokes elegiac themes and borrows elegiac diction. At the same time, however, he deprives her of the seemingly autonomous sexuality that characterized her predecessors, the women of Roman erotic elegy and their *lenae*. Through this strategy, Buchanan is able to construct the *lena* in such a way as to preserve her elegiac figuration while simultaneously depriving her of any sexual authority over male poets.[8]

The diction of the apologia is so heavily laden with borrowings from Latin elegy that, at first glance, it might appear to be simple plagiarism, just as late Latin writers stitched together quotations from Vergil to compose *centones* (literally, quilts) on subjects of great diversity. A closer reading of the *pro lena*, however, indicates that Buchanan appropriates all of the machinery of the elegy, then transforms it to suit his purposes. Buchanan's strategy is most apparent in his construction of the *lena*. She appears regularly in the comedies of Plautus and Terence and is derived from the tradition of Greek new comedy, particularly from Menander, where she is a stock figure, as implied by Ovid in the *Amores*:

> dum fallax servus, durus pater, improba lena
> vivent et meretrix blanda, Menandros erit.
> (*Am.* 1. 15.17–18)

> [As long as deceitful slaves, harsh fathers, shameful procuresses and pleasing courtesans live, Menander will survive.]

The elegists occasionally treat the word *lena* metaphorically as that which "packages" a woman. So, Ovid in the *Ars Amatoria* encouragingly explains that delay is the best *lena*.[9] Much more frequently, however, the *lena* is a literal procuress, whose insatiable greed is an impediment to the pure love of the poet and his *puella* ([girl]friend). Tibullus laments how a *lena* has corrupted his own beloved:

> haec nocuere mihi. quod adest huic dives amator,
> venit in exitium callida lena meum.
> (1.5.47–49)

[Her charms have wounded me. She has a rich admirer now; the sly procuress planned my destruction.]

Because of the *lena*'s interference, the elegiac lover finds that the riches of the rival (the *dives amator*) are preferred to his own extravagant passion.[10] Propertius 4.5 contains a long harangue against the rapacity of the *lena*, beginning and ending with the wish that her grave be covered by sharp spines or stones and curses (*verba mala* 78).[11] In Ovid, where she is represented as a witch, the spells belong to the *lena* herself.[12] Her "Aeaean songs" (from the island of Circe, *Amores* 1.8.5) turn back the rivers and have alienated the poet's faithless mistress from him with the promise of a wealthier suitor (*Amores* 1.8.19–34). Thus, in Roman poetry, the *lena* is a sexually ambivalent figure, both a facilitating procuress and an obstacle who threatens the poet's exclusive possession of his *puella* ([girl]friend).

Buchanan reconfigures the *lena* in his apologia, first by investing what he calls the *ars lenae* (the procuress's art) with the values and attributes of poets and poetry as described by Augustan elegy. If we analyze the diction of his poem, we will find a large number of words in the *pro lena* that occupy a privileged place in Augustan aesthetics.[13] At the same time, however, he simultaneously downplays the *lena*'s status as the procuress of sexual relations in such a way that her illicit "art" is at times indistinguishable from the connubial Venus she supposedly supplements. At *pro lena* 130–31, for example, Buchanan justifies the service of the *lena* to unmarried men on analogy with her usefulness to married couples, which he has just catalogued:

> Haec bona si doctae debent connubia lenae,
> Quantum illi coelebs debeat ergo torus?
> (131–32)

[If they owe this good marriage to the learned lena
How much more does a bachelor's bed owe?]

Buchanan is able to take this audacious step in his argument because, in the preceeding section, he quietly elides the sexuality represented by

Aphrodite with that of the *lena* in his depiction of feminine erotics (113–30). He had already laid the groundwork for such a step by comparing Aphrodite's work to that of the procuress:

> Anne aliud quam lena Venus, quam leno Cupido?
>
> (59)
>
> [Is Venus anything but a lena, and Cupid a leno?]

In so doing, he highlights the illegitimate aspect of Aphrodite's work as he implicitly elevates the status of the *lena*. At 131–32, however, he reverses the comparison. The *lena* here becomes Aphrodite and her art now stands synecdochically for all of Aphrodite's works, including the sexual relations of married couples. As such the *lena*/Aphrodite becomes a polyvalent figure directly or indirectly responsible for all positive aspects of sexual behavior. Her legitimate social status rises considerably during Buchanan's figurative transformation of her role, but at the cost of the obstructive power she had previously wielded over poet/lovers. The *lena* who is the joyous preserver of legitimate marital unions is far from the figure who plays a pivotal role in elegiac texts of controlling the access of poets to their beloved *puellae*.

Although there is a great deal of slippage between the *lena*'s different aspects in the *pro lena*, two images of her predominate, one explicit, the other implicit. First, her work is a duty (*officium*) both for individuals and for the state. Second, her work embodies the same sophistication as the poet's.

The procuress's *officium* can be seen from the beginning of the poem. Buchanan begins his inquest by defending the *lena* from the charge that her activities are a crime (*crimen*) in keeping with the judicial fiction that structures the elegy; in fact, he claims, she has been the "faithful agent of duty" [officii fida ministra, 28] for the city. His description of her civic mindedness has several referents both inside and outside of the apologia. First of all, it recalls the opening lines the poem:

> Non erit in Veneris, Valli, censura ministras
> Aspera.
>
> (7–8)
>
> [Vallius, there will be no harsh complaint against the agents of Venus.]

The parallelism of the adjacent passages suggests that the "agent of duty" [officii ... ministra] and the "agents of Venus" [Veneris ... ministras] are similar, if not identical. Moreover, Buchanan goes on to develop the theme of the *lena*'s special ministry in the rest of the poem. Her duty (*officium*) appears again a few lines later:

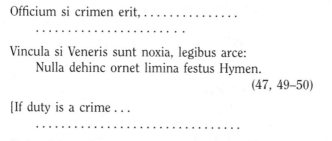

Officium si crimen erit,..............
....

Vincula si Veneris sunt noxia, legibus arce:
   Nulla dehinc ornet limina festus Hymen.
(47, 49–50)

[If duty is a crime ...
....

If the chains of Venus are injurious, forbid them with laws:
   From now on no festive marriage offering will decorate the doorway.]

The refutation of the charge that the *lena*'s duty is a crime is reiterated a little later where the poet claims that her *officium* has been wrongly labeled:

Sed vitii officio nomina falsa damus
(168)

[But we give to duty the false name of vice.]

Thus the juxtaposition of *officium* and crime is a part of the architecture of the poem that designates the *lena* as a citizen in the fullest possible sense, an idea that culminates later in the poem with the suggestion that, for all her benefactions, the *lena* should be given a citizenship award.[14] The representation of the *lena* as a model citizen, unfairly slandered, also accords with the judicial vocabulary that the poet appropriates.[15]

Buchanan integrates the ideas of *officium* and *crimen* thoroughly into the structure of his poem. Further parallels within the Latin literary tradition, however, suggest that Buchanan's construction is more complex. Seneca the Elder quotes the Roman jurist Q. Haterius for his unintentionally memorable formulation of the idea of *officium*:

> Memini illum, cum libertinum reum defenderet, cui obiciebatur quod patroni concubinus fuisset, dixisse: impudicitia in ingenuo crimen est, in servo necessitas, in liberto *officium*. Res in iocos abiit: "non facis mihi officium" et "multum ille huic in officiis versatur." Ex eo inpudici et obsceni aliquamdiu "officiosi" vocitati sunt.
> (Seneca the Elder, *Controversiae*. 4, pr. 10)

[I remember that when he (Q. Haterius) was defending a freedman who was charged with having been the lover of his patron, he said, "Unchastity is a crime (*crimen*) for the freeborn, necessity for the slave and duty (*officium*) for a freedman." The matter resulted in jokes: "You are not doing your 'duty' for me" and "He is really busy with his 'duties' for that man." As a result the unchaste and the obscene were for some time after called "dutiful."]

The collocation of *crimen* and *officium* both in the text of Seneca and in the *pro lena*, as well as the common erotic subtext, suggests that Seneca is the primary referent for Buchanan's poem.[16] Parallels from poetry are also suggestive. *Officium* is one of the typical serious Roman virtues that the elegists appropriated for their own purposes. Just as the *officium* of a respectable Roman noble is politics, so the *officium* of the poet is his erotic work. The word appears euphemistically in Propertius where the poet boasts that his "duty is strong all night long" [officium tota nocte valere 2.22.24]. Likewise, in *Amores* 3.7, the notorious poem in which Ovid bewails his recent impotence, he also uses duty to describe his former sexual prowess as he nostalgically looks back on his erotic career:

> at nuper bis flava Chlide, ter candida Pitho,
> ter Libas officio continuata meo est.

[But just recently blond Chlide twice, three times bright Pitho,
three times Lidas experienced my "duty."]

Thus, when Buchanan makes use of *officium* in his depiction of the procuress's art [*ars lenae* 138], he does not merely develop artfully a poetic conceit that forces the reader to accept the subject of the poem on the poet's unconventional terms. As I have shown, his choice of the word *officium* itself resonates strongly within the elegiac tradition and beyond.

George Pigman III has commented on the difficulty of distinguishing imitation in Renaissance poetry from unconscious reminiscence. That this could be a problem even in a contemporary context is clear from Petrarch's letter to Boccacio where Petrarch poignantly describes the effect of reading Vergil, Horace, and Cicero not once but thousands of times, with the result that these texts are affixed "not only in my memory but in the marrow itself" [non modo memorie sed medullis].[17] Nevertheless, Pigman's discussion of imitation in the work of Marco Girolamo Vida, the Italian Neo-Latin poet who reveled in his thefts from the ancients, shows that Vida's highly derivative work on poetic composition, *De arte poetica,* is an imitation of

Vergil that borrows more than just the words. In fact, Pigman argues, Vida appropriates Vergil's entire imitative practice. If this understanding of poetic imitation is correct, the problems Pigman raises concerning the possibility of unconscious reminiscence, while impossible to resolve fully, fade into the background, since they are imbedded in a poetics that appropriates the aesthetics of its source, as well as the diction.

I suggest that Buchanan's relationship to elegy is analogous to Vida's relationship with Vergil and that his use of the *lena* in the poem is an attempt to inscribe elegiac aesthetics into his own work. This is easy enough to demonstrate, for it is difficult to read more than a few lines without seeing the procuress's work described in the same terms that the Augustan poets use for their own creative work. As described earlier (pp. 291–92), Buchanan begins by identifying the procuress with the agents of Venus whom he will not allow to be slandered. He continues by praising the elegance of Venus and aligns it with that of the learned *Camoenae*, the Roman approximation of the Greek muses, whose qualities he describes:

> Sed facilis candor, doctisque exculta Camoenis
>   Pectora, quae saevae nil feritatis habent:
> Quae jocus & salibus capiat condita venustas,
>   quaeque juvent risus, gratia blanda, lepos.
>
>   (11–14)
>
> [But her kindness is easy to bear, and the cultivated breasts
>   of the learned Muses have no trace of cruel wildness;
> What joke or refined elegance can be witty without her,
>   What laughter pleases, what pleasant grace and charm
> remain?]

We shall now examine the diction of the passage in detail. The close connection between the *lena* and the *Camoenae* is never specified, still less justified. Nevertheless, it appears to be based on the procuress's evident sophistication, as the description that follows emphasizes.[18] The phrase "have no trace of cruel wildness" [quae saevae nil feritatis habent] is modeled on Ovid, *Tristia* 5.7, his description of the savage barbarians among whom the exiled poet finds himself.[19] The indignity felt by Ovid is clear from his self-description a few lines later: "I, the famous Roman bard" [ille ego Romanus vates (5.7.55)]. Worse than the savagery of the natives, however, is their inability to speak good Latin and, hence, appreciate Ovid's poetry. Thus, the line Buchanan borrows to describe the *Camoenae*, who inspire the writing of poetry, and to whom Venus and the procuress are conjoined, originates in a poem by Ovid that similarly explores the relationship between culture and the creation of poetry. Just as in the relationship between Vida and Vergil, so here also Buchanan imitates, not merely the words of his predecessors, but their aesthetics as well.

The pattern of imitation so established is virtually comprehensive. Jests (*iocus* 13) and wit (*sal* 13) are also common in Latin poetry as prerequisites for entrance into the cultivated elite for whom the poets claim to write. A representative early example is Catullus 16, a defense of neoteric poetic practice where the poet identifies wit (*sal*) and charm (*lepos*) as the key ingredients of his verses.[20] *Iocus* is more closely connected with conviviality, as in Catullus's admonition to Marrucinus Asinus, the dinner guest who stole his host's napkins "amid jests and wine" [in ioco atque vino (12.1–3)].[21] Ovid makes clear the same link in the *Ars Amatoria* (*The Art of Love*) where he also links *iocus* with the erotic locus of poetic creation:[22]

> proelia cum Parthis, cum culta pax sit amica
> et iocus et causas quicquid amoris habet.
>
> (2.175–76)
>
> [Let there be battles with the Parthians, peace with a learned girl-
> friend, and mirth and whatever else goes with love.]

Pleasant (*blanda*) and charm (*lepos*) are likewise poetic shorthand for the artistic values of the neoterics and their continuators. Charm figures most prominently in Catullus. It appears in poem 16, quoted, in part, above. Poem 50 shows similar aesthetic allegiances. It is addressed to friend and fellow poet Licinius Calvus, with whom he had spent the day extemporizing poetry:

> reddens mutua per *iocum* atque vinum.
> atque illinc abii tuo *lepore*
> incensus, Licini, facetiisque,
>
> (50.6–8)
>
> [exchanging (verses) amid jest and wine.
> I left there inflamed by your charm, Licinius,
> and by your jokes.]

Lepos and poetry are similarly combined when Martial imagines the whereabouts of a certain Canius Rufus:

> an otiosus in schola poetarum
> lepore tinctos Attico sales narrat?
>
> (3.20.8–9)

[Or is he at leisure in the school of the poets
telling clever stories with Attic charm?]

In both examples, the association of poetry with charm (*lepos*) is clear, and, further, its connection with wit and jest, as indicated by the copresence of *sal* and *iocus* (discussed above, pp. 295–96).

The passages cited above appear to connect the language of the *pro lena* with the sort of sophistication that was claimed for poetry in the Alexandrian tradition from Catullus onward. This claim was based on the premise that those with truly refined sensibilities should appreciate poetry that embodies similar principles.[23] As a result, there is a strong tendency for statements that on the surface appear to indicate a frivolous interest in the ephemera of stylish living to conceal rather more serious statements of poetic intent. This is accomplished in the Roman poets by the development of the highly integrated, self-referential vocabulary discussed above.[24] Buchanan appropriates this vocabulary of elegance for his defense of the procuress, along with its more complex meditations on the nature of poetry and on the best way of composing it.

Viewed in this light, the justification of prostitution is also implicitly a defense of poetry itself, as well as a learned compliment to the sophisticated humanist, Briand de Valeé, before whom the defense is enacted. The comparison of passages from the *pro lena* with their exemplars from Latin literature, taken together with the extraordinary move Buchanan makes in his argument—the startling assumption that the prosecution of the procuress is equally an attack on the learned Muses—reveal a complex poetic agenda coincident with the facetious defense of the procuresses' art. Thus Buchanan's extravagant praise of the procuress's art on the basis of its association with the Muses is finally a tacit defense of his own poetic practice.

The representation of the procuress in the *pro lena* is a tour de force in which the resources of the Latin literary tradition appear in a highly original construction. Buchanan is able to use the procuress both to resonate within the tradition and to continue it with wit and elegance. As a result, the real Renaissance procuress, about whom much was written by contemporary authors, is almost wholly obscured by a conversation among male poets, separated by a millenium and a half. The case of Buchanan's *lena* shows this process clearly: richly textured by Buchanan's profuse borrowings from the Latin literary tradition, she is never allowed to figure in the poem or to figure independently herself.[25] Buchanan inherits a representation of the procuress from antiquity where she is an ambivalent figure facilitating or frustrating the desire of the poet at her pleasure. He reconfigures her in a weaker form, however, using the materials of his predecessors to deprive her of the autonomous sexuality that is her most outstanding attribute in the literary tradition.[26] Buchanan accomplishes this process by linking her activity directly to the concerns of the city—her duty is, in fact, at one point said to be worthy of a civic crown (36)—and to the consummation of his own poetic desire.

Such a reading of the *pro lena* illustrates some of the difficulties in attempting to develop the suggestion of Elaine Showalter that "gynocritics begins at the point when we free ourselves from the linear absolutes of male literary history and stop trying to fit women between the lines of male tradition and focus instead on the newly visible world of female culture."[27] In the *pro lena*, however, this new world is hardly visible. There are no real women, only artificial, erudite versions of the cultural norms that Shari Benstock in *Textualizing the Feminine* describes as "woman-in-the-feminine."[28] Benstock's own analysis seeks to uncover what is lost or obscured by woman-in-the-feminine in literature and to use that unrepresented space as a tool to open up the more comprehensive category of self-difference within "the feminine." Again, the *Apologia pro lena* throws up formidable obstacles in the path of any such self-revelation, since the apologetic conceit, which leaves the defendant both passive and silent, deferring to the wisdom of her attorney, is the perfect vehicle for the expression of masculine control. The end of the poem is particularly revealing in this respect. Having been constructed without individual personality and in the singular throughout the course of the *pro lena*, the procuress at last comes before the tribunal to speak for herself. As soon as this happens, however, her voice is immediately elided into that of the generalized "combined procuresses" [cunctae lenae] who are called upon by the poet to address their judge:

> Finge tibi pariter cunctas astare puellas,
>   Oreque blandiloquo talia verba queri:
> "Aut una damnato omnes, aut crimine solve,
>   Juncta etiam nostris est tua caussa malis."
> Damna, si damnare potes, quae noxia nulli,
>   Grata sua multis sedulitate fuit:
> Quam nemo accusat, quam nemo coarguit, idem
>   Quin testis culpam publicet ipse suam.
> Illa potest mores, populo vel teste, tueri:
>   Legitimus quaestus nunc facit esse ream.
> Si vitium esse putes, poteris non credere factum:
>   Si factum credas, ne vitium esse putes.
>
>   (211–22)

[Have her stand beside all the girls
And speak such words as these with a pleasing voice:
"Condemn all together, or absolve us from crime;
Your own case is linked to our evils."
Condemn if you can condemn, what is harmful to none,
And pleasing with great service to many;
Whom no one accuses, whom no one convicts.
Let the witness truly publish his own guilt.
She can see the character of the crowd or the witness.
This inquest now makes her a defendant.
If you think it a vice you cannot believe in the deed—
If you believe in the deed, do not think it a vice.]

Even in the end the silent female does not speak for herself.[29] Passive and represented throughout the poem, when she finally is given a voice she is made to use it only as a means of subjoining her cause to that of the judicious male, representative of both his city and his gender, who will presumably judge in her favor so as to solve his personal dilemma of the final lines. Buchanan's *Apologia pro lena* belies its apparent intention to represent that part of women's experience that is found in the lives of procuresses, prostitutes, and courtesans. How, then does our reading contribute to the recovery of Renaissance women?

Karen Newman concludes her study of representations of women in English Renaissance drama by discussing the tradition of "specular reading," in which the critic situates him- or herself so as to see what has been missed by previous readings.[30] This tactic is the essence of most scholarly discussion, and, although valuable, it situates the specular reading within a scholarly tradition whose monolithic appearance can give the impression that the object under consideration in these successive specular readings remains the same. She quotes Louis Althusser on a particular kind of reading found in Marx's *Das Capital*, which begins by mirroring the incomplete readings of his predecessors, but ends up producing a transformation of the subject of investigation that may or may not be visible:

What political economy did not see is not a pre-existing object which it could have seen but did not see—but an object which it produced itself in its operation of knowledge . . . through the lacunary terms of its new answer political economy produced a new question, but *"unwittingly."* It made *"a complete change in the terms of the"* original *"problem,"* and thereby produced a new problem, but without knowing it. . . . It remained convinced that it was still on the terrain of the old problem, whereas it has *"unwittingly changed terrain."*[31]

Newman concludes:

> Readers of Renaissance plays and revisions of the canon that "see" the woman who has been overlooked leave intact a reading practice that depends on seeing more clearly than before, through a long genealogy of readers, each seeing what his predecessors overlooked. Such a practice of reading leaves unexamined the quality of literariness as well as its related hermeneutic practice of literary interpretation.[32]

This analysis of the *pro lena* cannot "see" the woman in Buchanan's text. Forced by the poem to abandon the specular reading designed to uncover the real women, we are compelled to refocus our attention on the sources that so clearly ground Buchanan's text. Nevertheless, by identifying and describing the literary structures that so thoroughly obscure the female, we can see what is not there and begin to grasp the efficacy of Buchanan's discourse and to contextualize it in light of other Renaissance writings by and about women. What we see is the lack, the lacuna. This change of terrain, in Louis Althusser's sense, this learning to see what is not there, is, in some ways, a more moderate goal to pursue, but one that nevertheless is not without value. We do not hear the voice of the feminine, nor do we invent it. We learn to hear its articulated silence. The resolution of the procuress's case takes place entirely within the masculine gaze, with the interests of the male foregrounded. In their final, collective speech before the tribunal, the procuresses are made to recognize that fact implicitly. We are not told what arguments they might have used in private.[33]

Notes

1. For a detailed reconstruction of the Bordeaux period in George Buchanan's career, see I. B. McFarlane, *Buchanan* (London: Duckworth, 1981), pp. 79–121.

2. George Buchanan, *Omnia Opera*, ed. Thomas Ruddiman (Edinburgh: Freebairn, 1715). For the early Renaissance institutionalization of prostitution followed by its suppression in the sixteenth century, see Kathryn Norberg, "Prostitutes," in *A History of Women in the West* ed. Natalie Zemon Davis and Arlette Farge (Cambridge: Harvard University Press, 1993), vol. 3, pp. 458–74; Margaret King, *Women in the Renaissance* (Chicago: Chicago University Press, 1991), pp. 77–80.

3. For the poem as a reconstitution of elegiac aesthetics, see Charles Platter and Barbara Welch, "The Poetics of Prostitution: Buchanan's 'Ars Lenae,'" *Celestinesca* 16.1 (1992): pp. 35–81.

4. The only exception is the chorus of procuresses, the *cunctae lenae*, brought before the judge to plead their case with a single voice (*pro lena*, 211–22). Even here, however, the individual voice of the *lena* is diluted by its multiplication.

5. For an English translation and commentary, see Platter and Welch, "Poetics of Prostitution," 1992.

6. For recent work on this topic, see Barbara K. Gold, "'But Ariadne Was Never There in the First Place': Finding the Female in Roman Poetry," in *Feminist Theory and the Classics,* eds. Nancy Sorkin Rabinowitz and Amy Richlin (New York and London: Routledge, 1993), pp. 75–95; Barbara K. Gold, "The 'Master Mistress' of My Passion: The Lady as Patron in Ancient and Renaissance Literature," in *Woman's Power, Man's Game: Essays on Classical Antiquity in Honor of Joy K. King,* ed. Mary DeForest (Chicago: Bolchazy-Carducci, 1993), pp. 279–304; Judith P. Hallett, "Martial's Sulpicia and Propertius' Cynthia," in *Woman's Power, Man's Game,* pp. 322–53; Maria Wyke, "Mistress and Metaphor in Augustan Elegy," *Helios* 16 (1989): pp. 25–47.

7. Since the procuress's interests are solely economic, she exploits the desire of men without any attachment, emotional or otherwise. Latin usage depicts prostitutes as wolves (*lupae*). See, for example, Livy's alternate interpretation of the story that Romulus and Remus were raised by a she-wolf: "Sunt qui Laurentiam volgato corpore lupam inter pastores vocatum putent: inde locum fabulae et miraculo datum" (1.4.7) [There are some who think that Laurentia was called a wolf among the shepherds in the sense that she prostituted her body; hence, the setting of the story and the marvel]. The noun *lupanar* and the adjective *lupanaris,* both etymologically derived from *lupa,* from a very early date refer to a brothel and the things connected with it, respectively. See also Juvenal 6.114–132, for the portrait of the Messalina who, according to Juvenal, defiled the imperial bed chamber with the *lupanaris odor* (the smell of the brothel). The idea becomes a commonplace in Renaissance depictions of prostitution. King, *Women in the Renaissance,* p. 78, quotes fifteenth-century humanist Giovanni Caldiera's reference to brothels as wolf dens (*lupanaria*) [neuter plural form of *lupanaris*], and Buchanan himself, in his satirical collection *Fratres Fraterrimi,* decries the debaucheries of Rome by cataloguing words etymologically related to *lupus* (wolf) and connected with Roman institutions (e.g., the *lupercalia*). He concludes the poem, *In Romam* (Against Rome), with the following:

Nihil comperies nisi LUPERCOS,
LUPERCALE, LUPOS, LUPAS, LUPANAR.
(*Omnia Opera,* pp. 335–36)

[You will find nothing except WOLF-PRIESTS
WOLF-CAVE, HE-WOLVES, SHE-WOLVES, WOLF DEN.]

8. That the institution of Renaissance prostitution should form the basis for a poetic challenge to female sexual authority may not be coincidental. In discussing the causes for the suppression of legalized prostitution, Norberg, "Prostitutes," pp. 461–62, suggests that, in addition to the changing societal expectations regarding male chastity found in both Catholic and Protestant circles, the economic independence of prostitutes and their adoption of both male and female dress "appear to reflect a new fear of female sexuality and a generalized anxiety over the blurring of gender and class lines."

9.   grata mora venies, maxima lena mora est;
        etsi turpis eris, formosa videbere potis;

(Ars 3.751–52)

[You will be welcome coming late; delay is the best procuress.
    Even if you are ugly you can seem beautiful.]

10. See Platter and Welch, "Poetics of Prostitution, pp. 61–63.

11.   quisquis amas, scabris hoc bustum caedite saxis
          mixtaque cum saxis addite verba mala.

(4.5.77–78)

[All lovers, strike this pyre with rough stones,
    and add curses to the stones.]

12. For further discussion of Buchanan's representation of the *lena,* see Virginia Chaney, "The Elegies of George Buchanan in Relation to those of the Roman Elegists and to the Latin Elegies of John Milton," (Ph.D. diss. Vanderbilt: 1961), pp. 54–55.

13. See Platter and Welch, "Poetics of Prostitution," pp. 52–55 *et passim,* for a fuller listing of Buchanan's borrowing from the Augustan aesthetic vocabulary.

14. Qui bene servati statuistis praemia civis,
        Ut premeret fortes querna corona comas.
    Illo debuerat mulier tam strenua nasci
        Tempore, virtuti cum suus esset honos.

(35–38)

[You who established rewards when a citizen's life was saved,
    So an oak crown would burden his strong head.
Such an industrious woman (the *lena*) should have been born
    When virtue had honor.]

The civic allusion is also strongly rooted in Buchanan's classical models, namely the honors traditionally paid to a Roman soldier who saved the life of a citizen in battle (for an account from imperial times, see Tacitus, *Annales* 3.21.8–10.). This precise passage, with its wreath of oak leaves (*querna corona* 36), is based on Ovid's *Tristia* (3.1.36) (as noted by Phillip Ford [*George Buchanan: Prince of Poets* {Aberdeen: Aberdeen University Press, 1982}, p. 61]), where the reference is to a crown given to Augustus, but the context here makes clear that Buchanan intends to apply to the procuress the traditional Roman appreciation of individual heroism in battle.

15. *reus* (defendant) 27, 45, 220; *agere* (hear a case) 26; *causa* (lawsuit) 26; *crimen* (crime) 45 (twice), 47, 68, 165, 174, 213, etc.

16. Buchanan's familiarity with the work of the elder Seneca seems clear also from his use of *Suasoriae* 6.27 at *Baptistes* 32. See *George Buchanan's Tragedies*, eds. Peter Sharratt and P. G. Walsh (Edinburgh: Scottish Academic Press, 1983), p. 270.

17. *Le familiari*, ed. Vittorio Rossi and Umberto Bosco (Florence: 1933–42) 22.2.11–14, quoted in G. W. Pigman III, "Neo-Latin Imitation of Latin Classics," in *Latin Poetry and the Classical Tradition*, eds. Peter Godman and Oswyn Murray (Oxford: Clarendon, 1990), pp. 200–01.

18. This is also suggested by the elevation of the procuress's work to the level of an art (*ars lenae*) during the course of the poem.

19.   quamque lupi, saevae plus feritatis habent.

             [They have more cruel savagery than wolves.]

20.   qui tum denique habent salem ac leporem,
             si sunt molliculi ac parum pudici,

                                                    (7–8)

             [(verses) which have then salt and charm,
             even if they are a little soft and scarcely chaste.]

21. Cf. also Catullus 50.6. in this sense and in the literary sense discussed below.

22. Elegance *(venustas)* is also connected with *sal* at Catullus 86.3.

23. Indeed, the defense of this idea is a familiar topos and forms the basis for the *recusatio*. The phrase *exculta Camoenis* itself is borrowed from a *recusatio* of Martial: "fila lyrae movi Calabris exculta Camenis," [I moved the strings of the lyre refined by the Calabrian Camoenae] (12.94.5).

24. For the line of argument Buchanan's elegiac borrowings suggest, see Platter and Welch, "The Poetics of Prostitution," pp. 43–81.

25. For a parallel appraisal of Propertius's Cynthia, see Gold, " 'But Ariadne,' " pp. 286–93.

26. This formulation of the procuress's role takes as central the perspective of the elegiac lover over whom she exerts an arbitrary authority. From a broader perspective, however, her position is not independent at all, as it is conditioned absolutely by the cultural forces that dominate women in ancient Roman society.

27. Elaine Showalter, "Toward a Feminist Poetics," in *Women Writing and Writing about Women*, ed. Mary Jacobus (London: Croom Helm, 1979).

28. Shari Benstock, *Textualizing the Feminine: On the Limits of Genre* (Norman: University of Oklahoma Press, 1991), p. xvi.

29. This analysis owes much to Edward Saïd's characterization of orientalist discourse as one whose greatest strength is its ability to speak in place of its object. Saïd comments on a speech of Balfour on the problems of British rule in Egypt: Balfour produces no evidence that Egyptians and "the races with whom we deal" appreciate or even understand the good that is being done to them by colonial occupation. It does not occur to Balfour, however, to let the Egyptian speak for himself, since presumably any Egyptian who would speak out is more likely to be "the agitator [who] wishes to raise difficulties" than the good native who overlooks the "difficulties" of foreign domination" (Edward Saïd, *Orientalism* [New York: Vintage, 1978], p. 33). So here, from Buchanan's perspective, the silence of the *lena* in deference to the good offices of her defender is a strong sign of her innocence and positive civic functions. To have her speak on her own behalf would probably only introduce numerous "difficulties."

30. Karen Newman, *Fashioning Femininity and English Renaissance Drama* (Chicago: University of Chicago Press, 1991), p. 145.

31. Louis Althusser, et al., *Reading Capital*, trans. Ben Brewster (London: New Left Books, 1970), p. 24.

32. Newman, *Fashioning Femininity*, p. 145.

33. I would like to thank Alysa Ward and my fellow editors, Barbara K. Gold and Paul Allen Miller, for their helpful criticisms and suggestions.

"She Never Recovered Her Senses":
Roxana and Dramatic Representations of Women at Oxbridge in the Elizabethan Age

Elizabeth M. Richmond-Garza

Neoclassical theories of tragedy privilege the plays of the seventeenth and eighteenth centuries, with their careful observations of neo-Aristotelian decorum in language, characterization, and staging. Certainly the praise accorded to John Dryden's experiments in the forms of classical tragedy has been quite substantial, and yet the earlier plays on the same theme often suffer from a scholarly love of restraint and measured heroic elegance. Even, as in the case of the Neo-Latin academic tragedy of *Roxana*, when Dryden merely revised the work of an earlier playwright, it is his later neoclassically purified version that will be remembered. If in 1642 the London Puritan City Council was able finally to achieve its goals of closing the doors of the dangerously entropic and vital Elizabethan, Jacobean, and Carolean stages, although only briefly, its conservative legacy perhaps extends even further. Critical doors are still closed on many plays of that period. Those plays that have suffered most are those that remain unrescued by the critical reception that saves a prominent name, that violate or offend, and that, either publicly or privately, affront both the substantive and the formal conventions that later periods will value. If T. S. Eliot can be offended by even *Hamlet*'s indecorous construction and hybridized content,[1] a much greater potential to affront is offered by the less canonized texts of the period. In their obscurity, both linguistic and archival, lies more than a boldness in style. These plays offer a false appearance of recondite disengagement with the polyphonic and often dissonant counterpoint of the public London stages, both those that we enjoy calling theaters and those that we place in the realm of official politics.

Any reading of a dramatic text in this period, or perhaps in any period, will involve a reading of its performance, that is to say of the complex cultural, political, and ideological material out of which the play's text is

223

constructed and with which the audience who attends its presentation is permeated. With drama we cannot limit the text to the words on the page but must, instead, assess the whole variety of semiotically overdetermined acoustic and visual appeals that the text makes when it is performed to an individual audience in a particular performance space. The elision of such performative considerations as audience expectations and visual iconography permits a privileging of the word as transhistorically and hermeneutically available to the modern reader without the need for a careful meditation on the performative implications of the play, which are connected to the historical. The connection between Elizabethan theater and the political debates of the period has often been noted, both by traditional and new historicist critics. And yet their conclusions have varied widely about the nature of this ideological and iconographic homology, depending very often on the care taken to reconstruct not only a reading of the text but also a subtly nuanced performative context and audience reception of that text.

For decades, modern university students have been trained in the history of the London stage, even as they have ignored other performances of the period. Informed by varying modern ideological agendas, whether following the optimistic universalism of critics like Alfred Harbage, the savage elitism of Ann Jennalie Cook, Martin Butler's proletarian refutations, or Andrew Gurr's careful reconstruction of a diversified and complex nexus of reception, modern scholars have been much concerned over the nature of the Elizabethan audience and of its immediate responses to the plays it witnessed.[2] This preoccupation has often superseded scholarly inquiry into the texts and performances themselves. *Roxana* offers a case in point of this appropriative strategy. Even such basic texts as the *Riverside Shakespeare*, while not adopting a particularly aggressive stance on the nature of this audience in social, political, economic, or gender terms, do place great emphasis upon the construction of the space of performance, if not in ideological at least in architectural terms. Along with the famous sketches and engravings of particular Elizabethan theaters like the Swan, a striking image of the role and positioning of the audience in period theaters is offered.[3] The small woodcut, which is taken from an edition of the largely ignored first *Roxana* play by William Alabaster, is enlarged from its two square inches to show a socially diverse audience, placed both in front of and in galleries to the side of the stage, viewing a performance taking place in the outer stage, which is divided from the inner by a transverse.[4] The popularity of this image for teaching theater history constitutes this play's only reception. Through its reinscription of the fantasy of Elizabethan social integration, the image ironically has been used to obscure the subversive content of the play that it covers. The return to the performative details, as well as the text itself, of the play promises a rescue from such ideologically informed modern conjecture. The original image is, moreover, always cropped in modern editions. Even those critics who concern themselves particularly with the university drama at most indicate that the image is but one of eight woodcuts from the frontispiece of the author's imprint of William Alabaster's *Roxana*.[5]

It is with these censored images that I wish to reintroduce not only a metonymic representative of a marginalized body of Neo-Latin dramatic texts but also another doubled and thus doubly excluded body, that of the woman and of the Oriental. The seven other images that constitute the full frontispiece include female and Oriental nudes in various suggestive and yet graceful postures. Clothed, but only partially, in the flowing garments of European fantasies of the luxurious East, these women have been excluded from the critical reception, such as it is, of the play. Already on the margins of the ideal image of the Elizabethan stage even in the original print, they have failed to infiltrate modern constructions of the Renaissance English stage. With our excluding focus on London theaters and politics, we have not been concerned with the academic experiments occurring only a few miles to the east and west of the capital, where the drama's academic status permitted experiments that would have startled not only later neoclassical formalists but also the contemporary government in London.

In addition to and precisely because of such opportunistic pedagogical manipulations of the image from this text, the play now elicits critical and theoretical scrutiny as a neglected site of ideological experimentation, one that at least Renaissance audiences found compellingly unbearable. Its modern critics however, are more contemptuous. F. S. Boas, for example, launches a threefold attack on *Roxana*, even as he seeks in his seminal study of the academic drama to rescue it from oblivion. The play, he claims, is not only unoriginal; it is indecorous, and it traumatized its original audience. Alabaster's play is derived and condensed from an Italian tragic original, Luigi Grotto's *La Dalida* published in Venice in 1567. Alabaster's play has been praised only for its elegant Latin verses, and not for its philosophical or dramatic content, by Thomas Fuller and Samuel Johnson, who were unaware of Alabaster's plagiarized source. Boas is only able to summon an interest in the play's language and a damningly invidious comparison to Shakespeare's *Titus Andronicus* that argues for *Roxana*'s ascendancy in brutality.[6]

William Alabaster entered Trinity College, Cambridge, from Westminster School in 1583 and went on to complete his M.A. at Oxford University in 1592. He was successively chaplain on the Cadiz expedition to the Earl of Essex (Queen Elizabeth's favorite and later her betrayer) and, after a brief period of conversion to Roman Catholicism, prebendary of St. Paul's, and rector of Tharfield. Indeed, one of his poetic productions, a "heroick song" of praise for Elizabeth entitled the *Eliseïs*, was even well received by his eminent contemporary, Edmund Spenser, in *Colin Clouts come Home Againe.*[7] Little more is known of Alabaster, and, indeed, even this much biographical information is uncommon for the authors of texts such as the university drama whose identities are often preserved in name alone. Although biographical criticism must be approached with care, the details of Alabaster's life are emblems, if not proofs, of the direct connection between the two great universities of Oxford and Cambridge and the expanding world of the early English empire under Queen Elizabeth. It is perhaps not surprising then that Alabaster, in an age preoccupied with empire and with the expansion of England's and Europe's frontiers, should appropriate an exotic story about queens and imperial confrontation, set no longer in Spain and England but now safely displaced to India and Bactria.

Clearly there lies within the plot and language of the play more than the stylistic elegance that Edmund Spenser and Samuel Johnson praised.[8] If the "content" of *Roxana* in both narrative and semiotic terms is the source for its denigration by earlier critics, I will suggest it, instead, as the site for remaking the play's challenge to both period and modern audiences. The basic outline of the story is as follows. The play is set at the royal court of Bactria (modern Afghanistan) where the king, Moleus, has been killed by his nephew, Oromasdes, who, in spite of a marriage to an Indian princess, Atossa, has taken Moleus's daughter, Roxana, as his mistress and has two children by her. To further his love for Atossa, Oromasdes' counselor, Bessus, tells Atossa of her husband's infidelity and brings Roxana and her children into Atossa's presence. After a disingenuous welcome, Atossa has Roxana tortured until she kills both herself and her children. Oromasdes has, in the intervening time, overheard Bessus boasting of his conquest of Atossa and had him executed. The play concludes with Atossa's invitation to Oromasdes to celebrate her birthday with a feast at which he is presented with the remains of Roxana and her children as the main dish. After the revelation of the events of the play, they murder each other with poisoned flowers and leave the chorus, senate, and audience to mourn the barbarisms.[9]

F. S. Boas concludes his commentary on *Roxana* with the detail from Fuller's contemporary assessment of the play which I have poached for my title, as being a summation appropriate to the play as a whole: "The soundest critic of *Roxana* is the nameless 'gentlewoman' who, we are assured, 'fell distracted' upon seeing it performed 'and never after recovered her senses.' "[10] While not accepting the patronizing rhetoric of the delicacy of female sensibility that this remark reflects (for after all Fuller also praises the play from the academic perspective of its male collegiate audience), I propose to connect this second, performatively excluded body, here foreign only in gender, with her counterparts on the page and stage who are foreign in both culture and ethnicity.

What might have caused one member of the audience to collapse and others to feel themselves academically edified by this savage little play that, in its marginal Cambridge setting, can place before its viewers' eyes images and interpretive challenges that both resonate with London's actualities and evade London's official censorship? The play in its special academic environment and its special academic language, uniquely combines a consideration of the representation of women, within the codes of marriage and diplomatic alliance, with an attempt to construct a view of "the East" for its English audience. Anticipating the comments of critics like Edward Saïd about the complicity of these two projects of subjugation and alienation, the play challenges its voyeuristic, and largely male, audience, who view these atrocities acted by and upon women necessarily within a perspective informed by the policies and self-construction of their own female monarch.

Edward Saïd and other critics like Gayatri Spivak have reminded us of the complicity of the twin projects of colonizing gender and race.[11] In an age that foretells the enormous imperialist expansions of the eighteenth and nineteenth centuries, Alabaster will challenge an audience deeply concerned with the questions of female rulership, marital autonomy, and the intimidating seductions of newly encountered alien cultures. Alabaster, like the great imperialists after him, was seduced by the twin Renaissance themes of knowledge and power that constitute the matrix for the fascination with the imperialist project.[12] Saïd would place Alabaster within the first wave of Orientalist appropriation, which included not only London's plays about the Ottoman empire but a thoroughgoing attempt to remake Western thought through the appropriation of Eastern Mediterranean philosophy and literature.[13] The Orient, in the early stages of imperialism, became "the stage upon which the whole East is confined . . . a closed field, a theatrical stage affixed to Europe."[14] Alabaster will even foreshadow Saïd's accounts of the eighteenth and nineteenth centuries as he maps foreign exoticism onto the construction of female identity, as both ruler and wife, at home in England. In the safely displaced and fascinatingly violent and exoticized setting of the Eastern Mediterranean, Alabaster will suggest a radical allegory of the contemporary conservative encroachments on the Tudor monarchy's attempts to modernize and liberalize the legal status of women through the existential presence of a female, unmarried monarch and an enlightened view of divorce.

The connection of academic drama to London politics is direct. Many of the plays addressed a London audience, even a female one. Within the exclusively male domain of the universities, at least one woman did consistently preside over and intervene in the dramatic productions of Oxbridge without fainting, and she often did so in eloquently idiomatic Latin:

> et ego quia nil nisi male agere possum, odi sane lucem, id est conspectum vestrum.

> [And I, because I can do nothing if not badly, wisely avoid the bright light, that is to say your faces.][15]

As she begins her royal address in 1566 to the assembled leaders of the University of Oxford, Elizabeth I adopts an iconography that she had systematically developed and caused to be associated with her person. As Roy Strong and Frances Yates have noted,[16] Elizabeth, through both her verbal and her iconographical articulations of herself as queen, emphasized her status as the Virgin Queen, as a modern day Diana or Cynthia who, like her mythological predecessor, could be immediately identified by her most recognizable attribute of chaste moonlight. And yet, in this self-introduction to the learned gentlemen of the University of Oxford the powerful virgin goddess/queen adopts a markedly self-deprecating tone, perhaps not so far from the other and anonymous representative of her gender who fainted. This second woman, Elizabeth, herself empowered with a thorough education and eloquence in Latin, defers to the academicians and, instead of invoking the moon's purity, insists upon its reflected secondariness. Even encased in the safety of her double self-construction as both virginal and essentially English, she hesitates to be on display visually and verbally. The risk of deprecation will be far greater for those foreign, denuded, displayed, and sexually provocative women who will be offered to at least one Cambridge audience for visual consumption. With the increasing political and economic centralization of England in the capital encouraged by a powerful female monarch, the remark is more than polite; it is doubly startling. Elizabeth presents herself, the representative of real political events, as a mere foil to Oxford's learning and shrinks from the brightness of its light. At the same time, she insists that her effort should in some way reflect, in the public scene, the insights of these doctors far removed from London's daily events.

Such a staging of herself, emphasized by her reference to the faces of her spectators (*conspectum*), is not peculiar for Elizabeth who consistently made elaborate royal visits throughout England.[17] What is curious is her tone and the relationship that she implies between London and Oxford. Although many critics place the universities on the margins of Tudor England, her remarks offer them, not only an important, but even a central position. Just as the words of academics uttered in Tudor lecture halls are often relegated to a secondary role, so the spectacles viewed in the two great university towns of Oxford and Cambridge have not yet received the attention that Elizabeth herself insists upon as their due. The spectacle of the queen's several visits to the universities was hardly the only one available to their students and dons. The image of the queen both appeared and presented itself before the faces of her academic subjects, and those academic subjects presented to the royal eyes another sort of spectacle, one which formed a central part not only of university life and training but also of that raw material and experience that went into many of the London plays. I refer here to the dramatic performances that took place at the universities of Oxford and Cambridge in honor of particular religious holidays and royal visits.[18]

The products of the university included not only future parliamentarians but also a rich and ignored textual production whose most outrageous texts were in the form of plays presented by, and for, academic audiences. Often more incendiary than anything that could have been placed on the London stage, which was always under the threat of censure and dissolution by the Puritan City Council, these legitimate exercises in rhetoric were praised and funded by the authorities. Consistently politically irreverent and even subversive in their content, all the plays present challenges to modern critical expectations of what material and which attitudes were permitted a public hearing. In the context of the long period of female control represented by Elizabeth's reign and of the rapid international commercial expansion of the Elizabethan economy, *Roxana* stands out as a text presented in an entirely male performance context and yet, nevertheless, also presented to a queen.

Like the students of the last quarter of the sixteenth century, we must place before our eyes these academic plays.[19] We must take stock of what neoclassical material is being offered to reassure and orient these student interpreters, who will soon stage their own actual political dramas in London. We must assess what experiments in ideology and staging the sacred space of a university uniquely accorded to, and even encouraged in, its participants.[20]

Elizabeth's evident ill ease at staging her royal spectacle for academic eyes is thoroughly understandable. She addresses a highly trained audience accustomed not only to the witnessing of staged events but also to their evaluation and manipulation for particular social ends. The inheritance of the university drama derives both from the official classical curriculum of the universities and from the increasing availability of Italian neo-Senecan poetics and plays such as *La Dalida*. The academic audiences were not only aware of classical materials, they were also involved in their detailed study.

A university play stands between the self-consciously academic humanist study of classical tragedy and the practice of commercial tragedy. It produces a uniquely powerful, irreverent, and classically trained collocation of writers, players, and viewers.

Traditionally fed by students aged fourteen or fifteen from grammar schools, the two universities grew greatly in the late sixteenth century. Moreover, their populations became increasingly elite and politicized.[21] Any consideration of activities at Oxford and Cambridge in this period thus must include an awareness not only of a growth in the size of the audience but also of the increasingly political and nonacademic nature of the university population. The many political and intellectual changes of the period, the increase of royal control, the influx of the sons of the nobility, and the growth of collegiate teaching and collegiate power within the university generated a lively intellectual environment, even if they did not radically alter the official curriculum. For the century of Tudor rule, the universities conformed far more to a materialist elitist description.

Nevertheless, what would emerge from the universities as a new radical politics in the seventeenth century was expressed in such controlled forms as academic drama in the sixteenth century. With the reinforcement of the new suggestions of Ramist logic, which gave substantial importance to literary exempla, and the incipient politicization of the universities, the students and dons were able to explore many topics that would have been censored on the popular stage. At the universities, participation in the drama would be defended on both pedagogical and ethical grounds.

Oxbridge students were under constant scrutiny and discipline from the surrogate parental figures of senior fellows, as in the case of Corpus Christi College, Oxford.[22] Apart from private lessons in some sports and modest recreation, student dramatic productions for Christmas, royal visits, and other special events were one of their few diversions.[23] The performing of plays, both as an expression of the wealth of the college and a display of obedience to the royal patron in attendance,[24] and as a sort of Bakhtinian carnival to release the entropic energies of the students, especially over the long winter vacation, was typical until well into the eighteenth century. The symbolic representation of obedience to the monarch through the mounting of elaborate entertainments was especially important under Elizabeth I. These entertainments usually included the staging of several plays for the queen, whose fluency in Latin and flair for royal pageantry were well flattered by the university celebrations. Unlike the London stages, which were always under threat from the Puritan City Council and were finally closed in 1642, the university plays constituted sound pedagogy.[25] Plays were regularly commissioned and lavishly produced by the colleges, which spent enormous amounts of money on sets and were even permitted the use of Queen

Elizabeth's own garments for costumes on occasion.[26] Indeed, some plays were accepted in partial fulfillment of the requirements for a degree.[27] While professional players had been banned in 1593 by the Privy Council, student players were rewarded as humanist rhetoricians. Furthermore, costumed in the ritual garments of real politicians and, at the same time, inspired by a saturnalian sense of irreverence and satire, they insisted upon the right to stage these spectacles.

This paradoxical role as the moment of release that later facilitates containment of subversive experimental ideas and images was well-known to the university authorities. Such contained radical content and performance ensured good behavior in the students for the rest of the academic year and, perhaps, even good citizenship for the rest of a political career. These "revels" were aimed at two sorts of political objectives. Ralph Holinshed describes Elizabeth's 1566 visit to Oxford as follows:

> The one and thirtieth of August the queenes majestie in her progress cam to the universite of Oxford and was of all the students which had looked for hir coming thither two yeares, so honorablie and joifully received as either loialness towards the queenes majestie or the expectation of their friends did require.[28]

The pair of objectives appear in the last clause: political loyalty and institutional harmony. On the one hand, the plays provided an outlet for the not-to-be-underestimated flamboyant and anarchic tendencies of university students and were far more effective than the attempts to impose penalties and rules on the students. The preserved text of *The Christmas Prince, A True and Faithful relation of the risinge and fall of Thomas Tucker, Prince of Alba Fortunata*, by Griffius Higgs (1607–08), St. John's College, Oxford, Ms. 52, gives a clear sense of the enormous destructive energy that was released in an only barely contained form at these performances and revels:

> But (as it often falleth out), the Freshmen, or patients, thinkinge the Poulderlings or agentes too busie and nimble. They them too dull and backwards in their duty, the Standers by findinge both of them too forwarde and violente, the sportes for that night for feare of tumults were broken upp, everye man betaking himself to his reste. . . . And wheras yt was hoped à nighte sleepe would have somewhat abated theyr rage, it contraryewise sett a greater edge on theyr fury.[29]

On the other hand, these performances were yet another example of the staging of the Elizabethan system of control. Elizabeth relied heavily upon display and pageant, upon her subjects receiving "honorablie and joifully as . . . their loialness . . . did require" the spectacle of the monarch that they had looked for so long.

It is in the context of these heavy burdens, of being an educative extracurricular student activity and serving a crucial double political role, that the academic drama must be seen. And yet, I do not wish to underestimate the entertainment value of these plays, with their sumptuous costumes from the Office of Revels and the lively interventions in Latin verse by the royal audience. Indeed, it is precisely because the plays are being used to so many different ends that they are so provocative and important. Each of the three goals, rather than discrediting the other two, emphasizes the interdependency of the three projects. All three must be kept in mind as we turn now to the play itself.

The appeal of a play such as *Roxana* was finally secured by its technically accomplished staging, which both dazzled the eyes and repeated the iconography of the real monarch in London. Like their counterparts in Italy and France, the English plays were always staged indoors.[30] According to Elliott,[31] for example, the stage at Christ Church was placed at the high table in the main hall and was highly raked, with the royal throne placed in the "Corridor" at the center of the hall with the courtiers in front of the stage and seated in boxes affixed to the side walls. The most advanced and fashionable dramatic technology, machinery, and later even set designers such as Inigo Jones were used for these lavish productions. This interior splendor not only matched the exterior display of the more overtly political royal entrances and progresses through the university towns but also conflated optically the two events. The real queen who entered Oxford or Cambridge at noon might very well watch a boy play another queen, perhaps an Indian one, in Elizabeth's own clothes, that same evening.

Only now, against this sketched background of the intensity of the intellectual, social, and political forces that converge upon the university drama, can such a play as *Roxana* be fully considered. Since it was not uncommon for the academic plays to assess particular current political and philosophical material, to offer in the safe space of festival entertainment and well-turned Latin verses scathing parodies or at least critiques of highly contested and even forbidden topics, *Roxana* suggests itself, with equal force albeit in a different genre, as an appropriate pair to *The Christmas Prince*. Its theatrically excessive violence, couched in the recognizably Senecan classical conceit of the myth of the Thyestean cannibalistic feast, appeals to more than a simple period taste for violence on the stage. It draws upon its audience's fascination with two threatening, unstable, and seductive terms, the eastern and the female. In a period replete with exotic and violent treatments of both of these topics,[32] *Roxana* brings them together in a particularly frightening way in which the "strangeness" (with its sixteenth-century meaning of both peculiar and other) of these women is not kept safely in the distance of a fictional eastern space but instead, in fact, negotiates crises all too familiar to the English audience itself.

Modern literary theory has only just begun to concern itself with preindustrial European culture and arts. A concern with an earlier period and with contemporary critiques of essentializing literary history that deifies either the author of his text or even the text itself as somehow hermeneutically self-contained and available to the modern reader, therefore, often involves an act of triangulation or at least adaptation. The modern model, intended to decode an artifact of the nineteenth or twentieth century, will demand adaptation to an earlier context. Fortunately, Edward Saïd's own text's discussion of later imperialist constructions of the "other" invites an interest in the textual production of the protoimperialist and yet already Orientalist period. Precisely because of the shared grand narrative of imperialism, whose beginnings in England occur under Elizabeth's rule, the suggestions of critics like Saïd, who are concerned with its height in the nineteenth century, enlighten the reading of its origins in the sixteenth. Far from a simple story of military domination and expansion, British imperial ideology spread by an apparently more benevolent method of cultural appropriation and alienation even as early as 1583. *Roxana*, with its combination of representing the East and speaking to England of its women, provides a prehistory to the Orientalism of the industrial age and hints at which attitudes might fill in the space between the crusades of feudal Europe and the great age of empire.

Indeed, the case for *Roxana* as a play especially suited to a reading through Saïd's lens becomes yet stronger if we look to the details of his account. Drawing upon Antonio Gramsci's work, which distinguishes the cultivation of the subaltern in the project of eighteenth- and nineteenth-century European imperialism from Europe's other brutally militaristic strategies of repression, Saïd suggests that there was, especially in the case of the Muslim Orient in which *Roxana*, too, is set, a systematic mapping of the characteristics of the feminine onto those of the Oriental so as to align both as objects of desire and domination.[33] For Saïd, nineteenth-century Orientalists, seduced by the exoticism of the East, consistently associated it with sex and the female, as well as with the culturally other:

> For Nerval and Flaubert, such female figures as Cleopatra, Salomé, and Isis have special significance; and it was by no means accidental that in their work on the East, as well as in their visits to it, they pre-eminently valorized and enhanced female types of this legendary, richly suggestive, and associative sort. . . . The Oriental

woman is an occasion and an opportunity for Flaubert's musings;
he is entranced by her self-sufficiency, by her emotional carelessness, and also by what, lying next to him, she allows him to
think. . . . Like the Queen of Sheba . . . she could say . . . "je ne suis
pas une femme, je suis un monde." [34]

There is an almost symbiotic (or should one say, parasitical) relationship
between the European male constructions of European female identity and
of the Oriental. Whatever is said of those gendered other is directly connected to those cultured other, and, in both cases, this mark of difference
is the site of domination of that otherness, whether "she" is coerced or
complicit. What will be important is the exact nature of the historical
details that are in crisis for a given period in the development of European
hegemonic power. Saïd carefully notes differences among the various
European centers of imperial power and among their peripheries and does
not suggest a monolithic, transhistorical, and rigid paradigm. I, too, hope
to suggest that a very particular form of the experiment he describes occurs
in *Roxana*, whose author and audience, like Flaubert lying by the side of
the Egyptian dancer, Kuchak Hanem, are surprised by "what they are allowed to think."[35]

Like Gerard de Nerval and Flaubert after him, Alabaster capitalizes
upon a deep period fascination with the culture and customs of the eastern
Mediterranean, with its exotica, its fantastical luxury, and its danger. The
play's first lines conjure, in the voice of the shade of Moleus, a Tartarean
nightmare of the sensually threatening East for the eyes of its scholarly
audience. And yet the speaking voice is not that of the Western interpreter
but of the sympathetically suffering Oriental who will soon speak of Bactria's
pain and humiliation by sin and the gods:

Utrumne noctis ille Tartareae vapor
Depinxit oculos ludicri mundi noctis
Vegetumq rerum examens errore implicat?
An hoc quod oculis haurio late meis,
Illa est scelesta et excreta Bactria? (1) [36]

[Is it some exhalation of the Tartarean night
Which has colored the eyes of the night in the sportive world
And entangles a multitude of lively things in uncertainty?
Or is it that which I everywhere devour with my eyes,
That is, the evil and damnable Bactria?]

Bactria's savage history has reduced her spiritual representative to introspective self-doubt and self-hatred. By contrast, however, with the victory

over the Spanish Armada, the period of 1588–99 was marked, not by a decrease in international economic ventures, but by an increase combined with a striking tone of "national isolationism," "narrow nationalism and militancy" especially in the drama of the London plays of the University Wits.[37] Alabaster's text also presents the spectacle of female foreign suffering to the voyeuristic *(oculos/oculis)* future politicians of London, who will soon join the audiences of great Orientalist plays such as *The Wars of Cyrus* and *Friar Bacon and Friar Bungay*, not to mention *Tamburlaine* itself. And yet, I hope to suggest that Alabaster uses this fashionable proto-Orientalist setting against the grain, as a displaced locus not for English self-congratulation for military and imperialist successes, but rather as a safely distant environment in which to critique that same English society.

The play will both invoke and frustrate a second fashionable trope, for Bactria's national humiliation will be played out in the suffering and crimes of its most powerful women, Roxana and Atossa. The period taste for explicit violence against women, especially foreign ones, whether Roman like Shakespeare's Lavinia in *Titus Andronicus* or Damascan like the virgins in Marlowe's *Tamburlaine*, is satisfied by the savage murders of both women. But this exoticism, while pandering to popular fantasies of the violence of non-English societies, does not wholly distance the play's narrative or thematic content from the English context. It provides a pretext for the performative aggression of the play that will permit Alabaster's topical commentaries on women and marriage in England, as well as abroad.

Not altogether unlike London dramatists, who were in this same decade experimenting with conventional New Comedy resolutions of family strife, especially of the conflict between father and daughter over the choice of a husband (here Moleus, Atossa, and Oromasdes) and representations of marriage in ethical and legal terms, Alabaster stages this same moment of crisis. He offers his student audience a double adultery and meditations on divorce. He explores this uniquely dangerous topic in the legal construction of familial and female identity in this period with unapologetic directness.

Rather than alienating us from the Bactrian context, he coerces us into this dark and unstable world, which reminds us of our own. No commentary on divorce, adultery, and the question of heirs is neutral in an Elizabethan context.[38] Again, it is the shade who will warn the audience of this content and of its chaotic consequences. The challenge to the viewer's preconceptions about marriage is presented in the unimpeachable voice of the prophetic ghost of a neo-Senecan revenge play. As he agonizingly foretells the death of Roxana, he constructs the scene as one of ideal maternity victimized by the gods:

Quid hoc? video natae capit?
Roxana salve: patris an amplexum veni
Solvet perire mortuis formae decus:
Sed crevit in te nata: quanto es pulchrior
Defunta (si non judico nimis pater.)
Et haec nepotum capita, de matre auguror
Patro nec ablunudunt, habent et quiddam avi:
Nepos generque gemina amicitiae nota. (8)

[What is this? Do I see the head of my daughter?
Greetings Roxana: If you come into your father's embrace
It will allow you to die in a way worthy of the dead:
But a daughter appears in you: how much more lovely you are
Dead (if I do not judge too much as a father)
And these heads of my grandchildren, I foretell, which neither by
    mother
Nor by father shall be expiated, have some hope from their
    grandfather:
A noble grandson and a twin-born sister famous for friendship.]

The move from the shade's speech to the play itself marks a move from the prophecy of a divine director to a scrupulous performance of just those events foretold. Even such conventional details as Counselor Bessus' later praise of Atossa's beauty [pulchra est (17)], and chastity [castitas moram dabit (17)], disorientingly recall descriptions of the conventionally idealized western female, whose worth is constituted through physical beauty and sexual purity. Even his sardonic and misogynist philosophy of love, which echoes 1 Corinithians 7 and reminds a modern audience of Hamlet's fiercely binary attack on Ophelia as a virgin/whore in the nunnery speech, confirms this stereotype by negation:

> Nulla amoris nescia est,
> Quae semel amavit: virgines quod non sciunt
> Amant, mulieres quod sciunt, et quod amant. (17)

> [No woman is innocent of love,
> When once she has been in love: virgins love what they
> Do not know; and wives love what they do know.]

Bessus' final connection of love to civil war which makes him "equally traitor to my king and myself" [regi et mihi/ pariter rebellis (17)] again invokes a conventional metaphor, that of the battle of love, and emphasizes both the inconstancy of women and the Renaissance doctrine of the husband as lord of his household and wife, ideas whose most notorious expression is perhaps contained in Katherina's last speech to Petruchio in *The Taming of the Shrew* (5.ii.136–79). In other contexts, this conventionalized language, with its superficiality and its underlying misogyny, might go scarcely noticed. And yet Atossa's foretold brutality, which conflates the stories of the revenging Atreus of Seneca's *Thyestes* and Euripides' jealous Medea, destabilizes the whole code of proper female behavior that is both presented and dismantled as the play opens. Atossa, though childless, is, like Medea, sexually betrayed and seeks revenge through the unwomanly act of infanticide. And yet the act is moved from the realm of the purely personal to that of the political; Atossa does not kill her own children for she has none. Instead, she destroys another woman's children who represent the only hope, albeit an illegitimate one, for an heir for Oromasdes. The invocation of the Medea archetype is especially striking, since Alabaster reverses the female antagonists, making the legitimate wife into the childless revenger who kills not only her rival's children but herself and her husband as well. The innovation is important because it displaces the monstrous actions of a witch and mistress onto the legitimate wife. The resonances with Elizabeth's own history are alarming, given the consistent Catholic argument, forwarded most aggressively by Mary Stuart, that she was herself, as the daughter of Henry VIII's second marriage after his dissolution of a first, arranged and childless marriage, just such an illegitimate child. If Medea attacks the code of marriage from the outside, Atossa attacks it from within. This system of arranged marriage, and the knowledge of its necessary companion of adultery, has transformed one who was modest, faithful, and gentle [pudica, fida, lenis, innocens fui (23)] into one who, victimized by her father and state obligations [patriae, sceptra, throno], has now ceded her legitimate marriage bed [thoro] to another and is thrown into a fit of murderous rage that frightens even the chorus of her ladies (25).

Such is the traumatic environment that sympathetically prompts Atossa's less sympathetic course of revenge, whose obscene results will horrify especially the woman who fainted at its premier in the audience. Indeed, even Oromasdes exists in this same fiercely rigid world. Delighted with his affair with Roxana, whom he claims genuinely to love, and with their children, who sadly only simulate heirs to his throne, he has yet to resolve the nightmare of the future. While, like Henry VIII, he has chosen a second love, and she has proved fertile, he is still encumbered by the burden of a first and infertile wife, who both threatens the directness of succession and forecloses the possibility of a second marriage. He meditates on this injustice, peculiar to kings, who must both agree to arranged marriages and secure legitimate heirs (27). Interestingly, his counselor,

Arsaces, insists that even children do not guarantee peace in either private or public life and cites the examples of Niobe, Belidus, Priam, Laius, and, prophetically, Thyestes. Children, he argues, are fragile and no cure for the king's nagging political fears (28).

The portrait is a horrifying one of instability and desperation, one that might well terrify an audience of the last years of the sixteenth century. Veiled under the exotica of Bactria, and apparently about an affair with the beautiful Bactrian, Roxana, not the elegantly francofied Anne Boleyn, Alabaster's play probes perhaps the greatest fear of the end of the Tudor period, the succession. There is a moment, however, which I have omitted so far, that linguistically betrays the analogy's exactness. The first solution that Oromasdes suggests to his dilemma invokes that word *divortium* (26), notorious for Elizabeth, whose claim to the throne hinged upon its legality. Unlike his English counterpart, however, this Bactrian king will be denied this option. Heeding the advice of his senate and religion, he will retreat from this desperate solution and give up his hopes of a happy second marriage and a cure to his sorrows.

And yet the word has been spoken in a period still divided as to the legality of divorce and concerned about the ramifications of their own queen being the product of a broken home. By the end of the sixteenth century, England was the only Protestant country that lacked some form of legalized divorce.[39] Five years after the writing of the play, the confusion in English divorce law, a result of the religious reversals of the century and perhaps of Elizabeth's own complex relationship to marriage, was only partially resolved by Archbishop Whitgift, who, while not directly stating that second marriages were adulterous, established a series of Latin ecclesiastical statutes which permitted separation but required of both parties a hundred-pound bond not to remarry during the lifetime of the spouse.[40] Lawrence Stone goes further to argue that, in spite of the events of Henry VIII's reign, there was in this period a concerted effort on the part of conservative clergymen and laymen to discourage divorce, against the grain of developments in Scotland and on the European continent.[41]

If we are troubled by the conservatism of the portrayal of the particular women, divided somewhat facilely into caring and virtuous mother and revenging and adulterous fury, we must nevertheless be struck by the aggressive and exact treatment of the matter of divorce. Along with the sensual naïveté and innocent exoticism of Roxana's presentation and speeches as she prays to the gods of the Night (30) and the almost strident presentation of Atossa's anger and hypocrisy as she dupes Roxana, whom she calls "mater" four times in her speech (33), there is a radical and unorthodox commentary on the negotiation of heterosexual liaisons. Displaced to Bactria, Alabaster's play refutes the developing official attitudes. The play even perhaps stages this displacement and the violent potentials of Orientalism itself. The play contains its own embedded Orientalism. Bactria is obsessed with India as the decadent fictional space characterized by Atossa's sensuality, violence, and sterility from which Oromasdes escapes to experience illicit sexuality. It offers its viewers, if they look carefully, an account of its own process of construction. Roxana precedes Flaubert's Kuchak Hanem by centuries and yet functions as a *mise-en-abîme* of the whole project of the fantasy, found at the imperial center, about life in the peripheries. India is Bactria's mystified East just as Bactria is England's. Here, however, Bactria is more than a sensationalist tactic to attract an audience that dreams of Ottoman sexuality and violence; it is also used as a mask to hide a structural critique of England's own legal move to limit the possibilities for divorce.

Almost with too much care, Alabaster creates a legitimate case for Oromasdes to divorce Atossa so as to heighten the agony of this missed opportunity from which a conservative politician, not unlike those in Elizabethan London, dissuades the king. Both natural affection and, more importantly, the capacity to produce heirs endorse this second would-be marriage as not only desirable personally but crucial politically. Henry VIII's case for the succession is repeatedly invoked, as is the threat of a kingdom torn [divisa regna (35)] by civil war, should Oromasdes fail to bring his house into order. Moreover, Atossa's crimes are made to square with the grounds for divorce, as she takes up an affair with Bessus and commits her many murders, culminating in that of Oromasdes himself. Finally, she even openly threatens treason, a charge that appears against Anne Boleyn as well in her trial, as she assures the chorus that she prays for civil strife along with all others who contemplate making any wars [quid bella aliud faciunt], and hope thereby to transform a personal ruin into a public victory, calling it the king's victory [hac gloria / regis vocatur, (54)]. Not only are the king's personal body and biological family under attack, but even his political body is threatened by her jealous fury. With so exact a repetition not only of the events of Henry VIII's life but also of what divorce law did exist, Alabaster seems to insist upon a comparison. Oromasdes' plight highlights the wisdom of Henry's choice of divorce, which at least deferred the civil war for a century and ultimately ensured Elizabeth's ascension to the throne and a period of peace.

While complicit in invoking a binary stereotype of female behavior for Atossa and Roxana, the play nevertheless hybridizes both the ideal mother, who is now a mistress, and the revenging fury, who stages the costs of the obligation to remain within painful and politically unstable arranged marriages. The analogy is quite precise, as is the interpretive challenge to the academic audience, which is encouraged to assess these dangerous and provocative issues. In a nightmarish experimental world set abroad, Alabaster stages, in terms of the codes of marriage and divorce that most constrained female identity in Tudor England, a liberal theory of female self-determination that connects the autonomous selection of a spouse not only to the fates of one woman and her children but to the preservation of the integrity and stability of the very state itself. Indeed, in seeking to account for the fainting spell at the play's performance, one might even push Alabaster's critique further and suggest that it is a play of great sympathy, if not for Atossa, although she, too, is presented as wronged by the system of marriages of political alliance, at least for Roxana, and for the women whose lives are destroyed by this thoroughly English inflexibility and atavism on the matter of marriage. Dare we suggest that the play offers a certain criticism not only of Oromasdes' treatment by the legal system but also of the treatment of Roxana and Atossa, figuring forth dramatically that female other who sometimes witnessed these university plays? Even as two women's fates are staged, at least one actual representative of that society collapses at the witness of her own tragedy, a tragedy that will remain unrescued from its severity until the legal reforms of the midnineteenth century.[42]

Alabaster's experiment, his lesson in rhetoric offered to a sophisticated audience of academic and political spectators, is couched in its academic Latin and in the seductive exotica of a foreign landscape that dissolves into the darkness of an awful sunset at the moment of Atossa's death (62). He invokes both as protections from reproof by the authorities, should they care to scrutinize this among so many other entropic, pedagogical exercises. He critiques neither, however, and, instead, manipulates them so as sufficiently to alienate its story from its most immediate and obvious implications. Replicating rather than critiquing a proto-Orientalist fantasy of the East, Alabaster strives, like Nerval and Flaubert after him, not to understand its otherness, but rather to use it as an intellectual and dramatic landscape in which to interrogate the others, whether constructed through a difference of religion, politics, or gender, that are closer to home. Those others will, in the space of *Roxana*, force the whole audience to "recover its senses." As for that ultimate other, the other of the East, "her" story of recovery has yet fully to be written.

Notes

1. T. S. Eliot, "Hamlet," *Selected Prose of T. S. Eliot*, ed. Frank Kermode (New York: Harcourt Brace and Jovanovich, 1975), pp. 45–49. Eliot famously calls the

play "most certainly an artistic failure" because of its "superfluous and inconsistent scenes" (47).

2. There is an ongoing controversy about the composition, in terms of class and gender, in particular, of the London theater-going audience. Alfred Harbage initiates the debate with *Shakespeare's Audience* (New York: MacMillan, 1941). Ann Jennalie Cook refutes Harbage's utopian construction of a thoroughly heterogeneously nonelitist audience in *The Privileged Playgoers of Shakespeare's London, 1576–1642* (Princeton: Princeton University Press, 1981), which is a development of her controversial article "The Audience of Shakespeare's Plays: A Reconsideration," *Shakespeare Studies* 7 (1974), pp. 283–305. Martin Butler explicitly rejects her arguments for a limited aristocratic, educated, and wealthy audience in Appendix II of *Theater and Crisis 1632–1642* (Cambridge: Cambridge University Press, 1984). Andrew Gurr carefully reconstructs, in sociological, literary, and historical terms, a complex audience that attended with varying frequency a highly diverse group of productions presented by a wide variety of companies in different sorts of performance contexts in his two studies *The Shakespearean Stage, 1574–1642* (Cambridge: Cambridge University Press, 1984) and *Playgoers in Shakespeare's London* (Cambridge: Cambridge University Press, 1987).

3. My argument here is that the *Riverside Shakespeare*, ed. G. Blakemore Evans (New York: Houghton Mifflin, 1974) constitutes a representative and frequent point of entry, especially for university students, to Shakespeare's plays and that it contains one page of particular interest. On the same page as the famous Johannes de Witt sketch of the Swan Theater (plate 8, after p. 494), it contains two woodcuts of particular stagings of minor plays, Nathaniel Richard's *Messalina* (1640) and William Alabaster's *Roxana* (from the 1632 author's edition).

4. William Alabaster, *Roxana* (London, 1632). My description is of the remarkable title page to Alabaster's own edition of the play, printed by William Jones. He published this edition in response to a plagiarized edition of the play, issued earlier that year by R. Badger for Andrew Crook. The play had been acted at Trinity College, Cambridge, in 1592. The image is widely reproduced as one of the Renaissance English stage. Both this and all future citations from *Roxana* are taken from the copy of Jones' edition in the Bodleian Library, Oxford, Douce A 399(1). All future page numbers are from this edition and are given in parentheses.

5. F. S. Boas, *University Drama in the Tudor Age* (Oxford: Clarendon Press, 1914), p. 288.

6. Ibid., pp. 286–88.

7. Ibid., p. 286.

8. Johnson, according to Boas, mentions Alabaster's *Roxana* as a model of Latin versification in his *Lives of the English Poets*.

9. There is a complete plot summary (with regrettably few comments on details of diction and image) in George R. Churchill and Wolfgang Keller, "Die

lateinischen Universitäts-Dramen in der Zeit der Königen Elisabeth," *Shakespeare Jahrbuch* 34 (1898): pp. 252–55. Boas also offers a brief, if evaluative, summary in the pages already noted.

10. Boas, *University Drama*, p. 288. The words in inside quotes are Fuller's exact period comments on the production as cited by Boas. Interestingly, the particular detail of the collapse of a female audience member during a performance is not unique to Alabaster's neo-Italian play. Perhaps the most influential of the Italian humanistic playwrights at Oxbridge, Giambattista Giraldi Cinthio, uses the same detail to initiate his account of the ethical and dramatic defense of the use of explicit horror in his seminal and notorious horror tragedy, *Orbecche*. To establish the performance context for his discussion of this play in his treatise on tragedy, *Discorso intorno al comporre delle comedie e delle tragedie*, (Venice: n.p., 1554), Cinthio recounts Fuller's scene almost exactly (202). What is surprising is that, in the midst of this persuasive and highly academic discussion, Cinthio's practical stage experience inserts itself in a startling little anecdote. At the premier performance of *Orbecche*, according to Cinthio, when the remnants of Oronte were brought on stage at the Thyestean climax of the play, the fiancée of the actor who had played the role was so overcome with horror at the sight that she fainted. There is a modern Italian edition available in G. B. Giraldi Cinthio, *Scritti Critici*, ed. Camillo Guerrieri (Milan: Marzorati, 1973). The above page numbers, however, are from the 1554 edition. Boas, *University Drama*, p. 240.

11. See Edward Saïd, *Orientalism* (New York: Vintage Books, 1978), and Gayatri Chakravorty Spivak, *In Other Worlds: Essays in Cultural Politics* (New York: Methuen, 1987).

12. Saïd, *Orientalism*, p. 32.

13. Ibid., p. 60

14. Ibid., p. 63.

15. This line appears early in Thomas Cole's compilation of documents from the 1566 visit of Queen Elizabeth to Oxford University, Bodleian Ms. Lat. misc. e. 105, ff 27–28.

16. Roy Strong, *Gloriana: The Portraits of Queen Elizabeth I* (London: Thames and Hudson, 1987), pp. 125–28; Frances A. Yates, *Astraea: The Imperial Theme in the Sixteenth Century* (original imprint, London: Routledge and Kegan Paul, 1975; second imprint, London, Boston, Melbourne, and Henley: Ark Paperbacks, 1985), pp. 29, 76–80.

17. Elizabeth visited Cambridge in 1564 and Oxford in 1566 and 1592. See Boas, *University Drama*, pp. 90–98, 98–108, 252–67. In addition to the plays and speeches presented to her, she always delivered an original speech in fluent Latin in the course of her reign.

18. I do not wish to suggest that the plays performed at the two universities represent the totality of academic drama in Britain in the Tudor period. Certainly, plays were produced at the Inns of Court in London, and some schools were

involved in the mounting of civic pageants. I intend only by limiting this topic to indicate my concentration, not to form an evaluation of the plays with which I shall not be concerned.

19. Certainly still the most important work to date on English academic drama is Boas' *University Drama in the Tudor Age*. Of particular use in the study of the history of the universities have been the following works: Boas, *An Introduction to Tudor Drama* (New York: AMS Press, 1933); Kenneth Charlton, *Education in Renaissance England* (London: Routledge and Kegan Paul, 1965); David Cressy, *Education in Tudor and Stuart England* (London: Edward Arnold, 1975); M. H. Curtis, *Oxford and Cambridge in Transition, 1558–1642: An Essay on Changing Relations Between the English Universities and English Society* (Oxford: Clarendon Press, 1959); Hugh Kearney, *Scholars and Gentlemen, 1500–1700* (London: Faber and Faber, 1970); J. K. McConica, *English Humanists and Reform Politics* (Oxford: Oxford University Press, 1965); Jan Morris, *The Oxford Book of Oxford* (Oxford: Oxford University Press, 1978); Joan Simon, *Education and Society in Tudor England* (Cambridge: Cambridge University Press, 1966); Lawrence Stone, ed., *The University in Society*, vol. 1: *Oxford and Cambridge from the 14th Century to the Early 19th Century* (Princeton: Princeton University Press, 1974). Of particular interest are Lawrence Stone's own essay "The Size and Composition of the Oxford Student Body, 1580–1909" (pp. 3–110) and James K. McConica's essay "Scholars and Commoners in Renaissance Oxford" (pp. 151–82). The work of two other scholars must here be mentioned particularly: Alan H. Nelson's encyclopedic edition and editorial apparatus for the Cambridge dramas, *Records of Early English Drama: Cambridge*, vols. 1: *The Records,* and 2: *Editorial Apparatus* (Toronto, Buffalo, London: University of Toronto Press, 1989) and the ongoing work of John R. Elliott, Jr., on both the Oxford drama and the Inns of Court plays. I have only seen this material in manuscript except for his article "Queen Elizabeth at Oxford: New Light on the Royal Plays of 1566," *English Literary Renaissance* 18:2 (Spring 1988): pp. 218–29.

20. I have offered a fuller account of the whole neoclassicist agenda of Oxbridge in this period in a chapter on the university drama that takes as its focus another Neo-Latin tragedy of the period, *Perfidus Hetruscus*. See Elizabeth Richmond-Garza, *Forgotten Cites/Sights: Interpretation and the Power of Classical Citation in Renaissance English Tragedy* (New York: Peter Lang, 1994), pp. 93–132. That chapter offers a diachronic reading of the relationship of these plays to earlier literary events, as well as a synchronic account of its political and literary context, both of which will be seen through the focus on a single text. With this reading of *Roxana*, I propose to shift the emphasis to a critique of particular ideologies as represented in a singular instance of this sort of theater to its academic audience.

21. Cambridge grew, for example, from 1,200 students in 1564, to 1,800 in 1573, to 2,000 in 1597, and 3,000 in 1620. See Charlton, *Education in Renaissance England,* pp. 136–37.

22. McConica,"Scholars and Commoners," pp. 151–82.

23. These events are briefly described in Boas, *University Drama* (see especially his fifth chapter on Queen Elizabeth's visits to Cambridge in 1564 and Oxford in 1566, pp. 89–108). Certainly the most recent and extensive account of the festivities for a royal visit, Elizabeth's to Oxford in 1566, is in John Elliott's article (see note 19). Elliott will also soon be publishing an extended study of sixteenth-century performance history and has kindly discussed with me much of the material for his chapter on college and university drama. All of the specific textual references in the section that will now follow, however, are a result of my own research in Oxford and Cambridge unless otherwise noted.

24. Unfortunately, although performances did continue under James I, the new king's lack of real capacity in Latin and far less compelling persona both reduced the opulence of the plays after 1613 and prompted a decline in the quality of the dramatic performances. James was even noted by one commentator to have fallen asleep during a production in 1605.

The accounts of Elizabeth's visit in 1566 by Twyne and Wood, Bodleian MS. Twyne 17, 161, and Bodleian MS. Wood F1/2, are both reprinted in Elliott's article (see note 19). Boas, *University Drama*, also has a long, but divergent, discussion of the various versions of the 1566 visit in his fifth chapter. Although the details of the accounts do not exactly coincide, they all seem to emphasize both the opulence and deference of the university productions and the energy and sophistication with which Elizabeth responded to them. There was a revival for the visits of Charles II in 1605 and 1636, however, and elaborate performances of both new plays and earlier Elizabethan ones were staged with elaborate set designs by Inigo Jones. See John Orrell, *The Theaters of Inigo Jones and John Webb* (Cambridge: Cambridge University Press, 1985), pp. 30 ff.

25. The London plays and drama in general were, in this period, being aggressively attacked by Puritan opponents such as Stephen Gosson and Joshua Reynolds. See Jonas Barish, *The Antitheatrical Prejudice* (Berkeley and Los Angeles: University of California Press, 1981), chapter 4. These criticisms went largely unheeded by university officials at Oxford and Cambridge. See John Barton, "The King's Readers," in *The Collegiate University*, ed. James K. McConica (Oxford: Oxford University Press, 1986), pp. 290–91, and McConica, "Elizabethan Oxford," p. 652. Even Leicester's letter to Congregation in July 1584, which endorsed various reforms at the universities, including the banning of professional players, made a specific exception for student plays. Leicester remarks that students' plays are "commendable and great furderances of Learning." He further recommends that the plays be "continued at set times and increased, and the youth of the Universitye by good meanes to be incouraged in the decent and frequent setting forth of them." Robert Dudley, (*Oxford University Annals*, Register L, fol. 242v). Similarly, the Privy Council letters sent to Cambridge in 1575 and 1592 and to Oxford in 1593 (*Oxford University Annals*, Register L fols. 262–62v) make no mention of the academic drama (Penry Williams, "Elizabethan Oxford: State, Church, and University," in McConica, *The Collegiate University*, pp. 404, 427). Elliott (see note 19) concludes from this information that, not only was university drama exempt from the general censure of the

drama, but also that the more frequent letters to Cambridge indicate a stronger hold there of Puritan attitudes. He further argues that Cambridge's more intense puritanism resulted in fewer plays being produced there. Although an interesting conjecture, such a claim, particularly about the numbers of plays, is hard to prove with only partial records.

26. Both Boas' (*University Drama*) and Elliott's (see note 19) discussions of the 1566 visit indicate that large sums were spent on the productions and that Elizabeth lent costumes to the university for the performances from her own wardrobe. A glance at any part of the financial records from the colleges indicates the expense of the productions. Nelson's edition of the records makes such information readily available. According to the college financial records, Christ Church College, Oxford, alone spent £148 2s. i3/4d., on the royal visit of 1566 (Rawlinson C878, cited in Boas, *University Drama*, p. 106). Most of the plays were staged by colleges like Christ Church and Magdalen. Both of these colleges had large financial resources and large numbers of undergraduates.

27. Elliott has noted that in 1512 a certain Edward Watson, college or hall unknown, was admitted to teach in the School of Grammar provided that he submit "100 hundred songs (*carmina*) in praise of the university and a comedy (*comedia*)" (*Oxford University Annals*, Register G, fol. 143). Elliott has further noted that Martin Llewellyn of Christ Church College, Oxford, records in a poem that he received a degree as a result of staging a play for the Dean. See note 19.

28. Ralph Holinshed, *Chronicle* (1577), quoted in Jan Morris, ed. *The Oxford Book of Oxford* (Oxford: Oxford University Press, 1978), p. 56.

29. Higgs St. John's College, Ms. 52, fol. 5.

30. See John Orrell, "The Theater at Christ Church, Oxford, in 1605," *Shakespeare Survey* 35 (1982): pp. 129–40; and John Bereblock's *Commentarij siue Ephemerae actiones rerum illustrium Oxonij gestarum adventu Serenissimae Principis Elisabethae*, Bodleian MS Add. A. 63, fols. 1–22 and Bodleian Ms. Rawlinson D1071, fols. 1–25.

31. See note 19.

32. Even Shakespeare provides many such examples of eastern themes that often included prominent treatments of the definition of appropriate female behavior. *Antony and Cleopatra*, *The Tempest*, *Othello*, and *The Merchant of Venice* are only the most obvious, and that most financially successful of all Elizabethan plays, Christopher Marlowe's *Tamburlaine*, is even set in the Ottoman context.

33. The argument that I shall be using is largely presented in Saïd's *Orientalism:* "Oriental Residence and Scholarship: The Requirements of Lexicography and Imagination," (pp. 149–166), and in his analysis of the texts of the end of the nineteenth century in Paris, especially those of Flaubert and Nerval (pp. 179–92). Much is being made of his suggestions in current subaltern studies, particularly of the largely nonaggressive presence of the British Raj in India.

34. Ibid., pp. 180, 187. I have taken material from several places in Saïd's text to foreground this particular issue, but I have not, I hope, distorted his original argument.

35. Interestingly, Saïd distinguishes English Orientalism from its continental counterparts by virtue of its "more pronounced and harder sense of what Oriental pilgrimages might entail," p. 192.

36. This and all other quotations are taken from the original edition of 1632. I have preserved the original idiosyncrasies in Latin orthography of the Renaissance text. This text is available through a modern microfilm of *Roxana* (New York: Readex Microprint, 1955). There is no published English translation of the text, and so I offer my own of this and future passages.

37. Gurr, *Playgoing*, p. 137. Gurr also singles out the two plays mentioned in the next sentence, one of which is set in Persia. Moreover many of the plays at Oxbridge choose as their settings the eastern Mediterranean either in classical or Ottoman times. Boas' Appendix IV includes more than a dozen such plays, most of which are tragedies, *University Drama*, pp. 385–90.

38. I need no source to make the case for Elizabeth I's own uneasiness about this terrifying triad: divorce, the Catholic ground for denying her the crown; adultery, the ground for her mother, Anne Boleyn's, execution; and inheritance, an insoluble problem for a virgin queen past the age for having children.

39. Lawrence Stone, *Road to Divorce, England 1530–1987* (Oxford: Oxford University Press, 1990), p. 301. With the rejection of the sacramental status of marriage by the Protestant churches, all other Protestant countries had adopted a policy that allowed divorce on the three grounds of wifely adultery, willful desertion for a period of years, and life-threatening cruelty. Stone, in this study and in his more recent and specialized *Uncertain Unions, Marriage in England 1660–1753* (Oxford: Oxford University Press, 1992), emphasizes the extreme and unusual conservatism of English attitudes, in general, towards divorce and argues for the exceptional nature of the few famous divorces that were secured in this period.

40. Stone, *Road to Divorce*, p. 305.

41. Ibid., p. 306.

42. Ibid., pp. 317–82.

Latin and Greek Poetry
by Five Renaissance Italian Women Humanists

Holt Parker

The ability to write Latin verse is one of the essential marks of an educated person.

Battista Guarini, *De ordine docendi et studendi* (1459)

We . . . have not that generous and liberal education, lest we should be made able to vindicate our own injuries. . . . If we be taught to read, they then confine us within the compass of our Mother Tongue, and that limit we are not suffered to pass.

Mary Tattlewell and Joan Hit-him-home,
The Women's Sharp Revenge (1640)

This is a project in making visible. The mere fact that there were women educated in the humanist tradition who could read and write Latin is itself only now becoming more generally known, thanks to the pioneering works of Mary Cannon, Myra Renolds, and Ruth Kelso, the seminal paper of Joan Kelly, and more recently through the research of Jean Brink, David Herlihy, Paul Grendler, Lisa Jardine, Margaret King, Patricia LaBalme, Albert Rabil, and others. Even within this revival of learning, the existence of Latin and even Greek poetry from the hands of women remains largely unknown. They are absent from anthologies of Neo-Latin poetry by reason of their sex and from anthologies of women's verse (and, indeed, most surveys of women writers) by reason of their language.

My paper aims at making the poetry of five women scholars more easily available. In addition, I want to point out some directions for future research. After a brief outline of the place and importance of verse composition in humanist education and life, I provide short introductions to five women poets, educated in humanism: Angela Nogarola (fl. circa 1400), Isotta Nogarola (1418–66), Costanza Varano (1426–47), Alessandra Scala (1475–1506), and Fulvia Olympia Morata (1526–55). The prose works of some of these remarkable women are now available in translation[1]; their poetry, however, is still unknown. To make them available to a wider audience, I have included the texts of the original poems, most of which are still difficult to procure, and added a literal translation.[2]

Latin Poetry and Renaissance Women

Poetry, that is, the study of the ancient Latin poets, only became a distinct discipline during the Renaissance.[3] The purpose of reading poetry as defended by the educators was threefold. First, as a part of grammar and rhetoric in the broad sense, poetry allowed a pupil to increase his understanding of the language and his command of public eloquence, through metrics, analysis of tropes, and the like. Second, poetry was held to teach virtue, less by providing allegories of Christian theology than by providing models both positive and negative of civic behavior. Third, poetry gave the reader practical knowledge of life and nature. As Leonardo Bruni summed up: "Knowledge of the poets is necessary, both for utility . . . and their wide acquaintance with many things and then for the most excellent splendor of their style."[4]

Among the few who believed that women would benefit from a secular and Latin education, there was considerable debate as to whether women should be allowed even to read poetry. Poetry as a source of knowledge of language or of the world might be suitable for women, although not as important as it was to men, since the women would not take part in public life.[5] Poetry for women was most important for teaching morals, though the educators were well aware of the corrupting influence poetry could have even on boys.[6] Thus, for example, Christoforo Landino in his commentary on the *Aeneid* (1488) explicitly acknowledges poetry's moral usefulness for women: "Virgil's poem expresses every type of human life, so that there is no class of human being, no age, no sex, finally no condition, which cannot learn from it its duties in their entirety."[7] Maffeo Vegio argues that Vergil provided Dido as a moral lesson for girls.[8]

So, Leonardo Bruni in *De studiis et litteris liber* (1423–26) included grammar, history, philosophy, and poetry in his plan for the education of women, but he exempted the public arts of oratory and disputation as useless and unbecoming and the comic poets and satirists as perhaps excessive for women.[9] Juan Luis Vives in *De institutione feminae christianae* excluded all poetry from his Latin reading lists for women and explicitly banished rhetoric and vernacular poetry.[10] Ludovico Dolce, following Vives, in his *Dialogo della institutione delle donne* (1545) conceded the necessity of Latin education for women who rule a kingdom, but, even for them, there is no mention of Latin poetry; only the vernacular works of Dante, Petrarch, and Pietro Bembo were allowed. Lauro Quirini, writing to Isotta Nogarola (1443–48), ignores everything except philosophy. Gregorio Correr, writing to Cecilia Gonzaga before she entered a nunnery in 1443, warned her against the poets; she must lay aside Vergil for the Psalms.[11] Sabba Castiglione, *Ricordi overo ammaestramenti* (1554),[12] would leave out poetry, especially the morality destroying works of Petrarch, even from women's vernacular education. Further, there is no mention of poetry in the records or curricula of any of the schools in Italy in which women received Latin instruction.[13]

It is not possible here to review the history and nature of humanistic education for women nor Renaissance Latin verse.[14] However, one important fact needs to be pointed out. The Latin education of the Renaissance, drawing on Medieval models and consciously basing itself on Quintilian, was a rhetorical education, that is, it had as its goal "the ability to speak extempore on any subject in classical Latin, the ability to compose formal letters to order in the classical idiom,"[15] skills necessary and valuable in the public arena. It was intended, therefore, to produce a good prose style. Now, although the rhetorical study of poetry held a central place in the curriculum, the composition of verse does not seem to have been a standard part of the boys' education. Thus, while the writing of prose paraphrases, declamations, and themes was a daily task, in Italy "overall pedagogical theorists did not mention verse composition, and teachers did not report that they taught it."[16]

This lack of a fixed and formal place for writing verse in the schools has several important consequences for the role and status of Latin verse in the literature of the Renaissance. First, generally, it is obvious that the ability to write poetry is proof of talent and linguistic competence at a high level. Second, specifically, poetry was properly considered to be the product not of the grammar schools but of the universities and of adults. Only mature talents are called to poetry; most boys fear it, and good schoolboy verse is proof of precocious abilities.[17] Latin verse was a vital art and subject to the standards applied to the work of any genuine poet working in a competitive and creative tradition. Third, poetry was a public act. As J. W. Binns notes: "Most of the Latin verse of [the Tudor and Elizabethan] period is formal and public; and it fulfilled a recognized social function in the life of the times." Brinsley, for example, mentions it only in connection with "occasions of triumph and reioyscing, more ordinarily at the funerals of some worthy personages." Poems were literally displayed on walls, pinned up in public squares, attached to statues.[18] Even the most lyrical and personal were circulated in letters, intended to be copied, passed from hand to hand, and then gathered into manuscript or printed collections.

As a consequence, while the role of reading poetry is at best problematic for women, writing poetry has no role at all. As a public act, it is unsuitable; as a private act, unnecessary. Among those who wrote about women's education, Bruni raises the question of a knowledge of metrics as useful for understanding and appreciating poetry and obliquely mentions composing verse, but the context is general and is rather clearly directed towards prose composition; further, it seems to imply that verse composition is only expected of men.[19] Only one author explicitly mentions verse composition for women and that is to condemn it. Indeed, Silvio Antoniano in his *Dell'educazione christiana e politica de' figliuoli* (1584), disapproved of girls learning Latin and Greek altogether and singles out pleading law cases and writing poetry as vainglorious for women.[20]

Renaissance Latin poetry was, in some sense, therefore, an extremely high-stakes game even for men. The reward for success was a place at the highest table of literature; the punishment for failure, derision in one's own chosen art form. Thus, when we can discover something of the women scholars who created Latin and even Greek poetry, we are seeing the handful who triumphed over extraordinary odds. Few women were literate; fewer received any formal education; fewer still were given a full humanistic training.[21] Even of these, only the most learned and courageous attempted the open act of poetry.[22]

Angela Nogarola (fl. circa 1400)

Though King and others have made Isotta Nogarola a well-known figure, her aunt, born into the earliest generations of humanism, remains obscure. She was of a distinguished Veronese family, the eldest child of Antonio Nogarola and his wife, Bartolomea de Castronovo.[23] We know almost nothing about her apart from the fact of her marriage in 1396 to Antonio II, Count of Arco,[24] and a portrait given by Philippo da Bergamo (Foresti) praising her learning and piety.[25] She may have been educated at least in part by Antonio Lusco (see following). Letters from his son, Niccolò Lusco (c. 1436), and Tobias Burgus (1438) to her nieces, Isotta and Ginevra, imply that she had died by that time.[26]

We have, however, from her hand a number of interesting poems, showing not only the results of a thorough humanistic education but also an acquaintance (perhaps through her husband) with many of the most powerful political figures of her day. She wrote poetry before her marriage and, in contrast to several other female humanists, continued to do so afterwards.[27] Her works show a fascinating mixture of public and private occasion.

A pair of elegiac couplets addressed to the humanist, Antonio Lusco (1365–1429),[28] dates probably before 1388, when Lusco left Verona, and seems to indicate a pupil/teacher relationship. Written at least eight years before her marriage, it is almost certainly a work of girlhood or adolescence.[29]

Dominae Angelae de Nogarolis ad Antonium Luschum

Si modo me veniens studiis iuvenilibus actam
solicitamque pilae vanisque intendere ludis
vidisti, te nulla quidem miratio facti
commoveat; labor stimulos frenare iuventae.

[To Antonio Lusco.

If coming in just now you saw me led by childish zeal,
Excited about a ball and intent on silly games,
Let no wonder at the behavior move you.
The labor is to rein in the goads of youth.]

In what also seems to be an early work, Nogarola privately addressed Pandolpho III Malatesta (1370–1427), ruler of Rimini. There is no date, but the references in Pandolpho's response would indicate a time before her marriage.[30] With a nice mixture of boldness and modesty, she requests the return of a book that she had loaned him and that he apparently had lost. The poem reveals a wide and intimate knowledge of the Latin poets both ancient and contemporary in the form of a complex cento of thirty lines of rhyming dactylic hexameters. A cento, literally "patchwork," weaves together individual lines or half-lines taken from another poet (most often Vergil). The cento is a playful form that allows the reader the pleasure of seeing familiar lines in new ways and allows the author the opportunity for unbridled showing off, since composing a cento takes a close knowledge of one's sources, as well as a certain wit and bravado.[31] Angela Nogarola uses a less common form, alternating entire lines of quoted poetry with rhyming lines of her own.[32]

Ad magnificum dominum, Dominum Pandulfum de Malatestis, pro recuperatione cuiusdam voluminis quo omnia opera Senecae moralium dogmatum patris illustris continebantur, per Angelam Nogarolis de Verona.

Nate dea, quae nunc animo sententia surgit?
Cor quo Caesareum generoso e pectore fugit?
qua merui culpa fieri tibi vilis, Achille,
ut mihi tam fulgens raperes, generose, monile?
usquam iusti<tiae> est et mens sibi conscia recti,   5
ut tua iam valeant lacrimis praecordia flecti.
vince animum mentemque tuam, qui cetera vincis
iacturamque meam prospectu conspice lincis.
deme supercilio nubem plerumque modestus
balteus et parvus mihi non rapiatur honestus.   10
nunc prece, nunc precio, nec vi, nec morte suprema,
deprecor, ut nobis reddatur fulgida gemma.
non domus et fundus, non aeris acervus et auri
poscitur at tremula flos lectus ab arbore lauri.
poscimus hanc avide, nihil est mihi pulcrius orbe,   15
et tibi nunc plena praestatur copia corbe.
pars mundi tibi nulla vacat, sed tota tenetur
tellus proque tuo placito sermone movetur.
quid vetat esse pium? munus leve, dulcia verba;
nempe repulsa magis quam mors credatur acerba.   20
da mihi te placidum dederisque in carmina vires,
at cadet ingenium mentis si murmur inires.
rumpor et ora mihi pariter cum mente tremescunt.
hi quotiens nostra flores non sede nitescunt,
pro somno lacrimis oculi funguntur obortis,   25
nec mea permulcet patientia pectora fortis.
has solas semperque habeo semperque profundo,
nec male namque mihi cessit sors aspera mundo.
sed iam siste gradum finemque impone labori,
princeps celse, meo magnoque medere dolori.   30

15 hanc *cf. Petrarca* : id *Abel sed haud sane propter metrum* 19 quid
vetat esse pium? munus leve, dulcia verba. *Petrarcha* : quid vetat esse pium
munus? tene dulcia verba, *Abel*

[To the magnificent lord, Lord Pandolpho de Malatesta.
For the recovery of a certain volume in which were contained all the
works of the illustrious father Seneca on moral teaching.[33]
By Angela Nogarola of Verona.

"O goddess-born, what thought now rises in your spirit?"
(Verg. *A.* 1.582)
Whither does the heart of a Caesar fly from your noble bosom?
"For what fault have I deserved to be held worthless by you,
Achilles," (Ovid, *Her.* 3.41)

That you stole, noble man, so shining a jewel from me?
"Is there justice anywhere and a mind aware of what is right,"
     (Verg. *A*. 1.604)   5
So that your heart can be moved by tears?
"Conquer your pride and thoughts, you who conquer all else,"
     (Ovid, *Her*. 3.85)
And behold my loss with your lynx-like gaze.
"Remove the cloud from your brow; do not often let my modest,"
     (Hor. *Ep*. 1.18.94)
Honest, little girdle be taken from me.[34]   10
"With prayer and entreaty (*not* force and capital punishment!)"
     (Hor. *Ep*. 2.2.73. Emphasis added.)
I beg that my shining gem might be returned to me.
"No house and farm, no pile of bronze and gold" (Hor. *Ep*. 1.2.47)
Do I seek, but the bloom picked from the trembling laurel tree.
"I ask for it eagerly, there is nothing in the world more beautiful
     to me" (Petrarch, *Ecl*. 4.72)   15
While abundance is offered to you with a full basket.
"No part of the world is without *you*, instead the whole earth
     is held" (Lucan 2.583)
And moved by your pleasing speech.
"What forbids you to be pious? Sweet words are an easy gift."
     (Petrarch, *Ecl*. 5.24)
Let a refusal be thought more bitter than death.   20
"Show yourself kind to me and you will give strength to my
     poems," (Ovid *F*. 1.17).
But my mind's talent falls, if you rouse a murmur.
"I am broken and my face together with my mind trembles."
     (Ovid, *Her*. 8.57)
As long as these flowers do not shine in my house,
"Instead of sleep, my eyes suffer with welling tears,"
     (Ovid, *Her*. 8.109)   25
Nor does strong patience soften my heart.
"These (tears) alone do I always have and always pour forth"
     (Ovid *Her*. 8.57)
For bitter fortune has fallen my lot in this world.
But now "halt your step" and "put an end to your labor,"
     (Verg. *A*. 6.465, 2.619)[35]
Great prince, and heal my great pain.]   30

This is not a polished product. The rhymes, though not to the taste of later humanist poetry, show a certain linguistic competence but *vincis . . . lincis* (7/8) is weak, and several of the lines fit awkwardly in their new contexts (9, for example, does not really make sense). But the poem does accomplish one of its goals: it allows Angela to show the extent of her reading and her knowledge of Latin. Here we can catch one of our first glimpses of an upper-class woman's education. Vergil is central; Ovid is represented by the *Heroides* (standard for boys also)[36] and the *Fasti* (not the *Metamorphoses*); Horace by the *Epistles* only; Lucan makes a show; surprisingly, so do the odd and allegorical *Eclogues* of Petrarch. Angela has made some clever modifications in her originals. In line 7 she alters *iram* to *mentem* to accuse Pandolpho of carelessness, not anger; she changes the last two of Horace's reiterated *nunc*'s to *non*'s (11) and Ovid's *tumescunt* to *tremescunt* (24), humorously underlining the contrast between his power (he can have all the books of the world for the asking) and the modesty of her request for the return of a single volume. It is a delicate response to a delicate situation.

The cento is an interesting choice for a woman poet, especially for one who is perhaps making her first appearance as a humanist poet, for the form simultaneously proclaims allegiance to a poetic tradition and independence from it. The power of Angela's poem lies in the way she has reappropriated, not only the lines of classical poetry, but specifically men's language about women. The tears that Ovid gave his heroines are no longer those of a woman weeping for her man (Briseis for Achilles; 3; Hermione for Orestes, 23, 25, 27) but a scholar bemoaning the loss of a precious book. She takes the traditional signs for woman and woman's vanity–a necklace [*monile* (4)], girdle [*balteus* (10)], jewels [*gemma* (12)]—and applies them to a copy of Seneca's moral works. In a small and subtle way, Angela Nogarola has become a true *voleuse de langue*.[37]

Pandolpho replied with a letter containing a short (17 line) hexameter poem of his own. His response is revealing, not least in that he did respond, as many did not, and as a poet to a poet. He employs the standard conceits for the learned woman: virago, the Phoenix, Egeria,[38] but they seem to have no hint of reproof or mockery. His claim that she seeks things better suited for men is intended as a compliment, and he takes up and takes seriously her statement that she prefers her volume of Seneca to any jewels. By responding he acknowledges her as at least a potential poet and fellow humanist.

She also publicly addressed Gian Galeazzo Visconti (1351–1402), the ruler of Milan and hated enemy of Pandolpho Malatesta. The hexameter epigram is dateable to 1387 by the events. Gian Galeazzo had sided with Padua in the war with Verona and then gone on to seize both Verona and Vicenza. It is impossible to determine precisely what shifting political alliances may lie behind the preceding poem and this one, but both appear to be sophisticated moves in the turbulent events of politics on the part of a still-unmarried girl or woman, welcoming the new ruler of her city.[39]

Per Angelam de Nogarolis D[omino] V[isconti] devotissimam ex
    abundanti gaudio tamquam corvum crocitantem.

Magne parens, qui cuncta regis per principis aulam
anguiferi, clarumque dedit cui maxima nomen
Virtus, praecipue Pietas et sancta Fidesque,
felicem longamque tibi dent numina vitam.
parva suos tibi commendat Vicentia cives   5
innumeris quassata malis supplexque precatur.
heu populo miserere inopi nimioque labori.

[To the Lord V., by Angela Nogarola, his most devoted servant,
From her abundant joy, even though she croaks like a crow.

Great father, you who rule all through the court of the prince
Who bears the serpent,[40] to whom greatest Virtue[41] has given her
Famous name, and especially Piety and holy Faith,
May the gods give you a long and happy life.
Poor Vicenza entrusts to you her citizens,   5
Shaken by innumerable evils, and as a suppliant she prays.
Alas, have pity on a people, poor and over-burdened.]

Seventeen years later, and eight years after her marriage, she wrote the
following panegyric to Jacopo da Carrara (1380–1406) in 1404. The Carrara
were the ruling family of Padua, who had wrested control of Angela's former
city of Verona from their former ally, Gian Galeazzo. The hexameters celebrate the passing of the rule of Verona from Francesco the Younger (ruled
1391–1404) to his son Jacopo.[42]

Incluto et glorioso principi domino Iacobo de Carraria
    domino suo singularissimo

Summe parens rerum, summi regnator Olympi,
aethera qui stabilis terras atque alta profundi
sidereosque polos aeterna lege gubernas,
nunc tua turicremis venerentur numina donis
grandaevi iustique senes trepidaeque puellae   5
et pueri castaeque nurus iuvenesque torosi.
obstrepat omne nemus, velemus tempora sertis,
atria festivis celebrentur plena choreis,
exultent proceres simul in turbisque popellus.
affluit alma dies lapsis felicior annis,   10
qua te, grande decus Patavi, clarissime princeps,
marmoreae rectorem urbis sceptroque potentem

vidimus. O totum lux concelebranda per orbem.
vive diu felix, divum certissima proles,
et summis confide deis rebusque secundis.   15
sub iuga prosternes populos gentesque rebelles,
ibit et in totum tua celsa potentia mundum.
O patriae sedes, patrii gaudete penates,
et civis laetare, precor, dominumque benignis
ulnis sume tuum, quo, credas, principe nostro   20
aurea Saturni remeabunt tempora mitis.
dulcia felices tractabunt otia gentes
et pia sedatas proteget concordia terras.
tristia concordes horrebunt proelia mentes
nec metus humanos agitabit cura pavorque,   25
sed cuncti pariter concordi pace fruemur.

> [To the famous and glorious prince, Lord Jacopo da Carrara,
> her own most singular lord

Highest father of the Universe, Ruler of highest Olympus,
You who make firm the air, the lands and the depths of the ocean,
You who govern the stars and poles with eternal law,
Now may they worship your power with gifts of burning incense,
Long-lived and just elders and trembling girls,   5
And boys and chaste young wives and brawny young men.
Let every grove resound, let us veil our temples with garlands,
Let full rooms be crowded with festive choruses,
Let the nobles exult together in crowds with the common people.
A kind day has flowed in, happier than the past years,   10
On which we have seen you, great glory of Padua, most famous
        prince,
Ruler of the city of marble,[43] mighty with your scepter.
O light to be celebrated throughout the whole world.
Live long and happy, undoubted offspring of the gods,
And be confident in the highest gods and in your good fortune.   15
Beneath the yoke you shall lay rebellious peoples and nations,
And into the whole world shall go your lofty power.
Rejoice, O homes of the fatherland, ancestral gods,
Be glad, I pray, O citizen, and take your lord
To your kind arms, with whom as our leader, you may be sure,   20
The Golden Age of gentle Saturn will return.
Happy peoples will enjoy sweet peace
And pious Concord will protect settled lands.

Concordant minds will shudder at cruel war
Nor will fear stir up mortals, care and worry,   25
But we all equally will partake of a concordant peace.]

The poem is in keeping with much of Renaissance verse and draws its language primarily from Vergil and the fourth *Eclogue*. Again, we see Angela Nogarola, in her role as countess of Arco, as a visible presence in the highest levels of political games-playing.[44]

We can also see the genuine possibilities of attack inherent in the open act of writing poetry in her own defense against the charge of plagiarism, frequently made against educated women.[45] In a damaged poem to a certain Niccolò de Facino, she responds.[46]

> Angela de Nogarolis Nicolao de Facino Vicentino,
> qui suspicatus est metra per eam sibi missa ipsam non composuisse
> sed aliunde mendicasse.

> Non aliena meis imponere vellera membris
> me iuvat et levibus circumdare brachia pennis
> alterius: picti nota est mihi fabula corvi.   4
> nec mihi virtutum laudes conscendere cura est,   3
> nec veterum lauros nobis ascribere vatum.   5
> Est pudor et virtutis amor mentisque decorum.
> sed mihi nulla movet mentem miratio, quod non
> follibus esse meis †ullo† conflata putentur
> et fabricata mea †avitis in . . . † negentur.
> Femineae morem coeperunt namque cohortes,   10
> tempore quod nullas latices gustasse moderno
> fertur Gorgoneos doctasque audisse sorores.
> At, natura, pari rerum ratione creatrix,
> femineam formare animam pariterque virilem
> diceris atque soles aequas infundere mentes.   15
> ergo tuum veteres non poscere, femina, vates.
> naturae munus sexum dotavit utrumque.

1–4 *a* 5–17 *divisit MS et aliquot eligos adiunxit* 4 *post* 3 *traieci* 5–6 *post* 2 *traicere voluit Abel* 5 nec *coni. Abel* : ac *MS* lauros] laudes *MS* 6 est *coni. Abel*: et *MS* 8 follibus esse metra ulla meis *conieci* 9 *lac. ind. MS* me(a) avitis *haud sane propter metrum* 17 naturae] naturaeque *MS et Abel*

[A. N. to Niccolò de Facino of Vicenza,
who suspected that she had not composed the poem
which she sent to him,[47] but had borrowed it from elsewhere

It does not please me to place others' clothes
On my limbs and to circle my arms with another's
Light feathers: I know the story of the painted crow.   4
Nor do I care to mount the praises for virtue   3
and to ascribe the laurels of the ancient poets to myself.   5
I have modesty and love of virtue and decorum of thought.
But no wonder moves my mind, that (the lines)
are not thought by anyone (?) to have been forged by my bellows
and are denied to have been made in my ancestral . . .
For the cohorts of women began their practice,   10
because in modern times it is said no woman has tasted
the Gorgons' waters and heard the learned sisters.
But Nature, creator of all with equal reason,
you are said to form the male and female soul equally
and are accustomed to infuse them with equal minds.   15
Therefore, you do not need, O woman, to call on the ancient poets.
Nature's gift has endowed both sexes.]

Despite the damage to the poem and the resulting uncertainties,
Nogarola here is making use of both Platonic and Biblical arguments to
claim a place for women in the great tradition of poetry. In the final lines
Nogarola is not, of course, proclaiming independence from classical models—an unlikely act for the author of a cento and an impossible act for a
humanist; indeed, her mention of the "Gorgons' waters" (12) is an allusion
to Propertius 3.3.32. On the contrary, she is asserting women's ancient and
honorable place in the canon. The reference to "modern times" draws on
the reader's knowledge of Sappho, Corinna, and the other commonly cited
exemplars of feminine creativity in ancient times. Women's own individual
gifts have no need of theft to bolster them. Here she claims a place for her
gender in modern poetry.

Nogarola's longest work (342 lines) is the elegiac poem, "The Book of
Virtues." Her talent, however, shows itself more in her shorter poems, and
this attempt at a sustained form is not a success. It is perhaps an early and
overambitious work. The construction is loose, the Latin is sometimes
strained, and the thought never rises above versified maxims.[48] Though
titled "The Book of Virtues," it deals more with their corresponding vices:
pride (1–66), envy (67–104), anger (105–42), despair (143–85), gluttony
(186–225), lust (226–52), avarice (253–300), ending with a summary and a
return to fidelity opposed to lust. In each category, though primarily addressed to men, women's faults are briefly singled out. The poem is extremely repetitious and shows little of an individual voice.[49] A translation of

the entire work would not be particularly useful, but the final section (317–42) reveals an insistence, in keeping with orthodox doctrine but seldom expressed, on fidelity on the part of both husband and wife and a view of marriage involving mutual aid, deriving again partially from the teaching of the church but also from the poetry of Verona's Catullus.[50] Her view of marriage, however, is conventional and orthodox: wives should be obedient to their husbands (328). This passage will also serve to give a taste of Nogarola's style—both the infelicities and the occasional fine touches—as well as show the damage the text has suffered.

> Templa Pudicitiae numquam fore tristia possunt,
>   numquam continua sol sine luce manet.
> saepe libido solet truculentos laedere vultus,
>   saepe solet pestis laedere membra latens.   320
> casta pio mulier veneratur amore maritum:
>   casta suum turtur novit amore parem.
> vir mulierque sibi servantes foedera crescunt:
>   servant alterutrum se relevando pedes.
> nil est nobilius quam vir mulierque pudici,   325
>   nil potius gemino lumine mundus habet.
> anulus ex rutilo gratus solet esse lapillo:
>   gratis habet proprium femina casta virum.
> nil nocet in tantum quam si mulier dominatur:
>   flamma larem proprium transgrediendo nocet.   330
> perditur igniferis iuvenis meretricis ocellis
>   sed pius agnus abest praerapiente lupa.
> non timet insidias vigili qui regnat in arce
>   inque Pudicitia vir quasi Caesar erit.
> stante Pudicitia gaudet caro mensque [˘ — —]   335
>   ceraque melque fluunt donec [˘ — ˘] apis
> virtu[. . . .
>   virtus plus vitio sollicitata potest.
> ferrea vicino vis saepe resolvitur igne,
>   nec vir erit stabilis cum muliere frequens.   340
> ⌐contineas igitur fugiasque libidinis ignes,
>   nam loca sana solent frigidiora fore.

332 sed] et *MS*   abest] obest *MS*   333 *fort.* vigilis

[The temples of Chastity are never able to become gloomy:
  the sun never stays without continuous light.

Often lust is accustomed to disfigure savage faces,
 often the lurking plague is accustomed to disfigure limbs.   320
A chaste woman honors her husband with pious love:
 the chaste turtle-dove knows its partner in love.
A man and woman by protecting the bond between them increase it:
 feet help the other by reducing their load.
There is nothing nobler than a chaste man and woman: 325
 the world has nothing better than this pair of eyes.
A ring made from red stone is usually pleasing—
 a chaste woman has her own husband for free.[51]
Nothing causes more harm than if a woman rules:
 a flame by going too far harms its own household god.   330
A youth is lost in the fiery eyes of a courtesan
 but a pious lamb stays away from the ravening she-wolf.
He who reigns on a watchful citadel does not fear plots
 and in chastity a man will be a Caesar.
With Chastity established, the flesh rejoices and the mind . . .   335
 Wax and honey flow until the bee . . .
Virtue . . .
 Virtue even when attacked is more powerful than vice.
Often the strength of iron is melted when a fire is nearby,
 nor will a man be faithful if he is frequently with a woman.   340
Therefore you should be self-controlled and flee the fires of lust,
 for healthy places are usually cooler.]

Isotta Nogarola (1418–66)

Isotta Nogarola's humanistic career and her difficult solution to its pressures have been extensively studied.[52] I wish only to add the text and translation of her pleasing "Elegy on the Countryside Around the Spring of Cyanum," an especially fine piece of Neo-Latin pastoral verse.

In 1451 Isotta had written her major scholarly work, the "Dialogue on the Equal or Unequal Sin of Adam and Eve," based on an exchange of letters with her friend, the humanist, Ludovico Foscarini.[53] Over a hundred years later in 1563, her grand-nephew, Count Francesco Nogarola, had it published by the Aldine press and dedicated it to Bernardo Navagero, who had just been created Cardinal of Verona. Francesco brought it out under Isotta's name and retained her text but made several additions to it. By way of compliment to his friend and patron, he added as a third character of the dialogue one of the cardinal's famous ancestors, Giovanni Navagero, who

had briefly been praetor of Verona in 1425, when Isotta was seven, and
again for a few months in 1434, when she was sixteen. He has the dialogue
take place at the Nogarola family's summer retreat of Castel d'Azzano just
outside Verona, whereas no setting is mentioned in the original. The Aldine
edition is our only source for this elegy, and the mention in it of Navagero
and the dialogue led Eugenius Abel to question whether the poem might
not be entirely a production of Francesco. Abel rightly concluded, however,
that, following his practice in the prose portions of the dialogue, Francesco
had only added a few verses to Isotta's own work, again with the intention
of making Giovanni Navagero present on the scene. There is no reason to
doubt the attribution: Isotta was highly regarded as a poet, and Francesco's
interpolation, devoting a full eighteen lines to Navagero's praise, is manifestly inorganic.[54] Further, as Abel notes, the references to visits by a ruling
Gonzaga and by Giovanni Pontano[55] are details unlikely to have been
invented.

In her elegy Isotta gives the Nogarola estate the poetic name of Cyanum
and, after a series of graceful compliments to Gonzaga and Pontano, creates
her own etiological myth. Following Ovid's telling of the story of the rape
of Persephone and the transformation of her companion, the nymph Cyane,[56]
into a pool of water (*Met.* 5.409–37, 462–70), Isotta adds the clever notion
of Cyane coming to rest on the Nogarola property.[57] This love of the particular setting is a marked feature of Renaissance verse,[58] and Isotta's poem
is a beautiful example of Neo-Latin elegy. Lines 43–50, in particular achieve
a splendidly Ovidian effect.

Elegia de laudibus Cyanei ruris

Salvete, O Cyani fontes dulcesque recessus
    in medioque alnis consita silva lacu.
Aonidum salvete choris loca grata sororum
    et quae cum Bromio Phoebus adire solet.
docta mihi quoties quaerenti carmina Musas   5
    profuit in vestro comperiisse sinu.
posthabito quoties Parnasi vertice Apollo
    Libethrique undis haec nemora alta colit.
haec quoque, dum sordent Nysae iuga celsa, feroces
    Liber agens tigres saepe vireta petit.   10
quot patuit domus ista viris virtutibus auctis
    insignique ortis hospitibus genere.
haec quoties Gonsaga et amore et sanguine iunctus,
    Mantua quo gaudet praeside, tecta subit.

huc quoque Pontanus Musis comitatus amoeni   15
    non semel accessit captus amore loci.
qui iam migrantes Latii revocavit ab oris
    Pieridas, magnae gloria Parthenopes.
[quis tacitum, quis Naugerum, Verona, relinquat,
    sceptra tenens nuper qui tibi iura dedit?   20
Hanc dum urbem regeret paribus moderatus habenis,
    quam praeclare illud, quam bene munus obit.
hunc sophiae imbutum studiis sub flore iuventae
    Cirrhaeis quondam Musae aluere iugis.
Dum rapidus mediam Veronae dividet urbem   25
    noster et Adriadas dum petit amnis aquas
Naugeri nobis nomen laudesque vigebunt
    haerebitque imo pectore semper honos.
nunc memini et meminisse iuvat quo tempore nostras
    non sprevit tantus praetor adire domos.   30
quam fausta illuxit caelo, quam candida nobis
    lux felix, cressa lux bona digna nota,
qua periucundo iussum est certamine quaeri
    patraritne Adam maius an Eva scelus.
ille viri partes, ego sum conata tueri   35
    femineas, quamquam femina quid poteram?]
Deliciae, O Cyanum, et Nogarolae gentis ocelle,
    Alcinoi atque hortis gratior Hesperidum.
non mirum si iam deserta sede Pelori
    Nympha suburbano constitit hoc Cyane.   40
Dux Erebi Aetneis quondam ferus abstulit oris
    Persephonem Cereris pignora cara deae.
Tinacris ingemuit raptam miserata; tulisset
    Persephonae, ah miserae, si potuisset, opem.
flumina creverunt lacrimis fontesque lacusque.   45
    flammarum evomuit latius Aetna globos.
quis credat? tunc Scylla etiam, tunc Scylla doloris
    latratu horrifico maxima signa dedit.
te quoque non solitas memorant fudisse querelas
    miscentem lacrimis, saeva Charybdis, aquas.   50
ipsae etiam nymphae confectae corda dolore
    errabant scissis lata per arva comis
ac veluti Euantes implebant questibus auras,
    tundentes palmis pectora et ungue genas.
quas inter forma egregia castoque pudore   55
    praeclari Cyane nominis emicuit.

fida una ante alias Cyane comes atque ministra
    haerebat lateri sedula Persephones.
Alma Ceres, dum maternas inviseret arces,
    "Natae," ait, "O Cyane, sit tibi cura meae.   60
hanc tibi commissam, Cyane, fidissima serves,
    nusquam absit, iussis pareat illa tuis."
utraque paruerat, cura utebatur eadem,
    utraque sed Stygiis est superata dolis.
quid faceret? quo se raperet perterrita custos?   65
    non erat et formae vis metuenda suae?
ipsa amens animi atque ingenti caeca dolore
    torpuit et nuda frigida sedit humo.
tum patriam fugere atque invisa excedere terra
    et petere Ausoniae litora certa fuit.   70
nulla mora. undisonum Siculas quod dividit oras
    finibus Hesperiae traiicit illa fretum.
post varios casus, post multa pericla quievit
    sedibus his longae fessa labore viae.
rus proprio "Cyanum" dixit de nomine, fontes   75
    admirata tuis hic, Arethusa, pares.
ex illo Cyanum prisci didicere parentes,
    sera hoc gaudebit nomine posteritas.
Nympha decus Siculi quondam formosa Pachyni,
    nunc Cyani et nostrae gloria magna domus.   80
floreat o utinam per saecula longa superstes,
    credita tutelae gens Nogarola tuae.
aemula sit vitae Nogarolo a sanguine creta
    atque pudicitiae femina quaeque tuae.
hanc oro tutare domum natosque nepotesque;   85
    incolume hoc serves, candida nympha, genus.
sic varios numquam flores mala frigora laedant,
    neve tuos nimius torreat aestus agros.
sic tibi sint liquidi fontes, vernantia circum
    prata nec anguinea sordeat unda lue.   90
quin ea, quot rutilas Pactolus fundit arenas
    vincat, quotque Tagi iactat Iberus opes.

[Elegy on the Countryside Around the Spring of Cyanum

Hail springs of Cyanum and the sweet recesses
    and in the midst of the lake a wood grown dense with alders.
Hail places beloved by the choruses of the Boeotian sisters[59]
    where Phoebus and Bacchus are accustomed to come.

How often, when I have been seeking learned songs, has it helped me　5
　　to have discovered the Muses in your bosom.
How often has Apollo ignored the peak of Helicon
　　and the waves of Libethra[60] to visit these high groves.
Liber[61] too, when weary of the lofty peaks of Nysa,
　　driving his fierce tigers seeks these green places.　　　　　　　　　10
How often has this house opened its doors to men endowed with
　　virtue and to guests sprung from noble families.
How often has Gonzaga, joined to me by love and blood,
　　in whose protection Mantua rejoices, come under this roof.
Here too Pontano, the comrade of the Muses, has come—　　　　　15
　　not just once!—captured by love for this pleasant spot,
Who called back the Pierides when they wandered
　　from the shores of Latium, the glory of great Parthenope.[62]
[Who could pass over Navagero in silence, till lately holding the
　　scepter with which he gave laws to you, Verona.　　　　　　　20
While he ruled that city, moderate with equal reins,
　　how famously, how well he discharged that office.
Steeped with the study of philosophy in the flower of his youth,
　　he was raised by the Muses on the Delphic ridges.
While our swift river cuts through the middle of the town　　　　25
　　of Verona and while it seeks the waters of the Adriatic,
the name and fame of Navagero will flourish for me
　　and his honor cling deep within my heart.
Now I recall and delight to recall the time when
　　so great a praetor did not disdain to visit our house.　　　　　30
How lucky the light shown in heaven, how bright for us,
　　happy light, light worthy of its chalk mark,[63]
on which we were ordered to examine in the most pleasant
　　debate whether Adam or Eve performed the greater sin.
He attempted to defend the men's side, I the women's,　　　　　35
　　though what could I, a woman, do?]
O Cyanum, the darling of the Nogarola family and the apple of their
　　eye,[64]
　　more pleasing than the gardens of Alcinous or the Hesperides,
no wonder if, her haunts on Pelorus[65] now deserted,
　　the nymph Cyane takes her place in this country villa.　　　　40
The cruel Lord of Erebus once carried off from the shores of Aetna
　　Persephone, the dear pledge of the goddess Ceres.
Tinacris[66] groaned in pity at her rape: ah, poor Persephone,
　　He would have helped her if he could.

The rivers created springs and lakes from their tears;   45
    Aetna spewed out balls of flames more widely.
Who would believe it: then Scylla, even Scylla gave the greatest
    proof of her grief in horrible howling.
They tell that you too, cruel Charybdis, poured out unaccustomed
    complaints, mixing tears with your waters.   50
The nymphs themselves heart-stricken with grief
    wandered in the broad fields tearing their hair
and like Maenads filled the air with complaints,
    striking their breasts with palms and their cheeks with nails.
Among these, of exceptional beauty and chaste modesty,   55
    Cyane of the famous name shone forth.
The one companion and servant faithful beyond the others
    she used to cling constantly to Persephone's side.
Nurturing Ceres, when she visited the maternal citadels,
    would say, "O Cyane, please take care of my child.   60
Entrusted to you, most faithful Cyane, keep her safe,
    let her never leave your sight, let her always obey your
    commands."
Both obeyed, both used the same care,
    but both were conquered by Stygian tricks.
What could she do? Where could the terrified guardian take herself? 65
    Was not the power of her own beauty a thing to be feared?
She herself mad in mind and blind with great pain
    grew weary and sat down frozen on the bare ground.
Then she decided to flee her fatherland and leave the hated country
    and to seek the shores of Italy.   70
No delay. She leapt across the wave-resounding strait
    which divides the Sicilian shores from the borders of Hesperia.
After varied misfortunes, after many adventures, she rested
    in this place, exhausted by the labor of her long journey.
She called the countryside "Cyanum" from her own name,   75
    delighted with springs the equal of yours, Arethusa.
From that time the parents of old have learned of Cyanum;
    posterity afterward will rejoice in this name.
The lovely nymph, once the crown of Sicilian Panychum,[67]
    now the glory of Cyanum and our house.   80
O may it flourish surviving throughout the long ages,
    The family of Nogarola entrusted to your protection.
May each woman born from Nogarolan blood
    be emulous of your life and modesty.

I pray that you will guard this house, its children and grandchildren. 85
    Keep this race unharmed, O shining nymph.
So may cruel frosts never harm your varied flowers,
    nor may excessive heat burn your fields.
May your spring be clear, your meadows be verdant all around,
    and your wave not be dirtied by snaky slime.   90
Rather may she outnumber all the golden sand the Pactolus pours forth,
    and all the treasure which the Spanish Tagus boasts.]

Costanza Varano (1426–47)

    Costanza Varano was the granddaughter of Battista da Montefeltro
Malatesta (1383–1450), herself a scholar, who helped educate her.[68] At the
age of sixteen, she delivered a public oration in Latin on the occasion of the
visit of her future sister-in-law, Bianca Maria Visconti, to Pesaro in 1442.
Two years later, in 1444, she married Alessandro Sforza, who had long been
in love with her and had bought Pesaro in order to win her. Any visible sign
of her studies ceased with her marriage, and she died in childbirth three
years later.

    In a letter, written in 1442, before her marriage,[69] she included a short
hexameter poem in praise of Isotta Nogarola. Costanza would have been
sixteen and Isotta twenty-four. It is of particular interest, showing the cir-
culation of such pieces not merely to established male humanists to attract
male acknowledgement but also between women in mutual recognition and
support.[70] Varano's claim that Nogarola has surpassed men in learning is
unique in this period, and the promise of continued learning in the female
line is especially interesting in light of Varano's and Nogarola's family histories of learned women ancestors. There is no reference to Isotta's equally
famous older sister Ginevra (c. 1417–1461/68), who would have been about
twenty-five and whose talents had been absorbed by marriage.

Ad Dominam Isotam Nogarolam

Est, Isota, meo tua dulcis epistola fixa
pectore nec poterit quam longa abolere vetustas.
O Verona, tuis urbs fecundissima pomis,
plus trahet haec laudis iam vate puella Catullo!
floruit ille quidem praeclarus alumnus in aevo,   5
quo studiis homines vigili indulsere Camenae,
hac aetate viros superas celeberrima doctos.
hinc tibi virtutum numero, quibus ipsa refulges,

coniunctam me nempe scias, nec secula nostra
iam tantum deiecta puto velut ante solebam.   10
luminis est etiam prisci tibi flamma reposta
mentis in arcano. felices quippe parentes
quam reor esse tuos, quibus addis nata decorem
et pariter morum dulcis pariterque sophiae.
et si quam omnipotens concessit forte sororem,   15
o faustam, poterit tua post vestigia recto
sumere calle viam facilique venire volatu
Parnassi ad sacros latices et docta sororis
munere blandiloquo componet carmina plectro.
egregiam scribet prosam plaudentibus astris.   20

[To the Lady Isotta Nogarola

Your sweet letter, Isotta, has been fixed
In my breast and no age, however long, will be able to destroy it.
O Verona, town most fertile with your fruits,
Now this girl will draw more praises than the poet Catullus.
For he, your famous child, flourished in an age   5
wherein men indulged the wakeful Muse with study;
in this age you are most famous for surpassing learned men.
Hence, for the number of your virtues with which you shine,
you should know that I am attached to you, nor do I think
our age is as decadent, as I used to.   10
The flame of the ancient light has been placed safe
In the hidden recesses of your mind. How happy, I think,
Are your parents, to whom you, their daughter, add elegance
equally of manners and equally of sweet wisdom.
And if the Omnipotent allowed by chance any sister,   15
O lucky girl! She will be able, following in your footsteps,
to take the way with the right path and come with easy flight
to the sacred waters of Parnassus, and taught by her sister's
gift she will compose poems with a sweet-speaking plectrum,
she will write exceptional prose as the stars applaud.]   20

Alessandra Scala (1475–1506)

Alessandra was the daughter of Bartolommeo Scala (1428–97), the
humanist and historian, an intimate of Lorenzo de' Medici, who became
Chancellor of Florence. She was educated in Greek by Iohannes Lascaris

and Demetrius Chalcondylas and in Latin by her father and Poliziano. She may even have attended lectures at the University of Florence. She was famed for having acted the title role in Sophocles' *Electra* in Greek at the age of eighteen and later married the equally brilliant Greek-born scholar and poet, Michele Marullo (Michael Tarchaniota Marullus).[71] This seems to have been the end of her studies, and after his death in 1500 Cassandra retired to a convent.

Besides a letter to Cassandra Fedele, all that has survived of Alessandra's work is a sixteen-line epigram in Greek, written in response to a similar epigram from Poliziano.[72] This indicates a remarkable level of learning, of a sort attained even by few men at that time.

οὐδὲν ἄρ' ἦν αἴνοιο παρ' ἔμφρονος ἀνδρὸς ἄμεινον
   κἀκ σέθεν αἶνος ἐμοί γ' οἷον ἄειρε κλέος.
πολλοὶ θριοβόλοι, παῦροι δέ τε μάντιές εἰσιν.
   εὗρες ἄρ'; οὐχ εὗρες γ', οὐδ' ὄναρ ἠντίασας.
φῇ γὰρ ὁ θεῖος ἀοιδός· ἄγει θεὸς ὡς τὸν ὁμοῖον.   5
   οὐδέν 'Αλεξάνδρη σοῦ δ' ἀνομοιότερον.
ὡς σύ γ' ὁποῖα Δανούβιος, ἐκ ζόφου ἐς μέσον ἦμαρ
   καῦθις ἐπ' ἀντολίην αἰπὰ ῥέεθα χέεις.
φωναῖς δ' ἐν ἱπλείσταις σόν τοι κλέος ἠέρ' ἐλαστρεῖ,[73]
   'Ελλάδι, 'Ρωμαϊκῇ, 'Εβραϊκῇ, ἰδίῃ.   10
ἄστρα, φύσις, ἀριθμοί, ποιήματα, κύβρις, ἰατροὶ
   'Ηρακλῆν καλέουσ' ἀντιμεθελκόμενα.
τἀμὰ δὲ παρθενικῆς σπουδάσματα παίγνιά τ' αἰνῶς
   Βόκχορις εἰ κρίναις, ἄνθεα καὶ δρόσος ὥς.
τοιγὰρ μήτ' ἐλέφαντος ἐναντία βόμβον ἀείρω·   15
   αἴλουρον Πάλλας καὶ σύ γ' ὑπερφρονέεις.

13 αἰνῶς cod. Vat. : φασί aldina : αἰνῶν fort.

[Alessandra to Poliziano

Indeed nothing is better than praise from an intelligent man.
And praise from you to *me*, what glory it raises!
Many are the pebble-throwing soothsayers, but few the prophets.
Have you found it? You have not found it, you have not even found a
   dream.[74]
For as the divine singer says: "God brings (like) to like,"[75]   5
and nothing is less like Alessandra than you.
For you, like the Danube, from the West to midday
And again to the rising of the sun,[76] you pour forth steep streams.[77]

In many languages your fame rides the air
in Greek, Latin, Hebrew, your own.   10
Stars, nature, numbers, poems, law,[78] doctors,
these things call you Heracles, pulling in different directions.[79]
But both a young girl's serious work and her really playful work,
if you play the part of Bocchoris,[80] become like flowers and dew.
So I do not trumpet before an elephant: 15
Like Pallas you also despise the cat.][81]

There are faults—elision at the diaeresis in pentameters, overuse of γέ to
avoid hiatus or make position—nevertheless, this is an exceptional piece.
The language is Homeric and use of rare forms is not a sign (as it might
be today) of a student's desperation, but is rather in keeping with much
of Poliziano's and others' new Greek verse. It is intended to delight the
scholarly reader with philological *doctrina*. An example is ϑριοβόλοι (3),
a word found only in Hesychius (that great repository of the obscure), set
into a reworking of a proverb that Alessandra would have known from
Plato (*Phaedo* 69c) and the *Greek Anthology* (10.106), or her elliptical
citation of Homer.

Fulvia Olympia Morata (1526–55)

Finally, in Fulvia Olympia Morata we reach one of the most learned
women of her age.[82] The time is ripe for a scholarly edition and a full
biography, to put in their proper historical and theological settings the life
and works of this remarkable woman, whose letters so impressed Goethe.[83]
She was born in Ferrara at the court of Hercole II d'Este. Educated by her
father, Fulvio Pellegrino Morato, an early convert to Calvinism, and later by
Caelio Calcagnini and Chilian Senapius (Kilian Senf), she was selected to be
a companion to Anna d'Este. She gave proof of her talent by writing a
panegyric on Scaevola in Greek at the age of thirteen and giving declamations on Cicero's *Paradoxa* at sixteen. In danger from the Inquisition for
her Protestant beliefs, she left the court and in 1550 married Andreas
Grunthler (Grundler), a physician and fellow Protestant, escaping with him
back to Germany. She continued to read, write, and even teach Greek.[84] Her
Latin letters offer a vivid picture of her times and harrowing adventures.
She lost all her books and most of her writings during the siege of her new
home of Schweinfurt (1553–54). Her health destroyed, she died a year later.
Her friends, especially Celio Seconde Curione (1503–69), collected the let-
ters that remained and poems that she had copied out from memory after

Schweinfurt. The work went through four editions, dedicated first to Isabella Besegna and then Elizabeth I of England.

Morata produced, both as a devotional exercise and as a demonstration of remarkable skill, Greek translations of Psalms 1, 2, 23, 34, 70, 125, and 150 in hexameters and of Psalm 46 in Sapphics (a rare meter even in humanistic circles), which her husband set to music. Like Alessandra Scala, she used the Homeric dialect. While tours de force, these translations are not perhaps of sufficient intrinsic interest to be included here.[85] However, several other poems in both Greek and Latin have survived.

In an epigram dating to her early period of study, Morata declares her independence from the traditional symbols of feminine accomplishment and makes a bold claim to be an equal citizen of Parnassus.[86]

ὈΟλυμπίας τῆς Μωράτης εἰς Εὐτυχὸν Ποντανὸν Κέλτην

οὔποτε μὲν ξυμπᾶσιν ἐνὶ φρεσὶν ἥνδανε ταὐτὸ
κοὔποτε πᾶσιν ἴσον Ζεὺς παρέδωκε νόον.
ἱππόδαμος Κάστωρ, πὺξ δ' ἦν ἀγαθὸς Πολυδεύκης,[87]
ἔκγονος ἐξ ταύτης ὄρνιθος ἀμφότερος.
κἀγὼ μὲν θῆλυς γεγαυῖα τὰ θηλυκὰ λεῖπον·   5
νήματα, κερκίδιον, στήμονα, καὶ καλάθους.
Μουσάων δ' ἄγαμαι λειμῶνα τὸν ἀνθεμόεντα
Παρνάσσου θ' ἱλαροὺς τοῦ διλόφοιο χορούς.
ἄλλαι τέρπονται μὲν ἴσως ἄλλοισι γυναῖκες.
ταῦτα δέ μοι κῦδος, ταῦτα δὲ χαρμοσύνη.[89]   10

4 ταύτῆς] αὐτῆς 1562 1570 Bonnet

[To Eutychus Pontanus Gallus[90]

Never did the same thing please the hearts of all,
    and never did Zeus grant the same mind to all.
Castor is a horse-tamer, but Polydeuces is good with his fist,
    both the offspring of the same bird.
And I, though born female, have left feminine things,   5
    yarn, shuttle, loom-threads, and work-baskets.
I admire the flowery meadow of the Muses,
    and the pleasant choruses of twin-peaked Parnassus.
Other women perhaps delight in other things.
    These are my glory, these my delight.]   10

Datable to 1547 or soon afterward is this elegant poem on the death of the great Venetian humanist, Pietro Bembo[91] (1470–1547).

Ὀλυμπίας τῆς Μωράτης εἰς Βεμβόν

κάτθανεν Ἀονίδων κῦδος μέγα παρθενικάων
Βεμβός, ὁ τῶν Ἐνετῶν φωσφόρος εἰναλίων,
ᾧπερ ἐνὶ βροτέοισι τὸ νῦν ἐναλίγκιός ἐστι
οὐδεὶς οὔτ' ἔργοις οὔτ' ἐπέεσσιν ἀνήρ.
οὐ θανέοντος, ἔδοξεν ἄμ' εὐεπίῃ πάλιν αὐτὸς   =
εἰσιέναι στυγερὸν Τούλλιος εἰς Ἀΐδην.

3 ᾧπερ : οὔπερ 1562 1570

[To Bembo

He has died, the great glory of the Maiden Aonides,
    Bembo, the morning star of the sea-going Venetians.
Among mortals now there is no man resembling him
    neither in words nor in deeds.
When he died, it seemed that together with eloquence   5
    Cicero himself went a second time unto hated Hades.]

Only a little of Morata's original religious verse survives, but she shows a strong talent for recasting biblical themes. For example, "On Christ Crucified" refers to John 3:14.[93]

Περὶ Χριστοῦ σταυροθέντος

ὡς ὀφέων ποτὲ τὸν κεκακωμένον ἕλκεϊ λυγρῷ
    χώρῳ ἐ'ν οἰοπόλῳ χάλκεος ἄθλεν ὄφις,
ὡς ὃν μὲν βροτολοιγὸς ὄφις δάκεν, ἄλθεται αἶψα
    εἰς θεοῦ υἱὸν ἰδὼν ὑψόσ' ἀειρόμενον.

[As once the brazen serpent cured those harmed
    by the painful bite of the serpents in the desert region,[94]
so the one bitten by the serpent who is the plague of man is
    cured quickly,
    when he looks upon the Son of God lifted up on high.]

Similarly she recasts John 3:16 in the following:[95]

Olympiae Fides

Sic deus humanam gentem vel semper amavit
    filium ut unigenam traderet ille neci.
sic genus humanum dilexit filius ipse,

solus ut aeternam fuderit ille animam,
ut qui pacifero possit confidere Christo 5
vivat nec saeva morte perire queat.

[Olympia's Declaration of Faith

So God always loved the human race
that he delivered his only-begotten son to death.
So the Son in turn loved the human race
that he alone poured out his eternal soul,
So that whoever can believe in Christ the Bringer of Peace 5
may live and not be able to perish in savage death.]

Another early work is the following:[96]

De vera virginitate

Quae virgo est, nisi mente quoque est et corpore virgo,
haec laudem nullam virginitatis habet.
quae virgo est, uni Christo ni tota dicata est,
haec Veneris virgo est totaque mancipium.

[On True Virginity

A virgin, unless she is a virgin in mind as well as body,
has no share in the praise for virginity.
A virgin, unless she is totally dedicated to Christ,
is a virgin of Venus and completely her slave.]

Morata wrote an elegy for Johannes Lindemann (1488–1546), Martin Luther's cousin and a preacher in Schweinfurt. The language of the poem is that of Homer, and the well-fitted epicisms add a quiet solemnity to a Christian poem.[97]

Ἐπιτάφιον εἰς Ἰωάννην Λινδεμαννόν, ἐκκλησιαστήν,

ἔνθα κατευνηθέντα ᾽βροτὸν κατὰ γαῖα καλύπτει,
ὃς ποιμαίνεσκεν πώεα καλὰ θεοῦ.
ὅς τ' ὀΐων ἕνεκα πλείστους ἐμόγησεν ἀέθλους,
τάς μὲν ῥυόμενος μαρνάμενος δὲ λύκοις.
Νῦν δὲ μιν ἀργαλέου καμάτοιο μύυνθ' ἀπολήγειν, 5
εὕδειν τ' ἐν τύμβῳ Χριστὸς ἄνωγε θεός.
ὄφρα μὴ ὅσσα γε κήδε' ἅπασι βροτοῖσιν ἐφῆπται,
ὀφθαλμοῖσιν ἴδῃ, μηδὲ κακόν τι πάθῃ,

ἀνστήσει δὲ Χριστὸς ἑὸν τάχα μηλοβοτῆρα
σήματος ἐξαγαγὼν ἤματι τῷ πυμάτῳ   10

[Epitaph for Johannes Lindemann, Preacher.

There the earth hides the mortal lulled to sleep,
    who shepherded the beautiful flocks of God,
who on behalf of his sheep suffered the greatest pains,
    rescuing them, while he fought with wolves.
But now Christ our God orders him to cease for a little   5
    from his hard labors and rest in a tomb,
lest he see with his eyes how many griefs hang over
    all mankind, or lest he should suffer any ill.
But Christ will soon raise his own shepherd,
    leading him out of that tomb on the final day.]   10

Shortly before her marriage in 1550, she composed this "Wedding
Prayer." The poem is cleverly constructed as a single sentence, with the
Christian doctrine of marriage (Ephesians 5:22–33) placed in the form of a
classical aretology.[98]

Εὐχαὶ γαμικαί

εὐρυκρείων ἄναξ, πάντων ὕπατε κρειόντων,
    ἄρσεν' ὃς ἔπλασσας θηλύτερόν τε γένος,
ὃς κἀνδρὶ πρωτίστῳ ἑὴν παράκοιτιν ἔδωκας,
    ὄφρα τάγ' ἀνθρώπων μή ποτ' ὄλοιτο γένη,
καὶ θνητῶν ψυχὰς νυμφὴν τεῷ ἔμμεναι υἱῷ,   5
    τὸν δ' ἔθελες θανέειν εἵνεχ' ἑῆς ἀλόχου,
ὄλβον ὁμοφροσύνην τε δίδου πόσει ἠδὲ δάμαρτι.
    θεσμὸς γὰρ πέλεται λέκτρα γάμοι τε τεός.

[Wedding Prayer

Wide-ruling Lord, highest of all rulers,
    who formed the male and the female sex,
You who gave to the first man a wife for his own,
    lest the race of man die out,
and wished the souls of mortals to be the bride of your Son   5
    and that he die on behalf of his spouse,
give happiness and harmony to husband and to wife,
    for the ordinance, the marriage bed, and weddings are yours.]

From the period of her final illness came this brief prayer.[99]

Olympiae votum

Dissolvi cupio, tanta est fiducia menti,
    esseque cum Christo quo mea vita viget.

The Prayer of Olympia

I long to be dissolved, so great is the confidence of my mind,[100]
    and to be with Christ in whom my life flourishes.[101]

Directions for Future Research

Besides these five, I wish to mention the lives and works of four other women Neo-Latin poets as possibilities for further research. The world of Spanish humanism is still largely unexplored; the role of women even less so.[102] Perhaps the most famous learned woman of Spain and Portugal was Luisa Sigea of Toledo (c. 1522–c. 1560) whose letter of 1546 to Pope Paul III, written in Latin, Greek, Hebrew, "Chaldean" (i.e., Syriac), and Arabic made her the wonder of the age.[103] Her Latin poem, "Sintra" (1545), a lovely bucolic describing the countryside around Lisbon, was widely read, but her posthumous fame has rested primarily on a pornographic work circulated under her name by Nicolaus Chorier.[104]

The poetry of Elizabeth Jane Weston (1582–1612), an English Catholic whose family went to Prague in exile, is just now being rediscovered thanks largely to the works of Susan Bassnett.[105] Of particular interest is Elena Lucrezia Cornaro Piscopia, intellectual patron of Vassar College, most famous as the first woman to earn the Ph.D. (Parma, 1678).[106] Her Greek, Latin, and Hebrew poems were collected in her *Opera* (1688).[107] Finally, as an example of the new discoveries that are being made, there is the case of Bathsua Makin (1600–74?), tutor to the Princess Elizabeth (daughter of Charles I) and author of *An Essay to Revive the Ancient Education of Gentlewomen*. She has only recently been identified as the prodigy, Bathsua Reginalda, whose collection of poems, *Musa virginea: greco-latino-gallica* (London, 1616: STC 20835), was published when she was sixteen.[108] Much exciting work remains to be done and many exciting discoveries are waiting to be made, but the final words of this paper should belong to a poet:

Gold which lies hidden in the mine does not cease to be gold,
although it is entombed; and when it is brought out, and worked,
it is as rich and beautiful as all other gold.
                            Modesta da Pozzo, *Canti del Floridoro* (1581)

Notes

1. Margaret L. King and Albert Rabil, Jr., *Her Immaculate Hand: Selected Works By and About the Women Humanists of Quattrocento Italy* (Binghamton, NY: Medieval and Renaissance Texts and Studies, 1983).

2. A brief *apparatus criticus* has been added to a few of the poems. This aims at giving only the places where I have departed from the previously published versions and does not represent all the variant readings; I have normalized spelling without comment. The translations are intended to be no more than calques; I have made no attempt at a poetic translation.

3. David Robey, "Humanist Views on the Study of Poetry in the Early Italian Renaissance," *History of Education* 13 (1984): pp. 7–25; Paul F. Grendler, *Schooling in Renaissance Italy: Literacy and Learning 1300–1600* (Baltimore, MD: Johns Hopkins University Press, 1989), p. 236.

4. Eugenio Garin, ed., *Il pensiero pedagogico dell'umanesimo* (Florence: Giuntine, 1958), p. 162; Gordon Griffiths, James Hankins, and David Thompson, eds., *The Humanism of Leonardo Bruni. Selected Texts* (Binghamton, NY: Medieval and Renaissance Texts and Studies, 1987), p. 246; Grendler, *Schooling,* p. 239. For the place of Latin poetry in Renaissance education, see Robey, "Humanist Views"; Grendler, *Schooling,* pp. 234–55.

5. On the goal of humanist education as the public role and the consequences for women, see Margaret L. King "Thwarted Ambitions: Six Learned Women of the Italian Renaissance," *Soundings* 59 (1976): pp. 280–304; Margaret L. King, *Women of the Renaissance* (Chicago: University of Chicago Press, 1991), pp. 164–72; Anthony Grafton and Lisa Jardine, *From Humanism to the Humanities: Education and the Liberal arts in Fifteenth- and Sixteenth-Century Europe* (Cambridge: Harvard University Press, 1986), pp. 29–57, esp. 32–33, 43–45, 56–57; Grendler, *Schooling,* p. 89.

6. For Italian examples, see Grendler, *Schooling,* pp. 236–37, 250–55 (on Terence, Horace, and Ovid).

7. Craig Kallendorf, "Christoforo Landino's *Aeneid* and the Humanist Critical Tradition," *Renaissance Quarterly* 36 (1983): pp. 525–26.

8. Grendler, *Schooling,* p. 238.

9. Hans Baron, ed., *Leonardo Bruni Aretino: Humanistich-philosophische Schriften* (Wiesbaden: Steiner, 1969, original 1928), pp. 5–19, esp. 11–16; William Harrison Woodward, *Vittorino da Feltre and Other Humanist Educators* (New York: Teachers' College Press, 1963, original 1897), pp. 126–33; Grafton and Jardine, *From Humanism,* pp. 32–33, Griffiths, Hankins, and Thompson, *Humanism,* pp. 240–51; King, *Women of the Renaissance,* p. 194; Hans Baron, ed., *The Crisis of the Early Italian Renaissance,* 2d. ed. (Princeton: Princeton University Press, 1966), p. 554 n. 23; and Grendler, *Schooling,* p. 87.

10. Juan Luis Vives, *Joannis Ludovici Valentini Opera Omnia*. 1523/1783: vol. 4, pp. 4, 5, 83–84, 87, 89. See Gloria Kaufman, "Juan Vives on the Education of Women," *Signs* 3 (1978): pp. 891–96.

11. Grendler, *Schooling*, p. 88; King and Rabil, *Her Immaculate Hand*, pp. 102–03, 114–16.

12. 95 r–v, cited from Grendler, *Schooling*, p. 88

13. Grendler, *Schooling*, pp. 87–102.

14. For the former, see the works mentioned above; for the latter, Jacob Burckhardt, *The Civilization of the Renaissance in Italy*, trans. S. C. G. Middlemore (New York: Harper and Row, 1868/1960), pp. 193–202. John Sparrow, "Latin Verse of the High Renaissance," in *Italian Renaissance Studies*, ed. E. F. Jacob (London: Faber and Faber, 1960), pp. 354–409; and Fred J. Nichols, *An Anthology of Neo-Latin Verse* (New Haven, CT: Yale University Press, 1979) provide excellent introductions.

15. Grafton and Jardine, *From Humanism*, pp. 23–24.

16. Grendler, *Schooling*, pp. 243–44. Maffeo Vegio mentioned verse composition only as an aid to a good prose style (*De educatione liberorum et eorum claris moribus libri sex*, ed. Maria W. Fanning and A. S. Sullivan, 3 vols [Washington, DC: Catholic University of America Studies in Medieval and Renaissance Latin, 1541/1933–36], p. 235; Woodward, *Vittorino da Feltre*, p. 232) as did Melanchthon in Germany (William Harrison Woodward, *Studies in Education During the Age of the Renaissance, 1400–1600* [New York: New York: Teachers' College Press, 1967, original 1906], pp. 219, 239). The situation was somewhat different in England, with John Brinsley (1627) and Charles Hoole (1660), in their ideal schools in any case, recommending a gradual progression from the standard practice of double translation (i.e., from Latin into the vernacular and back again; David Cressy, *Education in Tudor and Stuart England* [New York: St. Martin's, 1975], pp. 80–81), which in their schools would be applied to poetry, as well as prose, up to extemporaneous verse composition (John Brinsley, *Ludus Literarius or the Grammar Schoole* [Menston, Yorkshire: Scolar Press, 1968/1612], pp. 191–95; Charles Hoole, *A New Discovery of the Old Art of Teaching Schoole* [Menston, Yorkshire: Scolar Press, 1969/1660], pp. 156–63; T. W. Baldwin, *William Shakspere's Small Latine and Less Greeke*, vol. 2 [Urbana: University of Illinois Press, 1944], pp. 380–82, 385–400). The "rules of versifieing" mentioned by Harrison (Baldwin, ibid., p. 383) refer to scansion, a standard part of the curriculum (so, e.g., at Sandwich School, 1580, cited in Cressy, *Education*, p. 82; cf. Grendler, *Schooling*, pp. 240–43), not composition.

17. Brinsley, *Ludus Literarius*, p. 380; Baldwin, *William Shakespeare's*, p. 380; and Grendler, *Schooling*, pp. 243–44, citing the case of Maffeo Vegio.

18. J. W. Binns, *Intellectual Culture in Elizabethan and Jacobean England* (Leeds: F. Cairns, 1990), pp. 34, 35, 38, 40–45; Brinsley, *Ludus Literarius*, p. 191; Baldwin, *William Shakespeare's*, p. 380.

19. "Quas qui non tenet, quid ipse in eo genere de se polliceri aut quem gustum in poetis habere possit, non equidem intellego." [But what promise someone who doesn't know these things (the laws of quantity) might have in this genre, or what taste in the poets, I certainly don't know] (Baron, *Leonardo Bruni Aretino,* pp. 18–19; Woodward, *Vittorino da Feltre,* pp. 125–26).

20. Book 3, chap. 46; cited from Grendler, *Schooling,* p. 89.

21. For a review, see Grendler, *Schooling,* pp. 87–102; King, *Women,* pp. 164–213.

22. The learned women usually had had considerable support from male relatives and colleagues merely to get their education in the first place. They often, too, received extravagant, if occasionally condescending, praise (though hyperbole was the norm for Renaissance writing). However, the attacks that could await the learned woman who ventured into the public arena are demonstrated by the cases of Isotta Nogarola (accused inter alia of incest) and Cassandra Fedele. Public humiliation was the result of merely the passive failure of a male addressee to respond to a woman's making the immodest overture of writing. See King, "Thwarted Ambitions," pp. 284–85; Margaret L. King, "The Religious Retreat of Isotta Nogarola (1418–1466): Sexism and its Consequences in the Fifteenth Century." pp. 808–10; King, "Book-lined Cells: Women and Humanism in The Early Italian Renaissance" in Patricia H. Labalme ed., *Beyond Their Sex: Learned Women of the European Past* (New York: New York University Press, 1980), pp. 72–73, 76–77; Grafton and Jardine, *From Humanism,* pp. 37–38, 40–41, 51–52.

23. Eugenius Abel, ed., *Isottae Nogarolae Veronensis opera quae supersunt omnia,* 2 vols. (Vienna: 1886), repr. in microfilm, "History of Women," Reel 472, No. 3527 (New Haven, CT: 1975) vol. 1, p. vii.

24. Archival research, however, might help rectify this. For the date, see Abel, *Isottae Nogarolae,* p. xc. Other documents not included in Abel and still unedited are: Bologna, Biblioteca Universitaria, 3977: verse letter to Angela by Antonio Lusco (Paul Oskar Kristeller, *Iter Italicum,* vol. 1 [Leiden: Brill, 1963], p. 202); Perugia, Biblioteca Communale Augusta, Fondo Vecchio D53 (65v): Jo. Nicola Salernus, verses to Angela Nogarola (Kristeller, *Iter Italicum,* vol. 2 [1967], p. 55); Vatican, Vat. lat. 5223 (25v–26): poem of Antonio de Romagno to Angela Nogarola (Kristeller, *Iter Italicum,* vol. 2, p. 372).

25. (Frater Iacopo) Philippus Bergomensis (Foresti), *De plurimis claris scele(s)tisque mulieribus* (Ferrara, 1497), Chap. 159 (fol. 140); the relevant section is printed in Abel, *Isottae Nogarolae,* vol. 2, pp. 392–94.

26. Abel, *Isottae Nogarolae,* vol. 1, pp. 121–28, and vol. 2, pp. 351–59.

27. For this as a recurrent phenomenon in the life of humanist women, see King, "Thwarted Ambitions," pp. 293–300; King, "The Religious Retreat," pp. 814–15; King, "Book-lined Cells," p. 69; Grafton and Jardine, *From Humanism,* p. 36.

28. Luscus, de Loschis, Loschi. He was the author of "The Temple of Chastity," a poem in celebration of Maddalena Scrovegni that set the terms for praise of educated women. See Margaret L. King, "Goddess and Captive: Antonio Loschi's Poetic Tribute to Maddelena Scrovegni (1389), Study and Text," *Medievalia et Humanistica* 10 (1980): pp. 103–27; King and Rabil, *Her Immaculate Hand,* pp. 11–13.

29. Abel, *Isottae Nogarolae,* vol. 1, pp. i, ix and xcii, and vol. 2, p. 304.

30. *Virgo, puellis*: Abel, *Isottae Nogarolae,* vol. 2, pp. 296, vv. 1, 5.

31. Sparrow, "Latin Verse," pp. 365–67, has some excellent remarks on borrowing and imitation in Renaissance verse.

32. Abel, *Isottae Nogarolae,* vol. 2, pp. 293–95.

33. Note the way in which Seneca is made one of the doctors of the church.

34. The lines are obscure. In Horace, the phrase stops after *nubem,* and *modestus* is a substantive: "Take the cloud from your brow; often the modest man / looks like he's sneaky." Abel puts a comma at the end of the line, making *modestus* a nom. for voc.: "Take away, you modest man, . . ." All the adjectives, however, seem to modify *balteus,* but no reading properly links the final *honestus* to the rest of the sentence. For line 14, Petrarch's original is "poscimus hanc avide, toto nil pulchrius orbe"; Nogarola's "nihil est mihi pulcrius orbe" may be merely a false recollection or else a slight rewrite to make the line more emphatically personal. For line 15, Able's *id* does not scan, while Petrarch's *hanc* here is neatly made to refer to *flos.* For line 20, Abel reads: "quid vetat esse pium munus? tene dulcia verba": "What forbids your gift to be pious? Keep your words sweet." This is no improvement and since the original reading of Petrarch makes more sense in the context, *tene* is likely to be a misreading for *leve,* with concomitant mispunctuation.

35. Abel, *Isottae Nogarolae,* vol. 1, p. viii, and vol. 2, p. 294, following the manuscript and the early editions assigns this line to "Pindaro Thebano"!

36. Grendler, *Schooling,* pp. 254–55.

37. For the idea, see Claudine Herrmann, *Les voleuses de langue* (Paris: des Femmes, 1976); Alice Ostriker, "The Thieves of Language," *Signs* 8 (1982): pp. 68–90.

38. The nymph who married Numa and whom Martial 10.35.13 had used to refer to a woman poet, the younger Sulpicia. For the ambiguous nature of these tropes, see King, "Book-lined Cells," pp. 75–80; for Isotta's reappropriation of them, see Grafton and Jardine, *From Humanism,* pp. 38–39; also 48–50 (on Cassandra Fedele).

39. Abel, *Isottae Nogarolae,* vol. 2, p. 300. Similarly, Maddalena Scrovegni, a friend and correspondent of Angela (for her letter, see Abel, vol. 2, pp. 305–07), in the following year (1388) had written a Latin letter to Jacopo del Verme, publicly announcing her joy (and her family's) at the Visconti conquest of Padua. The letter was requested by her cousin, Ugolotto Biancardo, formerly an ally of the Carrara

family and now the governor of Vicenza for the Visconti. See King and Rabil, *Her Immaculate Hand,* pp. 33–35.

40. The arms of the Visconti featured a serpent from whose mouth a child issued forth.

41. Gian Galeazzo received the county of Vertus (in Champagne) as part of the dowry of Isabella of Valois. The pun on *virtus* was frequent among both friends and enemies.

42. Abel, *Isottae Nogarolae,* vol. 2, 298–99.

43. A reference, of course, to Carrara.

44. This could not have pleased Maddalena Scrovegni, who was exiled to Venice following the Carrara reconquest of Padua.

45. What Joanna Russ (*How to Suppress Women's Writing* [Austin: University of Texas Press, 1983], pp. 20–24) categorizes as "Denial of Agency."

46. Abel, *Isottae Nogarolae,* vol. 2, pp. 301–2. The manuscript gives lines 1–4 as a single poem, then 5–17 plus the following elegiacs as a different poem. The elegiacs are obviously separate, perhaps by another author. Both Abel (vol. 2, p. 302) and Kristeller assume, rightly, I believe, that the elegiacs are the response by Niccolò de Facino, though, rather than a recantation, it is merely an apology for not having written. Abel united the two hexameter fragments; he also moved 5–6 after 1–2, but this fails to give adequate sense. Line 4 clearly belongs after 2; this leaves two occurrences of *laudes* in two lines, which is not outside our poet's practice. However, it might be better to read *lauros* in 5. The *ullo* of line 8 apparently equals *ab ullis,* unless it agrees with something in the following lacuna; a neuter subject is needed, and I suggest *follibus esse metra ulla meis.* The meaning of *morem* in 10 is uncertain.

47. This poem is apparently lost unless it refers to the cento above, which then Angela presumably copied and sent to him for his approval. He may have deliberately misread her use of the form as theft.

48. However, Valerius Palermus in his oration on the death of Count Ludovico Nogarola in 1559 apparently has this work of Angela's in mind during his praise of the accomplishments of the Count's ancestors. See Abel, *Isottae Nogarolae,* vol. 1, lxxv n. 1 and xcii n. 17, for text.

49. N.B. the masculine adjective at line 9: *tacitus contemno.*

50. The use of *foedera* is almost certainly a Catullan echo; cf. 64.335, 373; 76.3; 87.3; 109.6.

51. Punning on *gratus* and *gratis.* The thought is that a ruby ring is desirable but may have to be earned dishonorably; a good husband is above rubies.

52. For her life see Abel, *Isottae Nogarolae*; D. M. Robathan, "A Fifteenth-century Bluestocking," *Medievalia et Humanistica* 2 (1944), pp. 106–11; King, "Thwarted Ambitions"; King, "The Religious Retreat." *Signs* 3 (1978): pp. 807–22;

King, "Book Lined Cells"; King, *Women*, pp. 4, 191, 194–98, 212; Kristeller, "Learned Women of Early Modern Italy: Humanists and University Scholars," in Labalme ed., *Beyond Their Sex*, pp. 96–97; Jardine, "Isotta Nogarola: Women Humanists–Education for What?" *History of Education* 12 (1983): pp. 231–44; Jardine, " 'O decus Italiae virgo' or The Myth of the Learned Lady in the Renaissance," *Historical Journal* 28 (1985): pp.799–820; Grafton and Jardine, *From Humanism*, pp. 29–57; and bibliography there cited.

53. See Abel, *Isottae Nogarolae*, vol. 2, pp. 187–216; King and Rabil, *Her Immaculate Hand*, pp. 57–69 for a translation. See also King, "The Religious Retreat," pp. 818–20.

54. Abel, *Isottae Nogarolae*, vol. 1, pp. lii–vi, cxxxvi–vii n. 69, for the sources. I have included the interpolations, in brackets, so that the reader can see how they were inserted. Further, there is a clear difference in style. One must conclude that Isotta was the better poet of the two. Francesco's use of *dum* three times in six lines (21, 25–6) is trite, and a better stylist would have used an answering *tum*. Note, too, the piling up of adjectives in 31–32 (*fausta, candida, felix, bona*), and the failure of sequence of tenses in 34 (where one might have written, e.g., *fecissetne, peccassetne*, or the like, and used a better idiom).

55. Abel, *Isottae Nogarolae*, vol. 1, p. lvi. Either Gianfrancesco Gonzaga, first Marchese of Mantua (1395–1444), patron of Vittorino da Feltre, or his son Ludovico, second Marchese (1412–78), both famous as learned rulers. See Kate Simon, *A Renaissance Tapesty: The Gonzaga of Mantua* (New York: Harper and Row, 1988), pp. 28–37, 38–55 for a popular account. Giovanni Pontano (1426–1503) was a humanist, poet, and secretary of state for Naples.

56. Grk. "spring, fountain."

57. The language also owes something to Ovid's Orpheus and Eurydice (*Met.* 10. 1–62) and Horace's "Fons Bandusiae" (*Odes* 3.13).

58. Nichols, *Anthology of Neo-Latin Verse*, p. 5.

59. The Muses: Aonia is a region of Boeotia including Thebes and Mt. Helicon: a favorite usage of Statius.

60. A spring on Mt. Helicon: Verg. *Ecl.* 7.21.

61. Bacchus, born on Mt. Nysa, usually said to be in India.

62. A name for Naples (Neapolis) in classical Latin poetry, derived from the name of a siren.

63. A reference to Hor. *Odes* 1.36.10: the Romans marked lucky days with white stones or chalk marks; cf. our "red-letter day."

64. A literary reference to the poetic vocabulary of Verona's Catullus; cf. esp. 2, 3, and 31.

65. The northeast corner of Sicily encompassing the regions where the myth of Persephone took place.

66. Sicily.

67. The southeast corner of Sicily.

68. For Costanza Varano (Constanzia Varanea Sfortia), see King "Book-lined Cells," pp. 75, 83 (with bibliography); King and Rabil, *Her Immaculate Hand*, pp. 39–44. The date of her birth is secured by the fact that she was sixteen at the time of her first oration on the occasion of the visit of Bianca Maria Visconti (Bernardino Feliciangeli, "Notizie sulla vita e sugli scritti di Costanza Varano-Sforza (1426–47)," *Giornale storico della letteratura italiana* 23 [1894]: p. 24 n. 1) and that Guiniforte Barzizza congratulates her on this oration in a letter of 2 June 1442 (King, "Book-lined Cells," p. 88 n. 42). So, King, "Book-lined Cells," p. 84 n. 13 (b. 1426; the oration in 1442); but King and Rabil, *Her Immaculate Hand*, p. 17 (b. 1428), p. 18 (b. 1426), p. 39 (oration in 1444); the oration need not be in the same year as her marriage. For Battista da Montefeltro Malatesta, see Woodward, *Vitorino da Feltre*, pp. 119–20; King and Rabil, *Her Immaculate Hand*, pp. 16, 35–38. She was, among other things, the addressee of Bruni's treatise on female education (see foregoing).

69. The letter is translated by King and Rabil, *Her Immaculate Hand*, (pp. 55–56); dated to 1442 by Feliciangeli (pp. 33–34).

70. Grafton and Jardine, *From Humanism*, p. 55 n. 79.

71. See Giovanni Presenti, "Alessandra Scala, una figura della Rinascenza fiorentina," *Giornale storico della letteratura italiana* 85 (1925): pp. 241–46; Armando F. Verde, *Lo studio fiorentino, 1473–1503* (Florence and Pistoia: Istituto nazionale di studi sul Rinascimento, 1973–77), vol. 3, pp. 36–37, 1141; Allison Brown, *Bartolomeo Scala, 1430–1497, Chancellor of Florence: the Humanist as Bureaucrat* (Princeton: Princeton University Press, 1979), pp. 210–12, 245–47; King, "Thwarted Ambitions"; King, "Book-lined Cells," esp. 66–67, 83 n. 4; Kristeller, "Learned Women," p. 97; Grafton and Jardine, *From Humanism*, pp. 53–55, citing part of Poliziano's description of the *Electra* performance. For Bartolommeo, see Brown.

72. King and Rabil, *Her Immaculate Hand*, pp. 87. For the texts, see Anthos Ardizzoni, ed., *Poliziano, Epigrammi Greci* (Florence: La Nuova Italia, 1951), pp. 37–38, App. I. Originals are the Aldine ed. of 1498 and Vat. gr. 1412, f. 62r, the autograph of her teacher Lascaris (ibid., xv; ital. trans. p. 66). Presenti, "Alessandra Scala," (pp. 79–80), assumes on no good evidence that Lascaris must have heavily reworked this epigram; more sensibly, he attributes some of the changes in the Aldine to Poliziano (though other changes are clearly merely errors). Poliziano's Epigram 28 (1493) is addressed to Alessandra, as well as 30 (to which she replies), 31–33, 48, 50.

73. A Homeric *hapax*: *Il.* 18.543.

74. Poliziano's epigram "To the Poetess Alessandra" (Ardizzoni, p. 21, no. 30) began, "I have found her, I have found the one I've wanted, the one I've always been

searching for, / the one whose love I've been asking for, the one I've been dreaming of."

75. Alessandra quotes the second half of Homer, *Od.* 17.218.

76. For the form, cf. *AP* 4.4.61 or Nonnus 25.98.

77. A Homeric phrase, *Il.* 8.369, 21.9, but moved to a different part of the verse.

78. κύβρεις, usually plural refers to the tablets/pillars on which laws were inscribed.

79. Poliziano had written to Alessandra: "For whom there was a rivalry between Temperance and the Graces, pulling her one way and the other." Borrowing a line from Antiphilus (on Medea!) *API.* 4.136 (cf. *API.* 4.139), he had apparently misunderstood ἀντιμεθελκομέν-ην as a transitive middle (competing for). Alessandra picks up the word and the conceit, using it in the same way.

80. A proverbially just Egyptian king, according to Ael. *NA* 11.11; another example of recherché learning.

81. A reference to the Greek proverb "Like a cat to Athena": said, according to Zenobius 2.25, "of those who make comparisons of the greater with the less because of some small similarity, as though comparing a cat to Athena because both have green eyes."

82. For Morata, see Jules Bonnet, *Vie d'Olympia Morata, épisode de la renaissance et de la réforme en Italie*, 3d ed. rev. et aug. (Paris: Meyrueis, 1856), with French translation of some letters and poems (texts are occasionally inaccurate); Lanfranco Caretti, ed., *Olimpia Morata. Epistolario (1540–1555)* (Ferrara: R. Reputazione di storia patria per l'Emilia e la Romagna. Sezione di Ferrara, 1940); Caretti, *Opere di Olympia Morata* (Ferrara: Deputazione provincile di storia patria. Atti e memorie, 1954); Dorothea Vorländer, "Olympia Fulvia Morata–eine evangelische Humanistin in Schweinfurt," *Zeitschrift für bayerische Kirchengeschichte* 39 (1970): pp. 95–113; Roland H. Bainton, *Women of the Reformation in Germany and Italy* (Minneapolis: Augsburg Pub. House, 1971), pp 253–68; King, *Women*, pp. 202–04; Rainer Kößling and Gertrud Wiess-Stählin eds. and trans., *Olympia Fulvia Morata. Briefe* (Leipzig: Reclam, 1991), with complete bibliography; brief mentions at Kristeller, "Learned Women," p. 97; and Bainton, "Learned Women in the Europe of the Sixteenth Century," in *Beyond Their Sex*, p. 120.

83. *Tagebuch* for 30 Jan. 1820, cited in Kößling and Wiess-Stählin, *Briefe*, p. 218.

84. Niklas Holzberg, "Olympia Morata und die Anfänge des Griechischen an der Universität Heidelberg," *Heidelberger Jahrbücher* 31 (1987): pp. 77–93.

85. For the texts, see in bibliography: Morata, *Orationes*, pp. 228–43; Morata, *Opera omnia*, pp. 224–39 (with Latin trans.); the Greek versions of Ps. 23 and 46 have been translated into German by Kößling and Wiess-Stählin, *Briefe*, p. 176.

86. Morata, *Orationes*, p. 248; Morata, *Opera omnia*, p. 242; Bonnet, *Vie d'Olympia Morata*, p. 38; Bainton, *Women of the Reformation*, p. 254. Contrast Morata's rejection of the symbols of femininity with Angela Nogarola's different tactic of refiguring them. For this conceit in Poliziano, see King, "Book-lined Cells," pp. 76, 89 n. 47; King, *Women*, p. 181; Grafton and Jardine, *From Humanism*, pp. 49–50 (to Cassandra Fedele). For more on this topic, see Diana Robin's paper in this volume.

87. A reworking of *Il.* 3.237.

88. A reference to Soph. *Ant.* 1126.

89. A biblical use: *LXX 1Kg.* 18:6, etc.

90. I have not been able to trace him; Κέλτης/Gallus may be an ethnic. Curione mentions a Gallus (Letter 69, 1555).

91. Morata, *Orationes*, p. 246; *Opera omnia*, pp. 240–42; Bonnet, p. 66.

92. By analogy to the Homeric θανέειν; the participle is regularly θανών.

93. Morata, *Orationes*, p. 244; Morata, *Opera omnia*, p. 238; Bonnet, *Vie d'Olympia Morata*, p. 272.

94. John 3:14 recalls the brazen serpent of Num. 21:4–9, Wisd. 16:5–8.

95. Morata, *Orationes*, p. 249; Morata, *Opera omnia*, p. 244; Bonnet, *Vie d'Olympia Morata*, p. 256.

96. Morata, *Orationes*, p. 249; Morata, *Opera omnia*, p. 243; Bonnet, *Vie d'Olympia Morata*, pp. 71–72.

97. Morata, *Orationes*, p. 244; Morata, *Opera omnia*, p. 240; Bonnet, *Vie d'Olympia Morata*, p. 159.

98. Morata, *Orationes*, p. 246; Morata, *Opera omnia*, p. 240; Bonnet, *Vie d'Olympia Morata*, p. 79; Bainton, "Learned Women," pp. 257–68.

99. Morata, *Orationes*, p. 249; Morata, *Opera omnia*, p. 244; Bonnet, *Vie d'Olympia Morata*, p. 257.

100. *menti* in *Orationes* and *Opera omnia*; perhaps we should read *morti(s)*: "so great is my confidence in death."

101. Cf. *Phil.* 2:23. She repeats this phrase in letters to Johannes Infantius and Curione in the summer of 1555; Kößling and Wiess-Stählin, *Briefe*, pp. 138, 142.

102. P. W. Bomli's *La Femme dans l'Espagne du siècle d'or* (Hague: Nijhoff, 1950) is a good introduction; Carolyn L. Galerstein and Kathleen McNerney's *Women Writers of Spain: An Annotated Bio-bibliography* (Westport, CT: Greenwood Press, 1986) is a thorough and much-needed tool. Manuel Serrano y Sanz's *Apuntes para una biblioteca de escritoras españolas desde el año 1401 al 1833* (Madrid: Atlas, 1975, original 1903) is not only a bibliography but contains many texts as well.

103. Aloysia Sigea, Sigaea, Sygea, Sigée. Only the Latin text of her famous letter was copied and has survived; see Léon Bourdon and Odette Sauvage "Recherches sur Luisa Sigea," *Bulletin des Études Portugaises* 31(1970): pp. 38–39, 80–82.

104. "Sintra" was published posthumously by her father in 1566. Bourdon and Sauvage, "Recherches," is the most complete study of her life and includes the text of 22 Latin letters (with a French translation) by or to Luisa Sigea. Paul Allut's *Aloysia Sygea et Nicholas Chorier* (Lyon: Scheuring, 1862) and Serrano y Sanz, *Apuntes,* remain invaluable; Allut reproduced the published text of "Sintra," Serrano y Sanz the manuscript version and a Spanish translation (by Menéndez Pelayo), as well as the full text of her *Duarum virginum colloquium de vita aulica et privata,* also edited and with a French translation by Odette Sauvage, *Luisa Sigée. Dialogue de deux jeunes filles sur la vie de cour et la vie de retraite (1552)* (Paris: Presses universitaires de France, 1970). For the forgery, see Nicolas Chorier, *Aloisiae Sigeae Toletanae Satyra Sotadica de Arcanis Amoris et Veneris sive Joannis Meurii Elegantiae Latini Sermonis,* ed. Bruno Lavagnini (Catania, Italy: Romeo Prampolini, 1660/1935).

105. Susan Bassnett, "Elizabeth Jane Weston: The Hidden Roots of Poetry" in *Prague am 1600* (Frankfurt: Luca, 1988), pp. 239–51; Susan Bassnett, "Revising a Biography: A new interpretation of the life of Elizabeth Jane Weston (Westonia), based on her autobiographical poem on the occasion of the death of her mother," *Cahiers elisabethains* 37 (April 1990): pp. 1–8; King, *Women,* p. 211; Donald Cheney, "Westonia on the Gardens of Barvitius," *ANQ* 5 (1992): pp. 64–67.

106. Nicola Fusco, *Elena Lucrezia Cornaro Piscopia* (Pittsburg, PA: US Committee for the Elena Lucrezia Cornaro Piscopia Tercentenary, 1975); Francesco L. Maschietto, *Elena Lucrezia Cornaro Piscopia 1646–1684: prima donna laureata nel mondo* (Padua: Antenore, 1978); Maria I. Tonzig, ed., *Elena Lucrezia Cornaro Piscopia: prima donna laureata nel mondo* (Vincenza, Italy: Gualandi, 1980); Kristeller, "Learned Women," p. 97; King, *Women,* pp. 211–12.

107. Kristeller ("Learned Women," p. 133 n. 41) said that Columbia University had acquired a copy in microfilm. However, OCLC shows no copy in the United States, and Columbia has no record of it. The Bibliothèque Nationale, Paris, holds a master microfilm.

108. Variously Bathsua, Bathusa, Bathshua; Reynolds, Reginald(a); Makin, Makins, Making, Metkins. The prosopographical work leading to the correct identification was first done by Vivian Salmon ("Bathsua Makin: A Pioneer Linguist and Feminist in Seventeenth-Century England," in *Neuere Forschungen zur Wortbildung und Historiographie der Linguistik: Festgabe für Herbert E. Brekle,* eds. Brigiette Asbach-Schnitker and Johannes Roggenhofer [Tübingen: Tübingen Beiträge für Linguistik, 1987], pp. 303–18) and supplemented by Jean R. Brink ("Bathsua Reginald Makin: 'Most Learned Matron,' " *Huntington Library Quarterly* 54 [1991], pp. 313–26); previous work needs to be corrected in its light. She was the daughter of the teacher and author, Henry Reynolds (latinized as Reginald[us]), and the daughter-in-law (not daughter) of Sir John Pell; the attribution to her of a tract, *The Malady and Remedy of Vexations and Unjust Arrests and Actions,* is incorrect. See Brink, ed. "Bathsua Makin: Educator and Linguist," in *Female Scholars: A Tradition of Learned Women before 1800* (Montreal: Eden Press Women's Publications, 1980),

pp. 86–100; Elaine Hobby, *Virtue of Necessity: English Women's Writing, 1649–88* (London: Virago, 1988), pp. 199–203; Maureen Bell, George Parfitt, and Simon Shepherd, *A Biographical Dictionary of English Women Writers* (Boston: G. K. Hall, 1990), pp. 131–32; King, *Women*, p. 179. Her Latin elegy on the death of Lord Hastings (1649) has been published and translated: H. T. Swedenberg, "More Tears for Lord Hastings," *Huntington Library Quarterly* 16 (1952): pp. 43–51. The *Essay* has been reprinted: Makin 1673/1980. A check of OCLC shows no copy of the *Musa virginea* in the United States.

Bibliography

Abel, Eugenius, ed. *Isottae Nogarolae Veronensis opera quae supersunt omnia*. 2 vols. (Vienna, 1886). Repr. in microfilm, "History of Women," Reel 472, No. 3527, (New Haven, 1975). Copies of this microfilm collection are available at Bryn Mawr College and the University of Cincinnati.

Abelard, Peter, and Heloise. "The Personal Letters between Abelard and Heloise." Ed. J. T. Muckle. *Mediaeval Studies* 15 (1953): pp. 47–94.

———. "The Letter of Heloise on Religious Life and Abelard's First Reply." Ed. J. T. Muckle. *Mediaeval Studies* 17 (1955): pp. 240–81.

———. *Historia calamitatum texte critique*. Ed. Jacques Monfrin. Paris: Vrin, 1959.

———. *The Letters of Abelard and Heloise*. Trans. Betty Radice. Harmondsworth, England: Penguin, 1974.

Agrippa, Henri Corneille. *De Nobilitate et Praecellentia Foeminei Sexus*. Ed. R. Antonioli, Ch. Béné, and O. Sauvage. Geneva: Droz, 1990.

Alabaster, William. *Roxana*. London, 1632. Bodleian Library, Oxford, Douce A 399(1). New York: Readex Microprint, 1955.

Alberici, Giacomo. *Catalogo breve de gl'illustri et famosi scrittori venetiani*. Bologna: Rossi, 1605.

Alberti, Leon Battista. *Ten Books on Architecture*. Trans. James Leoni. Ed. Joseph Ryckwert. London: Alec Tiranti, 1955.

Alexiou, Margaret. *The Ritual Lament in Greek Tradition*. Cambridge: Cambridge University Press, 1974.

Alighieri, Dante. *Divina Commedia nella figurazione artistica e nel seculare commento*. Vol. 1: *Inferno*. Ed. Guido Biagi. Turin: Unione Tipografico-Editrice Torinese, 1921.

———. *The Divine Comedy*. 6 vols. Ed. and trans. Charles S. Singleton. Bollingen Series 80. Princeton: Princeton University Press, 1970–76.

Allen, J. B. *The Ethical Poetic of the Later Middle Ages*. Toronto: University of Toronto Press, 1982.

―――. *The Friar as Critic: Literary Attitudes in the Later Middle Ages.* Nashville, TN: Vanderbilt University Press, 1971.

Allut, Paul. 1862. *Aloysia Sygea et Nicolas Chorier.* Lyon, France: Scheuring, 1862.

Althusser, Louis, et al. *Reading Capital.* Trans. Ben Brewster. London: New Left Books, 1970.

Angenot, Marc. *Les Champions des Femmes.* Montreal: Quebec University Press, 1977.

Antonioli, Roland. "L'image de la femme dans le *De nobilitate et praecellentia foeminei sexus* de H. C. Agrippa." *Acta Universitatis Lodziensis, Folia Litteraria* 14 (1985): pp. 27–39.

Appian. *Roman History.* 4 vols. Ed. and trans. Horace White. Loeb Classical Library. Cambridge: Harvard University Press, 1912.

Ardener, Edwin. 1978. "Belief and the Problem of Women." *Perceiving Women.* Ed. Shirley Ardener. New York: Halsted Press, 1978, pp. 1–17.

Ardizzoni, Anthos, ed. *Poliziano, Epigrammi Greci.* Florence: La Nuova Italia, 1951.

Aristotle. *Generation of Animals.* Trans. A. L. Peck. Cambridge: Harvard University Press, 1953.

Aschbach, Joseph. "Roswitha und Conrad Celtes." *Sitzungsberichte der Kaiserlichen Akademie der Wissenschaften.* Vol. 56: *Philosophisch-Historische Klasse.* Vienna: Kaiserlich-Konigliche hof- und Staatsdruckerei, 1867, pp. 3–62.

Asher, Lyell. "Petrarch at the Peak of Fame," *PMLA* 108 (1993): pp. 1050–63.

Astell, Ann W. *The Song of Songs in the Middle Ages.* Ithaca, NY: Cornell University Press, 1990.

Atkinson, Clarissa, W. " 'Your Servant, My Mother': The Figure of St. Monica in the Ideology of Christian Motherhood." In *Immaculate and Powerful: The Female in Sacred Image and Social Reality,* ed. Clarissa W. Atkinson, Constance H. Buchanan, and Margaret R. Miles: pp. 139–72. Boston: Beacon Press, 1985.

―――. *The Oldest Vocation: Christian Motherhood in the Middle Ages.* Ithaca, NY: Cornell University Press, 1991.

Augustine. *Confessions.* Ed. P. Knöll. Leipzig: Teubner, 1909.

―――. *The Confessions of St. Augustine.* Trans. F. J. Sheed. New York: Sheed and Ward, 1942.

―――. *City of God.* 7 vols. Ed. and trans. Philip Levine. Loeb Classical Library. Cambridge: Harvard University Press, 1966.

―――. *Confessions.* 2 vols. Trans. W. Watts. Loeb Classical Library. Cambridge: Harvard University Press, 1912, repr. 1977.

Bainton, Roland H. 1971. *Women of the Reformation in Germany and Italy*. Minneapolis, MN: Augsburg Publishing House, 1971.

———. "Learned Women in the Europe of the Sixteenth Century." In Patricia H. LaBalme, ed. *Beyond Their Sex: Learned Women of the European Past*, pp. 117–28. New York: New York University Press, 1980.

Baker, Moira. *"The Uncanny Stranger on Display:* The Female Body in Sixteenth- and Seventeenth-Century Love Poetry." *South Atlantic Review* 56.2 (1991): pp. 7–25.

Bakhtin, Mikhail. "Forms of Time and Chronotope in the Novel." In *The Dialogic Imagination,* ed. Michael Holquist, Trans. Caryl Emerson and M. Holquist, pp. 84–258. Austin: University of Texas Press, 1981.

Baldwin, T. W. *William Shakspere's Small Latine and Less Greeke*. Vol. 2. Urbana: University of Illinois Press, 1944.

Bamber, Linda. *Comic Women, Tragic Men: A Study of Gender and Genre in Shakespeare*. Stanford, CA: Stanford University Press, 1982.

Barish, Jonas. *The Antitheatrical Prejudice*. Berkeley and Los Angeles: University of California Press, 1981.

Baron, Hans, ed. *The Crisis of the Early Italian Renaissance*. 2d. ed. Princeton: Princeton University Press, 1966.

———. *Leonardo Bruni Aretino. Humanistisch-philosophische Schriften*. Leipzig and Berlin: Teubner, 1928. Repr. Wiesbaden: Steiner, 1969.

———. *Petrarch's "Secretum": Its Making and Its Meaning*. Cambridge, MA: The Medieval Academy of America, 1985.

Bartky, Sandra Lee. "Foucault, Feminity and Patriarchal Power." In Irene Diamond and Lee Quinby, eds. *Feminism and Foucault: Reflections on Resistance.* Boston: Northeastern University Press, 1988, pp. 61–86.

Barton, John. "The King's Readers." In James K. McConica, pp. 285–94.

Bassnett, Susan. 1988. "Elizabeth Jane Weston: The Hidden Roots of Poetry." In *Prague um 1600: Kunst und Kultur am Hofe Kaiser Rudolfs II,* pp. 239–51. Freren: Luca, 1988.

———. "Revising a Biography: A new interpretation of the life of Elizabeth Jane Weston (Westonia), based on her autobiographical poem on the occasion of the death of her mother." *Cahiers élisabethains* 37 (1990): pp. 1–8.

Becker, Marvin B. *Medieval Italy: Constraints and Creativity*. Bloomington: Indiana University Press, 1981.

Bell, Maureen, George Parfitt, and Simon Shepherd. *A Biographical Dictionary of English Women Writers*. Boston: G. K. Hall, 1990.

Bell, Rudolph. *Holy Anorexia*. Chicago: University of Chicago Press, 1985.

———. *Psychiatry and Mysticism*. New York: Humanities Press, 1976.

Benstock, Shari, ed. *The Private Self: Theory and Practice of Women's Autobiographical Writings*. Chapel Hill: University of North Carolina Press, 1988.

———. *Textualizing the Feminine: On the Limits of Genre*. Norman: University of Oklahoma Press, 1991.

Bereblock, John. *Commentarij siue Ephemerae actiones rerum illustrium Oxonij gestarum adventu Serenissimae Principis Elisabethae*. Bodleian MS Add. A. 63, fols. 1–22 and Bodleian MS. Rawlinson D1071, fols. 1–25.

Bergamo, Jacopo Filippo da (alias J. F. Foresti). *De plurimis claris scele(s)tisque mulieribus*. Ferrara, Italy: Laurentius de Rubeis, de Valentia, 1497.

Bergin, Thomas G. *Petrarch*. New York: Twayne, 1970.

Bernard of Clairvaux. *Sermones Super Cantica Canticorum*. Vol. 1–2: *Sancti Bernardi Opera*. Ed. J. Leclercq, C. H. Talbot, and H. Rochais. Rome: Editiones Cistercienses, 1957–58.

———. *In Laudibus Virginis Matris*. Vol. 4: *Sancti Bernardi Opera*. Ed. J. Leclercq and H. Rochais. Rome: Editiones Cistercienses, 1966.

Bernardo, Aldo S. "Dramatic Dialogue and Monologue in Petrarch's Works." *Symposium* 7 (1953): pp. 92–119.

———. *Petrarch, Scipio and the "Africa": The Birth of Humanism's Dream*. Baltimore, MD: Johns Hopkins University Press, 1962.

———. *Petrarch, Laura, and the "Triumphs."* Albany: State University of New York Press, 1974.

Bersuire, Pierre. *Metamorphoses ovidiana moraliter . . . explanata* (Paris, 1509). Intro. by Stephen Orgel. New York: Garland, 1959.

Bertini, Ferruccio. 1979. *Il "'teatro" di Rosvita*. Genoa, Italy: Tilgher, 1979.

Betussi, Giuseppe, trans. *Libro di M. Gio. Boccaccio delle Donne illustri*. Venice: Pietro de Nicolini da Sabbio, 1546.

Biblia sacra. Juxta Vulgatam Clementinam. Madrid: Biblioteca de Autores Cristianos, 1965.

Billanovich, Giuseppe. "Petrarch and the Textual Tradition of Livy." *Journal of the Warburg and Courtauld Institutes* 14 (1951): pp. 137–208.

Billon, François de. *Le Fort inexpugnable de l'honneur du sexe Femenin*. East Ardsley, England: S. R. Publishers; New York: Johnson Reprints, and The Hague: Mouton, 1970. Reprint of the 1555 edition.

Binns, J. W. *Intellectual Culture in Elizabethan and Jacobean England.* Leeds, England: F. Cairns, 1990.

Bishop, Morris. *Petrarch and His World.* Bloomington: Indiana University Press, 1963.

Blaise, Albert. *Le vocabulaire latin des principaux thèmes liturgiques.* Turnhout, Belgium: Brepols, 1966.

Bloch, Maurice. "Death, Women, and Power." In *Death and the Regeneration of Life,* ed. Jonathan Parry and Maurice Bloch, pp. 211–30. Cambridge: Cambridge University Press, 1982.

Bloch, R. Howard. "Medieval Misogyny." In *Misogyny, Misandry, and Misanthropy,* eds. R. Howard Bloch and Frances Ferguson, pp. 1–25. Berkeley and Los Angeles: University of California Press, 1990.

————. *Medieval Misogyny and the Invention of Western Romantic Love.* Chicago: University of Chicago Press, 1991.

Blume, Clemens, ed. *Analecta Hymnica Medii Aevi.* 55 vols. Leipzig: O. R. Reisland, 1886–1992.

Boas, F. S. *University Drama in the Tudor Age.* Oxford: Clarendon Press, 1914.

————. *An Introduction to Tudor Drama.* New York: AMS Press, 1933.

Boccaccio, Giovanni. *De claribus mulieribus.* Venice: n.p., 1480.

————. *De genealogia deorum.* Ed. Vincenzo Romana. 2 vols. Bari, Italy: Laterza, 1951.

————. *Concerning Famous Women.* Trans. Guarino A. Guarino. New Brunswick, NJ: Rutgers University Press, 1963.

————. *Il Filocolo.* Ed. Mario Marti. Milan-Naples: Rizzoli, 1969.

Bolgar, Robert. *The Classical Heritage and Its Beneficiaries.* Cambridge: Cambridge University Press, 1954.

Bomli, P. W. *La Femme dans l'Espagne du siècle d'or.* The Hague: Nijhoff, 1950.

Bonfante, Larissa, trans. *The Plays of Hrotswitha of Gandersheim.* Oak Park, IL: Bolchazy-Carducci, 1986.

Bonnet, Jules. *Vie d'Olympia Morata, épisode de la renaissance et de la réforme en Italie.* 3d. ed. rev. et aug. Paris: Meyrueis, 1856. Repr. in microfilm, "History of Women," Reel 245, No. 1634 (New Haven, 1975).

Bono, Barbara. *Literary Transvaluation: From Vergilian Epic to Shakespearean Tragicomedy.* Berkeley and Los Angeles: University of California Press, 1984.

Bordo, Susan. "Anorexia Nervosa: Psychopathology as the Crystallization of Culture." In Diamond and Quinby, *Feminism and Foucault,* pp. 87–117.

Børresen, Kari Elisabeth. *Subordination and Equivalence. The Nature and Rôle of Woman in Augustine and Thomas Aquinas.* Washington, DC: University Press of America, 1981.

Bosco, Umberto. *Francesco Petrarca.* Bari, Italy: Laterza, 1961.

Bourdieu, Pierre. *Outline of a Theory of Practice.* Cambridge: Cambridge University Press, 1977.

Bourdon, Léon, and Odette Sauvage. "Recherches sur Luisa Sigea." *Bulletin des Études Portugaises* 31 (1970): pp. 33–125.

Braunstein, Philippe. "Toward Intimacy: The Fourteenth and Fifteenth Centuries." In Georges Duby, ed. *A History of Private Life.* Vol. 2: *Revelations of the Medieval World.* Cambridge, MA: Belknap, 1988, pp. 535–630.

Brenkman, John. "Writing, Desire, Dialectic in Petrarch's *Rime* 23." *Pacific Coast Philology* 9 (1974): pp. 12–19.

Brink, Jean R., ed. *Female Scholars: A Tradition of Learned Women before 1800.* Montreal: Eden Press Women's Publications, 1980. Contains her article, "Bathsua Makin: Educator and Linguist," pp. 86–100.

———. "Bathsua Reginald Makin: 'Most Learned Matron,'" *Huntington Library Quarterly* 54 (1991): pp. 313–26.

Brinsley, John. *Ludus Literarius or the Grammar Schoole* (1612). Repr. Menston, Yorkshire, England: Scolar Press, 1968.

Brodzki, Bella, and Celeste Schenck, eds. *Lifelines: Theorizing Women's Autobiography.* Ithaca, NY: Cornell University Press, 1988.

Brown, Allison. *Bartolomeo Scala, 1430–1497, Chancellor of Florence: The Humanist as Bureaucrat.* Princeton: Princeton University Press, 1979.

Brown, Judith. "A Woman's Place Was in the Home." In Margaret W. Ferguson, Maureen Quilligan, and Nancy J. Vickers, eds. *Rewriting the Renaissance: The Discoveries of Sexual Difference in Early Modern Europe.* Chicago: Chicago University Press, 1986.

Brownlee, Marina S., Kevin Brownlee, and Stephen G. Nichols, eds. *The New Medievalism.* Baltimore, MD: Johns Hopkins University Press, 1991.

Bruère, Richard T. "Lucan and Petrarch's *Africa.*" *Classical Philology* 56 (1961): pp. 83–99.

Brumberg, Joan Jacobs. *Fasting Girls: The History of Anorexia Nervosa.* New York: Plume, 1989.

Bruns, Gerald. "What is Tradition?" *New Literary History* 22 (1991): pp. 1–21.

Buchanan, George. *Omnia Opera.* Ed. Thomas Ruddiman. Edinburgh: Freebairn, 1715.

Burckhardt, Jacob. *The Civilization of the Renaissance in Italy.* Trans. S. C. G. Middlemore. New York: Harper and Row, 1960.

Burgess, Henry E. "Hroswitha and Terence: A Study in Literary Imitation." *Proceedings of the Pacific Northwest Conference on Foreign Languages*. Corvallis: Oregon State University Press, 1968.

Burns, E. Jane. *Bodytalk: When Women Speak in Old French Literature*. Philadelphia: University of Pennsylvania Press, 1993.

Bush, Douglas. *Mythology and the Renaissance Tradition in English Poetry*. Minneapolis: University of Minnesota Press, 1932.

Butler, Judith. *Gender Trouble: Feminism and the Subversion of Identity*. New York: Routledge, 1990.

Butler, Martin. *Theater and Crisis, 1632–1642*. Cambridge: Cambridge University Press, 1984.

Butler, Sister Mary Margaret. *Hrotsvitha: The Theatricality of Her Plays*. New York: Philosophical Library, 1960.

Bynum, Caroline Walker. "The Spirituality of Regular Canons in the Twelfth Century." *Medievalia et Humanistica* 4 (1973): pp. 1–16.

———. *Jesus as Mother: Studies in the Spirituality of the High Middle Ages*. Berkeley and Los Angeles: University of California Press, 1982.

———. *Holy Feast and Holy Fast: The Religious Significance of Food to Medieval Women*. Berkeley and Los Angeles: University of California Press, 1987.

Caccia, Ettore. "Cultura e letturatura nei secoli XV e XVI," in *Storia di Brescia II. La Dominazione Veneta (1426–1575)*. Ed. Giovanni Treccani degli Alfieri. Brescia: Morcelliana, 1963, pp. 474–535.

Calcaterra, Carlo. *Nella selva del Petrarca*. Bologna: Cappelli, 1942.

Cameron, Averil, and Amélie Kuhrt, eds. *Images of Women in Antiquity*. London: Croom Helm, 1983.

Cannon, Mary Agnes. *The Education of Women during the Renaissance*. Washington, DC: National Capital Press, 1916.

Carby, Hazel. *Reconstructing Womanhood: The Emergence of the Afro-American Novelist*. New York: Oxford University Press, 1987.

Caretti, Lanfranco, ed. *Olimpia Morata. Epistolario (1540–1555)*. Ferrara, Italy: R. Reputazione di storia patria per l'Emilia e la Romagna. Sezione di Ferrara, 1940.

———. *Opere di Olympia Morata*. Ferrara, Italy: Deputazione provincile di storia patria. Atti e memorie. N.S. Vol. XI.2, 1954.

Carrara, E. *Francesco Petrarca, "Il mio segreto."* Florence: Sansoni, 1943. Trans. and repr. in David A. Carozza and H. James Shey, *Petrarch's Secretum: With Introduction, Notes and Critical Anthology*. New York: Peter Lang, 1989. pp. 245–49.

Carozza, David A., and H. James Shey. *Petrarch's Secretum: With Introduction, Notes and Critical Anthology.* New York: Peter Lang, 1989.

Casagrande, Giovanna. "Realtà Storica e Movimenti Religiosi in Umbria nel Secolo XIII e nella Prima Metà del XIV." In *Sante e Beate Umbre tra il XIII e il XIV secolo,* pp. 21–44. Foligno, Italy: Arquata, 1986.

Case, Sue-Ellen. "Re-Viewing Hrotsvit." *Theatre Journal* 35 (1983): pp. 533–42.

Cassirer, Ernst. *The Individual and the Cosmos in Renaissance Philosophy.* Trans. Mario Domandi. Philadelphia: University of Pennsylvania Press, 1972.

Cavazzana, Cesira. "Cassandra Fedele erudita Veneziana del rinascimento." *Ateneo Veneto* 29.2 (1906): pp. 73–91, 249–75, 391–97.

Cereta, Laura. *Epistolae.* Ed. Iacopo Filippo Tomasini. Padua, Italy: Sebastiano Sardi, 1640.

Chabaneau, Camille. "Poésies inédites de divers troubadours (G. d'Anduze, Raimon de Salas, G. d'Hautpoul, Joyos, Cavalier Lunel de Montech)." *Revue de langues romaines.* 4e sér. 33 (1889): pp. 117–21.

Chabaneau, Camille, and J. B. Noulet. *Deux manuscrits provençaux du XVIe siècle.* Montpellier: Au bureau des publications de la société pour l'étude des langues Romaines, 1888.

Chadwick, Whitney. *Women, Art, and Society.* London: Thames and Hudson, 1991.

Chaney, Viriginia. "The Elegies of George Buchanan in Relation to those of the Roman Elegists and to the Latin Elegies of John Milton." Ph.D. diss., Vanderbilt University, 1961.

Charlton, Kenneth. *Education in Renaissance England.* London: Routledge and Kegan Paul, 1965.

Cheney, Donald. "Westonia on the Gardens of Barvitius." *ANQ* 5 (1992): pp. 64–67.

Chorier, Nicolas. *Aloisiae Sigeae Toletanae Satyra Sotadica de Arcanis Amoris et Veneris sive Joannis Meurii Elegantiae Latini Sermonis.* Ed. Bruno Lavagnini. Catania, Italy: Romeo Prampolini, 1660, repr. 1935.

Churchill, George R., and Wolfgang Keller. "Die lateinischen Universitäts-Dramen in der Zeit der Königen Elisabeth." *Shakespeare Jahrbuch* 34 (1898): pp. 252–55.

Cignelli, Lino. *Maria, nuova Eva nella patristica greca.* Assisi, Italy: Porziuncola, 1966.

Cinthio, G. B. Giraldi. *Discorso intorno al comporre delle comedie e delle tragedie.* Venice: n.p., 1554.

———. *Scritti Critici.* Ed. Camillo Guerrieri. Milan: Marzorati, 1973.

Cixous, Hélène. "The Laugh of the Medusa." Trans. Keith Cohen and Paula Cohen. In Elaine Marks and Isabelle de Courtivron, eds. *New French Feminisms*, pp. 245–64. New York: Schocken Books, 1981.

Cixous, Hélène, and Catherine Clément. *The Newly Born Woman*. Trans. Betsy Wing. Minneapolis: University of Minnesota Press, 1986.

Coffman, G. R. "A New Approach to Medieval Latin Drama." *Modern Philology* 22 (1925): pp. 239–71.

Cole, Douglas. "Hrotsvitha's Most 'Comic' Play: *Dulcitius*." *Studies in Philology* 57 (1960): pp. 597–605.

Coleman, Dorothy Gabe. *The Gallo-Roman Muse*. Cambridge: Cambridge University Press, 1979.

Constable, Giles. "Petrarch and Monasticism." In *Francesco Petrarca Citizen of the World: Proceedings of the World Petrarch Congress, Washington, D.C., April 6–13, 1974*, ed. Aldo S. Bernardo, pp. 53–99. Albany: State University Press of New York, 1980.

Conte, Gian Biaggio. *The Rhetoric of Imitation: Genre and Poetic Memory in Virgil and Other Latin Poets*. Ed. and trans. Charles Segal. Ithaca, NY: Cornell University Press, 1986.

Cook, Ann Jennalie. "The Audience of Shakespeare's Plays: A Reconsideration," *Shakespeare Studies* 7 (1974): pp. 283–305.

———. *The Privileged Playgoers of Shakespeare's London, 1576–1642*. Princeton: Princeton University Press, 1981.

Coppini, Beatrice. *La Scrittura e il Percorso Mistico: Il "Liber" di Angela da Foligno*. Rome: Editrice Ianua, 1986.

Cornaro, Elena Lucrezia Piscopia. *Helenae Lucreziae (quae et scholastica) Corneliae Piscopiae . . . opera*. Parma: 1688. A microfilm copy is held by the Bibliothèque Nationale, Paris, OCLC 25289856.

Cottino-Jones, Margo. "The Myth of Apollo and Daphne in Petrarch's *Canzoniere:* The Dynamics and Literary Function of Transformation." In Aldo Scaglione, ed. *Francis Petrarch, Six Centuries Later: A Symposium. North Carolina Studies in the Romance Languages and Literatures: Symposia*. Vol. 3. pp. 152–76. Chapel Hill and Chicago: Department of Romance Languages, University of North Carolina and the Newberry Library, 1975.

Coulter, Cornelia C. "The 'Terentian' Comedies of a Tenth-Century Nun." *Classical Journal* 24 (1929): pp. 515–29.

Cressy, David. *Education in Tudor and Stuart England*. New York: St. Martin's, 1975.

Culham, Phyllis. "Ten Years After Pomeroy." *Helios* 13 (1987): pp. 9–30.

———. "Decentering the Text." *Helios* 17 (1990): pp. 161–70.

Curtis, M. H. *Oxford and Cambridge in Transition, 1558–1642: An Essay on Changing Relations Between the English Universities and English Society.* Oxford: Clarendon Press, 1959.

Curtius, Ernst Robert. *European Literature and the Latin Middle Ages.* Trans. Willard R. Trask. Bollingen 36. New York: Pantheon, 1953.

Dean, Stanley R., ed. *Psychiatry and Mysticism.* Chicago: Nelson-Hall Company, 1975.

de Crenne, Hélisenne. *Les epistres familieres et inuectiues.* Paris: Denis Janot, 1539.

———. *Le songe.* Paris: Denis Janot, 1540.

———. *A Renaissance Woman: Hélisenne's Personal and Invective Letters.* Ed. and trans. Marianna M. Mustacchi and Paul J. Archambault. Syracuse, NY: Syracuse University Press, 1986.

DeForest, Mary, ed. *Woman's Power, Man's Game: Essays on Classical Antiquity in Honor of Joy K. King.* Chicago: Bolchazy-Carducci, 1993.

de Lauretis, Teresa. *Alice Doesn't: Feminism, Semiotics, Cinema.* Bloomington: Indiana University Press, 1984.

Delehaye, Hippolyte. *Etude sur le légendier romain.* Brussels: Société des Bollandistes, 1936.

DeLuca, Kenneth. "Hrotsvit's 'Imitation' of Terence." *Classical Folia* 28 (1974): pp. 89–102.

Delumeau, Jean. *Sin and Fear: The Emergence of a Western Guilt Culture 13th to 18th Century.* New York: St. Martin's, 1990.

Derrida, Jacques. *Of Grammatology.* Trans. Gayatri Chakravorty Spivak. Baltimore, MD: Johns Hopkins University Press, 1976.

Diamond, Irene, and Lee Quinby, eds. *Feminism and Foucault: Reflections on Resistance.* Boston: Northeastern University Press, 1988.

Dio Cassius. *Roman History.* 9 vols. Ed. and trans. Earnest Cary. Loeb Classical Library. Cambridge: Harvard University Press, 1914.

Diodorus Siculus. *Library of History.* 12 vols. Ed. and trans. Francis R. Walton. Loeb Classical Library. Cambridge, Harvard University Press, 1957.

Donaldson, Ian. *The Rapes of Lucretia: A Myth and Its Transformations.* Oxford: Oxford University Press, 1982.

Douglas, Mary. *Purity and Danger: An Analysis of Concepts of Pollution and Taboo.* London: Routledge and Kegan Paul, 1966.

Douie, Decima L. "A Franciscan Mystic of the 13th Century." *Franciscan Essays* 1 (1932): pp. 120–29.

Dronke, Peter. *Abelard and Heloise in Medieval Testimonies.* W. P. Kerr Memorial Lecture, no. 26. Glasgow: University of Glasgow Press, 1965.

————. *Women Writers of the Middle Ages: A Critical Study of Texts from Perpetua (d. 203) to Marguerite Porete (d. 1310).* Cambridge: Cambridge University Press, 1984.

Dubrow, Heather. *Captive Victors: Shakespeare's Narrative Poems and Sonnets.* Ithaca, NY: Cornell University Press, 1987.

Duby, Georges, ed. *A History of Private Life.* Vol. 2: *Revelations of the Medieval World.* Cambridge, MA: Belknap, 1988.

Duckett, E. S. *Death and Life in the Tenth Century.* Ann Arbor: University of Michigan Press, 1967.

du Guillet, Pernette. *Rymes,* ed. V. E. Graham. Geneva: Droz, 1968.

Durling, Robert M. "Petrarch's 'Giovene donna sotto un verde lauro,'" *Modern Language Notes* 86 (1971): pp. 1–20.

————. "The Ascent of Mont Ventoux and the Crisis of Allegory," *Italian Quarterly* 18 (1974): pp. 7–28.

————. ed. and trans. *Petrarch's Lyric Poems: The "Rime Sparse" and Other Lyrics.* Cambridge: Harvard University Press, 1976.

Eco, Umberto, Constantino Marmo, R. Lambertini, and A. Tabarroni. "On Animal Language." In *On the Medieval Theory of Signs,* eds. Umberto Eco and Constantino Marmo, pp. 1–41. Philadelphia: John Benjamins Publishing Company, 1989.

Egnatius, Ioannis Baptista. *De Exemplis Illustrium Virorum Venetae Civitatis atque Aliarum Gentium.* Venice: apud Nicolaum Tridentinum, 1554.

Elias, Norbert. *The Civilizing Process.* Vol. 1: *The History of Manners.* New York: Harper, 1978.

Eliot, T. S. *Selected Prose of T. S. Eliot.* Ed. Frank Kermode. New York: Harcourt Brace and Jovanovich, 1975.

Elliott, John R., Jr. "Queen Elizabeth at Oxford: New Light on the Royal Plays of 1566." *English Literary Renaissance* 18.2 (1988): pp. 218–29.

Erler, Mary, and Maryanne Kowaleski, eds. *Women and Power in the Middle Ages.* Athens: University of Georgia Press, 1988.

Estrin, Barbara L. *Laura: Uncovering Gender and Genre in Wyatt, Donne, and Marvell.* Durham, NC: Duke University Press, 1994.

Evans, J. M. *"Paradise Lost" and the Genesis Tradition.* Oxford: Clarendon Press, 1968.

Fedele, Cassandra. *Epistolae et Orationes*. Ed. Iacopo Filippo Tomasini. Padua: F. Bolezetta, 1636.

Feliciangeli, Bernardino. "Notizie sulla vita e sugli scritti di Costanza Varano-Sforza (1426–1447)," *Giornale storico della letteratura italiana* 23 (1894): pp. 1–75 (quotations of her works on pp. 50–75).

Ferguson, Margaret W., Maureen Quilligan, and Nancy J. Vickers, eds. *Rewriting the Renaissance: The Discourses of Sexual Difference in Early Modern Europe*. Chicago: Chicago University Press, 1986.

Ferrante, Joan M. *Woman as Image in Medieval Literature: From the Twelfth Century to Dante*. New York: Columbia University Press, 1975.

Fisher, Sheila, and Janet E. Halley, eds. *Seeking the Woman in Late Medieval and Renaissance Writings: Essays in Feminist Contextual Criticism*. Knoxville: University of Tennessee Press, 1989.

Flynn, St. John E. "The Last Troubadour: Raimon de Cornet and the Survival of Occitan Lyric." Master's thesis: University of Georgia, 1989.

Foley, Helene, ed. *Reflections of Women in Antiquity*. London and New York: Gordon and Breach, 1981.

Ford, Phillip. *George Buchanan: Prince of Poets*. Aberdeen, Scotland: Aberdeen University Press, 1982.

Forestié, Edouard. *P. de Lunel, dit Cavalier Lunel de Monteg, troubadour du XIVe siècle, mainteneur des jeux floraux de Toulouse*. Montauban, France: Imp. Forestié, 1891.

Foster, Kenelm. "Medusa or Beatrice: The Penitential Element in the Canzoniere." In *Italian Studies Presented to E. R. Vincent*, ed. Charles Peter Brand, Kenelm Foster, and Uberto Limentani, pp. 41–56. Cambridge: Cambridge University Press, 1962.

Foucault, Michel. *The Birth of the Clinic: An Archeology of Medical Perception*. Trans. A. M. Sheridan Smith. New York: Vintage, 1974.

———. *La Panoptique*. Paris: Belfand, 1977.

———. *Discipline and Punish: The Birth of the Prison*. Trans. Alan Sheridan. New York: Vintage, 1979.

———. *The History of Sexuality*. Vol. 1. Trans. Robert Hurley. New York: Random House, 1980.

———. *The Use of Pleasure*. Vol. 2: *The History of Sexuality*. Trans. Robert Hurley. New York: Vintage, 1990.

Frank, Donald K. "Abelard as Imitator of Christ." *Viator* 1 (1970): pp. 107–13.

Frankforter, A. Daniel. "Hroswitha of Gandersheim and the Destiny of Women." *The Historian* 12 (1979): pp. 295–314.

———. "Sexism and the Search for the Thematic Structure of the Plays of Hroswitha of Gandersheim." *International Journal of Women's Studies* 2.3 (1979): pp. 221–32.

Freccero, John. "The Fig Tree and the Laurel: Petrarch's Poetics." *Diacritics* 5 (1975): pp. 24–40.

Fregosa, Battista (alias Campofregosa, alias Baptista Fulgosius). *Factorum Dictorumque Memorabilium Libri IX.* Venice: 1483. Repr. with a supplement by Julio Gaillardo Campo, Paris: apud Petrum Cavellat, 1578.

Friedman, John B. *Orpheus in the Middle Ages.* Cambridge: Harvard University Press, 1970.

Fulgentius. *The Mythologies: Fulgentius the Mythographer.* Trans. Leslie George Whitbread. Columbus: Ohio State University Press, 1971.

Fusco, Nicola. *Elena Lucrezia Cornaro Piscopia.* Pittsburg, PA: U.S. Committee for the Elena Lucrezia Cornaro Piscopia Tercentenary, 1975.

Galerstein, Carolyn L., and Kathleen McNerney. *Women Writers of Spain: An Annotated Bio-bibliography.* Westport, CT: Greenwood Press, 1986.

Galinsky, Hans. *Der Lucretia-Stoff in der Weltliteratur.* Breslau, Poland: Priebatsch, 1932.

Garin, Eugenio, ed. *Il pensiero pedagogico dell'umanesimo.* Florence: Giuntine, 1958.

Gayley, C. M. *Plays of Our Forefathers.* New York: Duffield and Co., 1907.

Gerosa, P. P. *Umanesimo cristiano del Petrarca: Influenza agostiniana, attinenze medievali.* Turin: Bottega d'Erasmo, 1966.

Gilder, Rosamond. "Hrotsvitha, a Tenth-Century Nun—The First Woman Playwright." In *Enter the Acress: The First Women in the Theatre,* Rosamond Gilder, pp. 18–45. London: Harrap and Co., 1931. Repr. Freeport, NY, 1971.

Gilson, Etienne. *Héloïse et Abélard.* Paris: J. Vrin, 1948.

Gold, Barbara K. " 'But Ariadne Was Never There in the First Place': Finding the Female in Roman Poetry." In *Feminist Theory and the Classics,* eds. Nancy Sorkin Rabinowitz and Amy Richlin, pp. 75–95. New York: Routledge, 1993.

———. "The 'Master Mistress' of My Passion: The Lady as Patron in Ancient and Renaissance Literature." In DeForest, ed. *Woman's Power, Man's Game,* pp. 279–304.

Gold, Penny Schine. *The Lady and the Virgin: Image, Attitude, and Experience in Twelfth-Century France.* Chicago: University of Chicago Press, 1985.

Goodich, Michael. *Vita Perfecta: The Ideal of Sainthood in the Thirteenth Century.* Vol. 25: *Monographien zur Geschichte des Mittelalters.* Stuttgart: Hiersemann, 1982.

Gourmont, Rémy de. *Le latin mystique*. Paris: Editions Crès, 1922.

Goux, Jean-Joseph. *Symbolic Economies: After Marx and Freud*. Trans. Jennifer Curtiss Gage. Ithaca, NY: Cornell University Press, 1990.

Grafton, Anthony, and Lisa Jardine. *From Humanism to the Humanities: Education and the Liberal Arts in Fifteenth- and Sixteenth-Century Europe*. Cambridge: Harvard University Press, 1986.

Gravdal, Kathryn. *Ravishing Maidens: Writing Rape in Medieval French Literature and Law*. Philadelphia: University of Pennsylvania Press, 1991.

Green, Gayle, and Coppélia Kahn. "Feminist Scholarship and the Social Construction of Women." In *Making a Difference: Feminist Literary Criticism*, ed. Gayle Greene and Coppélia Kahn, pp. 1–36. London: Methuen, 1985.

Green, Monica Helen. "Women's Medical Practice and Health Care in Medieval Europe." *Signs* 14.2 (1989): pp. 434–73.

Greene, Thomas. *The Light in Troy: Imitation and Discovery in Renaissance Poetry*. New Haven, CT: Yale University Press, 1982.

Greenfield, Concetta. "Studies in Fourteenth and Fifteenth Century Poetics." Ph.D. diss., University of North Carolina, Chapel Hill, 1971.

Greer, Thomas H. *A Brief History of the Western World*. New York: Harcourt, Brace, Jovanovich, 1987.

Grendler, Paul F. *Schooling in Renaissance Italy: Literacy and Learning 1300–1600*. Baltimore: Johns Hopkins University Press, 1989.

Griffiths, Gordon, James Hankins, and David Thompson. *The Humanism of Leonardo Bruni. Selected Texts*. Binghamton, NY: Medieval and Renaissance Texts and Studies, 1987.

Grimm, Jacob, and Johann Andreas Schmeller. *Lateinische Gedichte des zehnten und elften Jahrhunderts*. Göttingen: Dieterichschen Buchhandlung, 1838.

Grosz, Elizabeth. *Sexual Subversions*. Boston: Allen and Unwin, 1989.

Guldan, Ernst. *Eva und Maria: eine Antithese als Bildmotiv*. Graz-Cologne: Bölhau, 1966.

Gurr, Andrew. *Playgoing in Shakespeare's London*. Cambridge: Cambridge University Press, 1987.

———. *The Shakespearean Stage, 1574–1642*. Cambridge: Cambridge University Press, 1984.

Gusdorf, Georges. *La découverte de soi*. Paris: Presses universitaires de France, 1948.

———. "Conditions et limites de l'autobiographie." In *Formen der Selbstdarstellung: Analekten zu einer Geschichte des literarischen Selbstportraits. Festgabe für Fritz Neubert*, ed. Günter Reichenkron and Erich Haase, pp. 105–23.

Berlin: Duncker and Humbolt, 1956. Repr. in translation in James Olney, ed. *Autobiography, Essays Theoretical and Critical.* Princeton: Princeton University Press, 1980. pp. 28–48.

Haight, Anne Lyon. *Hroswitha of Gandersheim: Her Life, Times, and Works, and a Comprehensive Bibliography.* New York: The Hroswitha Club, 1965.

Haley, Shelley P. "Livy's Sophonisba." *Classica et Mediaevalia* 40 (1989): pp. 171–81.

———. "Livy, Passion, and Cultural Stereotypes." *Historia* 39 (1990): pp. 375–81.

Hallett, Judith P. "Martial's Sulpicia and Propertius' Cynthia." In DeForest, *Woman's Power, Man's Game,* pp. 322–53.

Hamilton, Edith, and Huntington Cairns, eds. *The Collected Dialogues of Plato.* Trans. Benjamin Jowett. Princeton: Princeton University Press, 1961.

Haraszti, Zoltán. "The Works of Hroswitha." *More Books: The Bulletin of the Boston Public Library* 20.3, 20.4 (1945): pp. 87–119, pp. 139–73.

Harbage, Alfred. *Shakespeare's Audience.* New York: MacMillan, 1941.

Heilbrun, Carolyn G. "Non-Autobiographies of 'Privileged' Women: England and America." In Brodzki and Schenck, *Lifelines,* pp. 62–76.

Heinrichs, Katherine. *The Myths of Love: Classical Lovers in Medieval Literature.* University Park: The Pennsylvania State University Press, 1990.

———. "Mythological Lovers in Chaucer's *Troilus and Criseyde.*" *Journal of the Rocky Mountain Medieval and Renaissance Association* 12 (1991): pp. 13–39.

Herlihy, David. "Alienation in Medieval Culture and Society." In *Social History of Italy and Western Europe, 700–1500, Collected Studies,* pp. 135–45. London: Routledge, 1978.

———. "Did Women Have a Renaisssance? A Reconsideration." *Medievalia et Humanistica* 13 (1985): pp. 1–22.

Herrmann, Claudine. *Les voleuses de langue.* Paris: Des Femmes, 1976. Trans. by Nancy Kline, *The Tongue Snatchers.* Lincoln: University of Nebraska Press, 1989.

Hesiod, *Opera* ed. Friedrich Solmsen. Oxford: Oxford University Press, 1970.

Hieatt, A. Kent. "Eve as Reason in a Tradition of the Allegorical Interpretation of the Fall." *Journal of the Warburg and Courtauld Institutes* 43 (1980): pp. 221–26.

Hirsch, Marianne. *The Mother/Daughter Plot. Narrative, Psychoanalysis, Feminism.* Bloomington: Indiana University Press, 1989.

Hobby, Elaine. *Virtue of Necessity: English Women's Writing, 1649–88.* London: Virago, 1988.

Hollander, Robert. *Boccaccio's Two Venuses.* New York: Columbia University Press, 1977.

Holzberg, Niklas. "Olympia Morata und die Anfänge des Griechischen an der Universität Heidelberg." *Heidelberger Jahrbücher* 31 (1987): pp. 77–93.

Homeyer, Helena, ed. *Hrotsvithae Opera.* Munich and Paderborn: Ferdinand Schöningh, 1970.

Hoole, Charles. *A New Discovery of the Old Art of Teaching Schoole* (1660). Repr. Menston, Yorkshire, England: Scolar Press, 1969.

Huizinga, Johan. *The Waning of the Middle Ages.* No trans. London: E. Arnold and Co, 1924.

Hyginus. *The Myths of Hyginus, Poetica Astronomica,* ed. and trans. Mary Grant. University of Kansas Humanistic Studies 34. Lawrence: University of Kansas Press, 1960.

Ijsewijn, Josef. *Companion to Neo-Latin Studies, Part 1: History and Diffusion of Neo-Latin Literature.* Atlanta, GA: Scholars Press, 1990.

Iliescu, Nicolae. *Il "Canzoniere" petrarchesco e Sant' Agostino.* Rome: Società Accademica Romana, 1962.

Irigaray, Luce. "This Sex Which Is Not One." Trans. Claudia Reeder. In Marks and de Courtivron, *New French Feminism,* pp. 99-106.

———. *This Sex Which is Not One.* Trans. Catherine Porter with Carolyn Burke. Ithaca, NY: Cornell University Press, 1985.

Jardine, Lisa. "Isotta Nogarola: Women Humanists—Education for What?" *History of Education* 12 (1983): pp. 231–44.

———. " 'O decus Italiae virgo' or The Myth of the Learned Lady in the Renaissance." *Historical Journal* 28 (1985): pp. 799–820.

Jarrett, Bede. *Social Theories of the Middle Ages, 1200–1500.* New York: Frederick Ungar, 1966.

Jeanroy, Alfred. "Raimon de Cornet, troubadour." *Histoire littéraire de la France* 38 (1949): pp. 31–65.

Joplin, Patricia Klindienst. "The Voice of the Shuttle is Ours." *Stanford Literature Review* 1 (1984): pp. 25–53.

———. "Ritual Work on Human Flesh: Livy's Lucretia and the Rape of the Body Politic." *Helios* 17 (1990): pp. 51—70.

Joran, Théodore. *Les féministes avant le féminisme.* Paris: Arthur Savaète, 1911.

Jordan, Constance. "Boccaccio's In-Famous Women: Gender and Civic Virtue in the *De mulieribus claris.*" In *Ambiguous Realities: Women in the Middle Ages and Renaissance,* ed. Carole Levin and Jeanie Watson, pp. 25–47. Detroit: Wayne State University Press, 1987.

————. *Renaissance Feminism. Literary Texts and Political Models.* Ithaca, NY: Cornell University Press, 1990.

Joshel, Sandra R. "The Body Female and the Body Politic: Livy's Lucretia and Verginia." In *Pornography and Representation in Greece and Rome,* ed. Amy Richlin, pp. 112–30. New York: Oxford University Press, 1992.

Juvenal and Persius, *Satires,* ed. and trans. G. G. Ramsay, Loeb Classical Library. Cambridge: Harvard University Press, 1979.

Kahn, Victoria. "The Figure of the Reader in Petrarch's *Secretum.*" *PMLA* 100 (1985): pp. 154–66.

Kallendorf, Craig. "Christoforo Landino's *Aeneid* and the Humanist Critical Tradition." *Renaissance Quarterly* 36 (1983): pp. 519–46.

————. *In Praise of Aeneas: Virgil and Epideictic Rhetoric in the Early Italian Renaissance.* Hanover, NH: University Press of New England, 1989.

Katsaros, Thomas, and Nathaniel Kaplan, eds. *The Western Mystical Tradition: An Intellectual History of Western Civilization.* New Haven, CT: College and University Press, 1967.

Katz, Stephen T., ed. *Mysticism and Philosophical Analysis.* Oxford: Oxford University Press, 1978.

————. *Mysticism and Religious Traditions.* Oxford: Oxford University Press, 1983.

Kaufman, Gloria. "Juan Vives on the Education of Women." *Signs* 3 (1978): pp. 891–96.

Kearney, Hugh. *Scholars and Gentlemen, 1500–1700.* London: Faber and Faber, 1970.

Keller, Carl. A. "Mystical Literature." In Katz, *Mysticism and Philosophical Analysis,* pp. 31–44.

Keller, Eckhard. *Petrarca und die Geschichte.* Munich: Wilhelm Fink Verlag, 1978.

Kelly-Gadol, Joan. "Early Feminist Theory and the *Querelle des Femmes,* 1400–1789." *Signs* 8 (1982): pp. 4–28.

————. "Did Women Have a Renaissance?" In *Becoming Visible,* ed. Renate Bridenthal and Claudia Koonz, pp. 136–61; 2nd ed., 1987, pp. 175–201. Boston: Houghton-Mifflin, 1977. Repr. in *Women, History, and Theory: The Essays of Joan Kelly,* pp. 19–50. Chicago: University of Chicago Press, 1984.

Kelso, Ruth. *Doctrine for the Lady of the Renaissance.* Urbana: University of Illinois Press, 1956.

Kieckhefer, Richard. *Unquiet Souls: Fourteenth Century Saints and Their Religious Milieu.* Chicago: University of Chicago Press, 1984.

King, Margaret, L. "Thwarted Ambitions: Six Learned Women of the Italian Renaissance." *Soundings* 59 (1976): pp. 280–304.

———. "The Religious Retreat of Isotta Nogarola (1418–1466): Sexism and Its Consequences in the Fifteenth Century." *Signs* 3 (1978): pp. 807–22.

———. "Book-lined Cells: Women and Humanism in The Early Italian Renaissance." In LaBalme, *Beyond Their Sex*, pp. 66–90.

———. "Goddess and Captive: Antonio Loschi's Poetic Tribute to Maddelena Scrovegni (1389), Study and Text." *Medievalia et Humanistica* 10 (1980): pp. 103–27.

———. *Women of the Renaissance*. Chicago: University of Chicago Press, 1991.

King, Margaret L. and Albert Rabil, Jr., eds. *Her Immaculate Hand: Selected Works By and About the Women Humanists of Quattrocento Italy*. Vol. 20. Binghamton, NY: Medieval and Renaissance Texts and Studies, 1983.

Kinnear, Mary. *Daughters of Time: Women in the Western Tradition*. Ann Arbor: University of Michigan Press, 1982.

Klapisch-Zuber, Christine, ed. *A History of Women in the West*. Vol. 2: *Silences of the Middle Ages*. Cambridge: Harvard University Press, 1992.

Kößling, Rainer, and Gertrud Wiess-Stählin, eds. and trans. *Olympia Fulvia Morata. Briefe*. Leipzig: Reclam, 1991.

Kristeller, Paul Oskar. *Iter Italicum*. Vol. 1: *Italy, Agrigento to Novara*. Leiden: Brill, 1963.

———. *Iter Italicum*. Vol. 2: *Italy, Orvieto to Volterra, Vatican City*. Leiden: Brill, 1967.

———. "Learned Women of Early Modern Italy: Humanists and University Scholars." In LaBalme, *Beyond Their Sex*, pp. 91–116.

Kristeva, Julia. *Desire in Language: A Semiotic Approach to Literature and Art*. Trans. Thomas Gora, Alice Jardine, and Léon S. Roudiez. New York: Columbia University Press, 1980.

———. *The Kristeva Reader*. Ed. Toril Moi. Trans. Harry Blake, Thomas Gore, Seán Hand, Alice Jardine, Léon S. Roudiez, and Margaret Waller. New York: Columbia University Press, 1986.

———. *Tales of Love*. Trans. Léon S. Roudiez. New York: Columbia University Press, 1987.

Krueger, Roberta L. *Women Readers and the Ideology of Gender in Old French Romance*. Cambridge: Cambridge University Press, 1993.

LaBalme, Patricia H., ed. *Beyond Their Sex: Learned Women of the European Past*. New York: New York University Press, 1980.

Labé, Louise. *Oeuvres complètes.* Ed. François Rigolot. Paris: Flammarion, 1986.

LaChance, Paul. *The Spiritual Journey of the Blessed Angela of Foligno According to the Memorial of Frater A.* Studia Antoniniana nr. 29. Rome: Pontificum Athenaeum Antoninianum, 1984.

————. *Angela of Foligno: Complete Works.* New York: The Paulist Press, 1993.

Lazard, Madeleine. *Images littéraires de la femme à la Renaissance.* Paris: Presses universitaires de France, 1985.

Lazzaro, Claudia. "The Visual Language of Gender in Sixteenth-Century Garden Sculpture." In *Refiguring Woman: Perspectives on Gender and the Italian Renaissance,* ed. Juliana Schiesari and Marilyn Migiel, pp. 71–113. Ithaca, NY: Cornell University Press, 1991.

Lefebvre, Henri. *The Production of Space.* Trans. Donald Nicholson-Smith. Oxford: Blackwell, 1991.

Lefkowitz, Mary R., and Maureen B. Fant. *Women's Life in Greece and Rome.* Baltimore, MD: Johns Hopkins University Press, 1982.

Lemay, Helen Rodnite. *Women's Secrets: A Translation of Pseudo-Albertus Magnus's "De secretis mulierum" with Commentaries.* Albany: State University of New York Press, 1992.

Lerner, Gerda. *The Creation of Feminist Consciousness: From the Middle Ages to the Seventeenth Century.* New York: Oxford University Press, 1993.

Levi, G. A. "Pensiero classico e pensiero cristiano nel *Secretum* e nelle *Familiari* del Petrarca." *Atene e Roma* 35 (1933): Trans. and repr. in Carozza and Shey, *Petrarch's Secretum,* pp. 227–38.

Little, Lester K. *Religious Poverty and the Profit Economy.* Ithaca, NY: Cornell University Press, 1978.

Livy. *Ab urbe condita.* 14 vols. Ed. and trans. Frank Gardner Moore. Loeb Classical Library. Cambridge: Harvard University Press, 1940.

Locke, F. W. "Ganelon and the Cooks." *Symposium* 20 (1966): pp. 141–49.

Lopez, R. S. *The Tenth Century.* New York: Holt, Rinehart, Winston, 1959.

Lucan. *The Civil War.* Ed. and trans. J. D. Duff. Loeb Classical Library. Cambridge: Harvard University Press, 1962.

Lydon, Mary. "Foucault and Feminism." In Diamond and Quinby, *Feminism and Foucault,* pp. 135–47.

Maclean, Ian. *The Renaissance Notion of Woman: A Study of the Fortunes of Scholasticism and Medical Science in European Intellectual Life.* Cambridge: Cambridge University Press, 1980.

Magliola, Robert. "Sexual Rogations, Mystical Abrogations: Some Donnés of Buddhist Tantra and the Catholic Renaissance." In *The Comparative Perspective on Literature*, Ed. Clayton Koelb and Susan Noakes, pp. 195–212. Ithaca, NY: Cornell University Press, 1988.

Makin, Bathshua Reginald. *An Essay to Revive the Ancient Education of Gentlewoman* (1673). Repr. Los Angeles: Augustan Reprint Society, 1980.

Mann, Nicholas. *Petrarch*. Oxford: Oxford University Press, 1984.

Mariani, Eliodoro, ed. *Leggenda della Vita e dei Miracoli di Santa Margherita da Cortona*. Vicenza: L.I.E.F., 1978.

Mariani, Ugo. *Il Petrarca e gli Agostiniani*. 2d ed. Rome: Ed. di storia e letteratura, 1959.

Marks, Elaine, and Isabelle de Courtivron, eds. *New French Feminisms*. New York: Schocken Books, 1981.

Martellotti, Guido. "Storiografia del Petrarca." In *Scritti petrarcheschi*, ed. Michele Feo and Silvia Rizzo, pp. 474–86. Padua: Antenore, 1983.

Martinelli, Bortolo. "*Feria sexta aprilis:* la data sacra nel canzoniere del Petrarca." *Rivista di storia e letteratura religiosa* 8 (1972): pp. 449–84.

———. *Petrarca e il Ventoso*. Bergamo: Minerva italica, 1977.

Martines, Lauro. *Power and Imagination: City States in Renaissance Italy*. New York: Random House, 1980.

Maschietto, Francesco L. *Elena Lucrezia Cornaro Piscopia, 1646–1684: prima donna laureata nel mondo*. Padua: Antenore, 1978.

Matter, E. Ann. *The Voice of My Beloved: The Song of Songs in Western Medieval Christianity*. Philadelphia: University of Pennsylvania Press, 1990.

Mazzotta, Giuseppe. "The *Canzoniere* and the Language of Self." *Studies in Philology* 75 (1979): pp. 271–96.

———. *The Worlds of Petrarch*. Durham, NC: Duke University Press, 1993.

McColley, Diane Kelsey. *Milton's Eve*. Urbana: University of Illinois Press, 1983.

McConica, James K. *English Humanists and Reform Politics*. Oxford: Oxford University Press, 1965.

———. "Elizabethan Oxford: The Collegiate Society." In McConica, *Collegiate University*, pp. 645–732.

———, ed. *The Collegiate University*. Oxford: Oxford University Press, 1986.

McFarlane, I. B. *Buchanan*. London: Duckworth, 1981.

McGowan, Margaret. *Ideal Forms in the Age of Ronsard*. Berkeley and Los Angeles: University of California Press, 1985.

McGuire, Brian Patrick. *The Difficult Saint: Bernard of Clairvaux and His Tradi-tion.* Cistercian Studies Series 126. Kalamazoo, MI: Cistercian Publications, 1991.

McLaughlin, Eleanor Commo. "Equality of Souls, Inequality of Sexes: Woman in Medieval Theology." In *Religion and Sexism: Images of Woman in the Jew-ish and Christian Traditions,* ed. Rosemary Radford Ruether, pp. 213–66. New York: Simon and Schuster, 1974.

McLaughlin, Mary Martin. "Abelard as Autobiographer: The Motives and Meaning of his 'Story of Calamities.' " *Speculum* 42 (1967): pp. 463–88.

———. "Peter Abelard and the Dignity of Women: Twelfth Century 'Feminism' in Theory and Practice." In *Pierre Abélard—Pierre le Vénérable: Les courants philosophiques, littéraires et artistique en occident au milieu du XIIe Siècle.* pp. 287–313.

McLeod, Glenda. *Virtue and Venom: Catalogs of Women from Antiquity to the Renaissance.* Ann Arbor: University of Michigan Press, 1991.

McNeill, J. T., and H. M. Gamer. *Medieval Handbooks of Penance.* New York: Co-lumbia University Press, 1938.

Menesto, Enrico. "Beate e Sante dell'Umbria tra Duecento e Trecento: Una Ricognizione degli Scritti e delle Fonti Agiografice." *Sante e Beate Umbre tra il XIII e il XIV Secoli,* pp. 61–87. Foligno, Italy: Edizioni del'Arquata, 1986.

Michalka, Erich. *Studien über Intention und Gestaltung in den dramatischen Werken Hrotsvits von Gandersheim.* Inaugural dissertation der Ruprecht-Karl-Universät zu Heidelberg. Clausthal-Zellerfeld, Germany: Bönecke-Druck, 1968.

Migne, J.-P., ed. *Patrilogia Latina.* 221 vols. 2d ser. Paris: J.-P. Migne, 1844–64.

Miller, Paul Allen. "Sive Deae Seu Sint Dirae Obscenaeque Volucres," *Arethusa* 22 (1989): pp. 47–80.

———. "Sidney, Petrarch, and Ovid, or Imitation as Subversion," *ELH* 58 (1991): pp. 499–522.

Milton, John. *Paradise Lost.* Ed. Merrit Y. Hughes. Indianapolis, IN: Bobbs-Merrill, 1962.

Mitterauer, Michael, and Reinhard Sieder. *The European Family.* Chicago: Univer-sity of Chicago Press, 1982.

Mohanty, Chandra T., and Satya P. Mohanty. "Contradictions of Colonialism." *Women's Review of Books* 7.6 (1990): pp. 19–21.

Moi, Toril. *Sexual/Textual Politics: Feminist Literary Theory.* New York and Lon-don: Routledge, 1988.

Mommsen, Theodor. "Petrarch and the Story of the Choice of Hercules." *Journal of the Warburg and Courtauld Institutes* 16 (1953): pp. 178–92.

Monfrin, Jacques. "Le problème de l'authenticité de la correspondance d'Abélard et d'Héloise." In *Pierre Abélard—Pierre le Vénérable,* pp. 409–24.

Montano, Rocco. "La prese di conscienza: Il *Secretum.*" *Lo spirito e le lettere.* Milano: Mazorati, 1970. Vol. 1: trans. and repr. in Carozza and Shey, *Petrarch's Secretum,* pp. 213–16.

Moorman, John. *A History of the Franciscan Order from its Origins to the Year 1517.* Oxford: Clarendon Press, 1968.

Moos, Peter von. "Cornelia und Heloise." *Latomus* 34 (1975): pp. 1024–59.

Morata, Olympia Fulvia. *Olympiae Fulviae Moratae foeminae doctissimae ac plane divinae Orationes, Dialogi, Epistolae, Carmina tam Latina quam Graeca.* 2d ed. Basil: 1562 (1st ed. 1558). Repr. in microfilm, "History of Women," Reel 62, No. 396 (New Haven, 1975).

———. *Olympiae Fulviae Moratae foeminae doctissimae ac plane divinae opera omnia quae hactenus inueniri potuerunt.* 3d ed. Basil: 1570. Repr. in microfilm, "History of Women," Reel 62, No. 397 (New Haven, 1975).

Morris, Jan, ed. *The Oxford Book of Oxford.* Oxford: Oxford University Press, 1978.

Muir, Edward. *Civic Ritual in Renaissance Venice.* Princeton: Princeton University Press, 1981.

Mulvey, Laura. *Visual and Other Pleasures.* Bloomington: Indiana University Press, 1989.

Murphy, Francis X. "Petrarch and the Christian Philosophy." In *Francesco Petrarca Citizen of the World,* ed. Aldo S. Bernardo, pp. 223–47. Albany: State University of New York Press, 1980.

Murray, Oswyn. "The Idea of the Shepherd King from Cyrus to Charlemagne." In *Latin Poetry and the Classical Tradition,* eds. Murray and Peter Goodman, pp. 1–14. Oxford: Oxford University Press.

Nagel, Bert. *Hrotsvit von Gandersheim.* Stuttgart: J. B. Metzler, 1965.

Nauert, Charles G., Jr. *Agrippa and the Crisis of Renaissance Thought.* Vol. 55. Illinois Studies in the Social Sciences. Urbana: Illinois University Press, 1965.

Nelson, Alan H. *Records of Early English Drama: Cambridge.* Vols. 1: *The Records* and 2: *Editorial Apparatus.* Toronto: University of Toronto Press, 1989.

Newlands, Carole E. "Hrotswitha's Debt to Terence." *Transactions of the American Philological Association* 116 (1986): pp. 369–91.

Newman, Barbara. "Authority, Authenticity, and the Repression of Heloise." *Journal of Medieval and Renaissance Studies* 22 (1992): pp. 121–57.

Newman, Karen. *Fashioning Femininity and English Renaissance Drama.* Chicago: University of Chicago Press, 1991.

Nichols, Fred J. *An Anthology of Neo-Latin Verse.* New Haven, CT: Yale University Press, 1979.

Nichols, Stephen G. "The New Medievalism: Tradition and Discontinuity in Medieval Culture." In Brownlee et al., *The New Medievalism,* pp. 1–26.

Nichols, John A., and Lilian T. Shank, eds. *Medieval Religious Women.* Vol. 1: *Distant Echoes.* Oxford and Kalamazoo, MI: Cistercian Publications, 1984.

Noferi, Adelia. *L'esperienza poetica del Petrarca.* Florence: Le Monnier, 1962.

Nolhac, Pierre de. *Pétrarque et l'humanisme.* 2d ed. 2 vols. Paris: Librairie Honoré Champion, 1965, first printed in 1907.

Norberg, Kathryn. "Prostitutes." In *A History of Women in the West,* ed. Natalie Zemon Davis and Arlette Farge, vol. 3, pp. 458–74. Cambridge: Harvard University Press, 1993.

Oliver, Kelly. *Reading Kristeva: Unraveling the Double-Bind.* Bloomington: Indiana University Press, 1993.

Olney, James. *Metaphors of Self: The Meaning of Autobiography.* Princeton: Princeton University Press, 1972.

———, ed. *Autobiography: Essays Theoretical and Critical.* Princeton: Princeton University Press, 1980.

Orrell, John. "The Theater at Christ Church, Oxford, in 1605." *Shakespeare Survey* 35 (1982): pp. 129–40.

———. *The Theaters of Inigo Jones and John Webb.* Cambridge: Cambridge University Press, 1985.

Ortner, Sherry. "Is Female to Male as Nature is to Culture?" In *Women, Culture, and Society,* eds. Michelle Z. Rosaldo and Louise Lamphere, pp. 72–83. Stanford: Stanford University Press, 1974.

Ostriker, Alicia. "The Thieves of Language: Women Poets and Revisionist Mythmaking." *Signs* 8 (1985): pp. 68–90. Repr. in *The New Feminist Criticism: Essays on Women, Literature, and Theory,* ed. Elaine Showalter, pp. 314–38. New York: Pantheon Books, 1985.

Ovid. *The Art of Love and Other Poems,* trans. J. H. Mozley, revised by J. P. Goold. Loeb Classical Library. Cambridge: Harvard University Press, 1979.

———. *Fasti,* ed. and trans. J. G. Frazer. Loeb Classical Library. Cambridge: Harvard University Press, 1976.

———. *Metamorphoses.* 2 vols. Ed. and trans. Frank Justus Miller. Loeb Classical Library. Cambridge: Harvard University Press, 1966.

———. *Amores, Medicamina Faciei Femineae, Ars Amatoria, Remedia Amoris*, ed. E. J. Kenney. Oxford: Oxford University Press, 1961.

Packman, Zola Marie. "Call It Rape: A Motif in Roman Comedy and Its Suppression in English-Speaking Publications." *Helios* 20.1 (1993): pp. 42–55.

Palma, Marco. "Laura Cereta." *Dizionario biografico degli italiani*. Rome: Istituto della Enciclopedia italiana, 1960.

Panofsky, Dora, and Erwin Panofsky. *Pandora's Box: The Changing Aspects of a Mythical Symbol*. Bollingen Series 11. New York: Pantheon, 1962.

Partner, Nancy F., ed. *Studying Medieval Women: Sex, Gender, Feminism*. Cambridge, MA: The Medieval Academy of America, 1993.

Pascal, Carlo. "Didone nelle letteratura d'Africa." *Athenaeum* 5 (1917): pp. 285–93.

Pascal, Paul. *Hrotsvitha, Dulcitius and Paphnutius*. Bryn Mawr, PA: Bryn Mawr Latin Commentaries, 1985.

Paxton, Frederick S. *Christianizing Death: The Creation of a Ritual Process in Early Medieval Europe*. Ithaca, NY: Cornell University Press, 1991.

Peradotto, John, and J. P. Sullivan, eds. *Women in the Ancient World: The Arethusa Papers*. Albany: State University of New York Press, 1984.

Personal Narrative Group, eds. *Interpreting Women's Lives: Feminist Theory and Personal Narratives*. Bloomington: Indiana University Press, 1989.

Peter the Venerable. *The Letters of Peter the Venerable*. Ed. Giles Constable. 2 vols. Cambridge: Harvard University Press, 1967.

Petrarca, Francesco. *Opera latina*. Venice: n.p., 1501.

———. *Opera latine*, Antonietta Bufano, ed. Torino: Unione Tipographica-Edizione Torinese, 1975.

———. *Africa*. Edizione nazionale delle opere di Petrarca. Ed. Nicola Festa. Florence: Sansoni, 1926.

———. *Secretum. Prose*. Ed. Enrico Carara. Milano: Riccardo Ricciardi, 1955.

———. *Rime e Trionfi*. Ed. F. Neri. Turin: Unione Tipografico-Edizione Torinese, 1966.

———. *Canzoniere*. Ed. Gianfranco Contini. Turin: G. Einaudi, 1964.

———. *Petrarch's "Africa."* Ed. and trans. Thomas G. Bergin and Alice S. Wilson. New Haven: Yale University Press, 1977.

———. *Letters on Familiar Matters, Rerum familiarum libri*. Trans. Aldo S. Bernardo. 3 vols. Vol. 1 Albany: State University of New York Press, 1975. Vols. 2 and 3. Baltimore, MD: Johns Hopkins University Press, 1982 and 1985.

———. *Poesie Latine.* Ed. Guido Martellotti and Enrico Bianchi. Torino: Giulio Einaudi, 1976.

———. *Letters of Old Age, Rerum Senilium Libri.* Trans. Aldo S. Bernardo, Saul Levin, and Reta A. Bernardo. 2 vols. Baltimore, MD: Johns Hopkins University Press, 1992.

Pierre Abélard—Pierre le Vénérable: Les courants philosophiques, littéraires et artistiques en occident au milieu du XIIe siècle. Colloques Internationaux du Centre National de la Recherche Scientifique, no. 546. Paris: Editions du Centre National de la Recherche Scientifique, 1975.

Pigman, G. W., III. "Neo-Latin Imitation of Latin Classics." In *Latin Poetry and the Classical Tradition,* eds. Peter Godman and Oswyn Murray, pp. 199–210. Oxford: Clarendon Press, 1990.

Pizan, Christine de. *The Book of the City of Ladies.* Trans. Earl Jeffrey Richards. New York: Persea, 1982.

Platter, Charles, and Barbara Welch. "The Poetics of Prostitution: Buchanan's 'Ars Lenae.' " *Celestinesca* 16 (1992): pp. 35–81.

Pliny. *Natural History,* ed. and trans. D. E. Eicholtz, Loeb Classical Library. Cambridge: Harvard University Press, 1962.

Plummer, John F., ed. *Vox Feminae: Studies in Medieval Women's Songs.* Kalamazoo, MI: Medieval Institute Publications XV, 1981.

Politian. *Prosatori latini del Quattrocentro.* Ed. E. Garin. Milan: R. Ricciardi, 1952.

Polybius. *Histories.* 6 vols. Ed. and trans. W. R. Paton. Loeb Classical Library. Cambridge: Harvard University Press, 1925.

Power, Eileen Edna. *Medieval Women,* Ed. M. M. Postan. Cambridge: Cambridge University Press, 1975.

Pratt, Mary Louise. "Dido as an Example of Chastity: The Influence of Literature." *Harvard Library Bulletin* 17 (1969): pp. 216–32.

Presenti, Giovanni. "Alessandra Scala, una figura della Rinascenza fiorentina," *Giornale storico della letteratura italiana* 85 (1925): pp. 241–67.

Proudfoot, Wayne. *Varieties of Religious Experience.* Berkeley and Los Angeles: University of California Press, 1985.

Quasten, Johannes. *Music and Worship in Pagan and Christian Antiquity.* Trans. Boniface Ramsey, O. P. Studies in Church Music and Liturgy. Washington, DC: National Association of Pastoral Musicians, 1983.

Quilligan, Maureen. *The Allegory of Female Authority: Christine de Pizan's "Cité des dames."* Ithaca, NY: Cornell University Press, 1991.

Rabil, Albert, Jr. *Laura Cereta: Quattrocentro Humanist.* Binghamton, NY: Medieval and Renaissance Texts and Studies, 1981.

Rabinowitz, Nancy Sorkin, and Amy Richlin, eds. *Feminist Theory and the Classics*. London: Routledge, 1993.

Raby, J. F. E. *A History of Christian-Latin Poetry from the Beginnings to the Close of the Middle Ages*. 2d ed. Oxford: Clarendon, 1953.

Radice, Betty. *The Letters of Abelard and Heloise*. Harmondsworth, England: Penguin, 1974.

Raimondi, Ezio. *Metafora e storia: Studi su Dante e Petrarca*. Turin: G. Einaudi, 1970.

Ravisius, Jean Tixier de. *De Memoralibus et Claris Mulieribus aliquot Diversorum Scriptorum Opera*. Paris: Simon Colinaci, 1521.

Rawles, Stephen. "Denys Janot, Parisian Printer and Bookseller (fl. 1529–1544): A Bibliographical Study." Ph.D. diss., University of Warwick, 1964.

Reynolds, Myra. *The Learned Lady in England*. Boston: 1920. Repr. Gloucester, MA: P. Smith, 1964.

Ricci, Charles. *Sophonisbe dans la tragédie classique italienne et française*. Grenoble: Allier Frères, 1904.

Rice, Warner G. "The *Paradossi* of Ortensio Lando." *Language and Literature* 8 (1931): pp. 59–75.

Richardson, Lula M. *The Forerunners of Feminism in French Literature of the Renaissance from Christine of Pisa to Marie de Gournay*. Johns Hopkins Studies in Romance Literatures and Languages, 12, Baltimore, MD: Johns Hopkins University Press; and Paris: Presses universitaires de France, 1929.

Richmond-Garza, Elizabeth. *Forgotten Cites/Sights: Interpretation and the Power of Classical Citation in Renaissance English Tragedy*. New York: Peter Lang, 1994.

Robathan, D. M. "A Fifteenth-century Bluestocking." *Medievalia et Humanistica* 2 (1944): pp. 106–11.

Roberts, Arthur J. "Did Hrotswitha Imitate Terence?" *Modern Language Notes* 16 (1901): pp. 478–82.

Robertson, D. W. *A Preface to Chaucer: Studies in Medieval Perspectives*. Princeton: Princeton University Press, 1962.

Robertson, Kim. "Heteroglossia, History, and Humanism: Bakhtin's Novel Perspective on the Renaissance." *Recapturing the Renaissance: New Perspectives on Humanism, Dialogue, and Texts*. eds. Diane S. Wood and Paul Allen Miller, Knoxville, TN: New Paradigm Press, 1996.

Robey, David. "Humanist Views on the Study of Poetry in the Early Italian Renaissance." *History of Education* 13 (1984): pp. 7–25.

Robin, Diana. *Filelfo in Milan.* Princeton: Princeton University Press, 1991.

———. "Cassandra Fedele." In *Italian Women Writers: A Biographical Sourcebook,* Ed. Rinaldina Russel, pp. 119–27. New York: Greenwood Press, 1994.

———. "Cassandra Fedele's *Epistolae* (1488–1521): Biography as Effacement." In *The Rhetorics of Life-Writing in Early Modern Europe: Forms of Biography from Cassandra Fedele to Louis XIV,* eds. Thomas Mayer and Daniel Woolf, pp. 187–203. Ann Arbor: University of Michigan Press, 1995.

Roche, Thomas P. "The Calendrical Structure of Petrarch's *Canzoniere.*" *Studies in Philology* 71 (1974): pp. 152–72.

———. *Petrarch and the English Sonnet Sequences.* New York: AMS Press, 1989.

Ronciere, Charles de la. "Tuscan Notables on the Eve of the Renaissance." In Duby, *History of Private Life,* pp. 157–307.

Rosaldo, Michelle Z. "Women, Culture, and Society: A Theoretical Overview." In *Women, Culture, and Society,* eds. Michelle Z. Rosaldo and Louise Lamphere. Stanford, CA: Stanford University Press, 1974.

Ross, James B. "The Middle Class Child in Urban Italy Fourteenth to Early Sixteenth Centuries." In *The History of Childhood,* ed. Lloyd de Maus, pp. 186–209. New York: Atcon, 1974.

Rubin, Gayle. "The Traffic in Women: Notes on the 'Political Economy' of Sex." In *Toward an Anthropology of Women,* ed. Rayna R. Rester, pp. 157–210. New York: Monthly Review Press, 1975.

Ruether, Rosemary Radford. "Misogynism and Virginal Feminism in the Fathers of the Church." In *Religion and Sexism: Images of Woman in the Jewish and Christian Traditions,* ed. Reuther. New York: Simon and Schuster, 1974.

Russ, Joanna. *How to Suppress Women's Writing.* Austin: University of Texas Press, 1983.

Saïd, Edward. *Orientalism.* New York: Vintage Books, 1978.

St. John, Christopher. *The Plays of Roswitha.* London: Chatto and Windus, 1923.

Salmon, Vivian. "Bathsua Makin: A Pioneer Linguist and Feminist in Seventeenth-Century England." In *Neuere Forschungen zur Wortbildung und Historiographie der Linguistik: Festgabe für Herbert E. Brekle,* eds. Brigiette Asbach-Schnitker and Johannes Roggenhofer, pp. 303–18. Tübingen, Germany: Tübingen Beiträge für Linguistik, 1987.

Sankovitch, Tilde. *French Women Writers and the Book: Myths of Access and Desire.* Syracuse, NY: Syracuse University Press, 1988.

Sauvage, Odette, ed. *Luisa Sigée. Dialogue de deux jeunes filles sur la vie de cour et la vie de retraite (1552).* Paris: Presses universitaires de France, 1970.

Sawicki, Jana. "Feminism and the Power of Foucauldian Discourse." In *After Foucault: Humanistic Knowledge, Postmodern Challenges,* ed. Jonathan Arac, pp. 161–78. New Brunswick: Rutgers University Press, 1988.

Saxer, Victor. *Le Culte de Marie Madeleine en occident, des origines à la fin du Moyen-Age.* 2 vols. Paris: Presses universitaires de France, 1959.

Scaglione, Aldo, ed. *Francis Petrarch, Six Centuries Later: A Symposium. North Carolina Studies in the Romance Languages and Literatures: Symposia.* Vol. 3. Chapel Hill and Chicago: Department of Romance Languages, University of North Carolina and the Newberry Library, 1975.

Schaller, Dieter. "Hrotsvit von Gandersheim nach Tausend Jahren." *Zeitschrift für die Philologie* 96 (1977): pp. 105–14.

Schiesari, Juliana. "In Praise of Virtuous Women? For a Genealogy of Gender Morals in Renaissance Italy." *Annali d'italianistica* 7 (1989): pp. 66–87.

Schiesari, Juliana, and Marilyn Migiel, eds. "Introduction." In *Refiguring Woman: Perspectives on Gender and the Italian Renaissance,* pp. 1–15. Ithaca, NY: Cornell University Press, 1991.

Schütze-Pflugk, Marianne. *Herrscher- und Märtyrerauffassung bei Hrotsvit von Gandersheim.* Wiesbaden, Germany: Steiner, 1972.

Seagraves, Richard. "The Influence of Vergil on Petrarch's *Africa.*" Ph.D. diss., Columbia University, 1977.

Sensi, Mario. "Incarcerate e Penetenti a Foligno nella prima età del trecento." In *I Frati penetenti di San Francesco nella società del due e trecento,* ed. Mariano D'Alatri, pp. 25–44. Rome: Istituto dei Cappuccini, 1977.

———. "Il movimento Francescano della penitenza a Foligno." In *Il movimento Francescano della penitenza nella società mediovale,* ed. Mariano D'Alatri, pp. 399–422. Atti del 3 convegno di studi Francescani a Padova. Rome: Istituto storico dei Cappucini, 1980.

———. "Angela nel Contesto Religioso Folignate." *Vita e spiritualità della Beata Angela di Foligno.* Atti del Convegno di studi per il VII centenario della conversione della Beata Angela da Foligno (1285–1985), pp. 43–58. Perugia: Schmitt, 1985.

Serrano y Sanz, Manuel. *Apuntes para una biblioteca de escritoras españolas desde el año 1401 al 1833.* Madrid: 1903. Repr. in Biblioteca de autores españoles, t. 268–271. Madrid: Atlas, 1975.

Seznec, Jean. *The Survival of the Pagan Gods.* Trans. Barbara Sessions. New York: Harper and Row, 1953.

Shakespeare, William. *Riverside Shakespeare.* Ed. G. Blakemore Evans. New York: Houghton Mifflin, 1974.

Sharrat, Peter, and P. G. Walsh, eds. 1983. *George Buchanan's Tragedies.* Edinburgh: Scottish Academic Press.

Showalter, Elaine. "Toward a Feminist Poetics." In *Women Writing and Writing about Women,* ed. Mary Jacobus, pp. 22–41. London: Croom Helm, 1979.

Silverman, Kaja. *The Acoustic Mirror, The Female Voice in Psychoanalysis and Cinema.* Bloomington: Indiana University Press, 1988.

Simon, Joan. *Education and Society in Tudor England.* Cambridge: Cambridge University Press, 1966.

Simon, Kate. *A Renaissance Tapestry: The Gonzaga of Mantua.* New York: Harper and Row, 1988.

Skinner, Marilyn B., ed. *Rescuing Creusa: New Methodological Approaches to Women in Antiquity. Helios* 13.2 (1986): Special Issue.

Smith, Louise Pearson. "Audience Response to Rape: Chaerea in Terence's *Eunuchus.*" *Helios* 21.1 (1994): pp. 21–38.

Smith, Sidonie. *A Poetics of Women's Autobiography: Marginality and the Fictions of Self-Representation.* Bloomington: University of Indiana Press, 1987.

Smith, Sidonie, and J. Watson, eds. *De/Colonizing the Subject: The Politics of Gender in Women's Autobiography.* Minneapolis: University of Minnesota Press, 1992.

Soja, Edward. *Postmodern Geographies: The Reassertion of Space in Critical Social Theory.* New York: Verso, 1989.

Sparrow, John. "Latin Verse of the High Renaissance." In *Italian Renaissance Studies,* ed. E. F. Jacob, pp. 354–409. London: Faber and Faber, 1960.

Spivak, Gayatri Chakravorty. *In Other Worlds: Essays in Cultural Politics.* New York: Methuen, 1987.

Stafford, Pauline. *Queens, Concubines, and Dowagers: The King's Wife in the Early Middle Ages.* Athens: University of Georgia Press, 1983.

Stallybrass, Peter. "Patriarchal Territories: The Body Enclosed." In Ferguson, Quilligan, and Vickers, *Rewriting the Renaissance,* pp. 124–42.

Stanton, Domna C. "Autogynography: Is the Subject Different?" In Stanton, ed. *The Female Autograph,* pp. 5–22.

———, ed. *The Female Autograph: Theory and Practice of Autobiography from the Tenth to the Twentieth Century.* New York: New York Literary Forum, 1984. Repr. Chicago: University of Chicago Press, 1987.

Sticca, Sandro. "Hrotswitha's 'Dulcitius' and Christian Symbolism." *Medieval Studies* 32 (1970): pp. 108–27.

———. "Sin and Salvation: The Dramatic Context of Hrotswitha's Women." In *The Roles and Images of Women in the Middle Ages and Renaissance,* ed. Douglas Radcliff-Umstead, pp. 3–22. Pittsburgh, PA: University of Pittsburgh Press, 1975.

————. "Sacred Drama and Comic Realism in the Plays of Hrotswitha of Gandersheim." In *Acta VI: The Early Middle Ages,* ed. William Snyder, pp. 117–43. Binghamton, NY: Center for Medieval and Early Renaissance Studies, 1979.

————. *The "Planctus Mariae" in the Dramatic Tradition of the Middle Ages.* Trans. Joseph R. Berrigan. Athens: University of Georgia Press, 1988.

Stone: Lawrence, ed. *The University in Society.* Vol. 1: *Oxford and Cambridge from the 14th Century to the Early 19th Century.* Princeton: Princeton University Press, 1974.

————. *Road to Divorce, England, 1530–1987.* Oxford: Oxford University Press, 1990.

————. *Uncertain Unions, Marriage in England, 1660–1753.* Oxford: Oxford University Press, 1992.

Strecker, Karolus, ed. *Hrotsvithae Opera,* 2d ed. Leipzig: Teubner, 1930.

Strong, Roy. *Gloriana: The Portraits of Queen Elizabeth I.* London: Thames and Hudson, 1987.

Stuard, Susan Mosher, ed. *Women in Medieval Society.* Philadelphia: University of Pennsylvania Press, 1976.

————. "The Sociobiological Model and the Medieval Evidence." *American Anthropologist* 86 (1984): pp. 410–12.

————, ed. *Women in Medieval History and Historiography.* Philadelphia: University of Pennsylvania Press, 1987.

Sturm-Maddox, Sara. "The Poet-Persona in the *Canzoniere.*" In Scaglione, *Francis Petrarch,* pp. 192–212.

————. *Petrarch's Metamorphoses: Text and Subtext in the "'Rime Sparse."* Columbia: University of Missouri Press, 1985.

————. *Petrarch's Laurels.* University Park: The Pennsylvania State University Press, 1992.

Suleiman, Susan. "Le récit exemplaire. Parabole, fable, roman à thèse." *Poétique* 32 (1977): pp. 468–89.

Swedenberg, H. T. "More Tears for Lord Hastings." *Huntington Library Quarterly* 16 (1952): pp. 43–51.

Tacitus, *Histories,* 4–5, *Annales* 1–3, trans. C. H. Moore and John Jackson, Loeb Classical Library. Cambridge: Harvard University Press, 1979.

Tarr, Judith. "Terentian Elements in Hrotsvit." In Katharina M. Wilson, ed. *Hrotsvit of Gandersheim: Rara Avis in Saxonia?* Ann Arbor, MI: MARC Publishing, 1987, pp. 55–62.

Tateo, Francesco. *Dialogo interiore e polemica ideologica nel "Secretum" de Petrarca.* Florence: Le Monnier, 1965. Trans. and repr. in Carozza and Shey, *Petrarch's Secretum,* pp. 251–71.

Thier, Ludger, and Abele Calufetti. *Il libro della Beata Angela da Foligno.* Rome: Grottaferrata, 1985.

Thomas, Keith. *Man and the Natural World: A History of the Modern Sensibility.* New York: Pantheon, 1983.

Tomasini, Jacopo Filippo. *Elogia Literis et Sapientia Illustrium ad vivum expressis imaginibus exornata.* Padua, Italy: ex Typographia Sebastiani Sardi, 1644.

Tonzig, Maria I., ed. *Elena Lucrezia Cornaro Piscopia: prima donna laureata nel mondo.* Vincenza, Italy: Gualandi, 1980.

Trapp, J. B. "The Iconography of the Fall of Man." In *Approaches to "Paradise Lost,"* ed. C. A. Patrides, pp. 223–65. Toronto: University of Toronto Press, 1968.

Trinkaus, Charles. *The Poet as Philosopher: Petrarch and the Formation of Renaissance Consciousness.* New Haven, CT: Yale University Press, 1979.

Ullman, B. L. "History and Tragedy." *Transactions of the American Philological Association* 73 (1942): pp. 24–53.

Van der Poel, Marc. "Agrippa von Nettesheim and Rhetoric: An Examination of the *Declamatio de Originali Peccato.*" *Humanistica Lovaniensia* 39 (1990): pp. 177–206.

———. "Review of Henri Corneille Agrippa's *De nobilitate.*" *Rhetorica* 10 (1992): pp. 303–11.

Vegio, Maffeo. *De educatione liberorum et eorum claris moribus libri sex.* Ed. Maria W. Fanning and Anne S. Sullivan. Catholic University of America Studies in Medieval and Renaissance Latin 1. Washington, DC: Catholic University Press, 1933–36.

Verde, Armando F. *Lo studio fiorentino, 1473–1503.* Florence and Pistoia: Istituto nazionale di studi sul Rinascimento, 1973–77.

Vickers, Nancy J. "Diana Described: Scattered Woman and Scattered Rhyme." *Critical Inquiry.* Winter 8 (1981): pp. 265–79.

———. "Widowed Words: Dante, Petrarch and the Metaphors of Mourning." In *Discourses of Authority in Medieval and Renaissance Literature,* eds. Kevin Brownlee and Walter Stephens, pp. 97–108. Hanover, NH: University Press of New England, 1989.

Vives, Juan Luis. *Joannis Ludovici Valentini Opera Omnia.* Ed. Gregorius Majansius. 8 vols. Valentiae: 1523/1783. Repr. London: Gregg Press, 1964.

Vorländer, Dorothea. "Olympia Fulvia Morata—eine evangelische Humanistin in Schweinfurt." *Zeitschrift für bayerische Kirchengeschichte* 39 (1970): pp. 95–113.

Wack, Mary Frances. *Lovesickness in the Middle Ages: The "Viaticum" and its Commentaries.* Philadelphia: University of Pennsylvania Press, 1990.

Walsh, P. G. "The Literary Techniques of Livy." *Rheinisches Museum für Philogie* 97 (1954): pp. 97–114.

———. *Livy: His Historical Aims and Methods.* Cambridge: Cambridge University Press, 1961.

Warner, Marina. *Alone of All Her Sex: The Myth and the Cult of the Virgin Mary.* New York: Vintage Books, 1983.

Waswo, Richard. *Language and Meaning in the Renaissance.* Princeton: Princeton University Press, 1987.

Wayne, Valerie. "Zenobia in Medieval and Renaissance Literature." In *Ambiguous Realities: Women in the Middle Ages and Renaissance,* pp. 48–65. Detroit, MI: Wayne State University Press, 1987.

Weedon, Chris. *Feminist Practice and Poststructuralist Theory.* Oxford: Basil Blackwell, 1987.

Weinstein, Donald, and Rudolph Bell. *Saints and Society.* Chicago: University of Chicago Press, 1982.

Wiesner, Merry. "Spinsters and Seamstresses: Women in Clothing Production." In Ferguson, Quilligan, and Vickers, *Rewriting the Renaissance,* pp. 191–206.

———. *Working Women in Renaissance Germany.* New Brunswick, NJ: Rutgers University Press, 1986.

Williams, Arnold. *The Common Expositor.* Chapel Hill: University of North Carolina Press, 1948.

Williams, Penry. "Elizabethan Oxford: State, Church, and University." In McConica, *Collegiate University,* pp. 397–440.

Wilson, Katharina M. "The Saxon Canoness: Hrotsvit of Gandersheim." In Wilson, *Medieval Women Writers,* pp. 30–63.

———. "*Figmenta vs. Veritas:* Dame Alice and the Medieval Literary Depiction of Women by Women." *Tulsa Studies in Women's Literature* 4.1 (1985): pp. 17–32.

———. *Hrotsvit of Gandersheim: The Ethics of Authorial Stance.* Leiden: E. J. Brill, 1988.

Wilson, Katharina M., ed. *Medieval Women Writers.* Athens: University of Georgia Press, 1984.

———. *Hrotsvit of Gandersheim: Rara Avis in Saxonia?* Ann Arbor, MI: MARC Publishing, 1987.

Wilson, Katharina M., trans. *The Plays of Hrotsvit of Gandersheim.* Garland Library of Medieval Literature, Series B, vol. 62. New York: Garland Publishing, 1989.

Winkler, John J. "Double Consciousness in Sappho's Lyrics." In *The Constraints of Desire: The Anthropology of Sex and Gender in Ancient Greece*, pp. 162–87. New York: Routledge, 1990.

Winterfeld, Paulus de (Paul von). *Hrotsvithae Opera.* Berlin: Weidmann, 1902.

———. *Deutsche Dichter des Lateinischen Mittelalters.* Munich: Oskar Beck, 1913.

Woodbridge, Linda. *Women and the English Renaissance: Literature and the Nature of Womankind, 1540–1620.* Urbana: University of Illinois Press, 1986.

Woodward, William Harrison. *Vittorino da Feltre and Other Humanist Educators* (1897). Repr. New York: Teachers' College Press, 1963.

———. *Studies in Education During the Age of the Renaissance, 1400–1600.* (1906) Repr. New York: Teachers' College Press, 1967.

Wyke, Maria. "Mistress and Metaphor in Augustan Elegy." *Helios* 16 (1989): pp. 25–47.

Yates, Frances A. *Astraea: The Imperial Theme in the Sixteenth Century.* Original imprint, London: Routledge and Kegan Paul, 1975. 2d imprint, London: Ark Paperbacks, 1985.

Young, Karl. *The Drama of the Medieval Church.* Oxford: Clarendon Press, 1933.

Zama, Piero. *Santa Umiltà: La Vita e i "Sermones."* Faenza, Italy: Fratelli, 1974.

Zeydel, Edwin H. "Were Hrotsvitha's Plays Performed During Her Lifetime?" *Speculum* 20 (1945): pp. 443–56.

———. "The Authenticity of Hrotsvitha's Works." *Modern Language Notes* 61 (1946): pp. 50–55.

Zufferey, François. *Bibliographie des poètes provençaux des XIVe et XVe siècles.* Geneva: Droz, 1981.

Zumthor, Paul. *Essai de poétique médiévale.* Paris: Seuil, 1972.

Contributors

Phyllis Culham is Professor of History at the U.S. Naval Academy. She is the author of three dozen articles on Greek, Roman, Merovingian, and early Christian history. She co-edited the volume, *Classics: A Discipline and Profession in Crisis?* (University Press of America 1989). Most of Culham's current work is on comparative questions of literacy and the transmission of texts. These topics lie at the heart of her book-in-progress, *Roman Records.*

Donald Gilman is Professor of French at Ball State University. He specializes in French, Italian, and Neo-Latin literature and literary theory of the late Middle Ages and Renaissance. Co-editor of *Louis Caron, Dialogues* (Droz 1986) and editor of *Everyman and Company: Essays on the Theme and Structure of the European Moral Play* (AMS 1989), he has published over twenty articles in the United States and Europe. He is currently working on a book-length study of Helen in Ronsard's *Sonnets pour Hélène.*

Barbara K. Gold is Leonard C. Ferguson Professor of Classics at Hamilton College. She has published widely on Augustan Latin poetry, Roman social history, feminism, poststructuralism, and women in the ancient world. Her book, *Literary Patronage in Greece and Rome,* was published by the University of North Carolina Press in 1987. She is now at work on a translation, commentary and series of interpretive essays on Juvenal's Sixth Satire, "On Women."

Saint-John Flynn is a doctoral candidate in comparative literature at the University of Georgia. He has given papers at several conferences dealing with the texts of Marie de France, Abbot Suger, and Raimon de Cornet.

Nancy A. Jones is Lecturer on Romance Languages and Literatures and History and Literature at Harvard University. She has written on the female voice in medieval pastourelle, Old French Romance, and Dante, and is co-editor with Leslie Dunn of *Embodied Voices: Representing Female Vocality in Western Culture* (Cambridge 1994). Her essay is drawn from a study-in-progress on female lamentation in medieval literature of the twelfth and thirteenth centuries.

Paul Allen Miller is Associate Professor of Classics and Director of Comparative Literature at Texas Tech University. He has published articles on lyric poetry in English, French, Latin, and Greek, and gender studies and literary theory. His book *Lyric Texts and Lyric Consciousness* was published by Routledge in 1994. He is co-editor of *Russian Literature and the Classics* (Harwood 1996), *Bakhtin and Ancient Studies* (*Arethusa* 1993), *Recapturing the Renaissance* (New Paradigm 1996), and of the journal *Intertexts.*

Holt Parker is Associate Professor of Classics at the University of Cincinnati. He has published on the Roman woman poet Sulpicia, on Martial's poetry about a woman of the same name, on ancient sex manuals in *Pornography and Representation in Greece and Rome* (ed. Amy Richlin, Oxford 1992). He is currently completing a book, *Coopting the Feminine: Male and Female in Roman Poetry.*

Charles Platter is Associate Professor of Classics at the University of Georgia. He has recently published a commentary on Buchanan's *Apologia pro Lena* as well as articles on Greek choral lyric, old comedy, Catullus, Propertius, and Buchanan's hendecasyllabics. He is co-editor of *Bakhtin and Ancient Studies* (*Arethusa* 1993) and of *Carnivalizing Difference: Bakhtin and the Other* (Harwood forthcoming). He is currently at work on a book on Aristophanic comedy and novelistic discourse.

Elizabeth Richmond-Garza is Associate Professor of English and Comparative Literature at the University of Texas. She has published several articles on drama of various periods as well as her book, *Forgotten Cites/ Sights: Interpretation and the Power of Classical Citation in Renaissance English Drama* (Peter Lang 1994). She is currently at work compiling a critical edition and translation of the Neo-Latin, academic play *Perfidius Etruscus.*

Diana Robin is Professor of Classics and Director of the Program in Comparative Literature at the University of New Mexico. She has been awarded the Rome Prize for Post-Classical Humanistic studies and two grants for research at the Newberry Library. He book, *Filelfo in Milan: Writings: 1451–1477,* was published in 1991 by Princeton. She has published widely on gender issues, Renaissance women's autobiographical letters, and humanist poetics.

Diane Wood is Associate Professor of French at Texas Tech University. She has published articles on Hélisenne de Crenne and is currently completing a monograph on her. She has also written on the literary climate for women during the Renaissance, the emblematist Gilles Corrozet, the misogynist Gratien Du Pont, and Renaissance translations and adaptations of ancient epic. She is co-editor of *Recapturing the Renaissance* (New Paradigm 1996).

Index

Abelard, 4-5, 17, 20-34; castration of, 22; fame of, 23-25, 28-29, 32; shame of, 22

Adam, and misogyny, 196–97. *See also* Eve

Agrippa, Heinrich Cornelius, 4, 10, 189–202

d'Ailly, Pierre, 78

Alabaster, William, 11–12, 224–26, 232–40

Alberici, Giacomo, 170

Alberti, Leon Battista, 166, 179, 180

Alexander of Hales, 126, 136n47

Alexiou, M., 28

Allen, J.B., 132n16

allusion. *See* imitation; intertextuality

Allut, P., 284n104

Althusser, L., 217, 218

Angela of Foligno, 6, 71–72, 75, 76, 78, 79, 80

Angenot, M., 202n1, 206n34

Antoniano, Silvio, 250

Antonioli, R., 203n12, 206n29

appropriation, 7, 156, 215, 233, 254

Aquinas, on gender, 126, 194, 195

Archambault, P., 206n32

Ardener, E., 69n83

Aristotle, as source for Cornelius Agrippa, 198

Aschbach, J., 43

Asher, L., 159n25

Astell, A.W., 108n29

Atkinson, C.W., 18, 34n4, 35n9

audience: for Abelard's letters, 37n23; for Alabaster's *Roxana*, 226–27, 233–40; for confessional literature, 82; for Elizabethan drama, 224, 226, 227, 228–30; for Hrotswitha, 50–51, 52, 57–61. *See also* the gaze

Augustine, 4–5, 8–9, 17–20, 32–33, 127; as source for Abelard, 36–37n20; in Petrarch, 139–56, 143–55; on gender, 194, 195

authorial intent, 74, 76, 152–53

autobiography, 4, 5–6, 9, 17, 21, 23, 45–53, 172–81; as subversive, 81; mediated, 71–83. *See also* biography; catalogues

Baker, M.P., 106n4

Bakhtin, M., 158n22, 230

Bamber, L., 134n32

Bartky, S.L., 77, 86n18

Barton, J., 244n25

Bassnett, S., 274

Beatrice, 34–35n5; tears of, 16

beauty, 114–15, 116, 129, 141, 144, 146–48, 151, 198, 236. *See also* materiality; seduction

Bell, R., 74, 87n31, n35, 88n40

Benstock, S., 45, 65n29, 216

Bergamo, Jacopo Filippo da, 169, 250

Bergin, T.G., 130n6, 133n28

Bernardo, A.S., 111 and 129n1, 124, 129–30n4, 131n7

Bernard of Clairvaux, 6–7, 93, 95–97, 99; identified with the Virgin Mary, 99–101

Betussi, Giuseppe, 170

Billanovich, G., 131n10

Binns, I.W., 249

biography, of women, 9, 167–72. *See also* autobiography; catalogues

Blaise, A., 107n23

Bloch, M., 15

Bloch, R.H., 13n5, 136n47, 139 and 156n2, 141–42, 158n16, n19, 161n42, 183n11, 205n22

Boas, F.S., 225, 226, 242n10, 243n19, 245n26

Boccaccio, 9–10, 116, 167–71

Bodo, Heinrich, 63n12